Household Encyclopedia

THE
GOOD HOUSEKEEPING
Household
Encyclopedia

Edited by Carolyn E. Forté, Associate Director

The Good Housekeeping Institute

HEARST BOOKS   NEW YORK

GOOD HOUSEKEEPING

Editor-in-Chief	John Mack Carter
Managing Editor	Mary Fiore
Executive Editor	Mina W. Mulvey
Deputy Editor	Susan Seliger

THE GOOD HOUSEKEEPING INSTITUTE

Director	Amy Barr
Associate Director and Director, Home Care and Textiles	Carolyn E. Forté
Associate Director	Delia Hammock, M.S., R.D.
Technical Director	Roger G. Cook
Director, Food Department	Mildred Ying
Director, Engineering Department	Richard L. Mastrangelo
Project Manager, Engineering Department	David Quentzel
Associate Director, Microwave Cooking and Food Appliances	Sharon Franke
Environmental Specialist, Bureau of Chemistry and Environmental Studies	Evan Pilchik
Manager, Textiles Department	Nancy J. Vozar
Associate Editor, Home Care and Textiles Departments	Kathleen B. Mulroy

Library of Congress Cataloging-in-Publication Data
The Good Housekeeping household encyclopedia/the editors of Good Housekeeping magazine
p.   cm.
Includes index.
ISBN 0-688-12036-9
1. Home economics.   I. Good Housekeeping   II. Title: Household encyclopedia.
TX158.G63 1993   93-1143T
640—dc20   CIP

Printed in the United States of America, First Edition,   2 3 4 5 6 7 8 9 10

The ideas and suggestions in this book regarding health/medical issues are not intended to substitute for the help and services of a trained professional. All matters regarding your health require medical consultation and supervision, and following any of the advice and procedures in this book should be done in conjunction with the services of a qualified health professional. In using any substances mentioned in the book, the reader is cautioned to follow the manufacturer's instructions carefully.

Produced by Smallwood and Stewart, Inc., New York City

CONTENTS

CHAPTER 1

HOME FINANCES
1

Managing Your Money Efficiently . . 2
Making a Budget
Month-by-Month Planning
Sample Monthly Budget
Checkbook Security

Getting Credit 6
How Credit Works
Your Credit Rating
All About Credit Cards
How to Organize
    Your Files
Where to Keep
    Important Papers

A Home of Your Own 13
Can You Afford It?
Home-Buyer's Checklist: What to Ask
    Before You Buy
Rules of the Game
Finding a Mortgage
Understanding Mortgages
Using Your Equity

Insuring Your Property 18
Shopping Around

Home-Owner's Insurance
Car Coverage
Is Your Insurance Agent Right for You?

CHAPTER 2

CLEANING
21

Saving Time 22
Cutting Out Clutter
Dirt Defense
Cleanup Calendar

The Right Stuff 25
Vacuum Cleaners
Vacuum Roundup
Vacuum Cleaner Attachments
Hand-Held and Stick Cleaners
Brush Basics
Broom Basics
Carpet Sweeper
Floor Scrubber/Polisher
Brushes
Brooms
Mops
Dust Cloths
Allergic Reactions
Cleaning Product Roundup

Furniture 33
Upholstery
Wood
Other Materials
Wood Furniture Polish Roundup
Fast Furniture Fix-Ups
Lamps and Lamp Shades
Mirrors and Picture Glass
Electronic Equipment

Floors 38
Wood
Resilient Surfaces
The Great Stain Rub-Out
How to Remove Floor Polish
Masonry
Rugs and Carpets
Vacuuming Oriental Rugs
Spot Cleaning Carpets
Deep Cleaning Carpets

Windows and Doors 44
Window Glass
Screens
Shades
Cleaning Your Fireplace
Blinds
Curtains and Draperies

Walls and Ceilings 47
Wallpaper
Wall Surfaces and Fixtures
Washable Walls

The Kitchen 49
Cabinets and Pantry
Sinks and Faucets
Cook Tops/Ranges

Anatomy of a Burner
Ovens
Refrigerators and Freezers
Dishwashers
Good Cooking Habits
Small Appliances
Dishes, Cookware, and Utensils

The Bathroom. 57
Tiles
Sinks and Faucets
Bathtubs and Showers
Toilet Bowls
Mirrors
Removing Skid Protection Strips

The Nursery. 59

Porches, Decks, and Patios 60
Outdoor Furniture
Barbecue Grills

CHAPTER 3

LAUNDRY AND CLOTHES CARE
61

Basic Equipment 62
Washers
Dryers

Laundry Products 63
Detergents
Soaps
Bleaches
Bleaching Dos and Don'ts
Bluing
Stain Presoaks
Prewash Stain Removers
Water Softeners
Fabric Softeners

Starches and Sizings
Guide to Fibers and Fabrics

Doing the Wash 68
Before You Start
Machine Washing
Setting Up a Laundry Room
Machine Drying
Air Drying
Before You Call for Repair
Special-Care Items

Laundering Vintage Linens and Lace
Hand Washing
Drying a Wool Sweater
How to Remove Stains

Ironing 78
Pressing
Caring for Your Iron
Irons: What to Look For
How to Iron

Dry Cleaning 82
Bulk Dry Cleaners

Sewing 83
Buttons and Fasteners
Mending and Altering
Darning
The Sewing Basket
Shortening Trousers
Sewing Buttons
Basic Stitches

Leather and Fur 89
Leather and Suede
Fur

Jewelry Care 91

Packing a Suitcase 92

Clothes Storage 93
Mothproofing
Hang or Fold?
Cottons and Linens
Furs
Leather Accessories

CHAPTER 4

FOOD AND THE KITCHEN
95

Eating Well 96
Protein
Carbohydrates and Fiber
Fats
Cholesterol
Vitamins
Minerals
Water
The Food Guide Pyramid
Understanding Vital Nutrients
Lowering Fats
Increasing Complex Carbohydrates
Vegetarians
Limiting Refined Sugars
Limiting Salt
Limiting Alcoholic Beverages

Smart Shopping 105
Negotiating the Market
How to Buy the Best: Meat, Poultry, and
 Seafood
Dollar Stretchers
Becoming Label Literate
Picking the Best Produce
Best Out-of-Season Buys
Herbs, Spices, and Other Flavorings

Cooking 115
Planning Meals
Making Healthier Meals
Beef, Pork, Lamb, and Whole Poultry Roasting
 Timetables
How to Prepare, Cook, and Store Food Safely
Grilling

Microwaving 122
Adapting Recipes to a Microwave
Microwave Cooking Table
A Cook's Tour of Cooking Terms
Kitchen Equivalents

Keeping Foods Fresh 128
Refrigerating
Freezing

Refrigerator Storage
The Cold Facts
Shelf Storage
How Long Is the Shelf Life?
Canning

Equipment 135
Pots and Pans
Basic Pots and Pans
Knives
Basic Small Appliances
Essential Knives
Useful Cooking Utensils
Basics for Bakers
Appliances
Surface-Cooking Options

Tableware 145
China
Flatware
Glassware
Traditional Place Setting
Tableware Glossary
Glassware Glossary
The Art of Napkin Folding

Entertaining 150
Parties for Adults
Parties for Teenagers
Parties for Children
Planning a Big Party
Party Timetable
Uncorking Champagne
Planning a Small Dinner Party
Party Ideas on a Budget
Setting Up a Bar
The Well-Stocked Bar

CHAPTER 5

DECORATING AND DESIGN
155

Doing It Yourself 156
Color
Four Steps to Sucess
The Color Wheel
Decorating Checklist
Style
Arrangement
How Long Will It Last?
How to Make a Floor Plan
How to Work with a Professional
Which Bulb is Best?
Lighting
Basic Bulbs
Six Classic Lamp Shades

Painting 165
Choosing Colors
Paint and Primer
The Right Equipment
Which Paint Finish
    Where?
Painting Dos and Don'ts
Special Paints
Getting Ready
How to Paint
Decorative Techniques
Step-by-Step Stenciling

Wallcoverings 172
All About Wallpaper
Hanging Paper
How to Hang Prepasted Wallpaper

Window Treatments 176
Curtains and Draperies
Measuring a Window for Curtains
Window Shades
Blinds and Shutters
Classic Curtain Styles

Floors 180
Carpeting
Understanding Your Options
Pile Possibilities
Area Rugs
Wood Flooring
Resilient Flooring
Nonresilient Flooring

Furniture 185
Shopping on a Budget
Antiques
Anatomy of an Upholstered Chair
Slipcovers
Buying a Mattress
The Well-Dressed Bed
Pillow Talk

Wall Decorations . 189
Framing
Caring for Framed Art
How to Hang Pictures
    and Mirrors

Storage 202
Children's Storage
Bedroom Storage
Wall Systems
Bookcases
Organizing Your Closets

CHAPTER 6

MAINTENANCE AND REPAIRS
205

Flowers 191
How to Arrange Flowers

The Kitchen 192
Cabinets
Countertops
Sinks
The Work Triangle
Appliances
Sink Types
Kitchen Storage

The Bathroom 199
Fixtures

The Home Office 200
Furniture
Lighting and Electronics
The Ideal Office

The Home Workshop 206
Safety
Nails, Screws, Bolts, and a Hook
What You Should Know About Ladders
The Basic Toolbox . . . and More

Mending China and Glass 210
Applying Glue
What Kind of Glue?

Restoring Wood Furniture *211*
Dents, Scratches, and Stains
Loose Chair Rungs
How to Mend Chair Rungs
Restoring a Wood Finish
Furniture Finishes

Wall and Ceiling Repairs *214*
Patching Plaster
How to Replace a Broken Tile
Plasterboard Holes

How to Hang Anything *216*
Lightweight Objects
Suspended Objects
Stud Finders
Putting Up Shelves
Shelves and Other Heavy Objects

Doors *218*
Fixing Scraping and Squeaks
Anatomy of a Door
How to Install a Lock Set

Windows and Screens *221*
Unjamming a Stuck Window
Screens
Anatomy of a Window
How to Replace Window Glass

Floors *224*
Restoring Wood Floors
How to Treat a New Wood Floor
Refinishing
Damaged Floors
How to Repair Wood Floor Scratches
Wood Floor Treatment Guide

Heating Systems *228*
Thermostats
Furnaces
Hot-Water Boilers
Steam Boilers
Heat Pumps
Portable Space Heaters
Fireplaces
Anatomy of a Fireplace

Cooling Systems *231*
All About Air Conditioning
Eight Cool Ways to Save Money
Built-In Fans

Weatherproofing *233*
Weather Stripping
Windows
Insulated Windows
Caulking Air Leaks
Where to Put Insulation

Plumbing 236
The Basic System
Thawing Ice in Piping
Plumbing Dos and Don'ts
How to Fix Leaky Faucets
Patching Pinhole Leaks
Faucet with a Washer
Clogged Drains
Cartridge Faucet
Toilet Problems
Anatomy of a Toilet

Electricity 241
Understanding Breakers and Fuses
Anatomy of a Lamp
Rewiring a Lamp
How to Replace an Outlet
Switches

Roof Repairs 243
How to Locate Leaks
Anatomy of a Roof
Troubleshooting Roof Problems

Gutters 245
Clearing Blockages
Fixing a Leaky Gutter
Anatomy of a Gutter
Home Repair Checklist

The Yard 248
Mowing
Mowing Safely
Fertilizing
Seeding
Reseeding
Mower Maintenance
Grass Seed
Basic Gardening Tools
Weed Killers
Using Chemicals and Pesticides
Hardy Grass the Natural Way
A Seasonal Guide to Lawn Maintenance
Home Pest Control
Snow Blowers

CHAPTER 7

CAR CARE
257

Preventive Maintenance 258
Safety Precautions
Anatomy of a Car
Car-Care Calendar
Self-Service Checks
A Kit for the Car
Changing Your Air Filter

Common Problems. 266
Car Won't Start
Engine Stalls
How to Jump-Start a Car
Engine Overheats

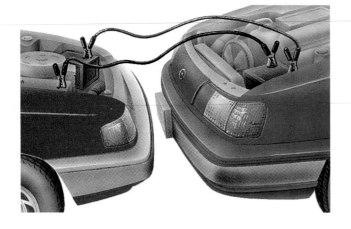

Car Starts But Won't Move
Minor Brake Trouble
Steering Trouble
Bulbs Burn Out
Fuses Burn Out
How to Change a Tire

Road Emergencies 272
Road Service Plans
Accidents
Accident Reports
Breakdowns
Overheating
Stuck in Snow, Ice, Sand, or Mud
Driving on Ice or Snow
Driving in Rain or Fog
Controlling Skids
Brake Failure
Child Safety

Keeping Up Appearances 277
Special Finishers
Paint Pointers

CHAPTER 8

SAFETY AND HEALTH
279

Safety First 280
Avoiding Falls
Preventing Fires
Where to Get Safety Information
Preventing Electrical Mishaps
Home Safety for Children and the Elderly
The Safe House

Emergencies in the Home 286
Fire
Putting Out Fires
Fire Extinguishers

Floods
Gas Leaks

Indoor Pollutants 289
Mildew, Molds, and Dust Mites
Formaldehyde
Carbon Monoxide
Asbestos
Get the Lead Out
Lead
Radon
Disposing of Toxic Household Products

The Secure House 292
Anatomy of a Lock

Emergency First Aid 295
The First Aid Kit
Emergency First Aid
Call EMS
Emergency: Fainting
Taking a Pulse
Emergency: Unconsciousness
Emergency: Choking
Emergencies: Heat Exhaustion and Hypothermia
Emergency: Heat Stroke

Emergency: Electric Shock
Emergency: Anaphylactic Shock
Emergency: Poisoning
Emergency: Heart Attack
Cardiopulmonary Resuscitation (CPR) Step by Step
The Heimlich Maneuver

Injuries 315
Bleeding
How to Make a Pressure Bandage
The Body's Pressure Points
Cuts and Abrasions
Puncture Wounds
Sprains and Fractures
Applying a Tourniquet
How to Make a Sling
Burns
Eye Injuries
Splinters
Animal Bites
Snakebites
Poisonous Snakes
Insect Bites

Index 324

INTRODUCTION

KEEPING A HOME CLEAN, WELL maintained, and running efficiently requires organization and time-management skills, technical and maintenance know-how, and an understanding of everything from nutrition to stain removal. And while our homes contain more and more "gadgets" to lighten our housekeeping load, putting them to the best possible use requires more new skills than ever before.

Since 1900, The Good Housekeeping Institute has been dedicated to making the task of running a home easier and more efficient for all of us and to eliminating much of the confusion we face as consumers in a complex marketplace. In our departments, which are staffed by scientists, engineers, home economists, and editors, we examine everything from bedding to barbecues, small appliances to stain-removal solutions, to develop information about products and their features and to discover the most effective techniques for our readers to use.

In *The Good Housekeeping Household Encyclopedia,* our experts have collected much of this information in a single volume. Here you'll find the best ways to paint a room, care for furniture, clean a carpet, or sew on a button; valuable consumer information on how to buy anything from a microwave oven to a mattress; and troubleshooting guides to help you deal with anything from a frozen pipe to a noisy washing machine. Throughout, we have provided the most up-to-date advice on such topics as obtaining credit and removing indoor air pollutants as well as the tried-and-true remedies for solving laundry disasters and even handling roadside emergencies—in short, help for the everyday and not-so-everyday challenges we all face.

Because time and money are so important to every homeowner, we have also included dozens of time-, money-, and energy-saving tips in every section of the book. Chapter by chapter, the margins are sprinkled with hints for smarter food shopping, for keeping decorating costs down, for cleaning more quickly and efficiently, saving energy in your home, and so on. Each time you open this book, you'll learn something new, whether you read an entire chapter, have time for just one page, or simply glance at a chart or tip.

Since more accidents occur at home than anywhere else, *The Good Housekeeping Household Encyclopedia* provides an invaluable section on health and home safety, with information on how to accident-proof your home and make it safe for all family members, including children and the elderly. A detailed illustration shows how to safeguard your home against burglary, and step-by-step instructions are included for handling kitchen fires, water damage, and gas leaks. Clear illustrations explain basic first aid such as how to accurately take a temperature or pulse, and how to perform CPR and the Heimlich maneuver. Help on handling injuries and medical emergencies is provided in a clear, easy-to-read, easy-to-locate format.

With Home Economics classes disappearing from school curriculums, and with spare time a rare commodity, we could all use a helping hand at home. We hope this collection of the best advice Good Housekeeping has to offer becomes a trusted reference and valued part of your household.

Carolyn E. Forté
Associate Director, The Good Housekeeping Institute

CHAPTER 1
HOME FINANCES

Sheets into Curt... Buffing Wood Fl... Larger, Ironing ... Creating a ☛M... Buy Produce, C... Dents, Unsticking Stacked Glasses, Making Rooms Look Larger, Ironing Pleated Skirts, Arranging Flowers, Jump-Starting a Car, Cleaning Tile Grout, Creating a Home Office, Fixing a Leaky Faucet ☛STEP-BY-STEP GUIDES: To Checkbook Security, Unblocking a Sink, Buying a Home, Successful Decorating, Performing CPR, Changing Flat Tires, Refinishing Furniture, Hanging Shelves, Lawn Mower Maintenance ☛MANAGING YOUR MONEY EFFICIENTLY: The household budget: solvency, reserves, and long-term plans. Calculating your income and expenses. How to balance your checkbook. Check-writing tips. ☛GETTING CREDIT: How credit works: open-ended, close-ended, and single-payment options. Protecting your credit rating. All about credit cards. ☛RECORD KEEPING: How to organize your files: ways to organize and de-clutter. Where to keep important papers. ☛A HOME OF YOUR OWN: Can you afford it? Home-buyer's checklist: What to ask before you buy. Rules of the game: terminology explained. Federal aid for home buyers. Understanding mortgages: Where to secure one; payment rates; how to apply. Using your equity. ☛INSURING YOUR PROPERTY: Insurance explained. How much is enough: home-owner and car insurance choices. Finding the right agent. Warranty terms. How to collect. ☛EVERYTHING YOU NEED TO KNOW: About Choosing Pots and Pans, Front-Wheel-Drive Cars, Making Healthier Meals, Vacuum Cleaners, Garden Tools, Upholstered Furniture, Your Credit Card Statement, Curtain Styles ☛MONEY-SAVING HINTS: How to Turn Bed Sheets into Curtains, Save on Car Repairs, Buy Produce, Choose Carpeting ☛HANDY TIPS: For Buffing Wood Floors, Preventing Carpet Dents, Unsticking Stacked Glasses, Making Rooms Look Larger, Ironing Pleated Skirts, Arranging Flowers, Jump-Starting a Car, Cleaning Tile Grout, Creating a Home Office, Fixing a Leaky Faucet ☛STEP-BY-STEP GUIDES: To Checkbook Security, Unblocking a Sink, Buying a Home, Successful Decorating, Performing CPR, Changing Flat Tires, Refinishing Furniture, Hanging Shelves, Lawn Mower Maintenance ☛DO-IT-YOURSELF: Create a Home Filing System, Make a Floor Plan, Measuring Windows for Curtains, Fix a Broken Bathroom Tile, Hang Pre-pasted Wallpaper, Install a Lock Set, Repair Runs in Woolens ☛WHAT TO DO: If Your Loan Application Is Denied, Your Brakes Fail, You Have Hard Water, a Fire Breaks Out, You

Any of these situations may alert you that it's time to take a closer look at your spending and make some adjustments:

☞ Your current monthly bank statement balance is considerably lower than your previous statement balance.

☞ Your current credit card totals are significantly higher than on your previous bills.

☞ The amount you budgeted for household cash disappears faster than usual.

☞ Your current utility bills are considerably higher than in the past.

EASY CONVERSIONS

Most budgets are done on a monthly basis. Here's how to convert figures to a monthly amount.

If your budgeting amount is:

Weekly: multiply it by 4.33

Biweekly: multiply it by 2.16

Semimonthly: multiply it by 2.00

Quarterly: divide it by 3.00

Annually: divide it by 12.00

MANAGING YOUR MONEY EFFICIENTLY

Running a household smoothly means taking control of your time, your budget, and your paperwork. The key to financial control is organization.

Planning ahead for large expenditures will save both time and money in the long run—but make sure you actually follow through. A few simple budgets and some good filing systems can be a surprising help.

MAKING A BUDGET

The first step in managing money well is to closely examine where it goes. The best way to do this is to make a budget—then stick to it (see sample budget opposite). To get an overview of your financial needs before making a budget, consider them in terms of simple, concrete goals. Make more ambitious, long-term plans after achieving a few basic ones.

Basic Goals

Solvency: Aim to have enough income to cover your current yearly expenses—without going into debt or having to borrow (except for such serious expenses as replacing a major appliance, sending a child to college, or buying a home or a car).

Emergency reserve: It's always wise to have credit cards, a line of bank credit, or funds set aside to cover unexpected bills; if possible, reserve at least three months' income.

Risk protection: While no one likes to have to plan for the worst, it is essential to have insurance to protect against finan-cial loss due to long-term illness, disabil-ity, property damage, liability, or prema-ture death.

Long-term Goals

Home ownership: This is a time-tested means to build equity—that part of the value of any piece of property that belongs to you and that you can borrow against and resell if you wish.

Investment plans: Investing money in financial plans like IRAs or Keoghs, savings bonds, or stocks allows you to build savings for retirement or for major expenses, such as a child's education.

Estate plan: The best way to ensure the transfer of your property and valuables to the people you wish after you die is to have a lawyer draw up a will. You may also want to set up trust funds for your beneficiaries.

MONTH-BY-MONTH PLANNING

For many people, a monthly budget makes the most sense because so many basic (essential) expenses, like rent, mort-gage and car payments, are billed monthly. Such expenses are called fixed expenses because the amounts are always the same.

Variable expenses are those that are also essential, such as groceries, utilities, and medical care, but are not set amounts month to month. It helps to break these out from fixed expenses because you must estimate them.

Discretionary expenditures are those you choose to make, but aren't absolutely

SAMPLE MONTHLY BUDGET

If you've never made a budget, try using the following sample as a model. It is easiest to start with fixed expenses because they are the same from month to month. You must estimate your variable expenses; round up to be on the safe side.

INCOME

SALARY	_____
RENTAL PROPERTIES	_____
INTEREST/DIVIDENDS	_____
OTHER	_____
TOTAL INCOME	_____

BASIC (ESSENTIAL) EXPENSES

FIXED:

RENT/MORTGAGE	_____
INSURANCE (CAR, HEALTH, HOME)	_____
CREDIT COMMITMENTS (BANK LOAN, CAR LOAN, ETC.)	_____
TAXES	_____
SCHOOL TUITION/LOANS	_____
TRANSPORTATION	_____
CHILD CARE	_____
OTHER (CABLE TV., HOUSEHOLD HELP, ETC.)	_____
TOTAL FIXED EXPENSES	_____

VARIABLE:

UTILITIES (ELECTRICITY, GAS, HEATING FUEL, WATER)	_____
TELEPHONE	_____
GROCERIES	_____
CREDIT COMMITMENTS (CREDIT CARD, ETC.)	_____
CAR CARE/GARAGE	_____
CLOTHING	_____
DRY CLEANING/LAUNDRY	_____
MAINTENANCE/REPAIRS	_____
MEDICAL/DENTAL CARE	_____
PERSONAL GROOMING (BEAUTY PARLOR, BARBER, ETC.)	_____
PET CARE	_____
OTHER	_____
TOTAL VARIABLE EXPENSES	_____

TOTAL INCOME		TOTAL BASIC EXPENSES (FIXED PLUS VARIABLE)		AMOUNT LEFT FOR DISCRETIONARY (OPTIONAL) EXPENSES
_____	**–**	_____	**=**	_____

essential, such as hobbies, entertainment, vacation, children's camp, and gym membership. These can differ greatly from household to household.

Four Easy Steps

To set up your monthly budget, you must:

1. *Estimate your available income.* Total all sources of income, including take-home pay, interest, dividends, bonuses, and receipts from rental property. If your income fluctuates, give yourself a cushion by underestimating your income (and overestimating your expenses in the next steps). Do not include any bonuses or overtime pay you are not positive you will receive.

2. *List your basic fixed expenses.* (Prorate [that is, divide proportionately] quarterly or annual expenses.) Be sure to include daily expenses like transportation. Total the amounts.

3. *Estimate your basic variable expenses you can control,* like food and clothing. Total the amounts.

4. *Add the amounts* in steps 2 and 3 and subtract from the total shown in step 1. If the sum is positive, you're in great shape! You can save or invest your surplus or increase the amounts you spend on discretionary items.

If the amount is negative, you'll have to cut back on your discretionary spending. You might postpone your vacation or cut down on some expenses, such as clothing or entertainment, in order to get ahead.

Consider brown-bagging instead of lunching out and try carpooling. Ask your family for their ideas.

SIGN HERE

☞ If cashing a check, wait to endorse it until you are at the bank; otherwise, it can easily be cashed if it falls into the wrong hands. When depositing, add "for deposit only." This helps to ensure that if lost the check cannot be cashed, only deposited.

BE ATM ALERT

☞ Automatic teller machines are convenient, but should be used with care. If the machine is in a secluded area, avoid it. Be aware of other patrons; if anyone looks suspicious, leave immediately.

BALANCING ACT

Balancing your bank statement each month will help you stay on a budget.

Here's how:

- Verify deposits and canceled checks by date and amount, making a check mark on the statement by each entry.

- Compare the amount of each canceled check or your carbon with both your checkbook and the bank statement.

- Check all deposits and withdrawals made at an ATM (automatic teller machine) against your receipt slips.

CONFIRMING YOUR BALANCE:

    _____ 1. Balance in your check book.

− _____ 2. Subtract service charges on statement.

= _____

+ _____ 3. Add any interest earned on account.

= _____ 4. New register balance.

THEN ENTER:

    _____ 5. Balance shown on bank statement.

+ _____ 6. Add deposits not on statement.

= _____

− _____ 7. Subtract total of checks written but not cleared and ATM withdrawals since your last statement.

= _____ 8. New balance (should match line 4).

CHECKBOOK SECURITY

KEEPING A CHECKBOOK CORRECTLY AND making sure it reconciles with your bank statement each month will help you catch any bank errors (and your own) and prevent overdrawn accounts. If you make a mistake on a check, correct it neatly and initial it; or, better yet, mark the check "void," rip it up, and start over. Write in permanent ink; don't use pencil or erasable pen.

CHECK NUMBER:
Note this on the receipt when paying bills.

PAYEE:
Write your own name, not "cash," when writing a check for cash. Otherwise, if the check is lost or stolen, anyone can cash it. Draw a line after the payee; avoid abbreviations.

DATE:
Most checks are valid for only a set period—usually six months. Postdating a check does not guarantee it won't be cashed sooner, because electronic scanners can't read the date.

FIGURES:
Print as close to the dollar sign as possible to prevent anyone from altering the amount.

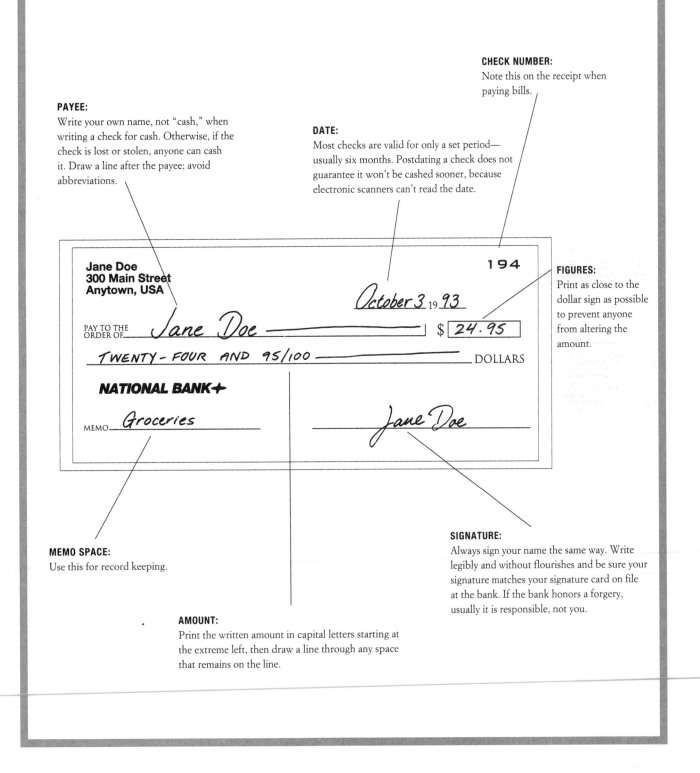

MEMO SPACE:
Use this for record keeping.

SIGNATURE:
Always sign your name the same way. Write legibly and without flourishes and be sure your signature matches your signature card on file at the bank. If the bank honors a forgery, usually it is responsible, not you.

AMOUNT:
Print the written amount in capital letters starting at the extreme left, then draw a line through any space that remains on the line.

GETTING
CREDIT

Credit allows you to buy needed items when they're on sale and to travel without carrying large amounts of cash. It also lets you delay or spread out payments for expensive items.

However, while money obtained through a bank loan or by using credit cards may seem like extra income, it's really a debt you must repay. As a general guideline, financial advisers suggest committing no more than 10 percent to 15 percent of your take-home pay for all consumer debts, excluding your home mortgage.

You may be tempted to buy more than you really need or to shop only at stores where credit is available instead of comparison shopping. If you do not pay your entire bill every month, habitual credit buying can add as much as 18 percent or more—the rate of many monthly interest charges—to your cost of goods and services.

Continually high monthly credit payments also reduce the amount of money available for basic needs.

HOW CREDIT WORKS

Credit is available in two forms:

Open-ended credit: Credit cards offered by a bank or retail store are an example.

They make money available—up to a specified limit—for purchasing products and/or services. You repay the amount when you pay the full sum shown on your monthly credit card statement.

If you don't pay the total amount, the unpaid portion is treated like a loan, and you pay a specified finance charge, which can vary widely, just the way you pay interest on a bank loan. There is no time limit on your payments, although there might be a minimum payment amount.

Close-ended credit: You might use this type of credit to pay for a large purchase such as a refrigerator, new furniture, or car on an installment plan.

When you sign for the loan, which may be offered by a bank or the place of purchase, you know the exact number of payments and the specific amount of each payment usually spread over many months.

Interest rates can vary widely, so it pays to compare. Before signing for this type of loan, be sure to ask about options for prepaying it. Some banks charge a prepayment penalty if you pay off the balance sooner than the stated time. (For more information on bank loans, see page 17.)

Single-Payment Options

Banks also offer single-payment close-ended loans. These allow you to borrow a specified amount of money for a specific amount of time, usually 30 days to one year. The total amount of the loan plus interest is due at the end of the period. They may also have a prepayment penalty.

YOUR CREDIT RATING

How well you've used credit in the past will affect whether or not you can get credit in the future.

Your credit history is based on how much income you have, how promptly you pay your bills, how long you have lived or worked in the same place, how much you owe, and your collateral—what you own that is worth more than the amount you want to borrow.

☛ Don't assume the government is keeping a correct record of your Social Security benefits. To check, call 1-800-772-1213 and ask for a personal earnings and benefit estimate statement request form (PEBS). Return the completed form to find out how much money you can expect to receive upon retirement (or in the event you are disabled), as well as the amount your spouse would collect if you died. Check this information against your own records.

☛ The Social Security Administration will not correct errors in records that are more than 39 months old, so it's to your advantage to complete the PEBS request form every three years.

Credit Records

If you have obtained credit in the past, your credit records are probably on file at a credit bureau near you. (Look under "Credit Reporting Agencies" in the Yellow Pages of your phone book.)

These reporting agencies receive and file records of credit transactions plus specific information from public records such as a contract suit, judgment, tax lien, or bankruptcy. They don't analyze the information, but rather make it available to creditors to help them decide if you are a good credit risk.

Credit bureaus are usually established and owned by local merchants and banks.

It is to your advantage to check your credit bureau file periodically for accuracy. You may have to pay a small fee, unless you inquire within 30 days of being denied credit. If you think the information is incorrect, ask the credit bureau to investigate.

Information proven to be incorrect must be removed. If you and the creditor disagree about the accuracy of the information, you can file a 100-word statement telling your side. It must be added to your file.

Both spouses should develop separate credit records so each will have access to credit in case of divorce or death.

ALL ABOUT CREDIT CARDS

Credit cards are popular and easy to use. Indeed, credit card issuers have been known to offer many incentives to encourage consumers to use their cards, including rental-car insurance and extended warranties on new products purchased with the card. The most important factors to consider, however, are the following:

Annual fee: the amount you pay once a year that allows you to use the card.

Grace period: the length of time after purchase before you are charged interest. The standard grace period is 25 days, but that may be applicable only if you have no outstanding balance from the previous month.

Interest rate: the percentage used to determine how much interest you pay on the unpaid portion of your bill. Interest rates vary by company and can be either fixed or floating. Issuers can change rates with as little as 15 days' notice, depending on state law.

Finance charges: interest added for balance due. There are different formulas used for computing finance charges. For example, a company may use an "average daily balance" method, in which your average daily balance in a pay period is multiplied by the monthly periodic rate.

Some allow a grace period, so that if you pay the full amount by the due date, there is no charge. Others calculate from the day of purchase.

Companies must tell consumers which method they are using, what the annual fee and interest rates are, and how long the grace period is.

Specialty Credit Cards

Two types of specialty credit cards are also available:

Affinity credit cards: may be offered from a university alumni association or a nonprofit organization or charity. A small portion of the purchase price of items charged to the card (usually 0.5 percent) is given to the organization, or the organization may receive a flat fee for each member who signs up for the card.

Secured credit cards: These are offered by some banks to help people who don't yet have a credit history or who want to erase a negative history due to past financial problems. To qualify for a secured credit card, you must keep a minimum balance—usually $500 to $1,000—on deposit. If you fail to pay the monthly bill, the bank withdraws the needed amount from your account. If you make the monthly payments, you can establish or improve your credit record and qualify for an unsecured card.

WHICH CREDIT CARD IS BEST?

The best credit card for you depends on how you plan to use the card and how you intend to pay the bill.

☛ If you are likely to use it often and to carry a balance from month to month, you'll save more over the year by concentrating on finding the lowest interest rate and longest grace period.

☛ If, on the other hand, you plan to pay off the balance in full every month, you can save more by ignoring the interest rate and finding a card with no (or a very low) annual fee.

FREE OF FEES

☛ If you are a good customer, you can ask the bank issuing your credit card to waive the annual fee, which can run as high as $50.

HOW TO ORGANIZE YOUR FILES

THE CHALLENGE IN ORGANIZING YOUR files is to keep the categories specific enough to be useful, yet general enough to be practical. Where you put items is less important than making sure material is returned to its designated spot. Make sure everyone involved understands the system. A good way to organize your files is to divide them into the following categories:

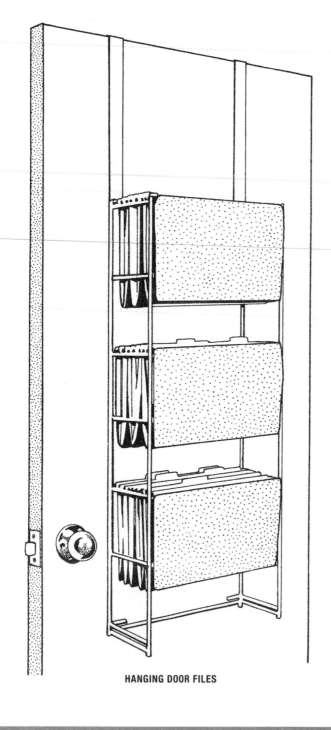

HANGING DOOR FILES

ACTION FILES:

Set up separate files for bills to pay, income/expense records, correspondence, upcoming events, organizational activities, and current projects. These files need to be readily available, but not immediately visible.

Clean out action files yearly but save:

- Tax records: Keep receipts, canceled checks, bank statements, and other documents used for income-tax deductions for six years. If desired, keep copies of income-tax returns indefinitely.

- Insurance policies: Keep these as long as they are current (but don't discard until checking for continuing benefits).

- Real estate records (initial cost, costs of improvement, selling costs): Keep receipts for seven years after you sell.

- Investments or property records: Keep receipts and pertinent documents for seven years after you sell.

- Records of major purchases: Canceled checks act as proofs of purchase. Keep these as long as service contracts and warranties apply.

REFERENCE FILES:

Material you need to find less frequently goes in these files. They can be as diverse as your interests and most useful when stored where you commonly use them. Typical categories include:

- Financial papers: Include canceled checks, receipts for tax-deductible items, and tax returns.
- Insurance policies and records of claims.
- Education, health, and employment records.
- Household papers: Include records of home improvements (important for later tax savings), appliance warranties and manuals, and decorating ideas.
- Car and travel records: Include owner's manual, service records, maps, brochures, directions to friends' homes, and clippings about places you want to visit.
- Yard records: Include warranties for tools, landscaping plan, improvements made, trees planted.

FAMILY FILES:

Depending on what's important in your household, you may want to create separate files for photographs and negatives, letters, recipes and party ideas, craft ideas and directions, personal writings, and genealogy lists.

ACCORDION FOLDER

STACKABLE DRAWERS

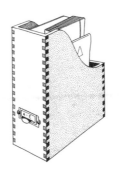

BOX FILE

KEEPING TAX RECORDS

☛ After filing a tax return, keep substantiating records for at least six years after filing. The Internal Revenue Service (IRS) has three years after the year of filing to audit a return; six years if the taxpayer omits more than 25 percent of gross income; and unlimited time if fraud is found.

LOSE THE CLUTTER

Storing file folders in a drawer or box works well for many people. Others prefer to use drawers, baskets, or other containers like those shown opposite. Use whatever works for you.

As you sort and organize, look for things you can throw out. Store the things you want in labeled containers. When possible, move them to the attic, basement, or a top or back closet shelf.

Many organizations that work with children welcome magazines and catalogs for cutting projects.

Libraries often take books and magazines for their own collections or for fund-raising book sales.

Ask social agencies if they know of any local groups that might be able to use items. Or set up an exchange program with neighbors and co-workers.

WHERE TO KEEP IMPORTANT PAPERS

*IT IS EXTREMELY IMPORTANT TO organize your financial and personal records well.
Keep whatever you don't immediately need on hand in a safe-deposit box; often-
used items should be neatly filed at home (see pages 8–9).*

WHERE	WHAT	WHY
Safe-Deposit Box	Abstracts of title and property deeds, mortgage, loan and title insurance documents (including cemetery plot)	To prove ownership; to aid title examiner
	Appraisals and photos of valuables; inventory of household goods	For insurance claims
	Contracts, leases, notes	To prove your debt or what is owed to you; important for interest deductions on tax returns and to prove that contract terms are fulfilled
	Military service records	For insurance, retirement, medical, and other benefits (to guard against loss, have discharge papers recorded by county recorder)
	Motor vehicle titles and purchase receipts	To prove ownership; needed for sale, proof of collateral for a loan, and in case of theft
	Personal records (adoption, birth, citizenship, death, divorce, and marriage certificates; passport, Social Security number)	For inheritance, insurance, and business matters; to prove citizenship, age, Social Security, etc.
	Stock, bond, and securities certificates	To prove ownership; attach purchase records to certificates: can be held by your broker
	Tax assessments and record of capital improvements to real estate	For tax purposes
	Wills (unsigned copies; leave the original signed copy with your lawyer or in a fireproof box at home)	To record your bequests

Where	What	Why
Carry with You	Personal identification (name, address, telephone number, names and telephone numbers of family members or friends)	For emergencies
	Auto insurance card (keep in your car)	To identify insurer in case of accident
	Credit, electronic banking cards	For identification; to charge purchases or make transactions
	Driver's license, car registration	For identification; to prove your legal eligibility to drive
	Health insurance card	For identification; to use during hospital admittance
	Medical information (allergy, blood type, diseases—diabetes, heart disease, epilepsy, etc.; donor card)	For emergency treatment
	Physician's identification card (name, address, telephone)	To contact in emergency
Home Files	Checking and savings account information (canceled checks, deposit slips and check registers, electronic transfer and telephone transfer ID numbers, extra checks, statements)	For tax and budget information
	Social Security card	For identification; to be able to provide number
	Credit records (bills and receipts, copies of contracts, loan statements and payment books, notification forms for lost or stolen credit cards)	For reference. In case of loss or theft, call the credit card company immediately to report, follow up with a letter; keep receipts to prove payment to return purchases
	Employment records (copies of contracts, fringe benefit information, pay stubs or statements, personal résumé, Social Security records)	For references

(continued)

(continued)

Where	What	Why
Home Files	Estate planning (instructions for survivors, unsigned copies of trusts, and other legal documents)	For reference and referral
	Household furnishings and appliances (guarantees/warranties, instruction manuals, place and date of purchase, receipts, repair records, serial/model numbers)	For reference and for use and care; useful for insurance or warranty claims
	Health (insurance records, records of immunizations, surgeries)	For reference
	Housing (copies of lease or rental agreements, property tax records, receipts for home improvements, record of mortgage payments, utility deposit receipts)	To compute capital gains/losses or income-tax basis in replacement residence; keep tax-related records for seven years after you sell the last house you own
	Income tax (copies of past returns, expenses in current year, records and receipts of income and deductibles, tax forms)	In case of auditing
	Insurance: auto, health, life, property (copies of policies, claim forms, receipts of payment)	For reference of coverage until policies have expired
	Investments: general, mutual funds, stocks and bonds, real estate (earnings statements, transaction slips)	For reference
	Vehicle information (registration receipts, repair and maintenance records)	To collect on a warranty or to resell car

A HOME OF YOUR OWN

Deciding to buy a home—be it a house, condominium, or co-op apartment—is among the most serious financial undertakings you will ever consider. Moreover, the matter can be somewhat complex because the housing market moves in cycles (not always predictable) of highs and lows.

When prices are depressed, for example, the traditional advantage of buying a home—that it is an investment you can borrow against or liquidate when you wish—is much less valid than when prices are high and sales brisk. If you buy during a low period and plan to sell your home in a year or two, the housing market may still be weak, and it might take you longer than expected.

The primary advantages to buying during a low period are the general trend to lower prices and lower interest rates. It is, therefore, a good time to buy if you aren't planning to sell right away. Most housing experts believe that if you plan to hold a home for ten years, you should make a substantial profit.

CAN YOU AFFORD IT?

If you decide to buy a home, take the following steps:

1. *Look at your budget.* Approximately how much can you afford to spend on a home? How much cash do you have available now for a down payment? How much can you afford to pay for a monthly mortgage payment?

One rule of thumb is that a house should cost no more than three times your annual gross income. Beyond that, many financial counselors recommend keeping your monthly payments, including mortgage, interest, taxes, and insurance (see page 15), at or below 25 percent to 28 percent of your monthly gross income.

However, you may be more comfortable taking on a smaller debt—especially if you have other financial obligations.

What you can afford to buy also depends on the initial amount of cash you have available for a down payment. Be sure to include in your calculations such related costs as moving expenses and closing fees, and anticipate some remodeling or redecorating costs.

2. *Study the market.* Read the real estate advertising section to familiarize yourself with what's for sale at what price.

Visit open houses. Drive around to get a feel for the neighborhoods where you think you might want to live.

Talk to a variety of real estate agents until you find one who seems to understand your tastes and price range.

3. *Talk to lending institutions.* For this you'll need some basic terminology (see page 15 for explanations). Compare interest rates, points, and customer service offerings. Find out what kinds of loans you are eligible for.

4. *Find a lawyer.* Ask friends, relatives, and realtors to recommend reputable real estate lawyers, or call the local bar association for help.

Buying a house is a legal action requiring your signature on legal documents. You will want a lawyer to review all written agreements before you sign them.

(see page 15), (see page 15 for explanations).

PREQUALIFYING

☞ Many lending institutions offer prequalifying consultations to help you understand the process of obtaining a mortgage loan. They can also help you identify the estimated amount you can afford to spend. Check to see if this service is available.

BUYER BEWARE

☞ Increasing pressure from courts, state legislatures, and the National Association of Realtors is pushing sellers to tell potential buyers about defects they might not otherwise discover until it's too late. Check for a disclosure form (some states require this).

HOME-BUYER'S CHECKLIST:
WHAT TO ASK BEFORE YOU BUY

WHEN BUYING A HOME YOU can do a lot to narrow down the choices by using this checklist. Ask yourself the following questions before you put down a deposit.

OVERALL IMPRESSIONS

☐ What do you like best about the house?

☐ What do you like least about the house? Can you fix that problem?

☐ Will this be a high-maintenance home? If so, will your budget be able to handle all the costs?

SPACE AND CIRCULATION

☐ Is there enough bedroom/closet/bathroom space? Can that space be added? It's often easier and cheaper to buy a larger home than to add rooms later.

☐ How is the traffic flow through the house?

☐ What obstacles do you face getting groceries from the car to the kitchen?

☐ How far do muddy or sandy feet have to go from back door to bathroom or utility room?

☐ How well do sounds carry throughout the house? Can you hear kitchen noises, like a dishwasher, in the bedroom? This can be a particular problem in split-level homes and apartments.

CONDITION

☐ How old is the roof? A properly installed roof should last twenty to thirty years.

☐ How many layers of shingles does the roof have? If it already has two layers, both of them will have to be removed the next time a new roof is needed.

☐ How old is the furnace? Depending on the type, if it's close to twenty years old, it will probably need replacing soon. Ask to see the past winter's heating bills. You may want to get an estimate from a heating contractor to replace the current system.

☐ If air-conditioning is provided, is it a central system or separate window units? Ask to see the past summer's cooling bills before accepting the seller's offer to leave window units in place; they may be more costly to operate than your budget can manage.

☐ How good is the garage? Is it big enough to hold cars, lawn care equipment and furniture, ladders, bikes, and sleds? If not, where can you store them?

☐ Are there any problems with asbestos, formaldehyde, lead, or radon (see pages 289–291) or material defects, such as a wet basement, bad septic system, or water damage?

☐ Are there any signs of termites or pest infestations? How much will it cost to solve the problems? Can any repairs safely be postponed to a later date?

NEIGHBORHOOD AND LOCALE

☐ What's the neighborhood like at different times of the day?

☐ How noisy is it during the busiest traffic times?

☐ Do you see children playing or are there toys in the yards? If not, will your children be lonesome?

☐ Are the schools nearby and up to your standards? If not, where and what are your educational options?

☐ Are you close to shops, dry cleaners, drugstores, video stores, and other conveniences?

☐ What does the house next door and across the street look like?

RULES OF THE GAME

Preliminary Negotiations

When you agree to buy a home, you first sign a **binder** or **purchase offer** to buy it and put up **earnest money**—the cash you pay as a deposit to show that you have the means to buy the property. It is usually 10 percent of the sales price. If you break the binder without a valid reason, you will forfeit this money.

Your lawyer should draw up a **contract** studded with **contingency clauses**, statements defining the conditions you expect to be met, such as obtaining financing or having the property inspected for defects.

Sellers may also include clauses to retain their rights to keep certain personal property, such as major appliances and light fixtures.

If you plan to buy, start thinking about a **down payment**—the amount you must pay in order to persuade a lender to give you a **mortgage**, the loan you get to make up the difference between the down payment and the sales price. Lenders usually want a down payment of 20 percent to 30 percent of the purchase price, less if you qualify for a Federal Housing Administration (FHA) or Veterans Administration (VA) mortgage or take private mortgage insurance. Your down payment represents the part of the property that you own. (The rest belongs to the lender.)

The Mortgage

A mortgage is both the loan and the legal contract stating the terms of the loan: the amount borrowed, the **interest rate** (a 7.5 percent interest rate means that your cost of borrowing the money is $7.50 per $100 still owed per year), and the length of the mortgage (see page 16).

Fixed rate mortgages come as thirty-year (the most popular), twenty-year, and fifteen-year loans. **Adjustable rate mortgages** may be written as six-month, one-year, or three-year loans. Other variations also exist.

The amount of the mortgage includes the **principal** (the amount you borrowed) plus the **interest** on that amount.

Each payment you make **amortizes** (pays off) part of the principal and part of the interest.

The longer your mortgage, the more each payment goes toward the interest and the less it goes toward the principal. Interest payments are tax deductible but the principal payments are not.

If you do not keep up with your mortgage payments, the lender can **foreclose** (take over) your home.

Points are an extra charge the borrower pays for the paperwork and processing of the loan. Each point is equal to 1 percent of the loan. (Two points on a $150,000 loan = $3,000.) The fee for points is paid at **closing** (when the property is officially transferred to you) and is not part of the mortgage. Sometimes an eager seller will pay a portion of the points.

Closing

Closing or settlement costs are additional costs you pay after the loan is approved and when it is officially closed. They include such items as appraisal fees, mortgage tax stamps, termite inspection, and title insurance. Sometimes, an eager seller will pay a portion of the closing costs.

FINDING A MORTGAGE

Banks, savings and loan institutions, credit unions, mortgage bankers, and private lenders (including sellers) all offer new mortgages. Eager sellers may also offer mortgages.

Doing Your Homework

All terms are negotiable. Make sure you do the following:

- Investigate a variety of institutions until you find the arrangement that suits you.

HELPING HAND FROM UNCLE SAM

☛ FHA and VA loans are government-sponsored mortgages offered through banks and other lenders.

☛ FHA mortgages are available to everyone. The down payment is only 3 percent of the first $25,000 and 5 percent of the remainder, but the amount of the mortgage is limited.

☛ VA mortgages are available to veterans who have served 180 days in peacetime or 90 days in wartime. No down payment is required, but the amount of the mortgage is limited. Check with your bank.

UNDERSTANDING MORTGAGES

Lenders offer two types of mortgages: **conventional** *and* **conventional-insured** *(sometimes called* **nonconventional***). The same lender may offer both types of mortgage, depending on the buyer's qualifications. Rules can vary from state to state.*

Conventional Mortgages

These require down payments of at least 20 percent but have comparatively low interest rates.

Conventional-Insured Mortgages

These accept lower down payments (sometimes 5 percent) but usually charge a higher interest rate to cover private mortgage insurance in case the buyer defaults on the mortgage.

MORTGAGE RATES:

Most mortgages have either a fixed rate or an adjustable rate.

Fixed Rate Mortgage (FRM):
Both the interest rate and the monthly payment remain the same over the life of the loan. This type of mortgage is the most common and is especially appealing to buyers who want stable payments.

Adjustable Rate Mortgage (ARM):
This type of mortgage has varying interest rates. Usually the starting or initial interest rate is lower than that of an FRM, but the interest rate is adjusted periodically.

If interest rates rise, your monthly payments rise, and if rates fall, your payments also fall.

The lender sets the adjustment periods. The most common are six months and one year. Longer adjustment periods tend to be more stable and so have a higher interest rate.

The interest rate is based on some financial index, such as interest rates paid on U.S. Treasury bills. The lender must tell you what index will be used before you sign the mortgage contract.

Be sure to ask the lender about the index's past performance and how those changes would affect your monthly payment.

The lender also may add from one to three points to the index. This margin will vary with the lender, but will be constant for the life of the loan.

You will also want to ask the lender how interest rate caps or payment caps will be handled. These are your insurance that drastic and abrupt index increases won't make

your monthly payments unaffordable. Be aware, too, that if an interest or payment cap keeps your monthly payment below the level required by the market interest rates that unpaid interest can be added to your remaining principal. That will cause your outstanding balance to increase instead of decrease.

Many ARMs also have a minimum interest rate called a floor.

Rollover Mortgage (ROM), or Renegotiated Rate Mortgage:
This is a type of ARM. The interest rate remains the same for a specified time, usually three to five years, then the rate is renegotiated.

The lender must offer you refinancing with minimum or no fees or you can look for more favorable terms from other lenders.

- Get good legal advice before you accept the seller's terms.

- Establish both points and interest rate and when they are set or locked in.

    Some lenders establish both at the time you apply for a loan. Others do so when your loan application is approved. Still others allow either or both points and interest rates to rise and fall with market demands until the final closing date.

    Be sure to get the agreement in writing as a letter of commitment or mortgage commitment.

- Find out how long the lock-in lasts and what happens if the lock-in period expires before your closing date.

- To ensure that an organization is financially sound, ask for copies of annual reports or quarterly financial statements.

- Check your library for publications from national bank-rating services such as Veribanc, Inc.

- Ask if it's possible to prepay the mortgage (repaying the mortgage before its term expires) or if a penalty would be incurred.

How to Apply

Although you can shop ahead of time, you can initiate a mortgage application only after you have a signed contract to buy, which you should obtain from your real estate lawyer.

Lending policies vary, but most lenders will ask for information they can verify to show that you are a good credit risk, including:

- Account numbers and balances, plus the names and addresses of institutions holding your checking and savings accounts, and of institutions or credit card companies to which you owe money.

- Information about any judgments, such as for bankruptcy, or other financial obligations such as child support that apply to you.

- Value of your personal property (cars, stocks, bonds).

- Statement showing your monthly income.

- Your Social Security number.

- Current and previous addresses.

- Proof of employment.

- Past tax returns if you are self-employed.

USING YOUR EQUITY

As you pay off the mortgage and as more of the value of your home flows from your lender's hands into yours, it becomes possible to borrow against that built-up equity.

You may do so through a **second mortgage,** a **home equity loan,** or (most popular today) a **home equity line of credit,** which allows you to write checks against a specified amount determined by your equity. Depending on where you live, your creditworthiness, and the property you own, you can borrow from 60 percent to 90 percent of your equity.

A home equity loan and a home equity line of credit share some similarities:

- The interest paid is tax deductible.

- If you can't make payments, the lender may foreclose.

- You will have to pay for a credit check and appraisal as well as some other fees.

Lenders usually charge points for a home equity loan, but not for a home equity line of credit. Your choice depends on why you want the money and how you intend to repay it.

For example, if you're planning a one-stage addition, you'll probably want a short-term loan to pay the contractors. If you're considering a series of improvements over several years, you'll save on interest by using the line of credit.

TURNED DOWN?

If your loan application is denied, federal law requires the lender to tell you in writing the specific reasons. Be sure to ask questions so you completely understand the reasons. You may be able to find alternatives that will satisfy the institution's standards.

Reasons for a turn-down may be:

☛ The down payment offered is too small.

☛ The mortgage amount is too high compared with the property's appraised market value.

☛ Your credit history is unstable or your current level of debt is too high.

POINT COUNTERPOINT

☛ Many lenders offer "no-points" mortgages now, but at higher interest rates than the same mortgages with points. If you can afford it, you'll be better off paying the points and getting the lower interest rate.

INSURING YOUR PROPERTY

Insurance plans for home and auto offer protection against financial catastrophes caused by loss, theft, property damage, and personal liability.

You pay a **premium** (fee) monthly, quarterly, or annually for coverage. Most policies have a **deductible** (the amount that you have to absorb before you are eligible for insurance payments). The lower the deductible, the higher the premium.

SHOPPING AROUND

Decide what coverage you need and then do some comparison shopping. Here's how:

- Talk to at least three insurance agents (see box page 20). Do their recommendations agree with your plans?

- Compare rates; nearly identical coverage policies can vary greatly. Ask your state's insurance department for a price list.

- Look at group plans offered by professional and social organizations.

What You Should Know

Learn all you can about the company issuing the policy:

- Is it licensed in your state? This is especially important if you are considering a no agent direct policy purchased by phone. Find out by calling your state insurance department.

- What do state regulators know about the company and its underwriters?

Have they seen many complaints about unpaid claims?

Read the fine print:

- Ask as many questions as necessary to understand exactly what the policy does and does not cover.

- Don't assume anything. If your situation is different from the examples given, ask how the policy would apply to you.

Ask about payment choices:

- Usually your total premium will be smaller if you pay annually instead of monthly. Plan ahead so you have the amount ready.

- Consider taking a larger deductible.

- Find out how you can qualify for lower premiums. Consolidating all your policies with one company is one way. Other discounts may be available if you have such safety features as smoke detectors in your home and an air bag in your car.

HOME-OWNER'S INSURANCE

Home-owner's insurance protects your house, other structures on your property, and your possessions.

Most policies also pay temporary living expenses if your home is destroyed or severely damaged by a fire or storm.

Depending on where you live, you may want to investigate separate policies—sometimes called endorsements—

to cover floods (available only if your community is included under a federal program) or earthquakes.

Be sure to ask about any discounts or credits that may be available for such safety measures as dead bolts, smoke detectors, and fire extinguishers.

How Much Is Enough?

A general rule is to insure your house for at least 80 percent of its replacement value—what it would cost to repair or rebuild the house at current prices.

To calculate how much insurance you need, start with the current value of your property minus the value of the land. You can get an appraisal, ask for advice from your insurance agent, get an opinion from one or more real estate agents, or determine a figure based on building costs in your area.

For example, a 2,000-square-foot house in an area where typical building costs are $60 per square foot would rate a $120,000 policy.

Taking Stock

Review your coverage every year or two. If it falls below the 80 percent replacement figure, you will receive only a prorated share for any claim you make. If your insurer automatically increases your coverage yearly, you may still want to review and double-check the values.

The top-of-the-line home-owner's policy offers "guaranteed replacement cost coverage," and will repair or replace your home even in excess of the policy's stated amount.

Covering Household Contents

In addition to covering the structure, the standard home-owner's policy covers furniture and other contents up to 50 percent of the total policy amount. However, this is often for only fire and theft and only in amounts reflecting the actual cash value of the items lost rather than the amount you originally paid or would need to buy replacements.

Full replacement coverage is usually best, even though it's likely to cost more.

Depending on your situation, you may also want to ask about endorsements or floater policies to cover specific valuables such as jewelry and art, or business property like computers.

Liability Coverage

Liability coverage protects you when visitors are hurt on your property, and when you or a family member damages someone else's property. A basic policy usually includes $100,000 personal liability.

You may want an umbrella policy with coverage of $1 million or more. This may be advisable if you have household helpers, including child-care givers.

If you have a swimming pool, play area, or other buildings on the property that might tempt uninvited, unsupervised visitors, you would do well with such a policy.

CAR COVERAGE

As with other types of insurance, comparison shopping for auto insurance can really pay off—your costs for the same coverage can vary considerably. You may also qualify for discounts that reduce your premiums.

State law may partially dictate the type of auto insurance you buy.

Typical Coverage

A number of different types of coverage are available within an auto policy:

Liability: This protects you when your vehicle damages someone or something. You and your family are covered, as well as anyone using the vehicle with your permission.

The suggested minimum coverage is $100,000 per injured person, $25,000 for property damage, and $300,000 total per accident.

Another option is single-limit coverage, which pays up to $300,000 or more per accident for injuries.

Many agents recommend purchasing an umbrella policy as protection against

KEEP A RECORD

One of the most important steps you can take toward collecting on a future claim is to prepare a detailed household inventory:
☛ Write down the date of purchase, brand and model number, appraised value, and price paid for everything you can.
☛ Document your belongings with photographs or videotape. Keep the documentation in your safe-deposit box.

INSURE THYSELF

☛ If you don't want to buy an insurance policy, create a self-insurance fund by investing money in a special savings account. This can be used to cover repairs or damages that otherwise would have been covered by a conventional insurance policy.

DO YOU RENT?

☛ Remember that the landlord's policy covers only the building structure. Protect your possessions with renter's insurance, which is similar to a home-owner's policy.

WHAT YOU SHOULD KNOW ABOUT WARRANTIES

Cars and appliances generally come with warranties, a policy that usually lasts for three years or 36,000 miles on automobiles and the first year of ownership on appliances.

Read all the terms carefully and ask questions about any parts that need clarification.

Misunderstandings are common. Be sure to find out:

• What is or is not covered.

• For how long.

• Under what conditions.

You must operate and maintain the car or appliance following the manufacturer's guidelines in order to be eligible for coverage on repairs.

Routine maintenance doesn't have to be done by the dealer, but replacements must meet or exceed the manufacturer's specifications.

An extended warranty is a form of insurance. Consider the extent of the manufacturer's warranty when deciding whether or not to buy it. You may find that you'll get a better return on your money by setting up your own repair fund.

liability lawsuits. A $1 million umbrella liability policy typically adds $100 to $200 to your premium.

Uninsured motorists: This pays for injuries to you and your passengers caused by hit-and-run, uninsured, or underinsured drivers. Some states require this coverage. Your health or collision policy also may include it. Typical coverage is $15,000 per injured individual and $30,000 total per accident. However, some recommendations go as high as $50,000 to $100,000 to cover lost wages or pain and suffering.

Medical: This pays for medical expenses incurred within a certain time period following an accident. Compare with your health insurance coverage to avoid paying for overlapping policies.

Collision: This pays for vehicle damage regardless of fault, but in amounts only in excess of the stated deductible (based on the current cash value of the vehicle).

Comprehensive: This pays for vehicle damage resulting from a wide range of causes, including fire, theft, and vandalism.

Payment is limited to the cash value of the vehicle and may not be needed, depending on what your car is worth.

IS YOUR INSURANCE AGENT RIGHT FOR YOU?

INSURANCE COSTS ARE a necessary part of your household budget. Some agents represent only one company; others work with many companies. Contact both types to compare options.

ASK YOUR AGENT:

• How long have you worked with the company you represent?

• What are the company's assets? How is it rated by professional rating organizations?

• What percentage of my premiums will you receive as a commission? Do all the products you sell have the same commission?

• How do you learn about changes in policies and programs? What kind of continuing education program is available from the company or companies you represent?

• What kind of insurance do you use?

ASK YOURSELF:

• Does the agent offer me more than one option? Can he or she clearly explain the differences and consequences?

• Does the agent ask enough questions about my situation to know my true needs?

• Is the agent accessible whenever I need help?

CHAPTER 2

CLEANING

Your Credit Card ... *NG HINTS: How to* *Turn Bed Sheets* ... *rpeting* ☛HANDY *TIPS: For Buffing* ... *Glasses, Making* *Rooms Look Lar...* ... *a Car, Cleaning* *Tile Grout, Crea...* ... *Curtains, Save on* *Car Repairs, Buy Produce, Choose Carpeting* ☛STEP-BY-STEP GUIDES: *To Checkbook Security, Unblocking a Sink, Buying a Home, Successful Decorating, Performing CPR, Changing Flat Tires, Refinishing Furniture, Hanging Shelves, Lawn Mower Maintenance* ☛DO-IT-YOURSELF: *Create a Home Filing System, Make a Floor Plan* ☛SAVING TIME: **How to set priorities and delegate. Cutting out clutter. Cleanup calendar: What to clean when.** ☛THE RIGHT STUFF: **Equipment to fit every need. Vacuum cleaners: choosing the right model. Wet mops, dry mops, brooms, and brushes. Cleaning and allergies. Cleaning product roundup.** ☛FURNITURE: **Vacuuming and cleaning upholstery. Wood furniture: when to dust, polish, and wax. Treating minor blemishes. How to clean lamps, shades, electronic equipment, and telephones.** ☛FLOORS: **Caring for wood, vinyl, and masonry. To wax or not to wax. Rugs and carpets: spot and deep cleaning. Oriental rug care.** ☛WINDOWS AND DOORS: **No-streak glass washing. How to clean shades, blinds, and shutters.** ☛WALLS AND CEILINGS: **How to clean paint, wallpaper, wood paneling, brick, and stone. Tackling stains: easy solutions.** ☛THE KITCHEN: **Cabinets, counters, drawers, sinks, and appliances. Ovens: self cleaning and standard. How to load your dishwasher. Small appliance care: cleaning and polishing. Tips on tarnish.** ☛THE BATHROOM: **Tiles, sinks, tubs, and showers. Removing rust and mineral stains. No-streak mirror cleaning.** ☛THE NURSERY: **How to keep it clean and fresh. Helping children clean up after themselves. Easy storage solutions.** ☛PORCHES, DECKS, AND PATIOS: **Mixing a deck-cleaning solution. How to care for outdoor furniture: aluminum, canvas, plastic, and wood. Grill maintenance.** ☛EVERYTHING YOU NEED TO KNOW: *About Choosing Pots and Pans, Front-Wheel-Drive Cars, Making Healthier Meals, Vacuum Cleaners, Garden Tools, Upholstered Furniture, Your Credit Card Statement, Curtain Styles* ☛MONEY-SAVING HINTS: *How to Turn Bed Sheets into Curtains, Save on Car Repairs, Buy Produce, Choose Carpeting* ☛HANDY TIPS: *For Buffing Wood Floors, Preventing Carpet Dents, Unsticking Stacked Glasses, Making Rooms Look Larger, Ironing Pleated Skirts, Arranging Flowers, Jump-Starting a Car, Cleaning Tile Grout, Creating a Home Office, Fixing a Leaky Faucet* ☛STEP-BY-STEP GUIDES: *To Checkbook Security, Unblocking a Sink, Buying a*

Saving Time

Cleaning house, while necessary for all, is a very personal issue. Don't worry about other people's standards. Decide what "clean" means to you and keep house accordingly. Above all, use your time effectively. Here's how:

Establish priorities: Identify which tasks absolutely have to be done, which ones should be done, and which ones would be nice to get done. Work on them in that order, and forget about all others.

Set time limits: You can accomplish quite a bit in several ten- or twenty-minute periods. Keep your cleaning schedule flexible so you can change it if something unexpected comes up. Do *what* you can *when* you can.

Delegate: Teach your kids how to fold laundry, vacuum, dust, unload the dishwasher, make their beds, and prepare their breakfasts, lunches, and snacks. Enlist teens to help with big jobs like washing windows and floors and cleaning cabinets and woodwork.

Finish tasks: Complete one project before you start another.

Reward yourself for a job well done.

CUTTING OUT CLUTTER

You probably spend about half your cleaning time picking things up and putting them away. Get rid of clutter to lighten your workload and shorten cleaning time.

- Designate one area or room where the inevitable clutter can accumulate: a place where puzzles can be left out, where the sewing machine can stay open, where model airplanes can wait for completion.

- Place containers where clutter collects: a large toy box in the playroom; a basket for newspapers and magazines in the living room; a file cabinet for mail that otherwise may collect on the kitchen counter or hall table.

- Put up easily accessible hooks and shelves for hats, coats, schoolbooks, and other everyday items that usually end up on the floor or a chair.

- Sort through your belongings a few times each year and give or pack away anything you haven't used recently.

- Place a wastebasket in each room.

DIRT DEFENSE

You can keep your house cleaner by preventing outdoor dirt from getting in. Use doormats and boot scrapers. As needed, sweep sidewalks, steps, and stairwells leading to your home.

If you have the space, set up a mud room where wet and soiled clothing and boots can be removed and stored.

To reduce airborne dust, regularly vacuum registers and radiators (see box page 30). Change the filters in your air conditioners and furnace, following the manufacturer's instructions. If you have severe allergies, hire a professional yearly to clean heating and ventilation ducts to reduce dust and molds.

When to Go Pro

Professional services can handle most cleaning needs, from frequent cleaning of the whole house to seasonal jobs such as carpeting, upholstery, draperies, and windows. Such services can be expensive, but they save time and energy, and may do a more thorough job than you can. Ask your friends for recommendations and be sure to ask for and check references. Get estimates from at least two services before you hire.

TWO TIMING

☛ Make double use of your time—straighten the coat closet while waiting for the car pool; clean kitchen counters while talking on the telephone.

A FAMILY AFFAIR

☛ Set aside at least two hours once or twice a week for cleaning. Write down all necessary tasks on slips of paper, and put them in bowls according to difficulty. Every family member chooses from the appropriate bowl. Enforce the rule that everyone helps with some cleaning task during that time.

SPILL SAVVY

☛ Wipe up spills as soon as possible. The sooner you clean up, the easier it is to remove stains completely.

CLEANUP CALENDAR

Most people hate to clean house. In these busy times, it makes sense to be flexible and do only what you need to so that you can maximize and enjoy your leisure time. This timetable can help you stay on top of the job.

	KITCHEN	BATHROOMS	THROUGHOUT THE HOUSE
Daily	• Dispose of trash and recyclables • Hand wash and dry dishes or place them in the dishwasher (machine wash them when a full load has accumulated) • Wipe table, countertops, and range top • Wash coffeemaker thoroughly after each use. • Run food disposer and clean the sink. • Sweep or vacuum floor and wipe up any spots with a damp paper towel. • Clean cutting wheel on can opener, if needed.	• Wipe fixtures, chrome • Straighten towels • Vacuum	• Put clothing, books, toys, and other items where they belong • Straighten living spaces and bedrooms • Make beds

	KITCHEN	BATHROOMS	THROUGHOUT THE HOUSE
Weekly	• Thoroughly clean range top and front, drip pans, control knobs, and back splash • Organize refrigerator and wipe up spills. Dispose of any leftover foods that may spoil • Wipe refrigerator sides and top • Clean items on countertop; move them away from walls to wipe under and behind them • Wipe cabinet doors and sides, woodwork, doors, and smudges off walls • Sweep and mop floor • Flush disposer with cold water • Wipe table and chairs.	• Scrub bathtubs and sinks • Clean mirrors • Clean and disinfect toilets and shower stalls • Clean toothbrush and soap holders • Wipe tile surfaces, walls, shower doors, and woodwork • Wash floors	• Mop floors • Dust, including books, pictures, lamp bases and shades • Vacuum • Wipe smudges off walls and woodwork • Empty wastepaper baskets • Change bed linens • Clean the mirrors, telephones, and electronic equipment

(continued)

(continued)

	KITCHEN	BATHROOMS	THROUGHOUT THE HOUSE
Occasionally	• Thoroughly clean microwave oven	• Wash throw rugs and shower curtains	• Vacuum wall hangings, curtains, draperies, and radiators
	• Wash inside of refrigerator and freezer	• Wash windows, blinds, shades, or curtains	• Wash windows, walls, and woodwork
	• Defrost freezer (if not an automatic defrost) when the frost is ¼ inch thick	• Clean medicine cabinet and closets	• Clean light fixtures.
	• Wash ventilating fan/hood filters		• Move and clean under furniture
	• Thoroughly clean cabinets and drawers		• Wax or polish furniture
	• Dust walls, ceiling, blinds, and shades		• Deep-clean rugs and carpets; clean and wax bare floors, if necessary
	• Wash curtains, windows, and screens		• Turn mattresses and vacuum mattresses and box springs; launder mattress pads
	• Clean light fixtures		• Straighten closets and give away unneeded items
			• Clean garage, basement, and attic

FORGET SPRING CLEANING

☞ Clean as needed.
☞ Systematic, regular cleaning minimizes the need for heavy-duty seasonal cleaning.

THE RIGHT STUFF

Cleaning is easiest and fastest when your equipment fits your cleaning needs and stows away in a closet or storage space. Be sure to keep all your vacuum attachments and small items like dust cloths accessible so you can find them when you need them. Start with the basics: a vacuum cleaner, broom, and mop. Then add specialty equipment as your needs dictate and budget permits.

VACUUM CLEANERS

A good vacuum is essential for household cleaning, so always invest in a high-quality machine with optional attachments—special brushes and crevice tools—for specific jobs.

Use it not only for carpets and floors, but also for draperies and bathroom fixtures, to dust windowsills, moldings,

GOOD VACUUM MAINTENANCE

☛ Empty the dirt receptacle or replace the disposable bag before it is ¾ full. (Check it; don't rely on the indicator.) If you vacuum fireplace ashes or use powdered carpet fresheners, change the dust bag more often; the powder seals the pores of the bag, which decreases effectiveness.

VACUUM ROUNDUP

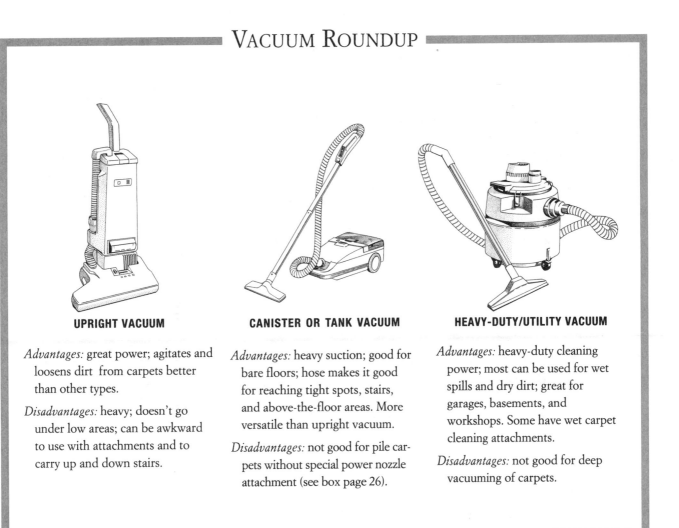

UPRIGHT VACUUM

Advantages: great power; agitates and loosens dirt from carpets better than other types.

Disadvantages: heavy; doesn't go under low areas; can be awkward to use with attachments and to carry up and down stairs.

CANISTER OR TANK VACUUM

Advantages: heavy suction; good for bare floors; hose makes it good for reaching tight spots, stairs, and above-the-floor areas. More versatile than upright vacuum.

Disadvantages: not good for pile carpets without special power nozzle attachment (see box page 26).

HEAVY-DUTY/UTILITY VACUUM

Advantages: heavy-duty cleaning power; most can be used for wet spills and dry dirt; great for garages, basements, and workshops. Some have wet carpet cleaning attachments.

Disadvantages: not good for deep vacuuming of carpets.

VACUUM CLEANER ATTACHMENTS

*UPRIGHT, CANISTER, HEAVY-DUTY, AND built-in central vacuums all come
with optional attachments for special cleaning needs. Most attach to a hose (6 to 8
feet long). Straight and curved wands help you reach places that normally
call for a step stool—ceilings, the tops of draperies, cabinets or high shelves, and
lighting fixtures. Use the extension wands with any of the attachments.
The following are especially useful:*

  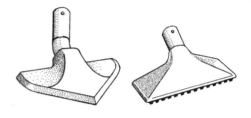

CREVICE TOOL

For vacuuming:
- Between radiator coils
- Cobwebs
- Drawers
- Filters, grilles, and air-condition-er fins
- Heating and air-conditioning ducts
- Refrigerator and freezer con-denser coils
- Underneath large appliances
- Upholstered furniture crevices

DUSTING BRUSH

For vacuuming:
- Baseboards
- Blinds
- Books
- Carved furniture
- Fireplace screens
- Lamps and lamp shades
- Piano keys
- Shelves
- Shutters
- Window and door moldings

UPHOLSTERY ATTACHMENTS

For vacuuming:
- Automobile interiors
- Carpeted stairs
- Curtains and draperies
- Hard-to-reach carpeted areas
- Mattresses
- Upholstered furniture fabric

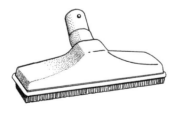

WALL/FLOOR BRUSH

For vacuuming:
- Bare floors
- Ceilings
- Flat rugs
- Walls

POWER NOZZLE

For vacuuming:
- Pile carpets and rugs (has motor-driven brush for deep cleaning)

and computer keyboards, to reach dirt in cracks and crevices, and to eliminate cobwebs.

Most vacuums can perform most jobs well, but some are better suited for specific tasks.

Upright

This is considered the best for wall-to-wall carpeting and large rugs; it uses suction and airflow to lift the carpet slightly off the floor and rotating brushes pick up deep dirt and dust. Some models provide a hose connection for above-the-floor cleaning.

Canister or Tank

This is a low-lying appliance; the canister, or tank—mounted on wheels or runners—is pulled along by the hose. The bag is in the canister. These cleaners are best suited for homes with many different surfaces and stairs to vacuum. A power nozzle is a must for vacuuming carpets.

Here are some extra features available on most uprights and canisters to make your vacuuming less of a chore:

• Adjustable suction

• Automatic pile height adjuster

• Bag-change indicator

• Built-in tool storage

• Edge-cleaning feature: removes embedded dirt near baseboards and around furniture

• Headlight

• Self-propelling feature: maneuvers the cleaner almost effortlessly

• Stair-cleaning handle on uprights

• Variable speed control: adjusts levels of suction and the brush speed; lower speed is used for delicate carpets, rugs, and bare floors

Built-in Central System

This system (generally installed when a house is being built) consists of a network of tubes built into the walls, floors, and ceilings with inlets located throughout the house.

To use it, you simply plug a long flexible hose into an inlet in each room; dirt is sucked into a receptacle located in the basement, utility room, or garage.

This system is expensive to install, particularly after a house is already built, but it is versatile, quick, easy, and clean to use.

Heavy-Duty/Utility

These hard-working vacuums are designed to pick up broken glass, nails, and wood shavings, which should never be cleaned up with a standard household vacuum. Many also pick up wet spills or with special attachments, clean carpet and upholstery.

HAND-HELD AND STICK CLEANERS

While not as powerful as full-size vacuums, these lightweight cleaners are easy to use for quick pickups and in-between big cleanings. Easy to store, they can be carried up and down stairs, or to the car. The dust cups are small, so you have to empty them regularly.

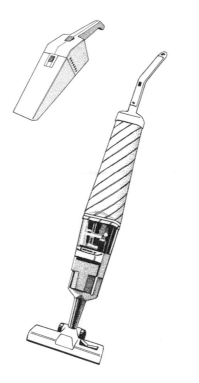

Brush Basics

SCRUB BRUSH
Use this short-bristled brush for general household cleaning.

TOILET BOWL BRUSH
Use this synthetic-bristled brush for cleaning all interior sections of the toilet bowl.

VENETIAN BLIND BRUSH
Use this multipronged padded brush for dusting venetian blind slats.

VEGETABLE BRUSH
Use this stiff-bristled brush for washing dishes and cooking utensils and a second one for scrubbing vegetables.

Broom Basics

GENERAL-PURPOSE BROOM
Use this for general cleaning; for sweeping large areas of floor, a large broom (10 inches wide by 14 inches high) is recommended.

WHISK BROOM
Use this small hand-held broom to remove lint from clothes or upholstery, and a second one for small amounts of dirt around plants, floors, and countertops.

PUSH BROOM
Use this squareback broom for sweeping the garage and basement floors, driveway, patio, and porch.

Cordless (battery-operated) and corded hand-held models are available. Many have tools or attachments (dusting brush, crevice tool, rotating brush) for greater versatility. Corded stick cleaners perform well on both bare floors and low carpets.

CARPET SWEEPER

The manual carpet sweeper is also lightweight and easy to store. In heavy traffic areas you can use it for quick pickups of surface dirt, lint, and crumbs before they work themselves into the carpet.

FLOOR SCRUBBER/POLISHER

If you need to scrub, wax, and polish floors or shampoo rugs, you can rent machines for these jobs.

The basic models will scrub and buff. More fully equipped models will scrub, wax, polish, buff, shampoo carpets, and even vacuum up the detergent and water solution. Combination machines are good for large areas of bare wood and resilient floors.

BRUSHES

Brushes are made with either natural (animal hair or palm fiber) or synthetic (nylon or less expensive plastics) bristles.

Natural bristles: sturdier and therefore best for scrubbing concrete, brick, and other hard or rough surfaces. Animal hair is useful for delicate fabrics.

Synthetic bristles: look better longer and dry faster.

- Wash brushes in warm, sudsy water to keep the bristles clean. Always dry them with the bristles down.

BROOMS

Stiff-bristled brooms work best outdoors—on sidewalks, stairs, and patios—while soft-bristled brooms will last longer if used indoors.

Natural bristles (such as palm): considered best—they last longer, but are also more expensive than brooms made from the traditional corn straw.

Synthetic bristles: are often flared to pick up more dirt and are angled to reach into corners.

- As they become dirty, rinse brooms under a hard stream of water. Shake the bristles to remove as much water as possible, then hang to dry.

MOPS

Wet Mops
These string or sponge mops, used with water, should have a wringing device to keep your hands dry, and readily available replacement heads that are easy to change.

- Rinse the mops well after each use and let dry.

String mop: much more maneuverable than sponge mops; good for tight corners and behind sinks and toilets. Choose a string mop with the head tied directly to the handle like a ponytail rather than a mop held with a metal clamp, which can scratch the floor.

- Wring the mop and hang it by its handle to dry. If possible, dry it in the sun.

Sponge mop: works well on large floor expanses, as in a kitchen. Look for "scrubber strips" on the sponge mop head to help remove tough stains.

- Wring the mop and turn it upside down to dry.

Dry mop

☞ Store products and equipment close to where you will use them. Duplicate supplies, if need be, to save time and energy, or keep all supplies in a tray or basket that you can carry from a central storage spot.

☞ Never store cleaning products where children or pets can reach them.

☞ Keep products in their original containers, away from where food is stored.

Dry Mops

These mops are made of synthetic or wool fibers. Both work well. Use a dry mop to dust bare floors when you don't want to use the vacuum cleaner. Spray with a dusting spray to avoid spreading dirt.

• Vigorously shake the mop outdoors after each use. Remove the head and wash it with dishwashing detergent and water. Rinse thoroughly, squeeze, then air dry before reattaching.

DUST CLOTHS

Use only clean cloths to dust. Wash or dispose of them as soon as they begin to look dirty. Never dry cloths that have been treated with wax or polish in an automatic dryer.

Treated cloths: recommended for easiest cleaning. Chemically pretreated cloths attract dust and dirt without leaving a film on furniture.

• Wash treated cloths as needed; the treatment remains on the cloth through many launderings.

Untreated cloths: use lintless cloths—cheesecloth, diapers, undershirts, or cotton flannel. Be sure to remove snaps, hooks, and buttons, which can scratch. Treat the cloth with a dusting spray. (A dry dust cloth merely spreads dust and scratches surfaces.)

CLEAN AND SAFE

When not used or stored properly, ammonia, bleach, cleansers, detergents, drain cleaners, furniture polish, oven cleaners, and other common household cleansers can cause rashes and respiratory ailments. To avoid problems:

• Read labels carefully.

• Use chemically based products sparingly; a small amount will often be enough to do the job.

• Don't mix household products; some create noxious fumes when combined.

ALLERGIC REACTIONS

MANY ALLERGY SUFFERERS are sensitive to dust mites, which live in carpets, bedding, and upholstered furniture (even clean homes have them; see page 289). Mites require moisture to survive. To lower the relative humidity in your house, use a dehumidifier, and be sure that your clothes dryer is vented outdoors.

• Dust and vacuum radiators, registers, vents, upholstered furniture, cushions, pillows, and carpets at least twice weekly if you're prone to allergies.

• Turn and vacuum your mattresses every two months. If pillows are not washable, put them in the dryer on the air-only cycle to eliminate the dust.

• Wash bedding frequently.

• Check to see whether your furnace has filters and whether they have been changed recently; they should be changed at least every two months to eliminate dust.

CLEANING PRODUCT ROUNDUP

*A*LL HOUSEHOLD CLEANING PRODUCTS COME *with directions detailed on the label; read and follow them and use the product only for recommended surfaces. You should take note of any warnings on the label.*

PRODUCT	GOOD FOR	HOW TO USE
Abrasive cleansers		
(powder)	Baked-on food residue, cooking utensils Tough stains on sinks and tub	Wet surface, apply cleanser; rub/scour as needed and rinse
(liquid)	Ceramic bathtubs, sinks, toilet bowls	Apply to surface; rub gently and rinse
Air, carpet, and room fresheners and deodorizers (aerosol, spray, powder, solid, heat-dispersed)	Counteracting odors in carpets, rooms, rugs, and upholstery	Sprinkle powdered carpet freshener on and leave for 10 to 15 minutes; vacuum; other forms, follow package directions
All-purpose cleaners		
(powder, liquid)	Appliance surfaces, glass ceramic and porcelain enamel range tops/cook tops, chrome, countertops, painted walls, painted and stainless steel, small plastic appliances, resilient and masonry floors, tile, window blinds/washable shades, painted woodwork	Mix with water or use liquids full-strength according to package directions. Generally no rinsing required, except for no-wax floors
(spray)	Appliances (spot cleaning and trim), chrome fixtures, laminate countertops, small washable areas, smudges on painted walls and woodwork, doors, and around switch plates	Spray on surface. Sponge, or wipe to clean; dry with towel or cloth
*Ammonia**	Chrome fixtures, combs and brushes, floors (resilient, ceramic, concrete), manually cleaned ovens, mirrors, painted walls, stainless steel, windows, painted woodwork **Do not use to clean plastic windows and on aluminum storm door windows. Clouding and pitting can occur**	You can control the cleaning strength by increasing the ammonia from ½ cup to 1 cup per gallon of water as the job difficulty increases. For spray bottle use: Mix 1 part ammonia to 16 parts water. For windows and mirrors: Use 1 tablespoon ammonia per 1 quart water
Baking soda	Baked-on food and odors in utensils, chopping boards, coffeepots, automatic waste disposers, freezers, refrigerators. Stains on plastic utensils and dishes, vacuum bottles. Bathtubs and sinks, ceramic countertops, chrome fixtures, fiberglass shower stalls, plastic laminate	*Paste:* Mix 3 parts baking soda to 1 part water. *Solution:* Mix 4 tablespoons baking soda per 1 quart water. *Dry:* Sprinkle straight from box. Rub with damp sponge or cloth; rinse and dry

(continued)

(continued)

PRODUCT	GOOD FOR	HOW TO USE
Carpet cleaners (liquid, foam, powder)	Rugs and carpets (spots and general cleaning)	Follow package directions. Some can be applied by hand; others require equipment
Chlorine bleach*	Disinfecting cutting boards, mildew on grout and ceramic tile, patio bricks, stains on hard surfaces, toilet bowls, wooden decks (see page 60)	Mix ¾ cup bleach to 1 gallon water Increase strength as needed
Drain cleaners (liquid, granular)	Dissolving grease, hair, soap-scum buildup. Sluggish drains—kitchen and bathroom	Follow package directions precisely
Dusting products (aerosol and pump, liquid, paste)	Furniture	Apply product to cloth; wipe over surface; buff to a shine
Glass cleaners (liquid, spray)	Chrome, mirrors, glass tabletops, doors, and windows. Do not use on acrylic plastic doors, windows, clock face protectors	Spray directly on windows or on cloth or sponge for mirror or picture glass. Wipe and dry.
Metal cleaner/polish	Various metals—brass, copper, silver, etc. Some contain antioxidant to protect cleaned surface from rapid retarnishing	Follow package directions
Mildew removers	Ceramic tile grout in showers, bathrooms (see page 57)	Follow package directions. Use in well-ventilated areas. Avoid contact with fabrics
Oven cleaners (liquid, sponge, spray)	Removing charred grease and food deposits from ovens and barbecue grills	Follow package directions
Scouring pads (soap impregnated)	Baked-on food, barbecue grills, broilers, cooking utensils, ovens	Wet and use
Toilet bowl cleaners (crystal, liquid, in tank)*	Cleaning; some also disinfect	Follow package directions
Tub, tile, and sink cleaners (liquid, spray)	Ceramic wall tiles, fiberglass, plastic, and porcelain bathtubs, shower stalls, and sinks, toilet bowl exteriors	Apply to surface, rub gently, rinse thoroughly, and wipe dry with cloth
Upholstery cleaners (liquid, aerosol spray, powder)	Upholstery fabric	Follow package directions. Test in an inconspicuous place on fabric
Vinegar (white)*	Automatic drip coffeemakers, appliance exteriors, chrome, glass windows and doors, mirrors, hard water deposits on bathtubs, shower stalls/curtains, sinks	Use full strength or diluted depending on use. To clean automatic drip coffeepots, fill reservoir with vinegar and water and run through a brew cycle; follow with a cycle of clear water to rinse (see page 54).

*Do not mix chlorine bleach with vinegar, ammonia, or a toilet bowl cleaner. Resulting toxic fumes may cause illness.

FURNITURE

All furniture needs frequent basic cleaning to keep it looking attractive. Treat your furniture kindly. Dust and polish wood frequently, vacuum upholstery before dirt weakens fabric fibers, and treat spots before they stain.

UPHOLSTERY

Many fabrics have protective finishes that resist soil and stains. Some repel water, others oil and water. But no fabric, treated or untreated, is soilproof.

- Vacuum regularly with the upholstery tool to extract dust and gritty dirt from smooth fabrics.
- Use the dusting tool for napped fabrics (velvets, velour, corduroy, and plush). To thoroughly clean, remove the cushions and vacuum the base, back, arms, and sides.
- Use a crevice tool in corners, areas between cushions that aren't removable, and along welted seams and in tufted surfaces.

Spots and Stains

Before cleaning upholstery, always spot test by cleaning a hidden area first. If you can, also check the cleaning code (see below).

- Blot up spills with absorbent towels, a cloth, or a sponge.
- Scrape up solids with a spoon or lift them off with a dull knife.
- Treat any remaining grease-based stains with a dry-cleaning fluid. Never use dry-cleaning fluid on furniture padded with foam rubber; it will damage it.
- For other soils, use a foam or spray upholstery cleaner. Follow the directions exactly, and test the cleaner in an inconspicuous place on the fabric for colorfastness before beginning.

Do-It-Yourself Cleaning

Vacuuming is the best cleaning method for upholstery, but there are occasions when the fabric will begin to appear soiled and you will need a do-it-yourself upholstery cleaner. If you use a cleaner, be gentle and use as little as possible. Vacuum first to remove surface dirt and soil.

There are various types to choose from: foam, powdered, and dry cleaning fluid, which has a solvent base. Different fabrics require different treatments. Select the

CLEANING CODES

The furniture industry has developed codes for cleaning upholstery fabrics. You will find the code on the piece of furniture and on sample fabric swatches.

W Clean the fabric with a water-based product, such as foam from a mild detergent or nonsolvent upholstery shampoo.

S Clean the fabric with a solvent-based cleaner.

WS Clean the fabric with a nonsolvent- or a solvent-based cleaning product.

X Have the fabric professionally cleaned.

appropriate type for your furniture and follow the package directions carefully. Always test the cleaner in a hidden area.

WOOD

Dust and grit may scratch the finish on wood furniture if it accumulates. Dust from once to several times each week, depending on your standards and the amount of dust in your home. Use the soft, round brush attachment on the vacuum cleaner for flat surfaces, chair rungs, table and chair legs. For light dusting, use cloths treated with an antistatic agent or a soft clean cloth and a dusting spray.

Never dry-dust. Not only do dry cloths scatter dust, but they also can scratch the surface, which will eventually dull the finish.

Start dusting at the top of each item, working down to the bottom. Remember to wipe the edges and fronts of drawers, doors, and cabinets. Follow the grain of the wood, gathering the dust into the cloth to avoid scattering it.

Polishing and Waxing

Creams, polishes, and wax not only protect and clean wood furniture, but they also enhance the wood's natural look.

Choosing the right furniture care product, however, depends upon the wood finish (shellac, varnish, lacquer, oil, and plastic laminates) and the amount of shine you want. Read the label. Once you have found the right product, stick to it. Using more than one—especially wax and oil—may damage the finish.

Before using a product for the first time, try it out on an inconspicuous spot to make sure it won't damage the finish. Use it sparingly and apply it to a clean, dry cloth; never put it directly on your furniture.

Be sure to wipe the surface dry; otherwise, the finish may streak. Always rub with the grain of the wood until all of the product is absorbed and the desired luster is achieved.

OTHER MATERIALS

Acrylic (Lucite and Acrylic Plastic) and Glass

Dust the surface with a clean, damp cloth or chamois, wiping gently. The damp cloth cuts down on friction, helping reduce static electricity which attracts and holds dust. Wash with a mild detergent and water solution for acrylic or with an ammonia and water solution or glass cleaner for glass.

Use a soft cloth or a clean sponge; the material scratches easily. Rinse with a clean, damp cloth and dry with a clean, soft cloth.

Chrome, Stainless Steel, and Wrought Iron

Dust with a clean, soft cloth or the dusting tool on your vacuum. Clean with a cloth soaked in a mild detergent and water solution, baking soda and water (4 tablespoons baking soda in 1 quart of water), or an all-purpose cleaner solution; rinse and dry with a clean, soft cloth.

For added protection to wrought iron, apply a thin coat of paste or liquid wax with a clean cloth.

Leather

Dust with a clean, soft cloth. Use a soft-bristled toothbrush or paintbrush if the leather is tufted and has buttons or piping. Wipe with a clean, damp sponge or cloth and mild soap. Dry with a clean, soft cloth.

Clean and polish sealed-leather tabletops with paste wax once or twice a year or when you do the surrounding wood.

Marble

Marble is not as durable as it appears. It is very porous and stains quite easily. Dust with a clean, soft cloth. Damp-dust occasionally with a clean sponge or cloth dampened in warm water. Dry the surface with a clean, soft cloth. Wipe up spills immediately.

Clean and restore marble with a marble polish, available in hardware and furniture stores. You can also apply a thin coat

---

CUSHION CARE

☛ To help upholstered furniture wear evenly, flip and turn the cushions every few months. Swap the far right sofa cushion with the far left cushion; switch two matching chair cushions.

WOOD FURNITURE POLISH ROUNDUP

Make your polish selection based on the amount of gloss you want, the amount of protection your furniture needs, and the amount of time the method requires. Wax provides the most protection; dusting sprays the least.

PRODUCT	GLOSS	PROTECTION	COMMENTS
Paste Waxes	Medium-Low	Superior	Time consuming to apply; long drying time. Buffing needed. Must be removed after 2 to 3 applications.
Liquids (*waxes*)	High	Very Good	Easier to apply than pastes. Most require some drying time and light rubbing.
(*oils—for use on unsealed wood*)	High	Good	Oils can smear and fingerprint if not completely dry. Waxes and oils should not be interchanged as they can build up and attract soil.
(*creams*)	Medium-High	Good	Same as oils.
Aerosols (*waxes*)	Medium-High	Very Good	Contain silicone for easy application and good shine. They also contain solvents to clean soil and remove previous coats of wax.
(*oils*)	Low-Medium	Good	As with liquids, aerosol waxes and oils should not be used interchangeably.
Dusting Sprays	None-Low	None	Help in removing dust without leaving anything on finish. Good for frequent dusting. Reduce the abrasive effects of dry-dusting.

of paste wax and polish while the wax is moist, but be aware that paste wax will cause white marble to yellow. Greasy stains may be removed by washing with ammonia; rinse thoroughly; dry.

Vinyl and Plastic
Use a sponge dampened with detergent to dust and clean vinyl and plastic; rinse and wipe dry with a clean cloth.

Wicker, Rattan, Bamboo, and Cane
Vacuum, using a brush to loosen dust and dirt. Sponge rattan, bamboo, and cane with a solution of water and hand dishwashing detergent; for wicker wash gently with a soft-bristled paintbrush or toothbrush. Rinse with a clean, damp sponge and dry the surface immediately. A light coat of furniture polish will renew natural or dark wicker, rattan, and cane. Avoid using on white or pastel colors.

Keep furniture out of direct sunlight and away from heat to keep the fibers from drying out and warping. To further prevent drying and splitting, wet wicker, rattan, and cane furniture periodically with a hose or put it under a bathroom shower and dry immediately.

Nutty Solution

☛ To camouflage a wood scratch, break the meat of a brazil nut, black walnut, or pecan in half and rub it in.

TRY THESE SOLUTIONS TO COMMON problems on wood surfaces (for cleaning materials see box page 37). All repair work should be followed with a coat of wax.

Alcohol: Alcohol has a tendency to dissolve most finishes, so blot the spot immediately, then put a few drops of ammonia on a damp cloth and wipe the area.

If the spot still remains, make a thin paste of boiled linseed oil and rottenstone, and rub it into the stain with your finger. Wax or polish.

Bloom or fog (whitening): This condition is often noticeable on wooden chair arms, backs or seats, around handles on wooden cabinets, or on bed headboards when the humidity is high. Clean the area with a creamy white appliance polish. If that does not work, add 1 tablespoon of cider vinegar to 1 quart of water; moisten a clean cloth and squeeze dry, rub the finish, and wipe dry. Rewax.

Candle wax: To harden the wax, rub an ice cube wrapped in plastic over the spill, then scrape the hardened wax off with a nonstick spatula or an expired plastic credit card.

Cigarette burn: For a burn that hasn't penetrated the wood finish, make a thin paste of pumice and boiled linseed oil, and apply it to the burned area. Wax or polish, working with the grain of the wood. If the burn is very deep and the damage too severe, professional refinishing may be necessary.

Heat mark: Blot the heat mark with a cloth dampened with boiled linseed oil and rub dry with a clean cloth. If the heat mark still remains, rub gently with fine steel wool dipped in a paste wax. Wipe off any excess and repolish.

Ink stain: Make a thin paste with rottenstone and boiled linseed oil. Apply it to the stain with your finger and rub with the grain of the wood. Wax or polish.

Milk: Wipe up spilled milk or food containing milk or cream with a damp cloth immediately. If spots remain, clean the area with a creamy white appliance polish. If further attention is needed, follow the suggestions given for removing alcohol.

Nail polish: If the spilled polish is still wet, blot clean and wipe any remaining residue with mineral spirits. Avoid nail polish remover—it contains solvents that can soften and dissolve the furniture finish.

Soak the stain for no longer than five minutes with boiled linseed oil, then scrape off the residue with a nonstick spatula or an expired plastic credit card. Repeat the process as needed.

Paint: Wipe fresh water-based paint with a cloth dampened with warm water. Scrape old water-based paint spots with a nonstick spatula or an expired credit card. Remove any remaining paint using a thin paste of boiled linseed oil and rottenstone. To remove fresh oil-based paint, rub the spot gently with a creamy white appliance polish. For old oil-based paint stains, cover the spots with linseed oil, soak for 5 minutes, then gently scrape with a nonstick spatula. Then wet another cloth with linseed oil and wipe over the area. Repeat, if necessary, or use the rottenstone and oil treatment.

Scratch: First try rubbing the scratch using a thick paste of boiled linseed oil with either pumice or rottenstone, depending on the depth of the scratch.

If the scratch is still noticeable, apply a paste wax and rub lightly with extrafine (000) steel wool (see page 211) in the direction of the grain.

For deeper scratches, wax touch-up sticks or furniture markers may be necessary. These are available in a selection of wood colors in paint or hardware stores.

Water mark: Wipe the water spot immediately, and rub a thin paste of boiled linseed oil and rottenstone over the spill. If this does not completely remove it, place a clean, thick blotter over the spot and press with a warm (not hot) iron; repeat this process until the ring disappears.

LAMPS AND LAMP SHADES

Dust the base of the lamp, the bulb, and the shade with a soft cloth or the dusting tool on your vacuum cleaner.

Clean the base with a damp sponge or cloth and the cleaning product appropriate for the material (see pages 31–32). Do not immerse the base in water as this damages the wiring.

Washable Shades (Sewn Trim)
Fill a deep tub or bathtub with enough warm water to cover the shade. Add an all-purpose liquid detergent. Dip the shade up and down in the sudsy water.

When the water gets dirty, change it. To rinse, repeat the process with clean water.

To dry, tie a string to the middle of the frame, then hang the shade over the bathtub or a clothesline (not in the sun) to drip-dry. Or put it in front of a fan to dry. To keep the metal frame from rusting, wipe it with a dry cloth and dry the shade as quickly as possible.

Plastic, Plastic-Coated, Laminated, or Parchment Shades (Glued Trim)
Wipe the shade with a damp cloth or dampened paintbrush and dry with a clean cloth. If the lamp has a reflector bowl, remove and wash it, using a warm water and detergent solution. You can also try a dough or a sponge type dry cleaner designed for use on wallpaper.

MIRRORS AND PICTURE GLASS

Use a commercial window cleaner, a solution of 1 tablespoon of ammonia per quart of water, or a solution of equal parts of vinegar and water.

Dip a sponge, paper towel, or cloth in the cleaner. Never spray it directly on the mirror or picture glass; the solution may damage the picture or the mirror backing.

Wipe dry with a lintless cloth, chamois, paper towel, or crumpled newspaper.

ELECTRONIC EQUIPMENT

Always unplug electronic equipment before cleaning. Avoid household cleaners containing chlorine.

Televisions
When the screen is cool, wipe it with a damp paper towel; towel dry. Dust and polish a wood cabinet as you would other wood furniture (see page 34). If the cabinet is plastic, wash it periodically with a mild detergent and water solution; rinse with a damp cloth and dry.

Clean metal or chrome trim and plastic or glass trim or doors with a soft cloth moistened with rubbing alcohol, white vinegar, or window cleaner; dry with a paper towel.

VCRs
Clean the exterior of a VCR as you would a TV. VCR player heads need intermittent cleaning. Refer to the owner's manual for the proper method.

Stereo Equipment
Vacuum the ventilation louvers of your stereo, tape deck, or CD player and speaker grilles every now and then to prevent dust buildup, which can cause overheating.

Keep records clean; surface dirt can be ground into the grooves when records are dropped during changing. Records collect static electricity, which attracts dirt and dust. A variety of products are available to help control the static charge.

Cassette heads need to be cleaned occasionally with tapes made specifically for that. But otherwise, cassettes and compact discs are rarely exposed to dirt, so they need little cleaning.

Computers, Word Processors, and Typewriters
Never use household glass cleaners on computer monitor screens. Instead, use a static-free product made for cleaning monitor screens or the same method used for TV screens. Keep static-free covers

SCREEN CLEAN

☞ Never use a liquid cleaner or an aerosol product to clean the television screen. Use a paper towel dampened with water.

SETTING OFF SPARKS

☞ When cleaning a computer, ground yourself by touching something metallic to discharge any static buildup before touching the equipment to avoid shock.

FURNITURE ELIXIRS

In addition to the common household products you probably already have, keep the following supplies (available in hardware, paint, or wallpaper stores) on hand for furniture repair.

Rottenstone is a fine, abrasive limestone powder used to create a hand-rubbed finish. It can also be used to remove minor blemishes.

Pumice, a harder abrasive than rottenstone, is used for deeper, more severe scratches—it may also leave a dull spot, in which case, a paste of rottenstone and boiled linseed oil is recommended.

Boiled linseed oil, a yellowish drying oil, provides color to cover minor scratches.

on the computer and printer when they are not in use.

Use the crevice tool on your vacuum to remove the tiny paper particles from the paper opening on the printer and to remove dust and dirt from the crevices in the keyboard On most keyboards, you can use a cotton swab dipped in alcohol or in a window-cleaning solution to clean between the keys. Special minivacs are available from computer stores to remove dust from these hard-to-clean areas.

Telephones

Wipe the handset and base or cradle of the telephone with a damp cloth and an all-purpose household cleaner. Wring the cloth out well to prevent water from getting into the unit. Unscrew the ear and mouth caps (if they are removable) and wash in a detergent and water solution. Dry them thoroughly before replacing. Use a moist cotton swab to clean under the dial or between push buttons.

Wipe the mouthpiece with a cloth sprayed with an aerosol disinfectant, wrung out in liquid disinfectant solution, or dampened with alcohol.

IS NO WAX
NO CARE?

☞ No-wax resilient floors require regular washing with all-purpose cleaners and rinsing to protect their finish. If you use specially formulated products to clean and shine them, and the floor has a dull appearance, it may need to be stripped (see page 40). If necessary, use a polish to fill in scratches, and add a protective shine.

CLEAN RINSES

☞ Keep a sponge mop just for rinsing floors; it is almost impossible to get all the cleaning solution out of a mop.

FLOORS

Of all the surfaces in your home, floors probably take the hardest beating. If floors are not kept clean, dirt underfoot can mar the surface or damage carpet fibers. Dirt doesn't stick to a clean surface as readily as it does to one that is soiled or rough from wear.

Wipe up spills as soon as they occur to prevent tracking and stains. Sweep, dust, or vacuum dry soil as often as needed and before mopping, waxing, and polishing.

A variety of products is available to make floor care easier and more effective. Floors can be damaged by using the wrong cleaner, cleaning method, wax, or finish, so choose carefully and read the label.

WOOD

Vacuuming and dust mopping on a regular basis are the best care you can provide for your wood floor. Vacuuming is especially good because it lifts dirt from seams between floor boards. Other general care tips are:

- Never pour water on a wood floor because it can cause warping and stains.

- Wipe up spills as soon as they occur.

- Place glides or floor protectors under furniture legs to prevent scratches.

- Use rugs in heavy-traffic areas to protect the floor.

- Keep high heels in good repair. Worn heels can destroy a wood floor.

- Use mats and throw rugs at doorways to prevent dirt from being tracked on the floor.

Caring for the Finish
The first step in caring for a wood floor is to know how it has been finished or sealed. To find out, try smudging the

surface in a hidden area with your finger.

If there is no smudge, the floor has been treated with a "surface finish" such as polyurethane.

If you see a smudge, the floor has been treated with a penetrating wax.

Surface Finish

Most new floors installed today have a surface finish and do not require waxing.

For general cleaning, mist a small area of the floor with a solution of ¼ cup of white vinegar to 1 quart of warm water, drying with a clean cloth as you go.

Never use oil soap, detergent, ammonia or any cleaning product that mixes with water because it can dull or damage the wood. Never wax a surface finish.

If the finish is dull, buff with a clean cloth to restore the luster. If this doesn't work, it may be time for a recoating.

Penetrating Wax

Penetrating wax soaks into the wood pores and hardens to seal the wood against dirt and stains and will not chip or scratch.

If your floor has been waxed and appears dull, try buffing a small area by hand with a clean cloth to see if you can restore the luster.

If this doesn't work, apply a solvent-based wax (available in paste, liquid, or liquid buffing/wax cleaner combination) specifically for wood floors. Such waxes, which have the odor of mineral spirits, should not have water listed as an ingredient.

Do not use a wax for resilient or tile floors because it can damage the finish and leave a dirt-attracting residue.

Apply a thin coat, which creates a more protective finish than a thick coat. Wax once or twice a year; more in heavy-traffic areas.

Complete refinishing, where machine sanding removes the old layers of finish and exposes new wood, may be necessary if a floor has been subjected to wear or neglect. This can be a difficult task and may best be left to a professional (see page 224).

RESILIENT SURFACES

Clean and protect resilient floors—no-wax vinyl, conventional vinyl, asphalt, and rubber tile—regularly. There are a variety of products available for doing so. Check the product label to make sure it is appropriate for the material.

To clean: Damp-mop at least once a week before the floor is badly soiled. Mix an all-purpose cleaning solution in a bucket.

THE GREAT STAIN RUB-OUT

ALWAYS WORK ON a stain on a waxed floor from the outer edge to the center, working with the grain, to prevent it from spreading. Be gentle. Repeat, if necessary. Never use the following methods on a floor coated with polyurethane or another surface treatment. Most spills wipe easily off these floors.

Alcohol: Rub the spot with a solvent-based wax, silver polish, boiled linseed oil, or a cloth slightly dampened in ammonia. Rewax.

Chewing gum, candle wax, and crayon: Apply ice until the material is hard and crumbles off. If the deposit remains, pour a solvent-based wax around the area (not on it) to soak under the deposit and loosen it.

Cigarette burn: Rub the burn with extra fine (000) steel wool (see page 211) dipped in a solvent-based wax.

Food and dried milk: Gently rub the stain with a slightly damp cloth. Rub dry and rewax.

Heel and furniture caster marks: Rub the mark with extra fine (000) steel wool (see page 211) dipped in a solvent-based wax; buff to a shine.

Oil and grease : Saturate cotton with hydrogen peroxide and place over stain. Saturate a second layer of cotton with ammonia and place over the first. Check after a few minutes. Repeat the treatment until the stain is removed.

Water mark : Rub the spot with extra fine (000) steel wool (see page 211) and rewax.

How to Remove Floor Polish

From time to time you need to strip polished masonry and resilient floors to prevent buildup, especially if using a new product or if you are unsure what product has been used before. Here's how:

1. Mix a solution of ¼ cup of powdered all-purpose cleaner, 1 cup of ammonia, and ½ gallon of cool water in a bucket. (Cool water helps ammonia retain its cleaning power.)

2. Puddle on the solution and use a sponge mop or cloth to spread the solution evenly over a 3' x 3' area. Let it soak for 3 to 5 minutes to soften the old polish. (On tile floors, let it soak 1 to 3 minutes.)

3. Scrub briskly with a stiff nylon or natural bristle brush to loosen the softened polish.

4. Wipe up the solution and the old polish with a clean cloth or a sponge mop. Rinse with a cloth or sponge mop dipped in plain water. Repeat for the remaining floor area. Let the floor dry.

FLOOR PHONE

☛ The National Wood Flooring Association provides a wood floor help line. Consumers can call 1-900-646-WOOD to ask any questions about maintaining or installing wood floors.

EASY RUG CLEANING

☛ At least twice a year, vacuum rug padding and the floor beneath it.

☛ Turn rugs around now and then so they wear and soil evenly.

☛ Stand on one end of a throw rug when vacuuming to keep it in place.

Dip in a mop; sponge, then wring some out (keep it damp enough to loosen dirt).

Clean the floor with slow, even strokes, using just enough pressure to loosen and pick up soil.

Rinse the mop or sponge frequently. Change the cleaning solution when necessary. Rinse the floor with a mop, sponge, or cloth dipped in clean water; allow to dry.

To shine: Pour a saucer-size pool of polish on the clean floor. Use a clean sponge mop, cloth, or polish applicator to spread it evenly over a 3' x 3' section.

Repeat until the entire floor is covered. Do not rinse. Let the floor dry for about 30 minutes.

On porous floors, wait at least a day for the polish to set. If you want a tougher finish, apply a second coat.

To refresh the shine periodically, damp-mop floors with ½ cup of polish added to 1 gallon of warm water. After 6 to 8 applications, or at least once a year, remove the polish and apply a new coat (see above).

To clean and shine: A product that cleans and shines combines cleaning agents for dirt removal with polish for shine and protection.

Pour a 10- to 12-inch puddle of it on the floor. Soak a damp sponge mop in the product. First mop with a scrubbing action, then with long strokes to even out the polish. For best results, rinse the mop in clean water between washing each 3- to 4-foot section of floor. Repeat until the entire floor is cleaned and protected. Remove these products after every 6–8 applications (see above).

MASONRY

Masonry floors—stone, marble, brick, terrazzo, unglazed ceramic tile, and quarry tile—are porous and susceptible to staining, so they should be sealed (except glazed ceramic tile) with a permanent sealer designed for use on this type of floor. Once sealed, care should be easy. Clean and vacuum them regularly. Many specific products are available for general floor cleaning and stain removal. Check with the flooring manufacturer or retailer and follow label directions. Grout, too, can stain easily, so it's a good idea to seal it also (see page 184).

RUGS AND CARPETS

More dirt settles into your carpets than in all the rest of your house. It's essential to remove surface dirt before it becomes ground in. Too much wet cleaning, however, can also cause damage and wear.

Vacuuming
Before vacuuming a carpet, pick up small objects, such as paper clips, coins, and buttons. Slowly move the vacuum over the carpet several times, going back and forth and side to side in parallel rows. Carefully go over areas in front of sofas, chairs, and doorways where soil from shoes collects and can be ground into the carpet.

- Move furniture as short a distance as possible to save your energy and time. Tip a chair back or to the side, move the end of a table an inch or two to

clean where the legs were, and then move it back.

- Once a month, vacuum the entire carpet thoroughly. Move furniture and vacuum all areas. Use the vacuum tools to clean the carpet adjacent to the baseboard, under and around heating and air-conditioning units/vents, in corners, and hard-to-reach areas.
- Check the vacuum cleaner bag often.

Deep Cleaning
Even if you vacuum carefully and consistently, heavy traffic and heavily soiled areas may require deep cleaning every six months (see page 43 for methods).

Often, a professional can do a more thorough job, with less risk of shrinking, fading, or staining the carpet due to over-wetting. You might alternate a professional service with do-it-yourself cleaning, or use a professional only for the dirtiest or most delicate areas. Always deep-clean Oriental carpets professionally.

Before hiring a service, get a reference from a friend or neighbor. Check to see if the service will give you an estimate, and if pickup and delivery services are included in the cleaning cost.

(see page 184).

(see page 43 for methods)

DEPRESSED CARPETS?

☞ Carpet dents occur when heavy furniture remains in one position for a long time. Periodically shifting the location of furniture helps prevent permanent damage. Furniture coasters are an even better idea.

☞ After the furniture is moved, brush the dented area with your fingertips to loosen and bring up the mashed tufts.

☞ If depressions are still noticeable after a few days, lay a damp terry cloth towel over them and press lightly with an iron using the wool or cotton heat setting. Leave the towel in place until dry. Remove it and the depression will be gone.

STAIR STRATEGIES

☞ To vacuum stairs, start at the top and work your way down.

☞ If you're not using a hand-held vacuum with rotating brush, use the upholstery tool of your vacuum to clean the carpet where the step and riser meet.

VACUUMING ORIENTAL RUGS

Oriental rugs, which are the most fragile of all area rugs, can be vacuumed safely—and should be as often as other carpets to keep them in peak condition. Vacuum as usual, except when approaching the fringe. With an upright cleaner, tip up the front of the cleaner slightly and push it completely off the carpet. This cleans the fringe without catching it in the agitator. With a canister use a floor brush or upholstery attachment for the fringe.

Spot Cleaning Steps

When spot cleaning carpets, follow these guidelines:

- Before treating, use a spoon or dull knife to pick up any excess solids. Always move from the outer edges toward the middle.

- Blot with a clean, white absorbent cloth or paper towel until dry. Never rub or scrub a stain.

- Be sure not to overwet the stain with the cleaning formula. Apply sparingly and, once again, blot with a white absorbent cloth or paper towel. Excess amounts could damage the backing and padding.

- Continue to blot the stain until it is gone and no more moisture can be absorbed. To remove excess moisture or stain residue, place an absorbent towel, weighted with a heavy colorfast object (like a book), over the cleaned area. Leave overnight.

- Allow the cleaned area to dry before walking on the carpet and attracting soil. Groom the pile by hand to restore it to its original condition.

- Many stains take time to respond to a cleaning formula and may even need repeated treatments.

Most spots can be treated if you attend to them as quickly as possible; the longer a stain has a chance to soak in, the harder it is to remove. Before you apply any cleaning formula, find a hidden spot and put a few drops on the carpet (or on each color if there is a pattern) and press with a white absorbent cloth or paper towel. Count to ten. If any dyes have bled onto the cloth call a professional cleaner.

CLEANING AGENTS

SOLVENT =	DETERGENT =	AMMONIA =	VINEGAR =
dry-cleaning solvent, available at a hardware store or supermarket	solution of 1 cup warm water and 1 teaspoon of mild, hand dishwashing detergent	solution of 1 cup warm water and 1 tablespoon of non-sudsing household ammonia	solution of 1 cup warm water and 2 tablespoons white distilled vinegar

How to Use This Chart:

Try the first method listed. Proceed to the second only if needed, and so on. Remember to rinse well and blot after each method tried. **Avoid using an ammonia solution on wool carpets.**

Asphalt/tar: solvent; detergent

Alcoholic beverages/beer/wine: detergent; vinegar. If any stain remains, apply denatured alcohol or a dry-cleaning solvent.

Berries: detergent; vinegar

Blood: sponge with cold water. Detergent; ammonia; detergent (ingredients must be cold).

Butter/oil: solvent; detergent

Candy (sugar): detergent; vinegar. If any stain remains, apply denatured alcohol or a dry-cleaning solvent.

Catsup: detergent; ammonia; detergent

Chewing gum: Freeze with an ice cube. Carefully remove as much as possible with a dull knife; apply solvent; wait several minutes; work residue out of fibers; blot; repeat if necessary

Chocolate: detergent; ammonia; detergent

Coffee/tea: detergent; vinegar. If any stain remains, apply denatured alcohol or a dry-cleaning solvent.

Cough syrup: detergent; ammonia; vinegar; detergent

Crayon: solvent; detergent

Dirt: detergent; ammonia; detergent

Egg: detergent; ammonia; detergent

Excrement: detergent; ammonia; detergent

Foundation makeup: solvent; detergent

Fruit juice: sponge with cold water; detergent; vinegar. If any stain remains, apply denatured alcohol or a dry-cleaning solvent.

Furniture polish: solvent; detergent

Glue (model, hobby): solvent. If stain remains, carefully apply non-oily nail polish remover.

Glue (white): detergent; ammonia; detergent

Gravy: solvent; detergent

Hair spray: solvent; detergent

Hand lotion: solvent; detergent

Ice cream: detergent; ammonia; detergent

Ink (ballpoint): solvent; detergent

Ink (fountain pen): detergent; vinegar; ammonia

Ink (permanent): detergent; ammonia; vinegar; detergent

Linseed oil: solvent; detergent

Machine oil/grease: solvent; detergent

Mascara: solvent; detergent

Mayonnaise: detergent; ammonia; detergent

Mercurochrome: detergent; ammonia; vinegar; detergent

Milk: detergent; ammonia; detergent

Nail polish: Apply a non-oily nail polish remover.

Paint (alkyd): solvent; detergent. If the stain remains, consult a professional cleaner.

Paint (latex): solvent; detergent

Rubber cement: solvent; detergent

Rust: detergent; vinegar. If any stain remains, apply denatured alcohol or a dry-cleaning solvent.

Shellac: Apply denatured alcohol; blot; repeat if necessary.

Shoe polish: solvent; detergent. If the stain remains, consult a professional cleaner.

Soft drinks: detergent; vinegar

Soy sauce: detergent; ammonia; detergent

Urine: detergent; ammonia; vinegar

Varnish/lacquer: solvent; detergent

Wax (candle): Treat as for chewing gum. If any remains, cover stain with 2 paper towels and use a warm dry iron to melt wax. Rotate towels to absorb stain. If, necessary, reapply solvent and blot.

DEEP CLEANING CARPETS

If you clean your carpets or rugs yourself, consider one of the following methods. Vacuum thoroughly before beginning. You can rent the necessary machines at your hardware store or supermarket.

METHOD	HOW TO USE	ADVANTAGES	DISADVANTAGES
Dry-cleaning powders	Sprinkle powder (granular "sponges" absorb soil) on. Work it into carpet pile with special machine or brush. Vacuum.	Easy, safe, fast; no water to wet carpet; no residue remains	Machine is not available for home purchase
Shampoo	Apply with sponge, mop, hand brush, electric rug shampooer, or manual applicator as label indicates. After carpet dries, vacuum away foam and dirt.	Economical	Machine may distort pile; can leave residue to attract soil
"Steam cleaning" (hot-water extraction)	Use a steam-cleaning machine to inject water and cleaner into the carpet. Solution and dirt are vacuumed into machine. Vacuum when carpet is dry—usually in less than 12 hours.	Maintains appearance of pile	Overwetting the carpet may shrink or discolor it

WINDOWS AND DOORS

PAINT POINTER

☞ To remove paint from window glass, soften it with a sponge dipped in warm, soapy water or warm vinegar. Gently scrape with a sharp single-edge razor blade. Clean the glass, rinse, and dry.

SCREEN TIME

☞ When you wash the windows from the outside each year, wash the screens, too. Before you remove the screens for the first time, use a permanent marker to write a number on the window or door frame and mark the same number on the corresponding screen. This makes it easy year after year to put each clean screen back where it belongs.

Wash windows, glass doors, and skylights when the sun is not shining directly on the glass. Working in direct sunlight causes streaks because the cleaning solution dries faster than you can wipe it off.

Many windows can be washed by pushing the bottom half up and the top half down, so you can reach outside. If you can reach windows from the ground, stand outside to wash them.

If you live in an upper-story apartment or a multilevel house, hire a window service to wash the windows. Never lean out of a window or stand on a windowsill.

WINDOW GLASS

Before washing window glass, vacuum the frame, sill, or track (sliding windows and doors) with the dusting and crevice tools on your vacuum cleaner.

Wash the frame, sill, or track every few months with a sponge dipped in an all-purpose household cleaning solution. Avoid using ammonia products on unpainted aluminum—they can cause pitting. Add chlorine bleach (except if it's an ammonia cleaner) to the mixture if the surface is stained with moss or mildew. Rinse and dry.

To clean the glass use either a commercial glass cleaner, or a solution of 1 tablespoon of ammonia per 1 quart of water.

Pour the ammonia solution in a pump spray bottle. Or wet a sponge or a soft, lintless cloth with the cleaning solution.

Wipe one pane of glass at a time. Wash the glass from side to side indoors. Then wash from top to bottom outdoors. If there are streaks, you can tell which side to rub again.

To clean corners use a cotton swab dipped in the cleaning solution. Dry with a squeegee, chamois, paper towel, or crumpled newspaper.

Kitchen windows and skylights may require a stronger cleaner if there is a heavy accumulation of grease and dirt. Use a more concentrated solution of the above.

HOW TO USE A SQUEEGEE

A squeegee should be used only on smooth, unbroken windowpanes. If a pane is cracked or chipped, the broken edges can take a nick out of the rubber blade, making it useless because it will leave a streak of water at the nick.

To use a squeegee, wipe the rubber blade with a damp cloth or sponge to help it glide easily across the glass. Hold the squeegee at a 45 degree angle against the side and upper corner of the pane and pull it horizontally across to the opposite side.

Wipe the edge of the blade. Place it at the bottom end of the dry strip and repeat until the window is dry. Wipe up remaining drops of water with paper towel or crumpled newspaper.

SCREENS

Clean screens outdoors or in a bathtub. Fill a large bucket with warm water and add all-purpose household cleaner.

Dip a scrub brush into the solution, scrub both sides of the screen, then wash the screen frame with the same brush.

Rinse both sides of the screen and the frame with clean water. Let the screen drip-dry for a few minutes, then wipe it with a dry cloth; stand it up to dry completely.

SHADES

At least twice each year, lower your shades and dust them on both sides with a clean cloth or vacuum cleaner and dusting tool.

Most shades are washable, but test them to be sure. Also test any trims that may be attached. Wipe a small section near the roller with a sudsy cloth or sponge. Rinse with a clean cloth or sponge and wipe dry. If it looks cleaner, but the color hasn't run, proceed.

Roller Shades

Clean washable roller shades, which are usually made of plastic, canvas, or treated fabric, with a mild detergent and water solution.

Lower the shade to spot-clean finger marks and smudges. For overall cleaning, take down the shade and unroll it on a clean flat surface covered with an old sheet, an old shower curtain, or an old plastic tablecloth. Place a heavy object on both ends of the shade to hold it open while you work.

Clean one section at a time, starting as close to the top as you can get, with a sponge or cloth wrung out in a detergent and water solution. If the shade has a rough finish, scrub it lightly with a soft brush. Rinse the section with a clean, damp sponge or cloth. Wipe dry and roll up the clean section.

Repeat the process until the whole shade is clean. Turn it over and wash the other side the same way. Hang the shade

CLEANING YOUR FIREPLACE

When they are cold, remove ashes in excess of 2 inches with a fireplace shovel or vacuum cleaner.

- Wash the hearth and front of the fireplace or stove exterior occasionally with a sponge or cloth dipped in an all-purpose household cleaner and water solution.
- Clean a cast iron exterior with a hand dishwashing detergent and water solution. Rinse with a clean, damp sponge or cloth and dry.
- Remove soot from brick or stone facing with a soft brush, then scrub with a strong solution of washing soda or trisodium phosphate (TSP) and water or all-purpose household cleaner and water. Old brick (more than 50

years old) should only be vacuumed to avoid crumbling.

SCREENS

Clean the mesh every few months with a vacuum cleaner and dusting attachment. To wash, use a sponge or cloth dipped in an all-purpose household cleaner and water solution; rinse and dry.

GLASS DOORS

To remove soot and smoke residue, scrape doors with a straightedge razor blade. Wash the glass with a sponge or cloth dipped in a solution made of equal parts of vinegar and water or 1 tablespoon of ammonia added to 1 quart of hot water; use paper towels or newspapers to dry the glass.

---

back on the window and pull it down. Let it dry thoroughly before rolling it back up.

For untreated fabric shades, take them down and launder if they are washable; if not, dry-clean them or use wallpaper dough cleaner (see page 47) to clean nonwashable shades.

Pleated Shades

To clean pleated shades, occasionally vacuum using the dusting attachment to clean both sides of pleated shades. Most are treated to resist soil, but if the fabric looks soiled, sponge with lukewarm water and mild suds or a foam upholstery cleaner. Sponge with clear water to rinse and dry with a clean towel. Do not immerse the shade or use commercial window-cleaning products or spot removers. Always work in a horizontal

PUTTING ASH IN ITS PLACE

☞ Sprinkle fireplace ashes with damp tea leaves or ½ cup of water with a teaspoon of dried rosemary in it. This will keep dust down and leave a pleasant fragrance.

direction, parallel to the pleats. Hang the shade partially open to dry. Excessive cleaning can remove the fullness and body from the pleated fabric.

BLINDS

Venetian and Mini Blinds

To dust: Use a special blinds brush (see page 28), vacuum dusting tool, or a soft cloth. Lower the blind. Dust the slats first when they are facing downward, then upward. If you are using the pronged blind-dusting tool, leave the blind open and slip the slats between the rollers.

To wash: wash blinds while they're hanging; lower and open them. Lay old cloths or newspapers under the window to catch any water drips. Remove nearby furniture.

Dip a sponge or cloth in a solution of all-purpose household cleaner and water and wring out. Start at the top and wash one slat at a time, folding the cloth or sponge around the slat, and sliding it from side to side. (Or use scissors to cut halfway through a thick flat sponge and use it the same way.)

Rinse with a damp cloth, sponge, or glove, using the same method as for washing; wipe dry.

Tapes and cords: scrub Venetian-blind tapes with a brush dipped into thick suds. Rinse with a clean, damp sponge or cloth.

Wipe each pull cord or wand with a folded sponge or cloth—first with suds, and then with clean water. Leave the blind lowered and open until it is completely dry.

Bathtub method: if you prefer, take the blinds down and wash them in a bathtub half filled with a warm water and household cleaner solution. Pull the cord so that the slats are open. Immerse the blind in the water, spreading it out.

Wash both sides with a sponge or cloth, and scrub the tapes with a brush. Drain the sudsy water and fill the tub halfway with clean water to rinse away any dirt and suds; repeat.

Drain the water. Dry with a cloth or towel. Place newspapers on the floor under the window and put the blinds back up. Lower them and keep the slats open until they are completely dry.

Outdoors: to wash blinds outdoors, hang them over a clothesline and clean in the same way as for hanging blinds. Rinse both sides with a garden hose. Drip-dry, then hang back up on the window.

Wood Blinds and Shutters
Wood blinds and shutters may warp if you clean them with water. Instead, wipe each slat with a cloth treated with furniture polish or use your vacuum cleaner with the dusting brush attachment.

CURTAINS AND DRAPERIES

Frequently remove dust from curtains and draperies using your vacuum cleaner and upholstery attachment. Pull the fabric taut and use a gentle suction. Work from the top to the bottom with firm strokes. They can also be "dusted" in your dryer on the "air fluff" setting (no heat) to freshen them periodically.

Most curtains are machine washable and dryable except those made with glass fibers (see page 72).

Draperies should never be washed unless indicated by the label. In either case, follow the care label recommendations. If there is no label, have your curtains and draperies dry-cleaned. Many cleaners will box-store them free of charge.

THE WHITE GLOVE TOUCH

☞ A good way to clean blinds is to wear a pair of cotton work gloves. Dip both hands into a solution of all-purpose household cleaner and water, and use your gloved fingers to wash the slats. You can also use pre-moistened glass-cleaning wipes.

WALLS AND CEILINGS

Periodically vacuum walls and ceilings using a clean dusting or wall-brush attachment. Begin at the ceiling and work down to the floor.

Painted walls and switch and outlet plates will look presentable longer if you clean fingerprints, smudges, and other marks soon after they appear.

Always test paint to make sure it is washable before beginning. With a sudsy sponge, wipe a small spot in a area. If the color and finish are unaffected, proceed.

To wash: Use a sponge and an all-purpose cleaner (follow package directions) or an ammonia and water solution (l cup ammonia per 1 gallon warm water). Wash a small section (2' x 2') of the wall at a time, starting at the bottom and working up to the ceiling to avoid streaks and drip marks. Overlap areas as you clean. When the section looks clean, rinse with a clean, damp sponge and water. (Rinsing is always advisable, even though manufacturers of some cleaners say it is not necessary.)

Wipe dry with a clean cloth. Change the wash and rinse waters frequently to prevent redepositing the dirt.

When the walls are done, wash the ceiling with the same all-purpose cleaner or ammonia and water solution and a sponge.

Standing on a stool or stepladder, start in one corner and clean as much as you can reach comfortably. When one part is clean, rinse and dry. Proceed to the next area.

WALLPAPER

Washable wall coverings include wallpaper (water resistant or plastic treated) and vinyl-coated or vinyl-processed coverings. The vinyls are the sturdiest.

Never wash untreated paper or coverings marked water sensitive. If you don't know how your wall covering should be cleaned, test a small spot in an inconspicuous place before beginning.

If the covering passes the test (the color didn't fade, run, bleed, disappear, or the paper isn't damaged), proceed.

To wash: For delicate paper, use clear lukewarm water. Wash most other coverings with a sponge dipped in a solution of hand dishwashing detergent and lukewarm water. Work from the bottom up, using as little water as possible. Clean one small area at a time and overlap your strokes. Rinse with a clean sponge dipped in cool water and gently wipe dry with a clean absorbent cloth.

Using wallpaper dough

Clean nonwashable coverings with a special dough available from wallpaper, paint, and hardware stores. Knead the dough in your hand until it is pliable, then rub it on the covering as you would a soft eraser. Overlap strokes and clean from top to bottom. As you work, fold the soiled surface of the dough to the inside, exposing a clean surface to use on the wall.

GET OUT THE COBWEBS

☛ Vacuum cobwebs with the crevice tool on your vacuum, or use a long-handled broom or pole with a clean cloth, such as an old pillowcase or T-shirt, attached to the end.

☛ With an upward lifting motion to avoid streaking the wall, remove as much of the cobweb as possible, repositioning the cloth frequently, as it becomes soiled.

CATCHING DRIPS

☛ Tie a washcloth around your wrist to catch wall-washing drips. An athlete's terry-cloth wristband works well, too.

WALL SURFACES AND FIXTURES

Keeping Up with the Woodwork

☞ Wash fingerprints, smudges, and marks at least once each month; it is much easier to wash off a little dirt than to wait until a lot accumulates. Work carefully to avoid soiling or wetting the bordering wall, ceiling, or floor.

Wood Paneling

Dust and remove fingerprints and other soil from paneling using a white appliance polish or a special product designed for paneled walls. Check that any product is suitable for the finish of your paneling. Wax and oil products should not be used interchangeably. Never wet clean paneling. Unsealed paneling should be dusted only.

To clean and polish oil-finished, varnished, or shellacked wood paneling, apply a mixture of ½ cup of turpentine, ¾ cup of linseed oil, and 1 tablespoon of vinegar; let it stand for 15 minutes, then rub until all the cleaner is removed.

Brick and Stone

Scrub brick and stone with a strong all-purpose cleaner and water solution. To remove stubborn stains, like soot (see box on page 45), scrub with an abrasive cleanser; rinse well.

Acoustical Tile

Acoustical tile should generally not be washed by wet methods. Clean tiles with a special dough, as you would nonwashable wall coverings (see page 47), or vacuum using the dusting brush attachment. If the tiles are vinyl-coated, they may be cleaned. Check with the manufacturer for the recommended method.

Fixtures

Ceiling fans: Wipe the blades weekly; dust and dirt build up quickly. Every three or four months, wash the blades with an all-purpose cleaner and water solution.

Light fixtures: Dust with the vacuum cleaner and dusting tool or a dusting cloth to remove dirt and cobwebs. Remove the globe or cover periodically; wash with a damp, sudsy sponge or cloth, rinse and dry. To clean lamp shades see page 37.

Chandeliers: Before cleaning, put a piece of plastic, then a layer of newspaper under the chandelier. To clean the fixture without removing all the pieces, use a specialized spray-on cleaner, a pre-moistened glass-cleaning cloth, or a small cup filled with the ammonia solution described below. After you "dip" each crystal into the cup held in one hand, towel dry with the other hand. If you are spraying, move or protect any furniture underneath.

If you prefer, take the chandelier apart, remove the crystal drops a few at a time, and wash them in the sink or a pan, using a hand dishwashing detergent.

Rinse in a solution of 1 tablespoon ammonia or vinegar to 1 quart of water.

Towel dry and replace the crystal drops immediately to make sure that they go in the right places.

Repeat for all the crystals. Wipe any permanent parts with a damp cloth and towel dry.

WASHABLE WALLS

If Your walls are washable, always test your cleaning solution on a hidden spot to make sure it won't damage the wall coloring or material. If it looks fine, proceed.

Stain	Take These Steps
Crayon marks	Wipe with a clean cloth and dry-cleaning fluid. If the marks remain, mix 1 teaspoon of liquid chlorine bleach in 1 cup of water. Apply the bleach with a cotton swab. Silver polish or liquid automatic dishwashing detergent works well on vinyl wall covering.
Grease	Blot a fresh grease spot with a clean paper towel. Then make a stiff paste of fuller's earth (an absorbent powder you can buy at a hardware store) mixed with spot remover (cleaning fluid). Apply a ¼-inch-thick coat of the paste over the spot and let it remain overnight. Remove by brushing with a soft brush or cloth. You can also try holding a clean white desk blotter on the spot and pressing with a warm iron, moving the blotter as it absorbs the grease.
Ink	Remove as for crayon marks. Or use a commercial ink remover or rubbing alcohol. Apply and blot.
Pencil	Lightly rub an art-gum eraser over pencil marks and other smudges.

THE KITCHEN

While the cleaning guidelines for furniture, floors, windows, ceilings, and other surfaces on pages 33–48 apply to all rooms of the house, the kitchen needs special attention to keep it clean and hygenic (as do the bathroom and nursery [see pages 57 to 59]). To keep your kitchen sanitary for food preparation, wash utensils and other equipment as you use them, and wipe up spills when they occur.

Minimize open storage to keep airborne dust and grease away from dishes, boxed or canned food, and utensils, especially near the stove where splattered food and grease are a constant problem.

CABINETS AND PANTRY

Clean your cabinets frequently; clean the interiors when they look dirty, but at least two or three times a year. Use the appropriate mild cleanser for your cabinets' surface.

It isn't necessary to empty the entire cabinet—do a shelf at a time and remove only half of the items on it. Dust and wipe shelves with a damp cloth, and move the items back into place.

If the top of the cabinet is exposed, clean it first, then move to the shelves. If the shelf is lined with paper, remove the contents, remove the paper, wipe the shelf, and reline it with new paper. Wipe the inside and outside of the door. If the door is greasy, use an all-purpose cleaner solution or one specifically recommended by the cabinet manufacturer. Avoid over-wetting wood cabinets. Rinse and dry quickly. Cabinet exteriors will need more frequent attention.

Drawers
Remove the drawer contents, then vacuum inside using the dusting brush or crevice tool. Wipe with a damp cloth. Be sure to clean the top, front, and bottom of the drawer as well as any knobs or handles. As with cabinet doors, use a mild cleaner or polish suitable for the exterior.

Countertops
Regularly move the items forward just far enough to be able to clean the counter and wall behind them. Most spills wipe up from most surface types with a spray all-purpose cleaner or warm solution of soap and water and a sponge or soft cloth.

If food sticks, lay a damp cloth or sponge over the spot to loosen it; do not use abrasive cleansers, plastic scrubbers, or steel wool because they will scratch the surface. Move the items back and clean the rest of the countertop. Every so often clean and remove countertop items. Clean underneath and behind them as well.

SINKS AND FAUCETS

Kitchen sinks need gentle daily cleaning. Before doing so, rinse them thoroughly and remove any waste. With a damp sponge or cloth, rub a nonabrasive powdered cleanser or a special product formulated for cleaning sinks over the basin, rim, and fixtures. Rinse with clean water.

Porcelain: You can remove stains from porcelain by filling the sink with lukewarm water and adding a small amount of liquid chlorine bleach. Leave the water in the sink for a while; drain and rinse.

Stainless steel: To make a stainless steel sink sparkle, clean and polish it occasionally with glass cleaner, metal polish, or a baking soda paste (3 parts baking soda to 1 part water). The paste is good for removing any stubborn stains

☛ From time to time, grind orange or lemon rinds in the disposer to keep it smelling pleasant.

TRASH CONTAINERS

Line trash containers with plastic or paper trash bags to make garbage removal easier and to keep the container clean longer. Wipe away finger marks and residue on the outside of the container (including the lid or cover) with an all-purpose household cleaner.

- To clean the interior, half fill the basket with warm, sudsy water, then scrub with a cloth or sponge. Rinse; wipe and let dry thoroughly before using it again. Don't let water soak into cardboard or wood baskets.

- Scrub the garbage can occasionally with a long-handled brush (a toilet-bowl brush works well) to keep it sanitary and odorless. Use this brush only for the garbage can. If odors persist, add a little ammonia or liquid chlorine bleach to the rinse water and rinse again, or tape a piece of orange peel to the inside of the lid. Turn the can upside down to drain and dry.

in the sink or around the rim. Towel dry to avoid water spots.

Don't worry about scratches; stainless steel is supposed to scratch and marks will eventually blend in. To avoid scratching, use a rubber mat.

Faucets: To remove soap and stain buildup from fixtures, dissolve 1 teaspoon of salt in 2 tablespoons of white vinegar. Rub the mixture on with a damp sponge. Be sure to rinse thoroughly and buff dry with a paper towel or clean cloth to avoid water spots.

Clog prevention: Never pour cooking grease down the drain. Once a month, pour a handful of baking soda into the drain and add ½ cup of vinegar. Cover the drain for several minutes, then flush with cold water.

Food disposer: Always use a heavy flow of cold water when operating your disposer. Cold water will congeal fats in the drain, which will aid grinding and help prevent clogging. Run the water before turning on the disposer and for 30 seconds after the grinding noise stops to make sure the disposer is completely empty and food debris has been flushed through the lines.

Once a week, flush the disposer drain by filling the sink with 3 inches of warm water and mixing in 1 cup of baking soda, then draining it with the disposer running. This should be enough to keep it clean. Never use detergent, lye, or a chemical drain cleaner.

COOK TOPS/RANGES

To care for your range top begin by reading the manufacturer's instructions. Then follow the guidelines provided below.

Porcelain enamel: Wipe up spills immediately. If the cook top is hot, use a dry paper towel or cloth. When the surface is cool, wash it with an all-purpose cleaner; rinse and polish with a clean, dry cloth. Avoid using cleaners and harsh abrasives, which may scratch.

Stainless steel: Clean with hot, sudsy water or a paste of baking soda and water

(3 parts baking soda to 1 part water). Rinse and towel dry. To polish, moisten a cloth with mineral oil; wipe the surface and towel dry to prevent streaks.

Glass and smooth-top glass ceramic: These surfaces are generally very easy to keep clean and recent improvements have made them even more so. Clean when cool with either dishwashing liquid, a paste of baking soda and water (3 parts baking soda to 1 part water), or a specially formulated cook-top cleaner. Apply with a paper towel or clean cloth.

Rinse thoroughly and towel dry. Do not use a soiled dishcloth or sponge to wipe the cook top. It may leave a film, which can cause discoloration the next time it is heated. If this occurs, remove the discoloration with a specially formulated cook-top cleaner.

Burned on soil can be removed with a razor-blade scraper. Avoid abrasive cleaners and pads.

Burners

Conventional electric coil: Most are self-cleaning. Turn the burners on high to burn off spills. Porcelain drip bowls under the units are dishwasher safe or can be cleaned in a self-cleaning oven. Wash aluminum/chrome reflector drip bowls in the dishwasher or by hand.

If spills are cooked on, the bowls require soaking in hot, sudsy water. Soap-filled scouring pads also work well to remove stubborn soil. Wipe the metal rings around the surface units or, if they're removable, wash them by hand or in the dishwasher.

Solid cast iron electric: These units are permanently sealed to the cook tops to prevent spills from seeping underneath. Wipe the area surrounding the burners with a sponge or cloth dipped in hot, sudsy water. To avoid rust spots, heat the units on a medium setting until they are completely dry. "Season" periodically with vegetable oil and heat for 3-5 minutes.

Conventional gas: When food boils over or is spilled, wipe the grate, burner,

ANATOMY OF A BURNER

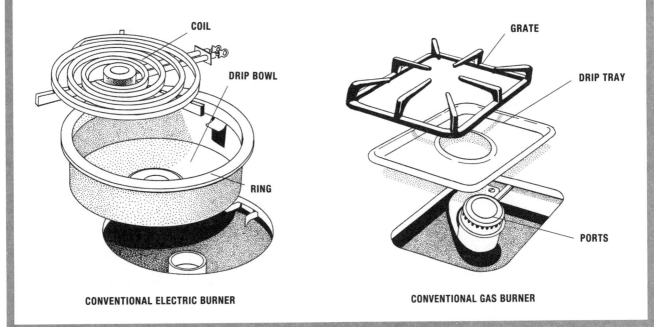

COIL

DRIP BOWL

RING

CONVENTIONAL ELECTRIC BURNER

GRATE

DRIP TRAY

PORTS

CONVENTIONAL GAS BURNER

drip pan, and drip tray as soon as they're cool enough to touch. Do not wash the grate or burner in the dishwasher. Clean burner caps with detergent and water or mild abrasive cleaners. To thoroughly clean the burner, lift out the parts (check your care manual for directions) and soak them in warm, sudsy water. Use a stiff brush to scrub off any burned-on food.

Clean the burner ports with a straight pin or a straightened paper clip. (Do not use a toothpick: It may break off and clog the port.)

Sealed-gas burner: These are easy to clean because the burners are sealed permanently to the cook top so boil-overs will not seep underneath. Wash burner caps and grates by hand in hot, sudsy water to prevent rusting of unfinished surfaces.

Knobs: Control knobs on most cook tops and ranges are removeable for cleaning. Pull them straight off, wash, rinse, and dry well. Replace firmly in the "off" position. Water should not be allowed to drip behind the knobs.

OVENS

Ovens have always ranked among the least favorite cleaning chores, but there are ways to simplify this messy job.

Racks: Soak racks in a solution of hot water and all-purpose cleaner containing ammonia (follow the container directions for the correct proportion) or in a solution of ½ cup of ammonia to 1 quart of hot water. Use soap-filled scouring pads to remove stubborn soil.

Broiler pan: Clean the broiler pan after each use. Remove the grill and dispose of the grease in an old can. Fill the pan with hot water. Replace the grill and pour dishwashing detergent on it. Cover with wet paper towels. Let stand for about 30 minutes. Then wash in hot, sudsy water, rinse and dry.

Front and sides: Remove any control dials/knobs, then wash them in hot, sudsy water or with an all-purpose cleaner. Wash the surface behind the control dials/knobs; rinse and dry well.

Periodically wash the sides of a freestanding range with an all-purpose household cleaner.

Glass doors: Use a glass cleaner, ammonia, or a solution of 50-50

BROILING WITHOUT SOILING

☛ To prevent burned-on grease, line the pan and the grill with aluminum foil punched with holes. After cooking, toss the foil and rinse the pan.

TEAKETTLES AND LIME DEPOSITS

☛ To remove lime deposits, boil a 50-50 mixture of vinegar and water. Simmer until the deposits disappear, then rinse thoroughly.

SHELF HELP

☛ To cut down on shelf cleaning, place clean plastic foam packaging trays from meats and vegetables under milk, juice, beverage, and other containers in the refrigerator that tend to drip.

FROST FIGHTERS

☛ Keep the freezer section of your refrigerator at least two-thirds full to help the appliance operate more efficiently. Don't overload the refrigerator or open the door more than necessary, especially during hot weather. Cover foods and liquids and wipe moisture from the outside of containers before placing them in the refrigerator. Moisture evaporates from the food and turns into frost.

SILVER TARNISHERS

Know that:
☛ Salt can corrode and discolor.
☛ Eggs, mustard, and mayonnaise are bad tarnishers.
☛ Contact with rubber can cause tarnish; avoid draining silver on rubber mats.
☛ Plastic wrap adheres to silver, which may damage the finish and create black spots that are difficult—if not impossible—to remove.
☛ Warm air will cause discoloration.

vinegar and water. Place a cloth or paper towel saturated with the solution (but wrung out) on the inside of the window with the door open; leave it for a half hour to loosen the soil. Never use an abrasive cleaner; it will scratch the glass. Use a plastic pad, if needed. Rinse well with clean water; dry with paper towels or a lint-free cloth.

Interior (standard): Clean a standard oven by applying a commercial oven cleaner, following the manufacturer's instructions. Or place ½ cup of undiluted ammonia in a cold oven for several hours or overnight. The fumes loosen baked-on soil.

Remove the oven door, if it can be lifted off, to make it easier to reach inside. Then wipe the oven walls and the floor of the oven with a wet cloth or sponge. Use a soap-filled scouring pad to remove stubborn soil. Rinse the oven well, then wipe it with a clean cloth dipped in a mild vinegar solution to remove any residue; rinse with warm, clean water.

After broiling in the oven or in a broiler compartment, wipe the walls with a hot, sudsy cloth to remove spatters.

Interior (self-cleaning [pyrolytic]): Wipe the oven frame and the portion of the door liner outside the oven gasket before using the self-cleaning feature. **Never clean the gasket; cleaning can damage it.** Use soap-filled scouring pads to remove stubborn spots; rinse well.

Follow the manufacturer's instructions for setting the self-cleaning controls. During the cleaning cycle, the oven soil is reduced to light ash. When the cleaning is completed, wipe up with a damp cloth.

Continuous clean: These ovens have a special surface that helps soil burn off gradually at temperatures above 400°F. Some manufacturers recommend occasionally operating the oven empty for an hour or so at 500°F to remove built-up soil. **The special surface on continuous-clean and self-cleaning ovens cannot be cleaned with soap, detergent, or most commercial oven cleaners; they cause permanent damage to the oven surface.**

Fans and range hoods: Ventilating fans and range hoods exhaust cooking odors and smoke and help circulate air. All of them have filters that need periodic cleaning.

Remove the wire mesh filters and clean them in the dishwasher or soak them in the sink in a solution of hot water and all-purpose household cleaner. Rinse well and let dry thoroughly. Before replacing a filter, wipe the fan blades with a clean, damp cloth.

REFRIGERATORS AND FREEZERS

A clean refrigerator helps prevent food spoilage because it harbors no food-spoiling organisms. Spoiled and strong-smelling foods cause bad odors that are picked up by other foods.

To absorb odors, place an open box of baking soda in the back of the refrigerator or on a shelf in the door. Replace it every two months.

Check the refrigerator for spoiled or questionable food just before shopping, when it is the emptiest.

You can keep major cleaning to a minimum if you wipe up spills as soon as they occur. Check the inside walls for residue and wipe them off. Sponge the front, sides, handles, and top regularly to remove fingermarks and greasy dust with an all-purpose cleaner solution.

Shelves: If you don't want to take the time to clean the entire refrigerator, do it in stages—one or two shelves at a time. Use a clean cloth or sponge dipped in a solution of 1 tablespoon of baking soda to 1 quart of warm water. Rinse the shelf and walls with clean water and wipe dry.

Condenser coils: These should be vacuumed regularly and the drip pan cleaned if your refrigerator has one. Check your use and care manual for the location and cleaning recommendations.

Drawers: Remove the drawers. Clean both inside and out using the baking soda solution described above. While the drawer is out, wipe the floor of the refrigerator and towel dry.

Gaskets and doors: Wipe the door gasket(s) and the rubber seal(s) around the door(s) with the baking soda solution, being sure to clean in the folds. If there's mildew on the gasket, use a chlorine bleach solution (¼ cup of liquid chlorine bleach to 1 quart of water) to remove it; rinse and towel dry. Wash the door shelves and the door frames with the baking soda solution.

Freezer

Empty and wash the freezer section at least once a year. Do not touch frozen surfaces with wet or damp hands; use a sponge or clean cloth dipped in a solution of 1 tablespoon of baking soda to 1 quart of warm water.

Defrost a manual refrigerator or freezer at least once a year. Don't let more than a ¼ inch of frost build up. Frost acts as an insulator, which makes the refrigerator use more electricity to maintain the proper temperature.

Wash the shelves and inside walls of the freezer with a solution of 1 tablespoon of baking soda to 1 quart of water. Be sure to clean the door gasket and remove any mildew with a chlorine bleach solution (¼ cup of chlorine bleach to 1 quart of water). Rinse well and towel dry. Return the food to the freezer when it is completely dry.

To protect the exterior finish of the refrigerator and freezer, particularly against rusting, and to make cleaning easier the next time, apply a coat of creamy appliance polish at least twice a year.

DISHWASHERS

Dishwashers generally get cleaned with the dishes and require minimal care. To remove lime deposits (the white granu-

BRIGHT FUTURE

☛ Cooking acidic foods such as tomatoes or rhubarb in an aluminum pan will brighten its finish.

HOT-WATER HINT

☛ If the dishwasher is located a distance from the hot-water heater, turn on the hot-water faucet in the kitchen sink before starting the dishwasher to clear the line of cold water.

GOOD COOKING HABITS

GOOD COOK-TOP HABITS

Foods may actually cook better on low heat and make less mess. You need high heat only to bring foods to a boil.

Using a larger pan when cooking foods that foam—pasta, rice, milk, dried beans—will help to keep them from boiling up and overflowing.

When frying or sautéing, use a small amount of fat and medium heat to minimize spattering and to brown foods more evenly.

Keep an eye on all food while it's cooking. If you must walk away, set a kitchen timer and carry it with you.

GOOD OVEN HABITS

To keep oven cleaning to a minimum, use a low temperature (325°F to 350°F) when cooking uncovered meats and poultry. There is less spattering, shrinkage is minimized, and the food will be juicy and flavorful.

To prevent boil-overs do not fill pans too full. Place a sheet of aluminum foil below the pan on a low rack to catch any drips. (Do not cover the entire rack with aluminum foil; it may affect browning.)

When using glass and glass-ceramic cookware, which absorb heat, set the oven thermostat 25° lower than you would for metal cookware.

☞ When loading the dishwasher, alternate plates of various sizes to prevent scratching and chipping.

☞ Leave adequate room between glasses; secure them between the cushioned prongs in the top rack and make sure that long stems don't interfere with the movement of the rack.

☞ Avoid nesting flatware, and be sure the spray arms aren't blocked by a fallen utensil, plate, or pot handle.

lar film that often appears in your dishwasher left behind by hard water [see page 65]), run an empty dishwasher through the full cycle with 2 cups of vinegar or 1 cup of citrus-flavored beverage or citric acid crystals (no detergent).

To remove brown rust stains from the interior, use citric acid crystals as for lime deposits, or use a special liquid product; following the package directions. If staining cannot be controlled, you may need to install iron-removal equipment in your home water supply.

Some dishwashers have filters/strainers (located in the bottom of the tub), which need to be removed and cleaned periodically. Check your manual.

Occasionally wipe the outside edge or rim of the door with warm, sudsy water or a solution of ¼ cup baking soda to 1 quart of water.

Wipe the door front with a solution of warm water and detergent; rinse and wipe dry. Avoid harsh or gritty cleaners or scouring pads that may scratch the finish. Every now and then apply a creamy appliance polish to protect the finish.

SMALL APPLIANCES

Before cleaning, unplug all small appliances and make sure they are cool. Never immerse an electric appliance in water. To avoid major cleanups, always wipe up spills with a damp paper towel, cloth, or sponge as soon after they occur as possible.

Do not use abrasive or harsh cleaners or scouring pads; they can cause damage. Instead, use a polyester or nylon mesh pad, a nonabrasive cleaner, or a paste made of 3 parts baking soda to 1 part water.

Sponge the exterior or base of a small appliance with warm, sudsy water. Polish chrome or stainless steel with a cloth moistened with white vinegar, club soda, silver polish, or a paste made with 3 parts baking soda to 1 part water. Rinse and dry.

To wash most electric appliances—blender, juicer, can opener, mixer, food processor—remove all parts and soak in warm, sudsy water. If recommended by the manufacturer, run them through the dishwasher. **Be careful with blender and food processor blades, can opener cutters, and other sharp objects. Don't allow them to sit in a sink of soapy water; it's dangerous to blindly search for them underwater, and they can rust.**

Microwave Ovens
If there is a turntable, remove it and wash in warm, sudsy water or in the dishwasher; dry. While the turntable is removed, clean the oven.

To clean the interior thoroughly, boil a cup of water for 3 to 4 minutes inside. The condensation will loosen any food soil on the walls or ceiling of the oven. Then wipe with a damp sponge or cloth, and dry. **Never use a commercial oven cleaner or remove the cover in the top of the oven interior for cleaning.**

To deodorize, wash the interior surfaces every few months with a solution of ¼ cup of baking soda to 1 quart of warm water; rinse and dry.

To clean the touch-control panel, open the oven to deactivate. Wipe the panel with a cloth dampened slightly with warm, sudsy water only; rinse, dry with a paper towel or soft cloth. Do not scrub or use any sort of chemical cleaners on the panel, and avoid using too much water.

If it is an over-the-range model with an exhaust fan, follow cleaning directions for fans/range hoods (see page 52).

Coffeemakers
Clean the serving container (percolator/drip/carafe) after each use to remove oils and residue that may affect the coffee's flavor. If recommended, put it in the dishwasher or wash it with hot water and detergent.

Automatic drip (ADC): These require periodic cleaning to remove mineral deposits. Pour ¾ cup of white vinegar into the water tank; fill the tank with cold water to the maximum fill line; brew the vinegar and water mixture. Rinse the machine twice by brewing with clean water only.

Percolator: Periodically remove the mineral and coffee stains that build up in the system. Fill the pot to the fill line with cold water and add 1 tablespoon cream of tartar. Insert the basket and pump assembly. Cover, plug in, and perk. Empty the solution and rinse well.

If you're planning to store the coffeemaker for more than a day or two, store the pot with the cover off.

Toasters and Toaster Ovens

Wipe crumbs off the outside regularly. To reach crumbs lodged inside the toaster or toaster oven, unplug the appliance, release the crumb tray latch, then shake the crumbs out. Wipe the tray with a damp cloth. Never cover the crumb tray with aluminum foil—it can catch fire—and never clean the inside of a toaster except for the crumb tray.

For a toaster oven, wash the bake/broil pan, the drain tray, and rack in hot, sudsy water or in the dishwasher after each use. Rinse and dry. Refer to the manufacturer's instructions for cleaning the interior; different finishes require different treatments.

DISHES, COOKWARE, AND UTENSILS

Cleaning dishes, silverware, and pots and pans is a daily chore. Here's help for some special items:

Aluminum

Wash aluminum utensils in clean, hot, sudsy water or the dishwasher unless the manufacturer's directions indicate otherwise.

To brighten the interior of an aluminum pan, fill it with water and add 1 tablespoon of cream of tartar to 1 quart of water. Boil the solution for 5 to 10 minutes.

Anodized aluminum, which is found on some pie and bread pans, beverage tumblers, cookware, and covers, may be affected by high temperatures and detergent ingredients. As a rule, do not machine wash.

Cast Iron

Cast iron utensils rust unless "seasoned" (see page 137). If your utensils are not preseasoned by the manufacturer, season them yourself before using them for the first time.

Never wash a cast iron utensil in the dishwasher; use baking soda to remove burned-on food residue. Always be sure to hand dry thoroughly to prevent rust.

China and Crystal

Most "everyday" china, crystal, ceramicware, and glassware can be washed safely in a dishwasher. If you're not sure a piece is dishwasher safe, check for a dishwasher-safe label. You can also try washing one piece for at least a month with your regular loads.

Always test antique china before running it through the dishwasher. China with metal trim, hand paint, or over-the-glaze patterns may fade. To be on the safe side, don't wash them in the dishwasher.

Special "china/crystal" cycles on dishwashers generally include one wash, two rinses, and a dry cycle. Depending on the

---

SMART LOADING

It is important to follow the manufacturer's instructions for loading a dishwasher because every model is designed differently. There's generally no need to rinse dishes, but do remove large and hard food particles before placing items in the dishwasher. Rinse dishes if they're going to sit for a while before being washed.

Store rinsed, soiled dishes in the dishwasher until a full load accumulates. Use only detergents designed for use in automatic dishwashers. Do not put detergent in the dispenser(s) until it is time to run the dishwasher; it can cake and fail to dissolve.

NO MORE DARK MARKS

☞ When a metal utensil or object scrapes across china, it often leaves a black or gray mark. To remove it, gently rub the mark with a mild abrasive cleanser or a plastic scouring pad. (Do not use abrasives on decorations.)

NO MORE WHITE FILM

☞ If you've had a problem with etching—cloudy white deposits on glassware from dishwasher detergent or very soft water— wash glassware by hand.

HOMEMADE BRASS AND COPPER CLEANER

☞ Dissolve 1 teaspoon of salt in 1 cup of white vinegar. Add enough flour to make a paste. Apply the paste; let stand for 15 minutes. Rinse with clean, warm water; towel dry.

UNSTICK STACKED GLASSES

☞ To separate stuck stacked glasses, fill the top or inner glass with cold water and dip the bottom or outer glass in hot water.

☛ Store china and glassware where they are easy to remove. Store stacked plates with paper towels, napkins, or doilies between each one. Never stack glassware. Store with rims upright, not down, to prevent trapping moisture inside. Never triple stack cups.

HOW TO CLEAN BURNED POTS

☛ After soaking the burned pot, sprinkle baking soda (or cream of tartar if it's an aluminum pan) on the burn, add a little water, and bring the solution to a boil. Let it cool, and wash as usual.

ELECTROLYTIC CLEANING FOR SILVER AND SILVER PLATE

This method depends on ion exchange in solution rather than on cleaning or deodorizing. It is not for raised patterns as it will remove the attractive coloration on the design, and it is not for cemented pieces, such as some knives, as the required soaking could soften cement.

Place silver on aluminum foil in a nonaluminum pan, add ¼ cup baking soda and 1 gallon of boiling water. Let stand while tarnish is removed, then rinse and dry.

manufacturer, the cycle may be shorter than the normal cycle and/or have less forceful water action.

If your dishwasher doesn't have a special setting for china and glass, use a short or light wash. Select the "no heat" or "energy saving" drying feature. Let the dishes cool before unloading the dishwasher. To minimize spotting, remove items at the end of the rinse cycle and towel dry.

Hand washing: Always be sure to use a plastic dishpan and sink mats to avoid chipping or breakage. When washing cold crystal, do not use water that is too hot; the glass cannot withstand drastic changes in temperature. Otherwise, rinse each piece in hot water. Air or towel dry.

Copper and Brass
Some brass and copper have a lacquered finish, which prevents tarnishing. Polish should be used only on tarnished (unlacquered) metals. These require more abrasive polishes than does silver. (**Never use copper and brass polish on silver.**) To clean, rinse in hot water, then apply a polish with a clean, damp sponge or cloth. Rinse and towel dry.

Nonstick Finishes
Cookware with nonstick finishes should be washed by hand. To remove stains, fill with a solution of 3 tablespoons of oxygen bleach, 1 teaspoon of liquid dish detergent, and 1 cup of water or 3 tablespoons of automatic dishwasher detergent in one cup of water. Simmer for 15 to 20 minutes; remove from the heat. Wash as usual. After washing, wipe the nonstick finish with vegetable oil.

Pewter
To prevent tarnishing, do not wash pewter in the dishwasher. Never use a harsh abrasive. To polish, use silver polish or combine 2 tablespoons of ammonia with 1 quart of hot, soapy water. Rinse in hot water and buff with a clean towel.

Plastic
Check the manufacturer's directions when you buy plastic cookware and utensils. Some types are marked dishwasher safe. And some "top-rack" only since they can dislodge and burn on contact with the heating element. Follow label recommendations.

If not, wash plastic items in hot, sudsy water. To remove stains, make a paste using 3 parts baking soda to 1 part water, then add 1 teaspoon to a pint of water. Soak each item in the solution for 5 to 10 minutes. Rinse and dry.

Stainless Steel and Silver
To minimize discoloration, wash items as soon as possible after use in hot, sudsy water or the dishwasher, or at least rinse well. Separate stainless from silver in the dishwasher. Silver will pit from contact with the stainless.

Stainless steel is not entirely stainproof. Use silver polish or a paste of 3 parts baking soda and 1 part water to remove the hazy white film some foods leave. To remove spots caused by minerals in the water, rinse and towel dry immediately.

Polishing: Follow the directions on the silver polish container. Rub silver gently. Rinse in clear water and wipe dry. To dry, rub each piece briskly with a clean towel—change towels frequently.

THE BATHROOM

To eliminate odors, dampness, mildew, and germs, be sure to clean your bathrooms regularly. Keep them as dry and well ventilated as possible. Use an exhaust fan (vented to the outside), a ceiling heater, or an open window to help evaporate moisture.

Keep shower doors ajar and leave gaps between the ends of the shower curtain and walls to let the air into tub or shower areas. After showering, wipe down the shower walls and doors with a towel to help to reduce mildew.

TILES

To remove soap spots or film, wipe tiles with a solution of 1 part water softener to 4 parts water, a commercial tile-and-basin cleaner, an all-purpose household cleaner, or a vinegar solution (1 part vinegar to 4 parts water or stronger, if needed). Rinse with clear water and buff dry with a soft towel or cloth to prevent streaking.

Clean the grout with a small stiff brush, an old toothbrush, or a nailbrush. If the grout is badly soiled or moldy, use a commercial tile and basin cleaner or apply a bleach solution (¼ cup liquid chlorine to 6 cups water or stronger, if needed).

Apply the solution with a cloth or sponge to help prevent spattering on clothes or nearby fabrics. After cleaning, rinse thoroughly. Use a white liquid appliance polish or wax on tiles, which will leave a shine on the surface and help prevent water spots.

SINKS AND FAUCETS

Clean ceramic, plastic, chrome, and stainless steel with a sponge or cloth. Use a tub and basin cleaner, a mild abrasive powder, baking soda, or a diluted ammonia solution (see page 31). Use full-strength vinegar to remove soapy film.

For a hard-to-clean faucet, soak a cloth in vinegar and wrap it around the fixture. Let it stand 5 to 10 minutes until the film loosens. Remove the cloth and wipe the fixture clean with a dampened cloth. Towel dry the sink and faucet after each use to prevent water spots.

Soap dish: Clean the residue by putting it in the dishwasher or soaking it in warm to hot water. To clean a built-in soap dish, place a wet sponge or cloth over it for 30 minutes. Wipe out the softened soap, rinse, and dry.

BATHTUBS AND SHOWERS

Use a sponge or a long-handled brush so you don't have to stoop. If you have a sunken tub, stand in it to clean.

MINIMIZING MILDEW

Mildew is one of the biggest bathroom cleaning problems. To remove it, wet the mildewed surface with water, then spray with a bleach solution of equal parts liquid chlorine bleach and water. (Or use a tile cleaner, according to directions, to remove mildew.)

Be careful not to get the cleaner on towels, rugs, or fabric shower curtains, because it can bleach the color out.

Be sure the room is well ventilated while using these products; noxious fumes can result. Rinse well and wipe dry.

REMOVING RUST AND MINERAL STAINS FROM TUBS AND SINKS

☞ To remove rust spots or mineral stains, soak the area in vinegar or lemon juice; let it stand 5 minutes. Rinse; then scrub using a mild cleanser. If the stain or spot remains, swab the stain with a dilute solution of oxalic acid, available in hardware and drugstores (1 part acid to 10 parts water).

☞ **Oxalic acid is poisonous; wear protective gloves.**

☞ For a vertical surface, mix the solution with cornmeal to make a thick paste. Apply the paste to the stain, then rinse quickly and thoroughly with water. Do not use a commercial rust-stain remover, it can damage the finish.

GETTING TO THE BOTTOM OF THINGS

☞ Be sure to clean the bottom of the tub or the floor of the shower stall and door track after cleaning the doors to remove any cleaner or soil that might have dripped down from the doors.

NO MORE RING

☞ To remove a bathtub ring (soap and mineral deposits), moisten a sponge or cloth with undiluted vinegar and rub. Use a packaged water softener in your bathwater to eliminate rings.

FILM-FREE SOAP DISH

☞ To prevent soap residue from building up, cut a thin cellulose sponge to fit the bottom of your soap dish, and use it as a soap rest. When the sponge gets soapy, squeeze it out in warm water and return it to the soap dish.

MIRROR BRIGHT

☞ Use rubbing alcohol to wipe dull hair-spray haze from a mirror.

Porcelain and fiberglass: Clean with a tub and tile cleaner, a mild nonabrasive cleanser, baking soda, or a water softener, using a damp sponge. Rub or scour the entire surface, letting the cleanser remain for a minute or so to dissolve the soap film and attack the soil and stains. Rinse thoroughly and dry.

Stall shower: Once a week use a liquid disinfectant cleaner or diluted liquid chlorine bleach (see container label for proportions) to clean the floor. Take care to clean cracks and crevices, which collect soil and harbor fungi and bacteria.

Shower doors: Clean with a solution of ½ cup water softener and ½ pail of water or vinegar and water (½ cup vinegar to 1 quart water). This will dissolve the cloudy film that accumulates on the doors.

You can also spray the door(s) liberally with a laundry prewash or tub and tile cleaner. Leave the cleanser on the door for a few minutes; wipe to remove any scum. Rinse well and towel dry.

Plastic shower curtain and liner: Stretch the curtain out after each use to let it dry and to prevent mildew. Machine-wash colorfast plastic curtains or liners periodically to remove built-up soap film. Use warm water and a nonprecipitating (check the label) water softener (about 1 cup) to dissolve the soap residue.

If the curtain is mildewed, add ¾ cup of liquid chlorine bleach to the wash cycle. Set the control for a 5-minute wash on the gentle cycle. Hang the curtain on a line or shower rod to drip-dry, making sure the bottom edge is inside the tub or shower stall and the curtain is well spread.

Rubber mat: Use disinfectant. Scrub the mat on both sides; rinse well. Between uses, remove the mat from the tub or shower and hang it to dry. Rubber mats can be machine-washed with bleach.

TOILET BOWLS

Clean the interior with a commercial bowl cleaner, sudsy water, or mild cleanser, using a toilet bowl brush.

Scrub all interior surfaces, especially the inside rim of the bowl and the trap. The holes inside the rim can clog with lime deposits.

To remove mineral buildup, plunge out and drain the toilet bowl completely, and wipe out all water with a sponge. Pour in one gallon of a 20 percent solution of muriatic acid (available at hardware stores), following the package directions (wear goggles). Brush the solution into the rinse holes and let it stand for 2 hours. Flush.

To disinfect the toilet, pour ½ cup of liquid chlorine bleach into the water. Let it stand for about 10 minutes; flush.

If you prefer in-tank cleaners, place one in the toilet tank. Most automatically release a measured amount of cleanser and deodorizer with each flush, lengthening the time between cleanings. Place these only in toilets that you use frequently.

Wipe the exterior of the bowl, base, and tank with a sudsy cloth or sponge. Do the same for the seat (both sides), the cover, and hinges.

MIRRORS

Water is the most effective cleaner for mirrors; add 1 tablespoon of ammonia per quart of water or equal parts vinegar and water to increase its cleaning power (or try commercial window cleaners).

Dampen a paper towel or cloth with the desired cleaning agent rather than spraying it directly on the mirror. This prevents moisture from damaging the mirror backing. Wipe the surface thoroughly; dry with paper towel, a lint-free cloth, crumpled newspaper, or a chamois.

REMOVING SKID PROTECTION STRIPS

To remove strips or appliqués carefully lift a corner or edge, making sure that you grip all layers. To get it started, use your fingernail, a chisel-pointed cuticle stick, or any rigid sharp-edged plastic or wood scraper. Do not use a metal or glass tool. Slowly pull up and peel back the strip, making certain that the top layer and clear film remain together, which may be difficult.

Should the layers separate and the film tear as you progress, lift other edges around the strips, working toward the center until all portions are free.

If the layers separate, an acetone nail-polish remover helps to loosen the film. Saturate a cloth with the remover and place it over the film for 15 minutes. Remove the cloth and peel off the film.

Remove the adhesive residue with a spray laundry soil and stain remover containing petroleum distillates or a dry-cleaning spot remover fluid. Allow the spot remover to soak the adhesive for 15 minutes, then wipe firmly with a coarse, dry cloth. Repeat if necessary until all adhesive is removed. Remove any residue with mild liquid dishwashing detergent.

THE NURSERY

A baby's room needs frequent cleaning to keep it hygienic. Change and launder the crib sheet, pads, and blankets daily (more often if needed). Once a week, wipe the crib, mattress, and bumpers with a damp sponge and an all-purpose household cleaner solution that disinfects. Rinse and dry.

- Wash washable stuffed toys in a pillowcase in the washing machine every week, or as needed, to keep them clean and smelling fresh.

- Vacuum or wipe other toys with a damp sponge and an all-purpose household cleaner.

- Empty wastebaskets often and dust furniture, windowsills, and other surfaces several times each week.

- Damp-mop or vacuum floors weekly or as needed.

CHILD'S PLAY

From an early age, children can clean their own rooms. Arrange the room to facilitate this. Install low horizontal shelves, cabinets, dressers, and other units instead of tall, vertical cabinets or storage units.

Keep toys and books that are used constantly on open shelves and favorite toys on a low, open shelf in the closet.

Periodically, you and your child should sort out toys that are broken or no longer interesting. This will reduce the number of toys and make it easier for your child to put toys away.

KEEPING A LID ON CHAOS

☛ Roomy catchall storage bins and baskets—laundry baskets, modular plastic storage cases or cubes, dishpans, and milk crates—are great for storing toys. Bright colors make the job more pleasant.

☛ A clothes hamper or a laundry bag makes depositing dirty clothes easy and convenient.

☛ A large conveniently placed wastebasket gives kids an easy alternative to throwing trash on the floor.

☛ Shoebags hung on the closet door at your children's height help them keep their shoes together.

PORCHES, DECKS, AND PATIOS

Porches, decks, and patios require basic cleaning as do interior spaces. Sweep as needed.

- Scrub decks and porches, even those made from pressure-treated wood, occasionally with a chlorine bleach and water solution to remove mildew, dirt, and stains. Rinse well with clean water.

- Scrub patios, especially those paved with brick, cement blocks, slate, or stone with a chlorine bleach and water solution or a cleaner (available in garden centers) developed to remove mold, moss, or algae. If mold isn't a problem, wash periodically with an all-purpose cleaner and water solution. Rinse well with clean water.

OUTDOOR FURNITURE

Lawn furniture—barbecue grills, blinds, and awnings—require care while in use and before seasonal storage.

Outdoor furniture receives a lot of abuse from the sun, rain, and wind. To protect it, follow these suggestions:

Aluminum

Although it does not rust, aluminum can become dull and pitted when left outdoors. To clean, restore the shine, and smooth the surface of aluminum chairs and chaise longues, scrub the frames with a plastic scrubber soaked in detergent or a soap-impregnated steel wool pad; rinse and towel dry.

Use a sponge soaked in detergent and water to wash tubular aluminum with baked-enamel finishes; rinse and dry. To maintain the luster of any aluminum surface (including baked enamel) and to make cleaning easier, wax the pieces from time to time with automobile paste wax.

Canvas

Soiled canvas seats and seat backs are usually machine washable; be sure to put them back on the furniture while they are still damp so they retain their shape.

Scrub large canvas pieces like awnings with a firm-bristled brush and an all-purpose cleaner and water solution. Rinse well with a hose. Air dry.

Plastic

Wash plastic furniture with an all-purpose cleaner and water solution, then rinse with water and dry.

Wood

Scrub stubborn soil with a brush and all-purpose cleaner and water solution; rinse well and towel dry. Wood furniture may need staining or to have a wood preservative applied periodically for protection.

BARBECUE GRILLS

Most grills will last many years if kept free of ashes and moisture. For extra protection against rust, paint with a heat-resistant enamel available at hardware stores.

To clean the rack, use an oven cleaner or soak it in a household ammonia and water solution; then scrub and rinse.

For gas-fueled grills, follow the directions in the owner's manual. To clean permanent briquettes, flip them occasionally, ignite the grill and, with the cover closed, allow it to burn at a high setting for about 15 minutes.

CHAPTER 3

LAUNDRY AND CLOTHES CARE

Sheets into Curt... HANDY TIPS: For Buffing Wood Fl... ...king Rooms Look Larger, Ironing ... ...ning Tile Grout, Creating a ☛ Mo... ...e on Car Repairs, Buy Produce, C... ...reventing Carpet Dents, Unsticking Stacked Glasses, Making Rooms Look Larger, Ironing Pleated Skirts, Arranging Flowers, Jump-Starting a Car, Cleaning Tile Grout, Creating a Home Office, Fixing a Leaky Faucet ☛ STEP-BY-STEP GUIDES: To Checkbook Security, Unblocking a Sink, Buying a Home, Successful Decorating ☛ BASIC EQUIPMENT: How to choose a washer and dryer. Tips on installation. ☛ LAUNDRY PRODUCTS: Which product when: soap, detergent, bleach, and starch. Testing for colorfastness. Tips for safe bleaching. When to use water softeners. Fabric care guide. ☛ DOING THE WASH: Advice on pretreating. How to use a washing machine and dryer. Setting up a laundry room. Air drying. What to do when your washer and dryer act up. Special-care items. Step-by-step cleaning for vintage linens and lace. Stain-removal guide. ☛ IRONING: How to get wrinkles out. Pressing techniques. All about your iron: How to buy one; how to use one. ☛ DRY CLEANING: How to get the best results. Safety measures. Using a bulk dry cleaner. ☛ SEWING: Buttons and fasteners. Repairing woolen runs. Fixing tears. Patches. Basic supplies. Step by step: shortening trousers, basic stitches, darning, and hemming. How to sew a on button. ☛ LEATHER AND FUR: Touch-up tips. Routine care for shoes, bags, and gloves. Proper storage. ☛ JEWELRY CARE: Keeping precious metals and stones bright and lustrous. How to unkink tangled jewelry chains. Tips on caring for pearls. ☛ PACKING A SUITCASE: What to pack and how to pack it. The carry-on bag: keeping important items handy. ☛ CLOTHES STORAGE: Mothproofing with cedar and other repellents. When to hang, when to fold. Careful fur and leather storage. ☛ EVERYTHING YOU NEED TO KNOW: About Choosing Pots and Pans, Front-Wheel-Drive Cars, Making Healthier Meals, Vacuum Cleaners, Garden Tools, Upholstered Furniture, Your Credit Card Statement, Curtain Styles ☛ MONEY-SAVING HINTS: How to Turn Bed Sheets into Curtains, Save on Car Repairs, Buy Produce, Choose Carpeting ☛ HANDY TIPS: For Buffing Wood Floors, Preventing Carpet Dents, Unsticking Stacked Glasses, Making Rooms Look Larger, Ironing Pleated Skirts, Arranging Flowers, Jump-Starting a Car, Cleaning Tile Grout, Creating a Home Office, Fixing a Leaky Faucet ☛ STEP-BY-STEP GUIDES: To Checkbook Security, Unblocking a Sink, Buying a Home, Successful Decorating, Performing CPR, Changing Flat

BASIC EQUIPMENT

KEEPING YOUR DRYER EFFICIENT

☛ Clean the lint filter before each use.

☛ Clean your dryer vent once a year to keep it working at its best. First, clear the vent flap at the outside of the house of leaves or other debris. Then, indoors—after disconnecting the duct by gently pulling it off the window vent—insert the crevice tool of your vacuum into the duct to draw out any accumulated lint.

DEALING WITH DECALS

☛ To prevent damage, turn T-shirts or other clothing with decals inside out before washing. Use cold or lukewarm water. Air dry or use the air-drying cycle on the dryer; heat can melt the decal.

D oing laundry is less of a chore and can fit into even the busiest schedules when good equipment is nearby. The laundry can be in the basement, a bathroom, kitchen, or even a closet as long as there is access to at least electricity, plumbing, and drainage, and your dryer can be vented to the outside of the house.

Proper Installation

Each appliance must have its own separate circuit. Like any major appliance, both washer and dryer must also be electrically grounded. Consult the manufacturer, a service expert, or utility company for proper procedures.

In addition, a gas dryer must also have access to natural or liquefied petroleum gas (LPG), and venting—through a window, wall, floor, or ceiling—is necessary for all dryers to carry lint and moisture outside.

If space is limited, consider a stacked washer/dryer combination.

WASHERS

Consider the following features when choosing a washer:

Capacity: If your wash loads are big, choose an extra large washer. (Smaller machines are labeled "large.") Top-loading machines have greater capacity than front loaders.

Water usage: To conserve water, choose a washer designed to use less water than others. Front-loading machines use less water than top loaders.

Cycles: Some machines come with electronically preprogrammed cycles to take the guesswork out of laundry, as well as custom cycles, which give you more control over the washing process than ever before. The standard cycles include:

Regular: for most items not needing special handling.

Permanent press: has regular agitation but includes a cold soak to minimize wrinkling during the wash cycle and before the rinse cycle.

Delicate: recommended for lingerie, knits, and other fine fabrics. It may have a shorter wash time and gentler agitation and spin speeds. If you have heavily soiled items, consider a machine with an automatic presoak (not a standard cycle).

Water controls: let you adjust water quantity when you do less than a full load.

Temperature controls: allow choice of hot, warm, or cold water. All automatic machines now have a final cold rinse, an important feature for energy conservation.

Bleach dispenser: automatically dilutes and adds bleach to the wash cycle.

Fabric softener dispenser: eliminates the need to add fabric softener when the final rinse cycle begins.

DRYERS

Consider the following:

Gas or electric: Both perform well, so base your decision on which hookup is more feasible inside your house and on fuel costs in your area.

Cycles: Most dryers have three basic cycles, all of which are necessary.

Regular: for items like jeans and towels.

Permanent press: has an extended cool-down period.

Air dry: tumbles dry without heat.

Some dryers also have a delicate setting, which is useful if you dry items such as knits or lingerie.

Controls: allow the dryer to stop when the clothes are properly dried. Every dryer works by one of the following systems:

Time control: lets you select the length of drying time.

Auto-dry control: time and temperature determine degree of dryness (more or less dry).

Electronic control: a moisture-sensing device measures moisture in the load.

Venting: Some dryers vent from more than one direction, making installation easier. A vent shouldn't be too long (no more than 50 feet) or have too many elbows.

LAUNDRY PRODUCTS

Products are available for every step of the wash process:

- Detergents and soaps for cleaning
- Bleaches and enzyme products for removing stains and whitening
- Water and fabric softeners for eliminating static cling and softening clothes and water
- Starches and sizings for restoring body to shapeless clothes

DETERGENTS

Unlike soaps, synthetic detergents contain surfactants, which increase water's wetting ability, loosen and remove soil, and suspend it in the wash solution. Some heavy-duty detergents also contain one or more "builders," which increase the surfactants' cleaning efficiency.

Depending on the brand, detergents may also incorporate fluorescent whitening agents, color-safe bleach, enzymes, and borax, which boost their basic cleaning power. Some include fabric softeners, eliminating the need to add softener to the rinse water or dryer.

Heavy-duty detergents, a good choice for very dirty clothes, can be used for all washable fabrics. Light-duty formulas are designed for laundering delicate fabrics and baby clothes.

"Ultra" detergents, also called compacts and superconcentrates, are a recent development in granular and liquid detergents. You need to use only a small quantity.

Detergents are available in both granular and liquid form. Liquids are especially effective for oily soils and are convenient for pretreating soil before laundering.

SOAPS

Soaps are mild and are natural fabric softeners, making them good for diapers and baby clothes. They are not good for items such as children's pajamas where soap residue can interfere with flame resistant properties.

In soft water, soaps are ideal for hand and machine washing delicate fabrics. In hard water, however, soaps combine with minerals to form a difficult-to-remove film. As a result, they are used less frequently than detergents.

SOAPS, DETERGENTS, AND THE ENVIRONMENT

☞ Soaps and surfactants, the most important ingredient in all synthetic detergents, are biodegradable. Other laundry product ingredients may not be biodegradable, but are designed to be compatible with both public sewage treatment systems and with septic tanks. These systems remove detergent ingredients so that those that are not biodegradable have little impact on the environment.

WASHING THE GREEN WAY

☞ Boost your detergent's cleaning power by adding ½ cup of washing soda (available in the laundry products section in your supermarket) to your wash load. This is an environmentally safe way to enhance your detergent's cleaning power. Washing soda may also be used with bleach.

BLEACHES

Use laundry bleaches as stain removers, whiteners, brighteners, and sanitizers to supplement soap or detergent. Bleaches are very powerful chemicals and should never be applied undiluted directly onto fabrics. (Before use, read "Bleaching Dos and Don'ts" below.) Use bleach only on white and colorfast washables.

There are two kinds of bleach:

Chlorine: This is potent, fast acting, and very effective for cottons, linens, and synthetics. If not used properly, however, it can weaken fibers, causing disintegration, even holes. To avoid damage, follow label directions carefully. Never use it on silk, wool, spandex, or fabrics treated with flame-resistant finishes.

If machine washing, add chlorine bleach manually or by bleach dispenser, if your machine has one, after the wash cycle has begun. If hand washing, add it to either the wash or rinse water, or both.

All-fabric/oxygen: Milder than chlorine bleach, this bleach is for fabrics needing gentle treatment. It is slower acting and less effective in restoring whiteness, but used regularly, it can help.

All-fabric/oxygen bleach, which comes in dry and liquid form, can be used with most washable silks and woolens—unless the garment manufacturer's label says "no bleach." Use liquid oxygen bleach to treat stains. Add oxygen bleach at the same time as detergent, before clothes are immersed in water.

BLEACHING DOS AND DON'TS

DO:

DON'T:

DO:	DON'T:
Wear rubber gloves when hand washing with bleach.	Let chlorine bleach come in direct contact with fabrics.
Read fabric and bleach labels.	Put all-fabric/oxygen bleach directly on wet fabrics without testing for colorfastness first.
Test bleach before use:	
Chlorine bleach: Mix 1 tablespoon bleach with ¼ cup cold water. Place a drop on a hidden area; leave for 1 minute; blot to see if there is any color change.	Use chlorine bleach if your household water supply has a high iron content. It can draw out the iron and deposit it as spots on clothes.
All-fabric/oxygen bleach: Mix 1 teaspoon bleach with 1 cup hot water. Place a drop on a hidden area; leave for 10 minutes; blot to see if there is any color change.	Use bleach and ammonia in the same wash. The combination can create hazardous fumes.
Thoroughly rinse out bleach.	Use more of either kind of bleach than recommended on the package or bottle label.
Keep bleach away from children.	

BLUING

Bluing helps restore whiteness. It's available in liquid form and contains blue pigment, which counteracts the yellowing that occurs with some fabrics. Dilute with water, as instructed on the label, before adding to the wash.

STAIN PRESOAKS

These powdered products, made with complex proteins known as enzymes, are effective spot and stain removers. Use them when soaking stained garments prior to washing or as a detergent supplement.

PREWASH STAIN REMOVERS

Use these products, which are available in pump spray, liquid, stick, or aerosol forms, to pretreat heavily soiled or stained areas. They work well on oil-based stains on polyester fibers.

WATER SOFTENERS

If you live in an area with hard water (see right), use water softeners to counteract the graying or yellowing effect of the water's minerals.

If your water is not very hard (less than 10.6 grains of hardness per gallon), soften the wash water simply by using extra detergent. Start by using half again the amount of detergent called for. If the wash is still not as clean as you like, you may need to install a mechanical softener.

Packaged dry softeners: Added to wash water with detergent, these remove the calcium and magnesium ions that cause yellowing. Nonprecipitating softeners contain phosphates. Precipitating or nonphosphate softeners are also available. These can leave residue that clings to fabrics and the washer.

Mechanical softeners: These are attached to the house water system (for more information see page 240).

FABRIC SOFTENERS

These make fabrics soft and fluffy, and help reduce static cling. They also reduce wrinkling and make ironing easier or unnecessary.

Liquid softeners: These should be added to the final rinse cycle by automatic dispenser if your washing machine has one, or by hand. Follow the label directions and measure carefully.

Dryer-added softeners: These come in two forms: paper-thin sheets and packets. Place the sheet type on top of the clothes; attach the packet to a fin in the dryer drum. To avoid buildup on towels, which reduces their absorbency, use fabric softener once every two to three washings.

If you use a detergent that contains fabric softeners (check the label), you don't need extra softener.

STARCHES AND SIZINGS

Starches and sizings restore body to fabrics that become limp, such as cotton and linen, when washed or dry cleaned.

Starch
Starch comes in powder, liquid, and spray forms. Mix the powder and liquid with water. If using the powder, mix to the desired thickness—thin for light starching, thick for heavy. When washing cottons and linens, add it to the final rinse. Spritz spray starches on during ironing.

Sizing
Lighter than starch, sizing is applied to some fabrics by manufacturers for protection and body. General wear, moisture, perspiration, and cleaning will break down sizing, but you can reapply it. Spritz it on before ironing.

IS YOUR WATER HARD?

To determine whether your water is hard, and if so, how hard, consult your local water-supply office.

If your water comes from another source, have it tested by a water treatment company.

There are several indications that you have hard water:

- Fabrics look dull and gray.
- Fabrics feel stiff instead of soft.
- Soaps and detergents don't lather well.
- A "ring" settles around your bathtub (for cleaning see page 58).
- A white residue appears, and remains, around drains and faucets and on glassware.

GUIDE TO FIBERS AND FABRICS

Use this chart as a general guide to choose the right cleaning method for your garments. Care varies based on colorfastness, weight, trimmings, linings, special finishes, fabric construction, and always read and follow the manufacturer's care label recommendations first.

Acetate Synthetic fiber. Dry-clean.
Acrylic Synthetic fiber. Machine-wash knits in warm water on gentle setting. Roll in a towel to absorb extra moisture, and dry flat; or dry at low setting in a dryer. Dry-clean woven acrylic fabrics.

Blends Fabrics of combined fibers: cotton/polyester, cotton/linen, silk/polyester, wool/polyester, and so on. Follow care guidelines for the more delicate or most prominent fiber in the blend.

Canvas Heavy, firm, tightly woven fabric, originally cotton or linen, now also made of synthetics or blends. Machine wash in cold water and tumble dry on low setting. Dry-clean if not colorfast.
Cashmere Undercoat hair of the cashmere goat. Treat as wool, and follow the care label.

Sweaters may be hand-washed with care, but it's best to dry-clean both knits and wovens.
Chiffon Thin, transparent fabric, usually silk, but can be of synthetic fibers. Hand wash as for Silk.
Chintz Glazed cotton, often printed. Dry-clean unless label states that glaze is durable and fabric can be washed; if so, wash as directed.

Corduroy Ridged-pile fabric that may be cotton, cotton/polyester, or rayon. Turn inside out and use warm water. Dry at normal setting; remove from dryer while slightly damp; smooth pockets and seams with hands. Hang until dry.
Cotton Natural vegetable fiber woven and knitted into fabrics of many weights and textures.

Hand-wash lightweight fabrics, such as batiste, organdy, and voile, and hang to air dry (or iron damp with a hot iron).

Machine-wash light-colored and white medium- and heavyweight cottons with warm water. Use cold water for bright colors that may bleed. Dry at low setting. Remove from dryer while still damp. Iron damp with hot iron.

Damask Jacquard-weave fabric; may be cotton, linen, silk, viscose, wool, or a blend. Hand-wash lightweight fabrics; see individual fiber listings. Dry-clean silk, wool, and all heavier weight fabrics.
Denim Strong, heavy twill-weave fabric, usually cotton, but can be a cotton/synthetic blend. Prone to shrinkage unless purchased preshrunk. Machine-wash in warm water. Traditional blue and other deep colors bleed the first several washings, so wash separately, as necessary. Dry at low setting to avoid shrinkage. Iron while damp with a hot iron, as needed.

Down Soft underplumage of water fowl, often combined with adult feathers (should be so labeled). Both machine-washable and dry-cleanable, but treatment depends on the fabric shell of the item; follow manufacturer's instructions carefully.

Do not air dry. Tumble dry on gentle setting (temperature no higher than 140° F). Fluff and turn often during drying.

Flannel Napped fabric in plain or twill weave. Cotton and synthetics may be machine washed. Dry at low setting and remove while damp or line dry. Wool should be dry cleaned.

Gabardine Firm, closely woven twill fabric, originally and often worsted wool; also made of cotton and synthetic fibers. Follow label directions or dry-clean.

Lace Open-work textile; may be cotton, linen, or synthetic. Hand-wash using a soap or detergent for delicate fabrics. Avoid rubbing. Squeeze out excess moisture; don't twist or wring. Shape by hand and hang to air dry or dry flat; do not tumble dry. Pin delicate lace to a cloth before washing.

Linen Natural flax fiber; light- to heavyweight fabrics. Hand-wash or machine-wash in warm water, if colorfast; use oxygen bleach, as needed. Iron damp on wrong side.

For heavy linens, use a hot iron; for lighter-weight linens, blends, and linens treated for crease resistance, use a lower temperature. Can also dry-clean (especially heavy linens).

Mohair Fiber from the angora goat. Treat as Wool.

Nylon Synthetic fiber used in fabrics of different weights, sometimes blended with other fibers. When used alone, it is both dry-cleanable and machine-washable; use warm water.

Tumble dry on a low setting, but can hang on plastic hanger and drip or air dry. To avoid permanent yellowing, keep away from sunlight or direct heat.

Organdy Sheer, lightweight, plain-weave cotton. Hand-wash; starch to maintain characteristic crisp appearance. Iron damp with hot iron. Can also dry-clean.

Polyester Strong synthetic fiber in fabrics of various weights and textures; often blended with cotton and wool. Does not shrink or stretch.

Wash in warm water. Tumble dry and remove promptly to prevent wrinkles. Iron at low setting. If garment is pleated, hand-wash and drip dry. If blended, follow guidelines for the more delicate fiber.

Ramie Natural fiber from ramie plant (similar to linen), used alone or blended, often with cotton. Machine-wash in warm water; tumble dry. Iron damp with hot iron. Can also dry-clean. Avoid excessive twisting.

Rayon A generic term for a man-made fiber including viscose and cuprammonium rayon. Some garment labels identify the fabric as "rayon," some as "viscose." Follow label care instructions. Dry-clean for best results.

Satin Fabric with a lustrous finish, traditionally silk, now also acetate, cotton, nylon, and polyester.

Dry-clean silk and acetate. Wash cotton, nylon, and polyester satins following fiber guidelines.

Seersucker Fabric with puckered stripes woven in during the manufacturing process; usually cotton, but also nylon, polyester, and silk versions. See fiber for washing. Drip or tumble dry. Iron on low heat, if needed.

Silk Natural fiber from the silkworm; in fabrics of various weights and textures. If recommended, hand-wash plain-weave crepe de chine, thin, lightweight, and medium-weight kinds in lukewarm water with mild soap or detergent or in cold water with special cold-water detergent. Do not use chlorine bleach.

Rinse several times in cold water until no trace of suds remains; towel blot. Dry flat. Iron on wrong side at warm (silk) setting. If so labeled, some silks can be machine washed; follow label directions carefully. Dry-clean heavier (suiting weight) silks, pleated silks, and those in dark colors, which may bleed.

Spandex Generic name for stretch fibers often added to other fibers to give them elasticity. Machine-wash in warm water on the delicate cycle (if exercise wear, wash after each wearing to remove body oils, which can cause deterioration). Do not use chlorine bleach. Line dry; do not use dryer. Do not iron.

Terry cloth Toweling fabric with looped pile made of cotton or cotton/polyester. Machine-wash in warm or hot water. Tumble dry or line dry.

Velour Napped fabric, originally wool, now also cotton, silk, and synthetics. Dry-clean unless manufacturer's label indicates it can be washed.

Velvet Soft pile fabric, originally silk, now usually rayon or cotton. Dry-clean.

Wool Natural fiber made of sheep fleece. Hand-wash sweaters and other knits in cold water with cold-water detergent. Rinse thoroughly. Squeeze; do not wring.

Towel blot and dry flat (see page 74). Machine-washable wools are so labeled; follow instructions carefully. Dry-clean woven wools and heavy sweaters.

DOING THE WASH

FIVE WAYS TO MINIMIZE SHRINKAGE

Always read the care label. If it indicates to dry-clean only, do so. For washable garments:

☞ Use cool or warm water, not hot.

☞ Use the most gentle wash method that achieves good results.

☞ Dry on the lowest dryer setting.

☞ Remove clothes from the dryer before they're completely dry.

☞ Drip dry or block into shape and lay flat to finish drying (see page 74).

MYSTERY STAINS

☞ For washable fabrics, apply pretreatment product or rub liquid laundry detergent into stain. Wash in warm, sudsy water with a few drops of ammonia added. For any remaining stain, launder again using an appropriate bleach. For dry-cleanable fabrics, sponge stains with dry-cleaning solvent.

Make organizing the wash everybody's job. Each person should be responsible for gathering his or her own soiled clothes and linens, presorting them, and taking them to the laundry room.

A laundry bag or small hamper in every clothes closet helps. It is best to treat stains quickly, so ask family members to turn in their heavily soiled items as quickly as possible.

BEFORE YOU START

For best results, separate:

• Dark from white or light-colored items.

• Lightly soiled from heavily soiled garments.

• Fabrics requiring different water temperatures (see machine washing below).

• Lint-shedding fabrics, such as terry cloth, from lint-attracting fabrics, such as corduroy, synthetics, and permanent-press fabrics. (Turn pile fabrics, such as corduroy or velour, inside out so they won't pick up lint.)

• Lingerie and delicate fabric from other garments and wash them in mesh bags.

• Any clothes where colorfastness may be a problem. Test (see instructions on page 64).

And before you wash, be sure to:

• Brush dirt and lint from the insides of pant and sleeve cuffs.

• Close zippers to prevent breakage and snagging.

• Tie straps, strings, and sashes to prevent tangling.

• Empty pockets (be sure to check children's).

• Remove nonwashable belts, shoulder pads, and trimmings.

• Mend tears and ripped seams; they are usually smaller and easier to fix before washing rather than after (see page 84).

Pretreating

Just before washing or presoaking, apply a paste made of powered detergent and water, or a commercial prewash stain remover to stains and soiled areas such as collars, cuffs, pocket edges, and seams, and rub in (or brush with an old soft toothbrush). Some commercial prewash stain removers can be applied as much as a week in advance of doing the laundry (see product label).

Before laundering, soak heavily soiled garments in a detergent solution in a sink or tub. If your washing machine has a presoak cycle, you can do this automatically.

Do not soak silk, wool, or noncolorfast fabrics.

MACHINE WASHING

First, select the appropriate water temperature:

Hot: for heavily soiled, colorfast clothes, diapers, sheets, and towels.

Warm: for cotton, washable woolens and knits, and moderately soiled items.

Cold: for lightly soiled, noncolorfast, and delicate fabrics. Use cold water for rinsing to save energy and reduce the

SETTING UP A LAUNDRY ROOM

THE IDEAL LAUNDRY ROOM HAS plenty of storage space, good lighting, venting, a no-skid, washable floor, and room for ironing, folding, and hanging and air drying clothes. If your space is limited, try a compact, efficient, closet arrangement.

FULL-SIZE LAUNDRY

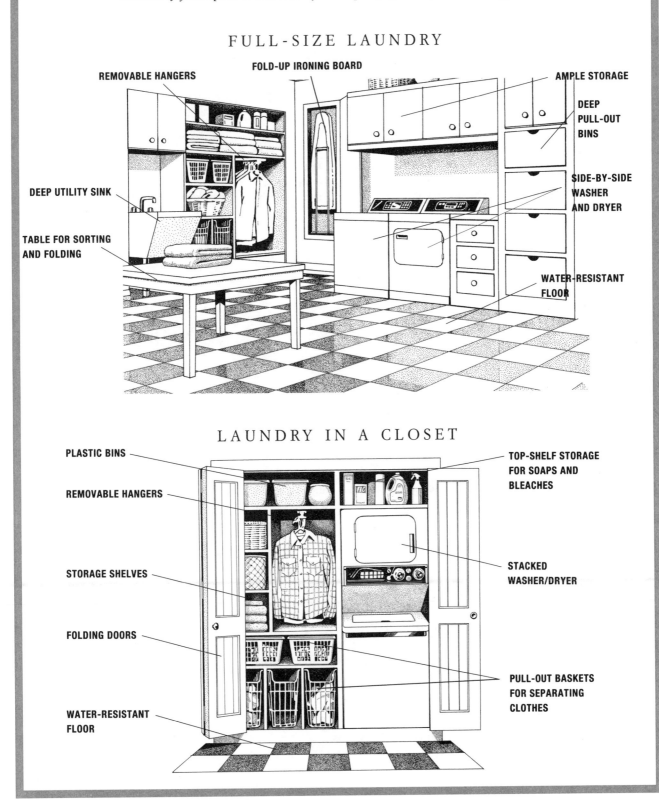

REMOVABLE HANGERS

FOLD-UP IRONING BOARD

AMPLE STORAGE

DEEP PULL-OUT BINS

DEEP UTILITY SINK

SIDE-BY-SIDE WASHER AND DRYER

TABLE FOR SORTING AND FOLDING

WATER-RESISTANT FLOOR

LAUNDRY IN A CLOSET

PLASTIC BINS

TOP-SHELF STORAGE FOR SOAPS AND BLEACHES

REMOVABLE HANGERS

STORAGE SHELVES

STACKED WASHER/DRYER

FOLDING DOORS

PULL-OUT BASKETS FOR SEPARATING CLOTHES

WATER-RESISTANT FLOOR

MACHINE DRYING

Before each wash, clean the lint filter to ensure better dryer performance.

- Separate any starched items and dry first in a cold dryer; turn the items inside out if they are dark colored.

- To reduce wrinkling, load the dryer cylinder no more than half full (preferably one-third full, which is the size of an average washer load), leaving ample space for tumbling.

  To dry evenly, put items of similar fabric weight, but mixed sizes in one load.

- For recommended drying times and temperatures, read the appliance manual and follow the suggestions on garment manufacturers' labels.

- As soon as the tumbling action ends, remove items to prevent wrinkles, and hang or fold.

  If clothes or linens are to be ironed immediately, remove them from the dryer while they are still damp.

AIR DRYING

Most cottons and linens can be line dried (which gives them a fresh-air scent no dryer can duplicate).

Hang washable garments on padded hangers and line dry indoors or out. If flat drying is recommended for sweaters or garments that may stretch (see page 74), roll the item in a towel to blot excess moisture, then shape the garment and place it on a towel to dry, away from the sun, which can bleach or discolor. When dry on top, turn it over, changing towels if necessary.

DELICATE MATTERS

☞ When machine washing or drying delicate items, place them in a net bag or a pillowcase (tied closed or pinned with rustproof safety pins).

STOP! DON'T PUT THAT IN YOUR DRYER

Do not put items in your dryer that are spotted with, or have been in contact with, paint, machine oil, gasoline, or any flammable fluids or solids. They are fire hazards, and their fumes can ignite. Line dry instead.

Once all traces of flammables and their fumes are removed, dry as usual.

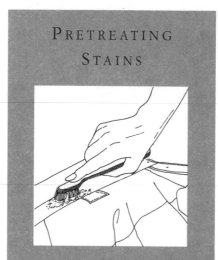

PRETREATING STAINS

To pretreat heavily soiled areas, use a soft brush or your hands to rub in liquid detergent or paste (an old toothbrush works well).

---

possibility of setting wrinkles in the fabrics.

- Add detergent or soap as the washer fills.

- Add any laundry aids such as bleach or water softener (according to package directions), as needed.

- Wait until the rinse cycle to add fabric softener, bluing, or liquid starch, as needed.

  Don't use fabric softener with other laundry products that contain softeners.

- Load the machine loosely—with enough items to fill, but do not overload.

  Distribute clothes evenly, balancing large and small pieces, and make sure that nothing is wrapped around the agitator.

- If you just want to starch selected items, remove them from the washer and soak in a basin in a starch solution (see page 65) for the time recommended on the starch package.

  Squeeze out excess moisture before placing them in the dryer.

BEFORE YOU CALL FOR REPAIR

If your washer or dryer isn't working, use the troubleshooting charts below and check your appliance manual. The answers may be right there, and the problems easily solved.

IS YOUR WASHER:	CHECK	REMEMBER
Not filling? *Not running?*	Is the cord plugged in? Is the "On" control button set? Are the fuse and circuit breaker intact (not blown or tripped)? Are the water faucets open? Is the water supply on? Have you depressed one—only one—water-level control button? Are the fill and drain hoses in proper position?	Some washer cycles pause, then restart. The permanent-press cycle cools down, then restarts.
Not spinning? *Spinning slowly?* *Not spinning out all water?*	Is the lid closed? Is the machine overloaded? Is the load properly balanced? Did you use a cold-water rinse?	Cold water is not as easily extracted from fabric as hot water.
Noisy? *Vibrating?*	After purchasing the washer, was it unpacked properly? Were all the shipping blocks removed? Was the machine installed on a level floor? Is the load properly balanced? Are any pins or nails caught in the basket?	It's normal for shifting gears to make noise at the beginning of wash and rinse cycles.

IS YOUR DRYER:	CHECK	REMEMBER
Not running? *Not heating?*	Is the cord plugged in? Is the door closed? Are the fuses and circuit breakers intact (not blown or tripped)? If a gas dryer, is gas turned on at the main line and at the dryer's gas valve?	An electric dryer has two fuses or circuit breakers in the main switch box; both must be working.
Not drying properly?	Are the controls set correctly? Is the lint screen clean? Is the dryer underloaded? Overloaded? Improperly vented?	The dryer should be only half full, and items of similar weights should be dried together. If it is underloaded, items may not tumble well; adding dry, lint-free towels will help.

LABEL LANGUAGE

Ever wonder what those symbols on garment care labels mean? Here are the most common ones:

MACHINE WASHABLE (RECOMMENDED WATER TEMPERATURE MAY APPEAR IN TUB).

DO NOT WASH.

HAND-WASH, LUKE-WARM WATER.

USE CHLORINE BLEACH WITH CARE.

DO NOT USE CHLORINE BLEACH.

TUMBLE DRY (YELLOW SYMBOL: USE LOW TEMPERATURE).

DRY ON FLAT SURFACE AFTER EXTRACTING EXCESS WATER.

DRIP DRY (HANG SOAKING WET).

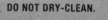

HANG TO DRY AFTER REMOVING EXCESS WATER.

DRY-CLEAN.

DO NOT DRY-CLEAN.

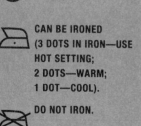

CAN BE IRONED (3 DOTS IN IRON—USE HOT SETTING; 2 DOTS—WARM; 1 DOT—COOL).

DO NOT IRON.

SPECIAL-CARE ITEMS

Area Rugs

Some small scatter rugs of cotton or synthetic fibers are machine-washable; check the manufacturer's label. Before washing, vacuum or shake out loose dirt.

If the rug is heavily soiled, use the soak cycle on your machine, or soak in a basin. Do not tumble dry if the rug has a rubber backing. Hang it on a line.

Bedding

Cotton and synthetic blankets, electric blankets, and bedspreads can be machine-washed if they are treated as delicate fabrics in both the washer and dryer. Always follow the manufacturer's recommendations.

Some quilts and comforters can be machine-washed, but only if securely stitched. If the filling isn't stitched through, it will shift and become lumpy.

Wash only one large bedding item at a time, distributing its bulk evenly around the agitator. Tumble dry or line dry.

If line drying, hang the item over two lines to bear the weight better, and turn and rehang at least once.

Cotton and Synthetic Knits

Close zippers and attach hook-and-eye fasteners. Turn the garment inside out. If the label says washable, machine-wash in warm water (cold water for dark colors). Tumble dry on a low temperature. Remove promptly.

Loose and open knits can be damaged by washer agitation. It is better to hand-wash these and dry flat after shaping.

Don't machine-wash wool knits, including sweaters. Follow the instructions for hand washing on page 74.

Down Jackets and Comforters

Down jackets and coats and down-filled comforters are machine-washable if their shell fabric is. Check the label.

It's especially important to mend tears and rips in the fabric before washing, since down (and feathers, if the filling

includes them) can even push through small holes.

Wash each item separately in warm water, distributing the bulk around the agitator. If the load is small, balance it with bath towels.

Never air dry down garments or bedding; the down will flatten and lump. Tumble dry at a low setting (drying will be slow). Add tennis balls or a clean sneaker to help fluff up the down.

Down items can also be dry-cleaned if the label recommends to do so. Use a reputable dry cleaner as dirty solvents can strip the natural oils in down and stain fabric.

Fabric Sneakers

Machine-wash fabric sneakers only if there is a care label that explicitly says to do so. Pretreat spots and stains (see pages 65, 68, and 70). Unless otherwise noted, use warm water and the regular wash cycle. Add several bath towels to balance the load. Place them on the drying rack, if your dryer has one, and use a low temperature setting, or stuff the shoes with paper towels so they retain their shape and air dry.

Don't machine-wash leather sneakers or those with leather trim. Instead, clean by hand with a small brush dipped in warm, sudsy water.

Glass-Fiber Textiles

Do not machine-wash or dry glass-fiber textiles, such as draperies. The glass particles can penetrate other fabrics. Hand wash and rinse carefully to avoid breaking the fibers. Line dry.

Pillows and Stuffed Toys

Before washing pillows or stuffed toys, check the manufacturer's label to see if they are machine-washable. Mend any tears or rips before washing.

Wash two pillows or toys at once for balance; one on each side of the agitator. Agitate 1-2 minutes on a gentle cycle.

Tumble dry feather pillows; they will become lumpy if you attempt to dry them

BEFORE YOU START

Never wash an antique or delicate quilt or textile without first showing it to a conservation or restoration specialist.

If you are washing an item with colored embroidery, consult a dry cleaner or professional hand launderer who works with vintage linens or lace about proper treatment.

If you are laundering items yourself, be sure to do the following:

• Remove any metal fasteners or decorations that might rust or discolor the fabric when wet.

• Protect small, delicate items by putting them in a net bag.

TO WASH

If you are working with a large item—such as a tablecloth, bed coverlet, or dress—use the bathtub for soaking, placing the piece on a stack of white towels or clean white cotton cloths to support it in the water.

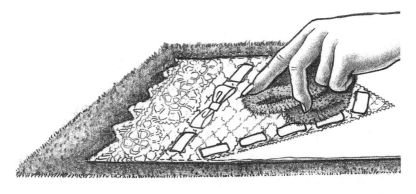

BLOT FRAGILE ITEMS DRY

1. Soak the item in a solution of a commercial cleaning paste designed for vintage fabrics and water or a solution of mild soap and water. The water can be cool or lukewarm, but not hot. Do not rub or wring the fabric while it is soaking.

2. As the water becomes dirty, change it, adding fresh cleaning paste or soap as often as necessary.

3. Rinse in fresh water several times until all traces of paste or soap are gone (any that remain can weaken the fabric). Lift the item out carefully after each rinse, holding the underside of the fabric.

4. If there are still stains and dirt, soak the item again in an all-fabric/oxygen bleach solution (follow package directions), and rinse again several times.

TO DRY

Blot the item with towels, and place flat on a fresh towel or a sheet to dry, gently blotting any excess moisture and pulling it into its proper shape.

TO PRESS

Use a low heat setting and a pressing cloth. Place lace and embroidered pieces facedown on a towel before pressing. (Lace may not need pressing.)

ANTIQUE LACE

To clean a fragile lace tablecloth, baste it with white thread to an old sheet before immersing it in water, and leave the two together until both lace and sheet have completely dried.

any other way. Fluff the items as they dry to separate lumps. Foam pillows should not be put in the dryer. Air dry only.

Woven Wools

Machine-wash only those wool garments and blankets with the Superwash label.

Follow directions carefully, and wash each item separately. Use the gentle cycle and lukewarm or cool water. Do not bleach.

Air dry or tumble dry at regular setting (120°F maximum) for 10 to 20 minutes. Remove while the garment still contains moisture and dry flat.

HAND WASHING

Always test for colorfastness (see page 64) before washing by hand and separate those items that run. Pretreat soiled areas such as collars and cuffs with an enzyme pretreatment product or liquid detergent, or rub with a bar of mild soap.

Dissolve soap or detergent in warm water, or use a detergent made especially to wash delicate fabrics in cold water. Soak and swish the garment in the suds for a few minutes, then squeeze out the water. Rinse at least twice in water the same temperature as the wash water. Squeeze out water after each rinse.

Roll the item flat in a towel to blot excess water. Except for sweaters and any items whose colors may run and streak, hang on a plastic hanger to dry (never wood or wire, which can rust or discolor wet fabric). Otherwise dry flat.

If the garment is to be ironed, partially air dry, and follow the care label.

JUST ADD VINEGAR

☞ When hand washing items other than silk, add a capful of white vinegar to the next to last rinse. The vinegar removes any soap or detergent residue in the water or on the fabric.

HOW TO CORRECT COLOR BLEEDING

☞ If color bleeding affects a washable white fabric, use a color remover (available where home dyeing products are sold). Run the item through another wash cycle immediately, adding the color remover according to package instructions to restore the original whiteness.

DRYING A WOOL SWEATER

BEFORE WASHING, USE a permanent marker to trace the outline of the sweater or other wool knit garment on a piece of clean paper. After washing, rinsing, and blotting the garment, place the paper pattern on a clean, dry towel; then gently pull or "block" the sweater into its original shape. Dry flat away from direct heat.

HOW TO REMOVE STAINS

ALWAYS READ THE MANUFACTURER'S LABEL before treating a stain. If the fabric is washable, follow the guide below. If there are any doubts, take the item to a dry cleaner (see page 82). Either way, act quickly. Since ammonia should be used sparingly on silk and wool, separate directions are provided, where appropriate. If no special care for wool or silk is noted, follow general directions. The longer a stain remains, the more likely it is to set permanently.

NOTE: ALWAYS TEST ANY METHOD OR SOLUTION ON A HIDDEN PART OF THE FABRIC FIRST.

---

*BLEACH BASICS

FOR WHITE FABRICS:

Mix 1 tablespoon chlorine bleach with 1 quart water; soak for 15 minutes.

FOR COLORED FABRICS, WHITE SILK OR WOOL:

Mix 2 tablespoons hydrogen peroxide in 1 gallon water; soak 30 minutes.

Alcoholic beverage Soak fresh stain in cool water. Wash in warm suds. Rinse. For old, brown stains or any remaining stain, soak in an appropriate bleach.* *Wool:* Place towel under stain. Gently rub with a cloth soaked in carbonated water (like club soda).

Antiperspirant Rub liquid laundry detergent into stain. Wash in warm suds. Rinse.

Blood Wash stain immediately in cold running water, rubbing with bar soap. Rinse.

For old stains or any remaining stain, soak for 15 minutes in a solution of 2 tablespoons ammonia to 1 gallon cool, soapy water. Soak any remaining stain in warm water with an enzyme detergent. Wash in warm suds with appropriate bleach.* Rinse.

Wool: Blot with a paste made of starch and water; rinse from the back with cold, soapy water.

Butter/margarine Stain usually comes out with ordinary laundering. If a greasy residue remains after washing, sponge or soak in dry-cleaning solvent, then wash in warm suds. Rinse.

Candle wax Harden the wax with an ice cube, then gently scrape off as much wax as possible with a dull knife. Sponge stain with dry-cleaning solvent to remove as much as possible. Place stain between paper towels. Press with warm, dry iron, changing towel as the wax is absorbed.

Launder as usual. If stain remains, use the appropriate bleach.*

Catsup/tomato sauce Soak fresh stain in cool water. Wash in warm

suds. Rinse. If a greasy residue remains after washing, sponge or soak in dry-cleaning solvent. For any remaining stain, use the appropriate bleach.*

Chewing gum Harden gum with an ice cube, then gently scrape off as much as possible with a dull knife.

Soak in dry-cleaning solvent until remaining gum is loosened and scrape again. Wash in warm suds. Rinse.

Chocolate/cocoa Wash stain in warm suds with a few drops of ammonia added. Rinse. If stain remains, sponge or soak in dry-cleaning solvent, then use the appropriate bleach.* *Wool:* Sponge with glycerine. If unavailable, use warm water.

(continued)

(continued)

Coffee/tea If cream was used, sponge with dry-cleaning solvent. Soak fresh stain in cool water. Wash in warm suds. Rinse. If stain remains, use the appropriate bleach.*

Crayon Place stain over paper towels and flush with dry-cleaning solvent until no further color is released.

Sponge remaining stain with a solution of 1 part alcohol to 2 parts water. If stain remains, use the appropriate bleach.* Launder as usual.

Cream/baby formula Sponge stain with cool water. Soak in enzyme detergent solution for 30 minutes. Sponge greasy residue with dry-cleaning solvent.

Launder as usual. Iron stains (from supplements or medicine) can be removed with a commercial rust remover (follow package instructions).

Fruits/berries Soak fresh stain in cool water. Wash in warm suds. Rinse. If stain remains, use the appropriate bleach.* Rinse well.

Grass Soak in an enzyme presoak, or rub some enzyme detergent directly on the stain. Launder as usual using the appropriate bleach.*

Grease/oil Sponge with dry-cleaning solvent. Pretreat with prewash stain remover or liquid laundry detergent. Launder as usual using hottest water safe for the fabric.

Ice cream Soak stain in cool water, then wash in warm suds. Rinse. For chocolate ice cream, first sponge with

dry-cleaning solvent or let soak in fluid 15 minutes. Launder as usual using the appropriate bleach.*

Ink (ballpoint) Sponge stain with rubbing alcohol. Launder as usual using the appropriate bleach.*

Other inks: Rinse stain freely in cool water, then wash in warm, sudsy water and a few drops of household ammonia. Launder as usual using the appropriate bleach.* (Some "permanent" ink cannot be removed.)
Wool: Soak stained area in cold water.

Lipstick Soak stain in dry-cleaning solvent or pretreat with prewash stain remover. Launder as usual using the appropriate bleach.*

Makeup Sponge or soak in dry-cleaning solvent. Launder as usual using the appropriate bleach.*

Mascara Rub stain with a liquid detergent or sponge with dry-cleaning solvent. Launder as usual using the appropriate bleach.* Some waterproof products cannot be removed.

Mildew Use a stiff brush to remove the mold spores. For fabrics that are safe to chlorine bleach, rinse and launder as usual, adding ½ cup chlorine bleach to the washer.

Otherwise, use oxygen bleach, or flush stain with a solution of ½ cup lemon juice and 1 tablespoon salt. Dry in the sun. Launder as usual.

Mud Allow stain to dry, then brush or vacuum. Pretreat with enzyme product or rub in liquid laundry

detergent. Launder as usual using the appropriate bleach,* if necessary.

Nail polish Sponge with acetone after first testing on a hidden part of the item. (Do not use acetone on fabrics containing acetate and triacetate; it will dissolve them.) Launder as usual using the appropriate bleach.*

Paint, *dried:* Gently scrape off as much paint as possible with a dull knife. Rub petroleum jelly into stain to soften. Soak in paint remover, rubbing occasionally, until stain has dissolved. Wash in warm, sudsy water. Rinse. Launder as usual using the appropriate bleach.*

Wet: Blot as much as possible with cotton cloth or tissue, then treat immediately as above.

Perspiration Rub liquid enzyme detergent into the stain and allow it to set for 30 minutes to 1 hour.

Wash in warm, sudsy water using the appropriate bleach,* if necessary. Rinse.

To restore any change to colored fabrics (other than wool or silk), hold stain over fumes of household ammonia, or sponge with white vinegar. To remove odor, soak 1 hour or longer in a solution of 3 tablespoons salt and 1 quart water.

Rust Use a commercial rust remover or soak 15 minutes in a weak oxalic acid solution (2 tablespoons to 1 quart water). Rinse 3 times, adding a few drops of ammonia to the final rinse water.

Traditional Method: Apply lemon

juice and salt and place in the sun. Keep area moist with lemon juice until stain disappears. Brush away dried salt. *Wool:* Sponge with weak solution of oxalic acid until stain disappears. Rinse with cold water.

Scorch mark Heavy scorch that has damaged fibers usually cannot be repaired. For slight scorch stains on washable fabrics, wash in warm, sudsy water using the appropriate bleach,* if necessary. Rinse.

Shoe polish Sponge stain with dry-cleaning solvent to remove grease. Wash remaining stain in warm, sudsy water using an appropriate bleach,* if necessary. Liquid shoe polishes may not come out.

Tar Gently scrape off as much as possible with a dull knife. Soften the remaining stain by rubbing in petroleum jelly. Let stand 15 minutes, then soak in dry-cleaning solvent. Wash in warm, sudsy water. Rinse.

Urine Flush stains with cold water. Launder in warm, sudsy water. Rinse. If the fabric color has been changed, soak area in solution of 2 tablespoons ammonia per cup water. If the color still has not been restored, sponge the area with white vinegar. Launder again as usual. *Wool:* Follow directions above, but don't use ammonia.

Vomit Scrape to remove solids. Soak stain in an enzyme detergent solution, then in warm, sudsy water with a few drops of ammonia added. Rinse. Launder as usual.

Water stains These rings occur when a water-based stain damages a fabric's finish. To remove, dampen the entire area and let dry, or hold the spotted area over the steam of a boiling kettle or use a garment steamer. Press the area with a steam iron while still damp.

Wine, *red:* Pour white wine onto fresh stain and launder as usual. If you don't have any white wine, rub table salt into stain and launder as usual with the appropriate bleach,* if needed. *White:* Blot excess. Sponge stain with cool water, then rub with liquid detergent and a few drops of white vinegar. Launder as usual.

Yellowing See rust. For white fabrics only, use commercially available color remover. For resin-treated white cottons that have yellowed from chlorine bleach, soak in a solution of 2 tablespoons sodium thiosulfate or sodium hyposulfite per gallon very hot water.

IRONING

GET ORGANIZED

☞ Iron according to the temperature needs of the fabrics (see pages 66–67). Since it takes longer for the iron to cool than to heat, start with silks and synthetics at the low-heat settings and increase the heat as you move up to linen.

STORING DAMP CLOTHES FOR IRONING

☞ If you are unable to iron all your damp clothes, and to prevent mildewing, store them in the refrigerator wrapped in a terry-cloth towel until you resume.

STEAM HEAT

☞ Allow the iron to heat long enough to generate steam before you press. Otherwise, there may be drips that can spot the fabric.

For smooth ironing, fabrics should be damp. If possible, bring garments from the dryer or line before they are fully dry and iron them immediately.

Sprinkle fully dried clothes with water, using your fingers or a clean spray bottle. Roll dampened pieces in a towel to distribute the wetness. To save time, use the spray feature on the iron as you go.

If you use spray starch or sizing, spray each section just before ironing it, and let the starch soak in. This prevents flaking and build-up on the iron soleplate.

Let freshly ironed things cool before putting them away. If handled while still warm, they can become wrinkled. Have a rack handy for hanging warm garments and a table for stacking linens.

Household Linens

Household cottons and linens, such as napkins, sheets, and pillowcases, may not need ironing if they are made of permanent-press fabrics or if you smooth them by hand immediately after drying.

If they do need ironing, gently pull them into shape first. To make ironing large items such as tablecloths and sheets easier, fold them first and iron in sections or drape them over a chair as you go.

PRESSING

Pressing is useful for smoothing wrinkles on a garment stored in a crowded closet or folded and crushed tightly in a drawer. It calls for short lowering and lifting motions, not the long gliding strokes used for ironing. Use the steam feature of your iron and select the appropriate temperature for the fabric.

Steam press lace, silk, and wool on the wrong side, when possible. When pressing on the right side, use a dry pressing cloth. Place metallic, beaded, and sequined fabrics facedown on a board covered with extra padding, such as one or two thick towels, and steam press on the lowest temperature setting.

Press only when and where there are wrinkles. Overpressing can take the life out of a fabric.

If your velvet or velveteen isn't wrinkled and the nap simply needs raising, steam it without pressing, moving the iron back and forth an inch or so above the fabric.

You can also hold the garment in front of a steaming kettle, hang it in the bathroom while hot water is turned on in the shower, or use a garment steamer.

CARING FOR YOUR IRON

A dirty iron or ironing-board cover can soil or damage your garments. Many irons now have nonstick soleplates that wipe clean with a damp sponge or cloth.

For irons without a nonstick soleplate, rub lightly with a sponge or cloth dipped in a detergent solution, followed by a clean cloth. Never use an abrasive pad or cleanser.

Remove spray-starch deposits on the soleplate of the iron by rubbing with a damp cloth sprinkled with baking soda, followed by a clean cloth. For stubborn starch that may have burned onto the sole plate, rub with a paste of cleanser and water, and steam over a cloth after cleaning and before ironing a garment.

Some steam irons clean automatically. By flicking a special switch after each use, steam and water are released to clean the vents and tank of the iron of minerals and lint. Be sure to hold the iron over a sink while you clean it. Always empty your iron of water after each use.

IRONS: WHAT TO LOOK FOR

THE FIRST THING to consider when buying an iron is safety. Make sure the model you choose has the UL (Underwriters Laboratories) mark, which assures that the iron meets national electrical safety standards. Any iron made by a major manufacturer will have it. Many irons are constructed largely of plastic, and are lighter weight than those made primarily of metal. You can use virtually any iron dry or with steam.

BASIC FEATURES
Be sure to test the weight and the grip, then choose the iron that feels best to you. Any good iron should have the following:

ADJUSTABLE THERMOSTAT with a choice of temperature settings for different kinds of fabrics

BUTTON GROOVES (indentations in the sides of the sole plate designed to fit around buttons)

SEE-THROUGH WATER TANK to show how much water is left as you steam press

SPRAY AND BURST OF STEAM CONTROLS

SPECIAL FEATURES
While fancy features aren't needed to do a good job, they can make ironing easier and safer. Consider these:

ADJUSTABLE STEAM LEVELS for different fabric needs

AUTOMATIC ELECTRONIC SHUT-OFF MECHANISM

DETACHABLE WATER TANK

EXTRA-LONG CORD

REVERSIBLE CORD (for left-handers)

HOT TIPS

Some irons have more steam vents than others (though that doesn't necessarily mean they emit more steam), and some are designed to give an extra surge or burst of steam when needed (often useful when ironing ruffles, gathers, pleats, and tucks).

Depending on your community's water system and the steam iron you choose, you may be able to use tap water for steaming or you may need to use distilled water.

Check before buying by questioning your city's water-supply office and studying the iron's label.

PRESSING MATTERS

☛ Use a damp, lint-free cloth, such as a handkerchief, diaper, or old cotton sheet, for a pressing cloth.

☛ You can cut your ironing time if you smooth seams, plackets, and pleats as garments dry on a hanger or line, or immediately after you take them from a tumble dryer.

SHIRTS AND BLOUSES

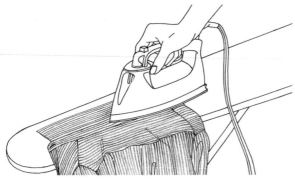

1. Start ironing at the top of a blouse or shirt. Begin or end with the collar, working toward the middle from the outer edges or points.

Lay one shoulder over the narrow end of the board and shift on the board. Iron one side of the front yoke, then the shoulder, across the back below the collar line, the other shoulder, and the remainder of the front yoke, shifting as needed.

2. Iron the sleeves and cuffs, working down from the underarm seams. (If you don't want a deep crease, shift the double layer of sleeve fabric and press out the creased line.)

Next, iron the body of the garment, moving from one half of the front around the back to the second half of the front.

If a blouse or shirt doesn't open, slip it over the end of the ironing board and iron front and back in turn.

PANTS

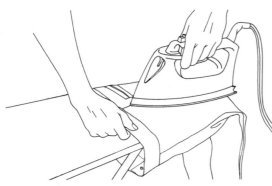

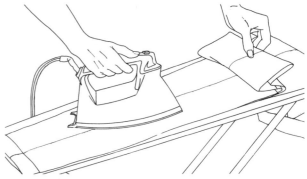

1. Turn the waistband inside out and pull the pockets out to iron first, then iron the zipper placket.

Turn back to the right side, iron the waistband and the remainder of the top all the way around.

2. Put the leg seams together in the middle and fold lengthwise. Lay the pants flat on the board, fold back the top leg, and iron the inside of the lower leg. Turn and iron the outside. Repeat the process for the second leg. Finally, iron the two legs (four thicknesses of fabric) together. If the pants have creases, press heavily on the folds.

DRESSES

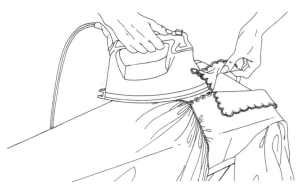 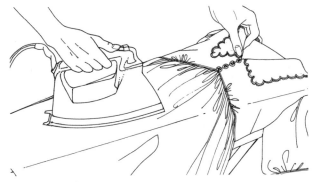

1. Iron the lining first. Then start at the top of the dress following the directions for ironing a blouse. If the dress doesn't open up the front or back, pull it over the end of the ironing board and iron front and back in turn. If there is a collar, lift and press underneath; then press the collar.

2. Iron the dress skirt last. For this, and for separate skirts, take lengthwise strokes—from hemline to waistline if the skirt is gathered at the waist.

Use a lifting, then lowering (pressing) motion to iron into the gathers.

PLEATED SKIRTS

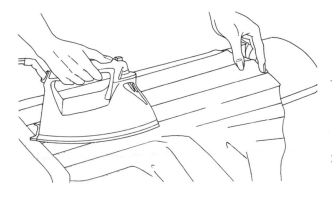

1. Arrange groups of pleats and hold in place or pin to the board as you iron in long strokes from top to bottom. Don't iron over pins.

SEQUINED GARMENTS

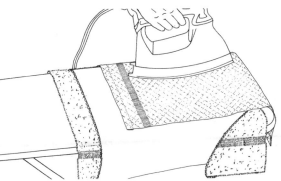

1. Turn the item inside out and place it carefully on the ironing board with the sequins (or beads) facedown on the towel. Put a pressing cloth on top and press with the iron on a gentle setting.

DRY CLEANING

☞ Although it's tempting to keep clothing in dry cleaners' plastic bags, they trap odors in clothes and the cleaning chemicals can cling to them. Recycle the bags by returning them to the dry cleaner. If you can't return them, destroy them. Keep them out of children's reach.

CAREFUL CLEANING

☞ Have all pieces of a suit cleaned at the same time even if only one piece needs cleaning. Cleaning fluids can affect the garment's dyes. This won't be noticeable if all pieces are cleaned together.

☞ Protect novelty and delicate buttons by covering them individually with a small piece of aluminum foil.

GET THE LINT OUT

☞ Wrap masking tape around your hand three or four times with the sticky side of the tape facing out. Pat or brush the garment with the tape.

Use dry-cleaning solvents only for stain removal, if that is the method advised for treating a particular stain. Leave full garment dry cleaning to the professionals.

Always dry-clean an item if it is:

- Made of sheer or delicate fabric.
- Made of fabrics with crimped or bouclé yarns.
- Made of an unidentified fabric that appears to contain wool.
- Made of noncolorfast silk (to determine colorfastness see page 64).
- Soiled with difficult or large stains.

The more you are able to tell your professional dry cleaner about your garment and the cause of any spots or stains, the better he or she will be able to determine the best method of cleaning.

Point out any stains and describe what they are, if you know. Even if no spots are visible but you remember spilling a beverage, show the cleaner where you think it might have landed.

If not treated, invisible spots can become visible later when it may be too late to remove them. If a garment is still stained, tell the cleaner not to press it. You may wish to try removing the stain yourself and pressing will only further set it.

Always consult your dry cleaner about:

- Clothes made of leather, fur, or suede, and clothes with leather, fur, or suede trim. They may need the attention of a leather-cleaning expert.

- Clothes with bead, sequin, and appliqué trims. Some trims, such as polystyrene beads and imitation pearls, can melt in the cleaning process. If trim is glued on, it can loosen and fall off.

Don't dry-clean too often. Too much cleaning can weaken fibers and shorten a garment's life. After each wearing, air dresses, suits, coats, jackets, or pants before hanging them up.

Brush thoroughly and often with a clothes brush to remove lint and loose dirt. (You can even vacuum heavy fabrics.) Check for spots and if you are experienced you may wish to try treating any you can yourself (see pages 75–77). Home stain removal methods are not always effective on dry-cleanable fabrics, and can sometimes even make matters worse. Proceed cautiously or consult your dry cleaner.

BULK DRY CLEANERS

Coin-operated dry-cleaning machines, in which clothes can be cleaned in bulk instead of individually, are available in some communities.

Bulk cleaners should be used as supplements to—not replacements for—professional dry cleaning.

Shrinkage sometimes occurs in these machines and (as in laundering) dyes can be transferred when a noncolorfast item is cleaned with others, so it's best not to use bulk machines for fine clothing.

Use them for older blankets, heavy wool sweaters, and other items that don't require pressing or professional attention.

SEWING

There are times in everyone's life when buttons must be attached, seams repaired, socks darned. If you can make minor repairs at home, you can avoid spending money on tailors and seamstresses.

While full-size sewing machines are useful for large jobs such as making clothes, and produce neater and more durable stitches than hand sewing for seam mending and other repairs, here are the basic hand sewing techniques to get you started.

BUTTONS AND FASTENERS

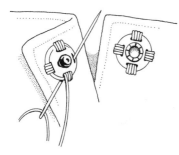

Sewing a snap fastener

Snap Fasteners

Snaps, meant to be invisible, are used where one section of a garment overlaps another. A snap has two parts—a ball and a socket.

1. Sew the ball half on the wrong side of the overlap section, keeping it at least ¼ inch from the edge.

2. Take a stitch under the edge of the snap, then push the needle through the fabric and one hole.

3. Take several stitches through each hole, then secure by knotting or back-stitching (see page 88).

4. Position the socket half on the right side of the underlapping fabric so that it meets the ball precisely.

5. Mark the exact spot before you begin by rubbing chalk on the attached ball and pressing it against the underlapping fabric.

6. Attach the socket as you did the ball.

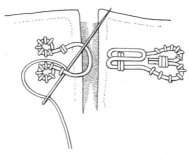

Sewing a hook-and-eye

Hook-and-Eye Fasteners

Use hooks and eyes for overlaps and where edges meet.

1. If attaching the fasteners at a waistband, sew the hook at the edge on the inside of the overlapping section and sew the eye on the outside of the underlap.

   If attaching them at a neckline or other area where edges meet, sew both parts on the wrong side (inside) of the garment. Sew the hook right at the edge and the eye, if curved, with the curve extending over the edge.

2. Sew down the two rings at the base of the hook (forming two thread-covered circles).

3. Take the threaded needle in a long stitch under the fabric to the curved end of the hook and secure to the fabric.

4. Finish with backstitches or a knot (see page 88).

5. Position the eye to meet the hook properly, and sew it through the fabric and around both rings at the base.

NO TIME TO SEW?

☞ Maybe you won't have to, with many of today's quick-fix products. Check the notions department of your variety or department store for no-sew hemming tapes, fusible powder that melts into the fabric when you iron, and ready-cut iron-on patches.

REPAIRING WOOLEN RUNS

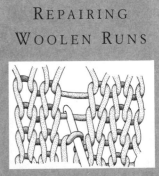

Use a narrow crochet hook to repair a run in a sweater.

Working on the outside of the sweater, pick up the loop at the bottom of the run.

Then pull the hook through the next loose stitch, bringing it through the loop.

Continue this procedure to the top of the run. Pull the broken yarn ends through the top loop to the inside of the garment.

Take tiny stitches with matching thread to sew the yarns together.

MENDING AND ALTERING

Tears

Cut a piece of fabric from an inner seam, the hem, or other hidden spot. The cut piece should be slightly larger than the area of the tear.

Place it beneath the tear, matching the direction of a pattern or grain of the weave as best you can, to the top surface, and secure it with pins or tape.

Working on the right side of the fabric, turn under the raveled edges of the tear and hem by hand with tiny stitches to make each one smooth.

Then sew each edge down onto the patch underneath, using small slip stitches.

Patching

Apply a hidden patch on the underside of a garment, as when mending a tear. For a visible patch, hem the patch edges on the machine or by hand with a simple running stitch (see page 88). Position the patch over the hole or tear, and pin or baste in place.

Then stitch around the edges with a plain or decorative stitch with thread that matches or contrasts with the patch or the garment. Remove pins or basting stitches (see page 88).

If using iron-on patches, follow the package instructions.

Rips

A rip, which is an opening along a seam, is usually easy to repair by machine or hand.

Turn the garment inside out and simply sew a running stitch (see page 88) along the original seam line.

Stitch an additional inch on either side of the opening to reinforce and to prevent the rip from opening again.

DARNING

DARNING IS USED TO REPAIR a hole by weaving in new threads, typically on sock heels or sweater elbows. Both cotton and wool can be darned. Use cotton thread when darning cotton, and wool thread with wool. Always use thread of the same thickness as the thread on the garment.

 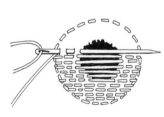 

1. Working with the appropriate thread, begin on the wrong side of the fabric by taking running stitches (see page 88) around the hole, enclosing the area to be darned. This prevents further raveling.

2. Make close parallel stitches across the hole, creating a thread "ladder." Try to keep threads as close as they are in the original fabric.

3. Weave across (over and under) these threads at right angles to them, keeping the stitches loose enough so they don't pull, but tight enough to fill the hole completely.

Secure the thread end on the wrong side with backstitches (see page 88).

THE SEWING BASKET

*K*EEP A BASKET IN OR *near your laundry room, with the following sewing basics,*
which are available in most notion departments and variety stores:

Battery-powered, hand-held sewing machine:
for mending seams quickly and hemming.

Fasteners:
both snaps and hooks and eyes in assorted sizes.

Scissors:
small for cutting thread; large, bent-handled for cutting fabric; pinking shears for cutting edges that won't ravel.

Straight pins:
for most pinning tasks; also safety pins, and a pin cushion.

Carpet thread:
for sewing buttons on heavy materials or restringing beads. (You can also use dental floss.)

Needles:
in different sizes, available in packets, and a thimble.

Spools of thread:
in a variety of colors and types. Both cotton-covered polyester and 100-percent polyester are all-purpose threads that can be used on all kinds of fabrics—natural and synthetic—knits and wovens.

They come in both regular and extrafine versions. Silk thread, though not necessary for sewing silks and other natural fabrics, is a good choice.

A 100-percent cotton thread is good for woven fabrics, but does not have sufficient stretch or strength for sewing knits and synthetics (use polyester or cotton-covered polyester).

Tape measure:
for hem and other measuring.

Chalk:
for marking hems.

Needle threaders:
if you have trouble guiding thread into a needle's eye, and a bodkin—a long needle with large eye useful for threading ribbon or elastic through an eyelet or casing.

Woolen yarns:
for mending sweaters and cotton yarns for darning socks.

Extra buttons:
both the extras attached to new garments by manufacturers and a miscellaneous selection.

Seam binding:
for finishing hems.

To make a stronger seam or to repair a seam that's hard to get to by machine, use a backstitch (see page 88).

Hemming Garments

The hem stitch (see page 88) is the basic stitch for putting in a new hem or repairing one that has pulled out.

Stitch until the hem is completed. You may want to stitch an inch or so past the beginning stitches to reinforce them. Finish with a backstitch or a flat knot (see page 88).

Changing a Skirt Hemline

To shorten a skirt, measure the fabric from the bottom up to the desired new length. Mark the place all around with pins or chalk.

Then remove the stitches from the original hem, cut off any excess fabric (more than is needed for the new hem), and finish the raw edge with seam binding.

Turn up along the pinned or chalked line, pin or baste in place, leaving 2 to 3 inches of fabric for the hem. Be sure to try on the garment before hemming to be sure the length is correct, then hem and steam or press.

To lengthen a skirt, remove the stitches in the hem and let the fabric down. Turn up to the desired line, pin or baste in place, and stitch.

Sometimes the crease left by the original hem can be pressed out, sometimes not. If the mark seems to be permanent, you may be able to camouflage it in some way depending on the fabric and the style of the garment.

COVER-UPS

☞ If a tear is still visible after it is repaired, and it is located appropriately, you can always camouflage it with a scarf or a pin. If it's on the skirt, perhaps conceal it with a flowing sash.

SHORTENING TROUSERS

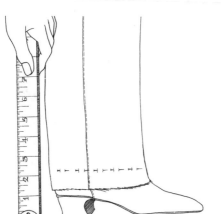

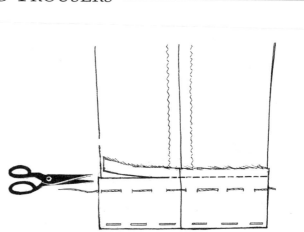

1. Measure the width of each leg's current hem; this will be your guide to an appropriate width for your new hem.

2. Remove the old stitches, unfold the hem, and straighten the fabric by steam pressing over the old hemline.

3. While wearing the trousers, have a helper mark the new length by placing pins around the leg (measure up from the floor at several points to assure the line of pins is even).

4. With the trousers off and turned inside out, fold the fabric up at the pin line and baste to hold in place while you measure the new hem width; try on the trousers again, and if the length is correct, cut off the excess.

5. If the fabric is thin, turn the cut raw edge under and stitch; if heavy, finish the raw edge with seam binding, then stitch. Repeat for the second leg.

SEWING BUTTONS

TO SECURE A button on heavy materials such as velvet or corduroy, use carpet thread. Dental floss and clear monofilament work well, too, but are best for shank buttons, where the stitches won't show. To reinforce, especially on coats and suits, hold a flat button on the opposite side of the fabric, and pull the thread through the holes of both buttons simultaneously.

SEW-THROUGH BUTTONS

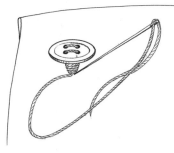

1. Start by taking 1 or 2 small stitches at the place where the button is to be sewn.

2. Pull the thread through the fabric and 1 hole of the button and position the button over the stitches.

5. Remove the toothpick. With the needle on the right side of the fabric, wind the thread around the threads under the button.

6. Take a few small backstitches (see page 88) under the button to secure the thread, knot, and cut excess thread.

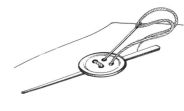

SHANK BUTTONS

3. To create a thread shank that will allow smooth buttoning, slide a toothpick or matchstick as a wedge between button and fabric.

4. Continue to push and pull the needle through each set of holes at least 6 times.

1. Begin by taking 2 small stitches in the fabric and then take at least 6 stitches through the shank loop and fabric together.

2. Finish as for a sew-through button.

(see page 88)

BUTTON, BUTTON...

☛ Always remove good-quality buttons before you discard a garment.

☛ If a pulled-off button leaves a tear in the fabric, reinforce the area by stitching a little patch on the underside before resewing the button.

☛ If your iron doesn't have button grooves, you can protect buttons by covering them one at a time with the bowl of a spoon as you iron around them.

BASIC STITCHES

HEMMING

A line of small, firm stitches.

1. On the wrong side of the garment, take a stitch in the hem edge.

2. Then take a stitch in the garment, picking up only one thread of the fabric, and bring the needle up through the hem edge coming out at least ¼ inch ahead. Continue in this manner.

BLANKET STITCH

Used for a decorative finish for edges.

1. Secure the thread at the left end of the edge you wish to sew by making a tiny stitch on the wrong side. Bring the needle out just under the edge.

2. Insert the needle ¼ inch in from the edge. Hold the bottom part of the thread in a loop.

3. Bring the needle up again on the edge, catching the thread loop under the tip. Pull the needle through the loop, forming a bar at the edge.

4. Repeat, placing your stitches at even intervals.

BLIND HEMMING

Stitches that are taken on the inside between the hem and the garment fabric, so that in the finished hem the stitches are not visible.

1. Fold back the hem edge, take a small stitch in the garment, then a small stitch in the hem edge.

2. Continue to alternate stitches from garment to hem, keeping the stitches about ¼ inch apart.

RUNNING STITCH AND BASTING

A running stitch is a line of short, even stitches used for seams. A basting stitch is a long running stitch used for gathering or to temporarily hold a hem or seam in place.

1. Push the needle through both layers of fabric, going in and out several times before pulling the thread through.

2. Keep the stitches short and close together for a seam, long and widely spaced for basting.

BACKSTITCH

Recommended for hand-sewn seams because it is so strong. It is also used as a finishing stitch.

1. Knot the thread and pull the needle through the fabric at the point where you wish to begin sewing. Insert the needle ⅛ inch behind the point on the seam line, and pull it down through the fabric.

2. Bring the needle up through the fabric ¼ inch in front of the first stitch and insert it again at the point where the needle first came out.

3. Continue stitching in this manner, always inserting the needle into the hole made by the previous stitch.

FLAT KNOT

Used to finish once stitching is completed.

1. Take a small stitch at the end of your row.

2. Run your needle through the loop that forms when you pull the thread, and repeat when another loop is formed.

3. Pull the thread taut.

LEATHER AND FUR

Leather, suede, and fur all need similar care. Store them in a ventilated area away from a heat source and protected from moisture. Always entrust dry cleaning to a professional who specializes in leather or fur cleaning.

LEATHER AND SUEDE

To keep leather supple, you must ensure that it isn't too dry or too wet. Give it room to breathe in the closet like other natural materials.

Drying out, which can result in cracking, is caused by the loss of natural lubricants. This happens in the course of normal wear, but it occurs much faster if the garment is exposed to heat or kept in a place where air can't circulate.

After wearing a leather garment in the rain or snow, dry it immediately; hang it on a padded hanger and let it air dry away from a direct heat source.

If leather remains wet or damp, mildew spots can form. Sponge them lightly with a solution of equal parts of rubbing alcohol and water. Then gently wipe the area with a commercial leather cleaner or with a damp cloth and mild soap and dry with a clean, dry cloth.

Touch-ups: Between professional cleanings, you can do touch-ups at home with a barely damp cloth and mild soap. To replenish lost lubricants, treat the garment with a commercial cleaner and conditioner especially formulated for leather. Check the ingredients to make sure they don't contain alcohol or petroleum distillates, which are harmful.

Some products made especially for cleaning leather call for application with fine steel wool (follow instructions on the container carefully). Don't attempt to treat leather with other waxes or silicone products. Instead of helping, they clog pores and interfere with leather's natural breathability. Never use solvents.

Suede

Suede is leather reversed and brushed to a nap finish. Like other leathers, it should be protected from moisture and dryness, kept from heat, and given space to breathe. To keep the nap raised, brush after each wearing with a stiff clothing brush. Try removing stains with a kneadable eraser or with jeweler's fine-grain sandpaper.

Shoes and Boots

When they are brand new, precondition leather shoes and boots.

Smooth or grained leathers: Apply a neutral polish (such as mink oil).

Suede: Use a silicone spray after testing on an inconspicuous area to make certain that it doesn't affect color. The silicone will resist stains and water spots.

When shoes get wet: take them off as soon as possible. Stuff them with newspaper or paper towels and allow to dry away from heat.

When they are thoroughly dry (twenty-four hours for leather, a few days for suede), polish smooth leather and brush suede. If only partially wet, eliminate the possibility of a water line by dampening the entire shoe with a wet sponge.

KEEP LEATHER COLLARS CLEAN

☛ Like collars of other materials, the collars of leather and suede jackets and coats become dirty faster than other areas of the garment. To keep your collar clean longer, consider wearing a scarf to shield it. If the collar becomes soiled, wipe it with a commercial leather cleaner or with a damp cloth and mild soap.

REMOVE WINTER SALT STAINS

☛ Mix equal parts of vinegar and water or use a commercial de-salter, and lightly sponge on smooth or grained leather shoes. This solution will remove dirt and winter salt stains.

HIDING SCUFFS

☛ When scrapes happen, it is sometimes possible to glue down the leather. If not, cover up the spot with matching polish or indelible ink.

Routine Care

- Change shoes daily, giving each pair a chance to air between wearings.

- When not in use, keep shoes in shape by inserting shoe trees. Wooden trees can be expensive, but they have the advantage of absorbing moisture.

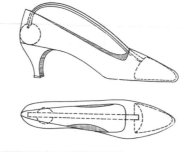

SHOE TREES

- Crumpled-up tissue paper can be substituted for shoe trees, especially when trees don't fit well, as in sandals and other open-toed shoe styles.

- Keep shoes in cloth shoe bags or in boxes to avoid contact with dust.

- Keep your shoes in good repair by having heels replaced as soon as they begin to wear down and replacing the soles when they wear thin.

- To keep leather shoes smooth and supple, polish them regularly. Begin by brushing off loose dirt. Then use clean cloths and brushes and cream polishes to enrich the leather.

  Vigorously rub the polish into the shoe until the cream penetrates. (If you run your hand over the polished surface, it should come away clean.) Liquid polishes, which contain alcohol, have a drying effect if used too often. Remove laces before polishing to avoid staining them.

- For quick emergency touch-ups of smooth leather, use applicators permeated with polish—some purse size—available at shoe repair shops.

- Rub suede with terry toweling after each use. If the nap is flattened, steam

shoes by holding them over a teakettle, and brush in one direction.

- Treat shoes of exotic leathers—snakeskin, lizard, alligator—with a special neutral-color conditioner that both cleans and conditions. Go with the grain of the overlapping scales.

- Clean patent leather shoes by lightly wiping with a sponge dipped in soapy water, then wipe with a dry cloth. To prevent drying and cracking, use petroleum jelly. Apply a little with one cloth; polish with a dry cloth. Avoid wax products, which can cause cracking.

Handbags, Briefcases, and Belts

Condition new handbags, briefcases, and belts with a neutral leather polish to protect them from rain spots and bruising.

Polish regularly (about once a month during the season being used) with cream conditioner or polish. Use only neutral polish; dark or colored polish may rub off onto clothing.

Gloves

To wash unlined leather gloves, put them on your hands, then proceed as if you were washing your hands using cool or lukewarm water and a mild soap. Give extra attention to spots by rubbing with the soap.

Rinse in clear water. Roll the gloves in a towel to blot excess water. Smooth into shape, and dry—either flat on a clean towel or hang on specially made hand-shaped glove dryers.

Lined gloves—with silk, acrylic, cashmere, or fur—should be professionally dry-cleaned. Between cleanings, keep gloves looking their best by pulling them back into shape after each wearing.

FUR

Keep fur in a well-ventilated area, never near direct heat. If it gets wet, shake out the excess water and hang dry. Leave repairs to professional furriers. (For fur storage see page 94.)

WOODEN HEELS

☛ If your shoes have wooden, rather than leather-covered heels, polish them with furniture wax.

JEWELRY CARE

Jewelry made of precious metals and/or semiprecious or precious stones is valuable and should be taken care of accordingly.

Annually, have a jeweler check the pieces you wear on a regular basis to make sure they're secure in their settings. Stones can become loosened easily, especially if you are active in sports. Have clasps and safety chains checked on occasion also. Replace as necessary.

When jewelry is not being worn, keep it in its original boxes or in other well-padded containers. Separate pieces to avoid scratching. Fasten the clasps of chains and other necklaces to help prevent tangling. Don't sleep or bathe with your jewelry on.

Gold
Wash gold jewelry that has no stones in a lukewarm mild detergent and water solution with a little ammonia or a jewelry cleaning solution. Soak for a few minutes. Rinse in warm water. Dry on a terry towel, lint-free cloth, or chamois.

Never expose gold to chlorine—either when cleaning or in a swimming pool. Chlorine can cause pitting and discoloration.

Silver
Apply silver polish, as directed on the polish container, with a dampened sponge or soft cloth (never a paper towel). Rinse, and polish with a soft cloth. For quick touch-ups or intricate pieces, cloths permeated with polish are available at jewelers.

Precious Gems
You can clean diamonds, emeralds, sapphires, and rubies with commercial cleaning products available at jewelry stores. However, soaking them briefly in an ammonia solution is just as effective. If necessary, scrub gently with a soft brush, rinse, and pat dry. This treatment is also suitable for amethysts, aquamarines, garnets, jade, topaz, and tourmaline.

Pearls
Wipe pearls after each wearing, using a damp cloth or sponge, to remove perspiration acids. Cosmetics, hairspray, and perfume have a dulling effect on pearls, so preserve their luster by putting your jewelry on last.

Wash pearls periodically with a solution of lukewarm water and mild soap. Rinse and pat dry. Pearls are easily scratched, so never use household cleaners on them.

Store pearls separately, away from other jewelry. Pearls, like other beads, should be restrung frequently because strings can weaken with wear and break.

Opals
Among the most fragile gems, opals should be cleaned by wiping with a dampened cloth, then dried with a soft cloth. Composed mostly of water, opals are naturally subject to moisture loss and subsequent cracking. To restore moisture, rub the stone gently with your finger.

Changes in temperature can affect opals, causing cracks. Avoid wearing an opal when you will be going from one temperature extreme to another.

Amber, Coral, and Lapis Lazuli
Avoid soaking these stones. Keep them clean by simply wiping with a soft cloth after each wearing.

GETTING THE KINKS OUT

If a jewelry chain becomes knotted, sprinkling it with talcum powder or cornstarch may make it easier to untangle.

Or insert a straight pin into the center of the knot and, with another straight pin, gently twist and turn to loosen the snarls.

If it's an especially tight knot, place it in a few drops of baby oil on a piece of waxed paper to make it easier to work with.

To remove the oil, dip the chain in a warm water/detergent solution, followed by clear water. If you still can't unravel it, take the chain to a jeweler.

PEARLY WHITES

☛ Never pull or stretch pearls. When they are freshly strung they will appear tight. Hang them up to store and eventually they will loosen.
☛ Never wear pearls while bathing or swimming.

PACKING A SUITCASE

WRINKLE-FREE WOOLENS

☛ Of the natural fibers, wool requires the least care. Wrinkles will hang out if you give the garment a little time and space to air. Don't hang or fold wool knits unless they're heavy or bulky; roll them before storing or packing.

Start with a checklist of what you want on your trip, and assemble everything. You may decide to eliminate some things as you pack if you find there's too much for your suitcases.

Have a supply of white tissue paper to layer between garments for wrinkle reduction, and plastic storage bags for shoes and cosmetics. Pack a few extra bags to carry home wet bathing suits and dirty laundry.

- Place shoes, except those you plan to wear the first day, and other heavy items in the suitcase first. Because wool fabrics are easier to free of creases and wrinkles than other fibers, they can also be put in or near the bottom of the bag.

- Pack those items you plan to wear on your first stop last so they'll be easy to find and wrinkles will be minimal. Pack the shoes you'll need first within easy reach—along the sides of the suitcase. For balance, place one at each side.

- Make as few folds as possible.

  Roll jerseys and other lightweight knits, as well as underwear and night clothes.

  After buttoning or fastening dresses, jackets, blouses and shirts, and heavy sweaters, fold them lengthwise, in thirds, turning back each side, including sleeves.

  If necessary—such as for a full-length dress—fold crosswise only at one point to fit the suitcase. Fold pants crosswise only once.

- Pin skirt pleats so they will lie flat and unwrinkled, or pull a pleated skirt through an old cut-off stocking or panty-hose leg. Some items, such as a straight skirt, pair of shorts, or sleeveless blouse, may be laid flat without folding.

- If packing more than one pair of pants, place one pair with the waist at one end of the suitcase, the next with the waist at the opposite end, and so forth.

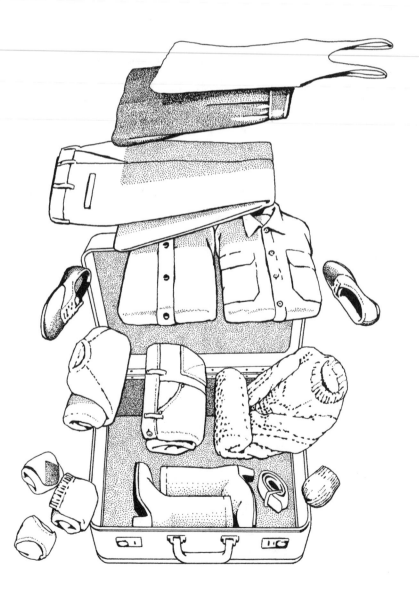

This prevents the buildup of too much bulk at one end of the suitcase and helps keep everything level.

- Stuff small things in other items to save space and help maintain the shape of larger pieces. For instance, rolled underwear and pantyhose can be stuffed in shoulders; rolled socks and belts can go in shoes.

Carry-On Bags

A carry-on bag is a necessity for air travel, when checked bags don't always arrive with you.

Pack in it medicines, toiletries, vitamins, an extra pair of glasses, nightclothes, extra change of underwear, blouse or shirt, folding umbrella, thin roll-up raincoat, and a miniature sewing kit.

Keep jewelry, passport, other important documents, including eyeglass and other prescriptions, and essential medication in your purse or briefcase.

CLOTHES STORAGE

Before storing any item it is essential that it be cleaned thoroughly. Although moths can destroy any unprotected woolens, clean or soiled, they (and other insects) are more attracted to soiled woolens and even synthetics and blends with stains.

Also, some spots, invisible when put away, can surface during the storage period. By the time they are discovered, they may be impossible to remove.

MOTHPROOFING

The traditional method—storing in or with cedar—has yet to be improved upon. A cedar-lined closet is an ideal enclosed area.

If your house doesn't have one, attach cedar panels and planks, available at home center stores, to an existing closet interior. A cedar chest is perfect for folded items.

Although they are less effective, you can also try cedar coat hangers, drawer strips, balls and cubes, and chips or shavings that can be put in little drawstring bags and hung on coat hangers or from closet hooks.

Other fragrant natural moth repellents include lavender and dried orange peel.

Although mothballs contain camphor, which can be dangerous if ingested, they do repel and kill moths, unlike cedar, which simply repels them. To be effective all repellents must remain in an enclosed space.

HANG OR FOLD?

Keep hanging clothes clean by covering them with cloth storage bags or old sheeting. (Cut a hole at the center for the hanger hook to go through.) Cloth covers are preferable to plastic bags, which prevent ventilation that fabrics and leathers need.

- Hang a suit on a hanger made for two pieces. Fold the trousers along the creases and double over the hanger bar. Pad the bar with fabric, if necessary, to prevent an unwanted crease

BUCKLES AND BEADS

☛ To keep belt buckles and metal trim on bags from tarnishing, give them a coat of clear nail polish.

☛ The weight of the beads can pull and distort the shape of a beaded garment, such as a sweater or a dress. Fold and store flat instead of hanging.

mark across the legs. Hang skirts by their loops.

- Don't hang knits, including jerseys. Their natural tendency to stretch is increased by gravity, so they soon lose their shape. Instead, roll thin knits and tuck them in the corner of a chest or drawer, just as you would when packing for a trip. Fold heavy or bulky knits.

COTTONS AND LINENS

Wrap white cottons and linens—and all fragile and old fabrics—in white acid-free tissue paper or place in acid-free boxes before storing. (Acid-free products are available at most art supply stores.)

Ordinary tissue paper and boxes have acidic properties that can cause delicate fabrics to deteriorate and white fabrics to become discolored.

Old bed sheets, free of their original sizing, or unbleached cotton, can substitute for acid-free paper.

If possible, roll tablecloths, bedspreads, and coverlets, especially antique pieces. If you fold them, remember to refold periodically so the lines don't create

permanent creases. Never starch before storing because it may yellow and attract insects.

FURS

Take your fur to a furrier for summer storage at the proper temperature. Professional cleaning and routine repairs can be done at that time. If you cannot get to a furrier, cover your fur with a fabric garment bag.

LEATHER ACCESSORIES

Simply shape and smooth clean gloves and lay them flat, wrapped in tissue, in a drawer or storage chest.

Shoes, boots, and handbags should be stored clean. Brush off surface dirt, sponge off spots, and treat with a conditioner.

Use shoe trees or stuff shoes and bags with tissue paper, and store, preferably in individual boxes. If you don't have boot trees, which can be expensive, improvise with rolled and tied newspapers, magazines, or cardboard tubes. They will keep the legs straight and upright.

CHAPTER 4

FOOD AND THE KITCHEN

Floors, Preven ~~ng Rooms Look~~ *Larger, Buffing* Glasses, Making *Rooms Look Lar* *a Car, Cleaning* *Tile Grout, Crea* Curtains, Save on *Car Repairs, Buy* Floors, Preventing *Carpet Dents, Unsticking Stacked Glasses, Making Rooms Look Larger, Ironing Pleated Skirts, Arranging Flowers, Jump-Starting a Car, Cleaning Tile Grout, Creating a Home Office, Fixing a Leaky Faucet* ☛ STEP-BY-STEP GUIDES: *To Checkbook Security, Unblocking a Sink, Buying a Home, Successful Decorating* ☛ EATING WELL: *Understanding vital nutrients. Using the food guide pyramid to plan a balanced diet. Hints for healthy snacking. Good sources of vitamins and minerals. Suggested fat intake levels. Reading a nutrition label. The importance of complex carbohydrates. Balanced diets for vegetarians.* ☛ SMART SHOPPING: *Negotiating the market. How to select the best meat, poultry, and seafood. Coupons explained. Becoming label literate. Picking good produce: tips on ripening and out-of-season buys. Herbs, spices, and other seasonings.* ☛ COOKING: *Planning meals: how to save time and effort. Hints for healthier meals. How to prepare, cook, and store meat, poultry, and seafood safely. Roasting timetables. Ensuring freshness in foods. Grilling.* ☛ MICROWAVING *Adapting recipes. Cooking timetable. Safety tips. A glossary of cooking terms. Measuring equivalents. Common recipe substitutions.* ☛ KEEPING FOOD FRESH: *All about refrigerating and freezing. Choosing the right container. Freezing fruits and vegetables. Freezer timetable. Shelf life and storage. Canning foods at home.* ☛ EQUIPMENT: *Basic pots and pans. Essential knives. Sharpening a dull knife. Nonstick cookware facts. The convenient kitchen. Useful utensils; basics for bakers. All about ranges, ovens, cook tops microwaves, refrigerators, freezers, and dishwashers. Energy efficiency. Tips for efficient cooking.* ☛ TABLEWARE: *Choosing china. Traditional table settings. An illustrated guide to silverware and glassware. Four steps to folding a napkin. Caring for fine crystal.* ☛ ENTERTAINING: *Planning a successful party: adults, teenagers, and children. Arranging a small dinner party. Beverages: setting up and stocking a bar. How to open Champagne. Serving the right wine.* ☛ EVERYTHING YOU NEED TO KNOW: *About Choosing Pots and Pans, Front-Wheel-Drive Cars, Making Healthier Meals, Vacuum Cleaners, Garden Tools, Upholstered Furniture, Your Credit Card Statement, Curtain Styles* ☛ MONEY-SAVING HINTS: *How to Turn Bed Sheets into Curtains, Save on Car Repairs, Buy Produce, Choose Carpeting* ☛ HANDY TIPS: *For Buffing Wood Floors, Preventing*

Eating Well

Food is the fuel that keeps the body running. Over time (not every day), you need about forty different nutrients to stay healthy.

Because no single food provides all the essential nutrients, a well-chosen variety is an important part of healthy eating. A basic understanding of what your body needs and what the foods you eat contain can help you plan your diet for optimum nutrition as well as good taste and easy preparation.

PROTEIN

After water, protein is the most abundant substance in the body and has nearly limitless functions, from building and maintaining tissue to forming antibodies, your main mechanism for fighting infections.

Complete proteins, or those that contain the essential amino acids in the proportions needed by humans, are most commonly found in animal products, including meat, fish, poultry, eggs, and dairy foods.

Vegetable proteins are usually low in essential amino acids and must be eaten in a great variety or in combination, such as beans with rice, to form complete usable protein. Therefore, adult vegetarians who eat a varied diet can get all the protein they need (see pages 98–99).

Although protein is critical, you actually need relatively little of it. In fact, six ounces of meat per day will provide the required amount. This is good news because many of the most common protein sources, such as meat, eggs, and dairy products, are also relatively high in fat; most people can cut back on these without risking a protein deficiency.

In addition, animal protein is one of the most expensive items in our diet, so if you cut back you can be healthy and save money, too.

CARBOHYDRATES AND FIBER

Carbohydrates are a nutrient group that includes starches, sugars, and dietary fiber. Starch and sugar are the body's main sources of energy, and are found in many foods, but especially in fruits, vegetables, and grains.

Dietary fiber, the bonus from plant sources of carbohydrates, is not itself a nutrient, but does provide bulk to facilitate digestion and encourage regular elimination of wastes. It is also thought to play a role in the prevention of some types of cancer.

Soluble fiber is found in fruits, some vegetables, beans, and oats. Some evidence indicates that soluble fiber may help lower blood cholesterol and thus help prevent heart disease.

Insoluble fiber is found in fruit, vegetables, whole grains, and wheat bran. It adds bulk to the diet, facilitates digestion, and may help protect against colon cancer and other digestive disorders.

Rather than rely on a single source of fiber, eat a wide variety of foods to ensure a balanced diet of fiber and other nutrients.

Carbohydrates used to be considered fattening, but it is now known that most of that reputation was due to additives—sour cream on the baked potato, butter on the bread, or cream sauce on the pasta.

FATS

Fats provide energy and carry essential fat-soluble vitamins such as A, D, E, and K.

EATING RIGHT IN RESTAURANTS

☛ Ask for undressed salads with oil and vinegar on the side.

☛ At salad bars, load up with fresh vegetables and avoid cheese, bacon bits, and high-fat salad dressings.

☛ Remember that it's not necessary to clean your plate. "Doggie bags" are fine.

☛ Order fresh fruit for dessert or order one dessert for the table and share it.

Fats are composed of the same elements as carbohydrates, but in a much denser, more concentrated form. Consequently, they have many more calories per gram than carbohydrates or proteins. Though essential to our diet, fats are a known contributor to obesity, heart disease, and possibly some forms of cancer. Their intake should be limited.

Fats are made up of fatty acids. Saturated fatty acids are found mainly in fats from meat and dairy products and in some vegetable oils, including coconut and palm.

Monosaturated fatty acids are found mainly in olive, peanut, and canola oils.

Polyunsaturated fatty acids are found mainly in sunflower, safflower, soybean, and corn oils, and in some fish.

Saturated fats are most often associated with heart disease because they tend to raise blood cholesterol levels. All three types of fat should be limited, however.

CHOLESTEROL

Cholesterol and fat are not synonymous. Cholesterol is a fatlike substance found only in animal products. It is necessary for hormone and cell membrane formation, but the body manufactures all the cholesterol it needs, and no extra intake is necessary.

Cholesterol is present in all meats, poultry, some seafood, dairy products, and egg yolks. Eating a diet high in cholesterol, especially since it is usually associated with high saturated fat levels, often causes elevated blood cholesterol levels.

VITAMINS

Vitamins are a group of organic substances present in almost all foods (see pages 100–101). Used by the body in very small amounts, they help release energy from proteins, carbohydrates, and fats, as well as facilitate other important chemical reactions in the body.

Many processed foods, in particular breads and cereals, are fortified with vitamins, especially B vitamins and vitamin C.

If you eat a well-balanced, varied diet, you probably don't need a vitamin supplement. Despite claims to the contrary, megadoses of vitamins do not have any magical effects. In fact, the overuse of some vitamins can be dangerous. Large doses of vitamins should be taken only with the advice of a physician.

MINERALS

Minerals, like vitamins, are also needed in minute amounts generally supplied by a balanced diet. The body uses minerals to build strong bones and teeth, and to produce hemoglobin in red blood cells, as well as to maintain an optimum fluid balance and help in other chemical reactions.

WATER

Water—often called the forgotten nutrient—actually accounts for most of our body weight and is our major means of transporting nutrients, eliminating wastes, and regulating body temperature. Because we constantly lose water, it must be adequately resupplied each day.

Water needs vary depending on climate, exercise, and individual differences, but drinking about eight glasses of water or other liquid daily is a good goal.

EATING RIGHT AT HOME

☞ Serve more pasta and rice; use low-fat fresh tomato and vegetable sauces.

☞ Serve beans and legumes as a meatless main course.

☞ Experiment with favorite dishes to try to lower fat content without sacrificing taste. Nonstick skillets and vegetable cooking sprays are an easy start.

☞ Keep lots of fresh fruits and vegetables on hand for snacking.

THE FOOD GUIDE PYRAMID

The Food Guide Pyramid is the newest FDA standard for balancing the diet. It is an easy-to-use visual guide of what to eat each day, but it is neither a rigid formula nor a collection of current fads.

The pyramid is "built" on a foundation of complex carbohydrates in the form of bread, grains, pasta, rice, cereal, vegetables, and fruits. These supply important nutrients and fiber; recent evidence strongly suggests that they may also help to prevent heart disease and some cancers.

The pyramid shows that we should consume dairy products and animal proteins, but in limited quantities. The small portion at the top of the pyramid shows that fats, oils, and sweets provide little but empty calories and should be eaten sparingly. These fats, oils, and sweets are also present in other foods.

Each of the lower blocks in the pyramid has a recommended range of serving portions. The flexibility allows for variations in calorie and nutrient intake according to age, sex, weight, and level of physical activity.

For example, pregnant or lactating women need more calcium, teenagers need more calories, and people with medical conditions may have special dietary needs. It is important to eat at least the lowest number of recommended servings each day, and it is equally important to vary these choices over time.

Children over six should eat the same serving sizes as adults; children between two and five should eat two thirds of an adult serving. Consult a physician for children under two.

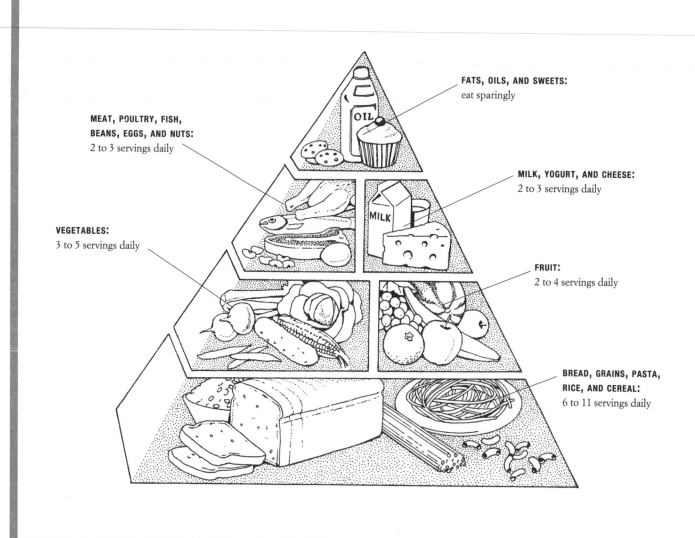

FATS, OILS, AND SWEETS: eat sparingly

MEAT, POULTRY, FISH, BEANS, EGGS, AND NUTS: 2 to 3 servings daily

MILK, YOGURT, AND CHEESE: 2 to 3 servings daily

VEGETABLES: 3 to 5 servings daily

FRUIT: 2 to 4 servings daily

BREAD, GRAINS, PASTA, RICE, AND CEREAL: 6 to 11 servings daily

SAMPLE SERVING SIZES

BREAD, CEREAL, RICE, AND PASTA

Choose high-fiber grains that are low in added sugar. Go easy on high-fat spreads, sauces, and gravies on rice and pasta.

1 serving =
1 slice bread, or
  1 ounce dry, ready-to-eat cereal, or
  ½ cup cooked cereal, rice, or pasta

VEGETABLES

Eat a variety of deep-green leafy, deep-yellow, starchy, and legume vegetables.

1 serving =
1 cup raw leafy vegetables, or
  ½ cup cooked or chopped raw vegetables, or
  ¾ cup vegetable juice

FRUITS

Eat whole fruits often as they are higher in fiber than fruit juices. Remember that fruit punch contains a lot of sugar and very little real fruit juice.

1 serving =
1 medium apple, banana, orange, or
  ½ cup cooked or canned fruit, or
  ¾ cup fruit juice

MEAT, POULTRY, FISH, DRY BEANS, EGGS, NUTS, AND SEEDS

Choose lean meat, skinless poultry, fish, dry beans and peas. Limit egg yolks to 4 per week, including those in sauces and baked goods. Remember that peanut butter, nuts, and seeds are high in fat.

1 serving =
2 to 3 ounces cooked lean meat, poultry, or fish, or
(½ cup cooked dry beans, 1 egg, or 2 tablespoons peanut butter count as 1 ounce of meat)

MILK, YOGURT, AND CHEESE

Choose skim milk, nonfat yogurt, low-fat cheeses, and frozen desserts such as ice milk or frozen yogurt. Cottage cheese is lower in calcium than most cheese; 1 cup of cottage cheese is the equivalent of ½ cup whole milk.

1 serving =
1 cup milk or yogurt, or
1½ ounces natural cheese, or
2 ounces processed cheese

COMPLETE PROTEINS FROM GRAINS AND VEGETABLES

Combine dry beans or peas (legumes) and:

- Barley
- Corn
- Oats
- Rice
- Seeds (such as sesame or sunflower)
- Wheat

Dry beans include kidney, navy, pinto, lima, black, and pink.

Dry peas include chick-peas, split peas, and black-eyed peas.

Wheat includes pasta, bread, and cereals.

BETTER SNACKS

- Crudités
- Fat-free frozen yogurt
- Fat-free unflavored yogurt with fresh fruit
- Fresh fruits
- Low-fat bran muffins
- 100% fruit juices
- Plain baked potato seasoned with herbs or topped with yogurt
- Rice cakes
- Unbuttered air-popped popcorn
- Unsalted pretzels

UNDERSTANDING VITAL NUTRIENTS

*Of the thirteen known vitamins, nine are water soluble: vitamin C
and the eight B vitamins, including folic acid, niacin, pantothenic acid, and biotin.
Most are stored in the body in only small amounts, so you need to
eat foods rich in them regularly.*

*The four fat-soluble vitamins—A, D, E, and K—are stored in body fat until used.
To avoid toxicity, do not take large doses.*

VITAMINS

	WHAT IT DOES	GOOD SOURCES	USEFUL INFORMATION
Vitamin A/Beta Carotene	Essential for normal vision, healthy skin, hair, and nails, and resistance to infection. Eating foods rich in beta carotene may reduce the risk of developing certain types of cancer as well as heart disease.	Liver, egg yolks, whole milk, butter, and fortified margarine and skim milk. Beta carotene, which is converted to vitamin A in the body, is found in dark-green leafy vegetables, deep-yellow and orange vegetables, and fruits.	Large doses of vitamin A can cause toxicity and liver or nervous system damage. Can also cause birth defects if consumed before or during first months of pregnancy. Large doses of beta carotene can cause skin to yellow.
Vitamin B₁ (Thiamine)	Helps body convert carbohydrates into energy and metabolize protein and fat. Promotes proper nerve function.	Whole grains, bran, wheat germ, enriched breads, pork, liver, dry beans and peas, peanuts, and orange juice.	Sensitive to heat and easily leached into cooking water.
Vitamin B₂ (Riboflavin)	Helps body use proteins, fats, and carbohydrates to produce energy. Supports normal vision and healthy skin.	Meat, fish, chicken, dairy products, spinach, broccoli, legumes, enriched breads, cereals, and almonds.	Easily destroyed by light.
Vitamin B₆ (Pyridoxine)	Helps form red blood cells. Promotes proper nerve function. Important in metabolism of protein, fat, and carbohydrates.	Meat, poultry, fish, wheat germ, whole wheat flour, and some fruits and vegetables such as bananas, watermelon, potatoes, and spinach.	Large doses can cause toxicity with severe nervous dysfunction, including numbness and difficulty in walking.
Vitamin B₁₂	Plays role in formation of red blood cells and helps maintain nervous system.	All animal products (meats, dairy products, eggs, liver, fish, and shellfish).	Strict vegetarians should take a B₁₂ supplement or eat foods fortified with B₁₂.

Food and the Kitchen • EATING WELL

	WHAT IT DOES	GOOD SOURCES	USEFUL INFORMATION
Folic Acid	Essential for normal cell division and red blood cell formation. Recent research suggests that adequate intakes of folic acid may protect against cervical dysplasia (precancerous changes in cells of the cervix).	Green leafy vegetables, dry beans and peas, orange juice, avocado, asparagus, fortified breakfast cereals, and liver.	Large doses can mask a B_{12} deficiency. Adequate intake of folic acid in the first few weeks of pregnancy lessens the risk of neural-tube birth defects.
Niacin	Prevents pellagra and helps cells use oxygen to release energy in the metabolism of glucose, fat, and alcohol.	Whole grains, enriched breads and cereals, meat, fish, poultry, peanuts, and mushrooms.	Large doses can cause side effects that range from uncomfortable skin flushing to liver damage.
Pantothenic Acid and Biotin	Aid in carbohydrate, fat, and protein metabolism.	Widespread in foods.	Made in the body by intestinal bacteria.
Vitamin C	Prevents scurvy. Helps heal wounds by promoting collagen formation, and strengthens resistance to infection. Eating foods rich in vitamin C may reduce risk of some cancers.	Citrus fruits, other fruits and vegetables, especially red and green peppers, dark-green leafy vegetables, brussels sprouts, broccoli, cabbage, white and sweet potatoes, cauliflower, kiwifruit, strawberries, and liver.	Large doses can cause nausea and diarrhea, interfere with the ability of white blood cells to fight infection, and interfere with some medical tests and drugs. Heavy smokers have lower blood levels of vitamin C.
Vitamin D	Essential for proper formation and maintenance of bones and teeth.	Fortified milk and margarine, liver, butter, and fatty fish; also produced by the body when skin is exposed to sunlight.	Large doses can cause calcification of soft tissue.
Vitamin E	Acts as an antioxidant to protect certain tissues and substances from effects of oxygen.	Nuts, seeds, whole grains, vegetable oils, and dark-green leafy vegetables.	
Vitamin K	Essential for normal blood clotting.	Dark-green leafy vegetables, peas, cauliflower, soybean oil, liver, dairy products, and meat.	Made in the body by intestinal bacteria.

(continued)

(continued)

MINERALS ARE NUTRIENTS THAT ARE essential to a host of vital processes in the body. Most are readily available in a balanced diet, so if you eat right, your body will receive adequate amounts. Here are some of the most important minerals:

MINERALS

	WHAT IT DOES	GOOD SOURCES	USEFUL INFORMATION
Calcium	Essential for building bones and teeth, maintaining bone strength, and proper muscle and nerve function. Adequate intake throughout life plays a role in preventing osteoporosis.	Whole and low-fat dairy products, canned sardines and salmon (including bones), clams, oysters, tofu, blackstrap molasses, almonds, and calcium-fortified juices.	Not all calcium supplements are equally effective, so check with your doctor and pharmacist about which ones are best for you.
Iron	Combines with protein to form hemoglobin, which carries oxygen in the bloodstream.	Meats, poultry, fish, shellfish, dark-green leafy vegetables, dry peas and beans, blackstrap molasses, prunes, dried peaches, dried apricots, and enriched breads and cereals. Foods cooked in cast iron cookware.	Consuming foods rich in vitamin C in conjunction with eating iron-rich foods increases body absorption of the mineral. For example, drink orange juice with your iron-fortified breakfast cereal.
Phosphorous	Combines with calcium to strengthen bones and teeth and helps the body convert food to energy.	All dairy products, eggs, meat, poultry, fish, nuts, dry peas and beans, whole grain cereals, and breads.	
Potassium	Helps maintain balance of body fluids. Essential for proper nerve and muscle function.	Fruits, vegetables, milk, yogurt, meat, poultry, seafood, and legumes.	Diuretic (fluid-releasing) drugs can deplete the body of potassium.
Sodium	Helps maintain balance of body fluids.	Table salt, naturally occurring salt in foods, and salt added to foods during processing.	Excessive sodium can lead to edema (fluid retention), as well as aggravate hypertension.

Other important minerals: Magnesium, zinc, selenium, iodine, copper, chromium, and fluoride are found in common food sources in a well-balanced diet and are needed in minute quantities.

LOWERING FATS

The U.S. Department of Agriculture, after much research, now recommends that fats represent no more than 30 percent of our daily caloric intake. Currently, most Americans consume about 35 percent to 40 percent of their calories as fats. Fat contains more than twice the calories of an equal amount of carbohydrates or protein.

Simple ways to reduce fat and cholesterol are :

- Reduce consumption of red meat. Choose lean cuts, trim fat, and keep portion sizes to about 3 ounces of cooked boneless meat.

- Have at least one meatless day per week. (Beware of meatless dishes, such as quiche, full of high-fat dairy products.)

- Substitute ground turkey for ground beef in meat loaf, burgers, and chili.

- Cook with a minimum amount of oil. Use nonstick cookware or a light coating of nonstick spray instead of oils and other fats.

- Remove skin from poultry before eating.

- Skim all grease from homemade stocks, soups, and stews.

- Avoid fried foods.

- Limit your consumption of egg yolks to four per week. To cut back painlessly, try some of the cholesterol-free liquid egg substitutes now available.

- Roast, bake, or broil meats and poultry on a rack or in ridged pans. Discard fatty drippings.

- Substitute unflavored fat-free yogurt for sour cream in dips.

- Substitute mustard for mayonnaise as a sandwich spread.

- Buy low-fat or fat-free salad dressings or sprinkle your salad with lemon juice or balsamic vinegar and fresh herbs.

- Eliminate fatty deli meats. Replace with roast turkey or extra-lean ham.

- Be aware that many processed and packaged foods contain large amounts of fat. Read labels carefully.

NUTRITION LABELING

Nutrition labeling containing information on salt, fat, carbohydrates, sugar, and cholesterol content is required on all packaged food as of May 1994. This example is from a package of macaroni and cheese.

NUTRITION FACTS

Serving size = ½ cup (144 g)
Servings per container = 4

Calories 260   Calories from fat 120

Amount per serving	% Daily value*
Total fat 13 g	20%
Saturated fat 5 g	25%
Cholesterol 30 mg	10%
Sodium 660 mg	28%
Total carbohydrates 31 g	11%
Sugars 5 g	—
Dietary fiber 0 g	0%
Protein 5 g	—

Vitamin A 4%, vitamin C 2%, calcium 15%, iron 4%

*Percents (%) of a daily value are based on a 2,000-calorie diet. Your daily values may vary higher or lower depending on your calorie needs:

Nutrient		2,000 Calories	2,500 Calories
Total fat	Less than	65 g	80 g
Sat. fat	Less than	20 g	25 g
Cholesterol	Less than	300 mg	300 mg
Sodium	Less than	2,400 mg	2,400 mg
Total Carbohydrate		300 g	375 g
Fiber		25 g	30 g

1 g fat = 9 calories
1 g carbohydrate = 4 calories
1 g protein = 4 calories

ROUGH 'N' TOUGH

Good sources of fiber include:
- ☛ Bran cereals and bran bread products
- ☛ Dried fruit
- ☛ Fresh fruits
- ☛ Legumes, such as dry beans, lentils, and dry peas
- ☛ Nuts and seeds
- ☛ Potatoes and other vegetables with skins
- ☛ Vegetables, especially broccoli, brussels sprouts, corn, peas, spinach, and string beans
- ☛ Whole grains and whole grain products

☞ Legumes are plants with seed pods that split along both sides when ripe. Beans, lentils, peanuts, peas, and soybeans are some of the most common ones. Legumes are high in protein and a staple in many vegetarian diets.

Calculating Fat

To figure out how many grams of fat will provide 30 percent of your diet, multiply your total daily caloric intake by 0.30. (Example: 2,000 calories x 0.30 = 600 calories from fat.) Then divide these calories from fat by 9 to get the grams of fat per day. (Example: 600 calories from fat divided by 9 = 67 grams of fat as the daily limit.)

INCREASING COMPLEX CARBOHYDRATES

It is recommended that 55 percent to 60 percent of our caloric intake come from carbohydrates—mainly from complex carbohydrates and naturally occurring sugars. To increase complex carbohydrates, try the following:

- Include a selection from the bread, cereal, and grain group in each of your three meals. For example, have high-fiber cereal for breakfast, whole grain bread for lunch, and pasta or rice for dinner. Eat 6 to 10 servings each day.

- Don't think of grains as a side dish. Make them the base for main dish casseroles, soups, and cold salads. Use them to extend meat entrées. Try a variety: bulgur, barley, buckwheat groats, wild rice.

- Keep leftover cooked grains in the refrigerator to use in instant meals.

- Thicken sauces and soups with pureed beans, rice, or potatoes.

- Have at least one vegetable or fruit at every meal, aiming for 2 to 4 servings daily.

- Make legumes a regular part of your diet. Add them to soups and salads, substitute them for meat in stews, chili, and spaghetti sauce.

LIMITING REFINED SUGARS

Simple sugars, such as table sugar, brown sugar, molasses, maple syrup, and corn syrup, provide calories but few vitamins or minerals. Moreover, high-sugar foods, such as desserts and pastries, are also often high in fat.

Here are a few tips for limiting sugar intake:

- Brew coffee with a small piece of cinnamon stick or vanilla bean to add flavor without sugar.

- Sweeten desserts, pancakes, and waffles with pure fruit purees instead of sugar or syrup.

- Limit soft drinks. Try mineral water or seltzer with a splash of fruit juice.

- Be aware that many processed foods contain substantial amounts of added sugar. Read labels carefully.

LIMITING SALT

Salt, while an essential part of a good diet, is usually used to excess. For those who have or are predisposed to hypertension, salt is often restricted since it is a major factor in the fluid retention that increases

VEGETARIANS

Strict vegetarians, or vegans, consume no animal products, including dairy and eggs. Lactovegetarians eat no animal flesh, but do eat dairy products, while ovovegetarians don't eat meat, but do eat eggs. Semivegetarians, perhaps the largest and most loosely defined group, eat little meat, poultry, and fish, but do not eliminate them entirely.

Vegetarians who eat dairy products or eggs have a relatively easy time maintaining a healthy, balanced diet. Even very small quantities of animal proteins provide all the nutrients needed by the body.

Vegans, however, need to be careful about avoiding nutritional deficiencies. The complete proteins and some of the vitamins and minerals in animal products are not present in plant foods in the same way (see the chart on pages 100–102). Vegan children must be especially careful to get enough protein while they are growing rapidly.

If a meat-eating family has one vegetarian member, it is still possible to prepare a healthy, tasty menu for everyone by including a variety of foods—grains, fruits, vegetables, legumes, seeds, and nuts—in each meal.

blood volume and, therefore, creates greater pressure as the blood is pumped through the arteries.

A sodium intake of about 1,100 to 3,300 milligrams per day is considered safe and adequate for healthy adults. One teaspoon of salt contains about 2,000 milligrams of sodium.

Here are a few tips for cutting down on sodium:

- Taste food before adding salt.

- Cook with spices and herbs as flavoring instead of salt.

- Reduce the amount of salt called for in a recipe by half. When you become used to that taste, decrease the quantity to one fourth.

- Try out different commercial salt substitutes, "light" salt products, and herb/spice blends until you find one you like.

- Be aware that many commercially processed foods contain high quantities of salt.

LIMITING ALCOHOLIC BEVERAGES

Drink alcohol in moderation. Studies show that one or two drinks daily may lower the risk of heart attack, but heavy drinking can cause many health problems. Alcohol, like other simple sugars, provides calories but few nutrients.

Pregnant women should abstain from alcohol.

SMART SHOPPING

Food is probably the most variable component of your home budget. Shop well, and you'll eat well and save money, too.

NEGOTIATING THE MARKET

- Avoid shopping when you're hungry and can be tempted to make impulse purchases. When you need a single item, buy it and leave the store.

- If you can arrange it, make major shopping trips without small children. Markets often encourage impulse buying by children by putting sugary cereals and candy at their eye levels.

    If you must take your child, bring a toy or book to keep him or her occupied.

- Take note of shelf labeling and unit pricing (price per ounce) if the market

practices this policy. Otherwise, invest in a pocket calculator to figure the actual unit cost of an item available in several sizes or to compare different sizes and prices of competing brands.

- Check expiration dates, especially of perishables such as dairy products and packaged meats and poultry. Older dates are usually up front in a display case.

- Shop the aisles first to minimize potential spoilage while items are unrefrigerated. Most markets are laid out so that the meat, dairy, and frozen food sections are at the end and sides.

- Double-check the cash register at the checkout. Mistakes can be made even with computerized scanning.

- Have groceries packed with like items together. If all frozen items are in one bag, they will help keep one another cold on the trip home.

WEEKLY STAPLES

☞ If you own a computer, make a list of basic staples and run off a stack. Use one weekly and check off what you need.

COOL IT

☞ When purchasing perishables, go directly home to unpack and refrigerate or freeze items. Many foods deteriorate quickly at room temperature.

BUYING IN BULK

☞ Cooperative buying, in which people join together to buy groceries in bulk, can save you money. You may have to contribute several hours a month to do your share of purchasing and paperwork.

HOW TO
BUY THE BEST:

Meat

Beef: Look for meat that is firm, slightly moist, and light to bright or dark red in color. Bones should be red and porous. Fat should not be overly thick in proportion to meat.

Lamb: Look for meat that is firm, pink to light red in color, and fine textured. Bones should be red and porous. Fat should not be overly thick in proportion to meat.

Pork: Look for meat with a lot of grayish-pink to light red meat in proportion to bone and fat. Smoked pork products include ham, smoked hocks, and bacon.

Hams are usually sold fully cooked except for bone-in country hams, which need to be soaked and cooked like raw pork before eating.

Veal: Look for meat that is white or very pale pink. The redder the meat, the older and tougher the veal. Fat should be thin in proportion to meat.

Poultry

Chicken: Broiler-fryers (1½ to 4 pounds) are all-purpose chickens that can be broiled, fried, braised, roasted, or stewed. Roasters are 3½ to 6 pounds and meaty and tender. Stewing chickens are older, weigh 5 to 6 pounds, and need to be cooked slowly to make them tender.

Capon (neutered roosters): These birds weigh 6 to 8 pounds and have especially tender meat.

Turkey: Although modern toms are as tender as hens, hens usually cost more per pound. Look for plump birds with substantial meat over the breastbone. Two 12-pound birds are sometimes a better choice than one 25-pounder.

Duck: These birds are usually two months old and weigh 6 to 7 pounds. One duck will serve four people.

Geese: The tastiest and tenderest geese weigh 12 pounds or less and are no more than 6 months old. Allow about 1 pound per serving.

Seafood

Fish: While most seafood on the market is safe and wholesome, it's always best to buy from a reliable source whose suppliers are equally reliable.

The federal government has safety regulations for seafood, but the nature of commercial fishing makes it difficult to apply the same stringent standards that regulate meat and poultry quality.

In whole fish, look for clean gills, clear eyes, and undamaged skin. In fillets and steaks, look for glistening flesh. Watery or dried edges indicate previous freezing or poor handling. Odor should be briny, but not pungent—no strong or fishy smells.

Shellfish: Except for shrimp and scallops, fresh, uncooked shellfish should be alive when bought, and cooked within one day.

BUYING MEAT: MAKING THE GRADE

☛ Prime meats are more marbled with fat and are most tender. They are often available in restaurants and are sometimes sold to the public.

☛ Choice meats are also tender but have less fat. They are most commonly found in stores.

☛ Good meats are least tender and are usually not sold retail.

DOLLAR STRETCHERS

HERE ARE SOME ways to keep grocery costs under control.

Read the weekly ads in the newspapers. Specials can often be a source of economical inspiration for meals, but be realistic about your needs. A large family can quickly consume a 5-pound bag of potatoes, but a single person will watch the spuds grow sprouts long before they're used.

Consider buying nonfoods such as aluminum foil, paper towels, and detergent in bulk if it's cheaper (and you have storage space).

SAVING WITH COUPONS

You can often save money with coupons; here are some pointers:

- Check expiration dates before shopping. Some coupons have short terms; others are unlimited.

- Star the coupon items on your shopping list as a reminder.

- Buy nonperishable items (pet food, toilet paper) once a month at a store that offers double coupons.

- Ask for a rain check if the coupon item is out of stock.

- Send in coupons for rebates. It may be time consuming, but it can save money.

BECOMING LABEL LITERATE

THE FOOD AND DRUG ADMINISTRATION (FDA) constantly reviews its labeling regulations to update information and make it easier for consumers to read and comprehend data. Manufacturers must note the product name, the net contents or net weight (including liquid in canned goods), and the name and address of the manufacturer, packager, or distributor.

LIST OF INGREDIENTS

Ingredients appear by common names in descending order according to weight. Manufacturers must list additives, but in some cases they use general language such as "artificial color" or "artificial flavor."

NUTRITION INFORMATION

The FDA requires nutrition information when a manufacturer adds a nutrient (other than protein and certain vitamins and minerals) to a food or makes a claim such as "low-calorie." A typical nutrition label is shown on page 103.

STANDARDIZED ITEMS

The FDA has adopted standards of identity for such common foods as jams, jellies, peanut butter, and milk. Once a standard has been set, no other product can call itself by that name. For example, a beverage that is not 100 percent fruit juice cannot be called juice. Ingredients must be listed on packaging for all other foods.

FEDERAL-INSPECTION STAMP

All fresh and processed meat and poultry products that are shipped interstate must bear a federal-inspection stamp showing that they meet federal standards. Meat that does not cross state lines must meet comparable state-inspection standards.

GRADING

Some foods carry a grade on their labels that is not necessarily a grading of their nutritive value. Eggs, milk, and milk products in most states carry a "Grade A" label based on FDA sanitary standards. For instance, butter is usually graded "AA."

The U.S. Department of Agriculture (USDA) sets grades for all meat and poultry based on characteristics of taste, texture, and appearance. Gradings for meat, such as prime, choice, and good, are optional. The National Marine Fisheries Service grades fish products in a similar manner.

PRODUCT DATES

Expiration dates specify the dates by which a product is best purchased or used.

CODING

Mostly used on shelf products, coding is primarily for the manufacturer and indicates when and where a product was packaged. This is important to the consumer in the case of recall.

UNIVERSAL PRODUCT CODE

UPC, the series of large and small bars that appear on a lot of packaging, is primarily used for computerized inventory, pricing, and store checkouts.

SPECIAL SYMBOLS

The symbol ® means that the trademark on the label is registered with the U.S. Patent and Trademark Office.

The symbol © indicates that the content of the label is protected under copyright laws.

The letter K inside the letter O indicates that the food is kosher.

The word "pareve" indicates that neither meat nor dairy was used in the product's preparation.

PICKING THE BEST PRODUCE

*While many fruits and vegetables are grown
year-round in temperate areas, they still have a preferred buying period during
which the produce is generally more flavorful and less expensive. Seasonal ranges
(shown in parentheses) allow for climate variations and peak harvest times.*

VEGETABLES

Artichokes (spring): Compact, plump, heavy, with thick, green, tightly closed leaves. Avoid if blemished or hard-tipped.

Asparagus (spring to early summer): Straight stalks with closed, compact tips and full green color, except for white ends. Avoid if shriveled or have spreading tips.

Avocados (all year): Shiny green or mottled purplish-black (depending upon variety); yield to gentle pressure. Ripen in a paper bag at room temperature.

Beans, green and wax (all year): Firm, crisp, bright color without blemishes.

Beans, lima and fava (late summer and early autumn): Firm, crisp, smooth skins without blemishes.

Beets (all year, but best from summer to late autumn): Firm, small to medium-sized, bright colored, smooth skins; preferable with fresh green tops attached. Avoid if bruised, soft, or overly large (signs of decay).

Broccoli (all year): Dark-green, firmly clustered buds on firm, but not thick stalks.

Brussels sprouts (autumn through early spring): Firm, tightly wrapped green sprouts free of black spots.

Cabbage (all year): Firm, heavy for its size, with brightly colored (green or red) outer leaves and no black blemishes.

Carrots (all year): Firm, straight, with bright orange color, preferably with fresh green leaves attached. Avoid if limp or cracked.

Cauliflower (all year): Firm heads with tightly packed creamy-white clusters and fresh-looking green leaves. Avoid those with blemishes or black spots.

Celery (all year): Crisp, pale-green stalks with fresh-looking leaves. Avoid stringy, bruised, or limp stalks.

Chayote (all year, but best in summer): Small, firm, unblemished.

Corn (late spring through summer): Medium-sized ears with plump, milky kernels, smooth green husks, and soft silk ends.

Cucumbers (all year, but best in summer): Medium to small, with bright green color. Avoid soft ends, blemishes, or wax coatings.

Eggplant (all year, but best in summer): Firm, glossy purple or white with fresh green cap, heavy for its size. Avoid if soft, wrinkled, or very thick skinned.

Endive (all year, but best autumn through spring): Small, compact, snowy-white leaves edged in pale green. Avoid wilted leaves.

Fennel (autumn to early spring): Firm, unblemished white bulbs with fresh-looking feathery leaves attached.

Garlic (all year): Firm, unblemished heads with tight, compact cloves. Papery skin should be soft, not brittle.

Kohlrabi (spring through late summer): Small, young bulbs with fresh-looking stems and leaves.

Leeks (all year, but best in autumn): Firm, unblemished white base with fresh-looking green leaves.

Lettuce, greens (all year): Crisp, unblemished leaves; color depends upon variety. Avoid brown edges or blemishes.

Mushrooms (all year, but peak for wild mushrooms like oyster or shiitake depends on variety): Firm, plump, unblemished with tightly closed caps and fresh-looking stems. Select carefully, avoiding mold. Best bet: Buy exotic mushrooms from a good gourmet produce store.

Okra (spring through early autumn): Young, firm, tender green pods.

Onions (all year, but certain varieties best in late spring or early summer): Clean, dry, firm with papery husks, and no sprouts or soft spots.

Parsnips (all year, but best in late summer): Firm, smooth, small to medium-sized. Avoid those with gray soft spots or large roots (signs of age).

Peas, green (spring through early summer): Firm, bright or light green, with well-filled pods. Avoid swollen, wrinkled, or immature dark green pods.

Peppers (all year): Firm, shiny, thick-fleshed with bright color, green, red, orange, or yellow (depending upon variety). Avoid blemishes, soft spots, or darkened stem ends.

Potatoes (all year): Firm, smooth-skinned, well shaped, with no sprouts or blemishes.

Radishes (all year): Firm, smooth, bright color, red or white, with fresh-looking leaves. Avoid blemishes or black spots.

Spinach (all year): Bright green, fresh, tender leaves with no yellowing or wilted ends.

Squash, also called **summer** or **soft-skinned,** such as **zucchini, yellow, straightneck, patty pan** (all year, but best in summer): Smooth, bright skin, bright color, green or yellow (depending on variety), heavy for its size.

Squash, also called **winter** or **hard-skinned,** such as **acorn, butternut** (all year, but best in autumn): Unblemished, rich color, green, white, yellow, or gold (depending on variety), heavy for its size, with hard skin and stem end attached.

Sweet potatoes (all year, but best in late autumn): Firm, uniform shape with even color and no blemishes. Avoid very large ones (signs of age).

Tomatoes (all year): Firm, plump with unblemished skin; color and size depends on variety.

Turnips and rutabaga (all year, but best in autumn and winter): Firm, unblemished, heavy for their size with fresh-looking tops.

(continued)

MICROWAVING FRESH VEGETABLES

☛ Cooking vegetables is one of the things the microwave does best. Fresh vegetables cook quickly with a minimum amount of water, so they retain nutrients, taste, and color.

(continued)

FRUIT

Apples (all year, but best in autumn): Firm, crisp, full color with no bruises, soft spots, or shriveled skins.

Apricots (June and July): Golden-yellow to orange-yellow, plump, and firm enough to yield only slightly to pressure. Avoid soft, shriveled, or dull-looking fruit. Ripen in a paper bag at room temperature.

Bananas (all year): Solid yellow or lightly flecked with brown. If soft and with spotted or brown skin, mash and use for baking. Ripen hard green fruit in a paper bag at room temperature.

Blueberries (June through August): Plump, firm with dusky blue color.

Cantaloupes (all year, but best in summer): Pleasant perfumelike aroma; heavy for their size; no stem at end. Rind should yield to gentle pressure. Ripen at room temperature. They're ripe when the skin beneath the webbing has turned from green to beige.

Cherries (June and July): Plump with bright color, red or purplish-black (depending upon variety); fresh stems (not discolored or dry).

Coconuts (all year, but best in late autumn): Heavy for their size, with lots of juice that sloshes when fruit is shaken. Avoid moldy or wet "eyes."

Cranberries (October through December): Plump, shiny, firm with bright to dark red color.

Figs (summer to early autumn): Smooth and yielding to gentle pressure, but not soft. Ripen at room temperature.

Grapefruit (all year, but best in winter): Firm and heavy for their size, with no discoloration at stem end.

Grapes (all year, but best from late summer to late autumn): Plump, colorful, from deep purple to pale green; smooth, firmly attached to fresh-looking stems. Avoid shriveled or discolored fruit.

Honeydew melons (late summer to early autumn): Firm, creamy-white smooth surface; slightly soft at blossom end; heavy for their size. Ripen at room temperature. They're ripe when they smell perfumed.

Kiwifruit (all year): Slightly firm, fuzzy, yielding to gentle pressure. Ripen at room temperature. They're ripe when they smell fruity.

Kumquats (winter): Small, bright orange, with shiny green leaves. Avoid blemished or shriveled fruit.

Lemons (all year): Firm, shiny, heavy for their size. Avoid shriveled or hard fruit.

Limes (all year): Firm, shiny, heavy for their size. Avoid shriveled or hard fruit.

Mangoes (all year, but best in spring and summer): Yellow-orange to reddish skin that may be slightly mottled, yielding slightly to gentle pressure. Avoid bruised or shriveled fruit. Ripen at room temperature.

Nectarines (summer): Plump, rich-colored yellowish to reddish skin, with slight softening on stem end. Avoid shriveled, rock-hard, or bruised fruit. Ripen in a paper bag at room temperature.

Oranges (all year, but best in winter and early spring): Firm and heavy for their size. Avoid spongy or dry-looking fruit.

Papayas (all year, but best in spring and summer): Greenish-yellow to yellow and smooth; yield to gentle pressure. Avoid shriveled or bruised fruit. Ripen in a paper bag at room temperature.

Peaches (May through September): Yellow or creamy color with red blush (depending on variety), slightly fuzzy; fairly firm, but yield to gentle pressure. Avoid shriveled or bruised fruit. Ripen in a paper bag at room temperature.

Pears (all year, but best in late summer to early winter): Color depends on variety, no discoloration at stem end; firm, but yield to gentle pressure. Avoid bruised or overly soft fruit. Ripen in a paper bag at room temperature.

Pineapples (all year): Firm fruit, heavy for its size, with fresh-looking leaves; plump and glossy eyes; fragrant aroma. The color will depend on variety, but usually dark green indicates that fruit is not fully ripe (once picked, they will not ripen further). They're ripe when you can pull out a leaf with a gentle tug.

Plums (summer): Bright color, green to red to purple (depending upon variety); plump, slightly firm, but yield to gentle pressure. Avoid shriveled or overly soft fruit. Ripen at room temperature.

Raspberries and blackberries (summer and early autumn): Plump; dry, rich color, from red to black. Select carefully and avoid moldy or mashed fruit.

Rhubarb (April and May): Firm, crisp, fairly thick stalks. Avoid soft stalks.

Strawberries (all year, but best in early spring through summer): Firm with bright color and fresh-looking leaves and stems. Select carefully, and avoid moldy or mashed fruit.

Tangerines (late autumn to early spring): Bright orange color; heavy for their size. Avoid bruised or overly soft fruit.

Watermelon (May through September): Smooth skin; rich red or yellow flesh, with no brown or black seeds; heavy for its size.

BEST OUT-OF-SEASON BUYS

FROZEN		CANNED	DRIED
Blueberries	Raspberries (for sauces)	Cherries	Apples
Corn		Corn	Apricots
Cranberries	Spinach	Peaches	Dates
Green peas	Strawberries (for sauces)	Pineapple	Figs
Lima beans		Tomatoes	Pears
Okra			Prunes
			Raisins

GETTING IT RIPE

Tomatoes classify as both a fruit and a vegetable. Therefore, the following tips also apply to them:

☛ Many fruits are picked well before their peak to allow for long-distance transport with the least amount of damage. Some ripen better than others once they are picked.

☛ If the ethylene gas that fruits give off during ripening is contained, the ripening process is hastened. Simply place the fruit in a loosely closed paper bag, a plastic bag with holes punched in it, or a commercial ripening bowl. Do not wrap airtight or moisture will accumulate and the fruit will spoil. Apricots, mangoes, melons (except watermelon), papayas, peaches, pears, plums, and tomatoes take especially well to this process.

☛ Some fruits, like tomatoes, stop ripening once they've been refrigerated, so ripen them at room temperature before refrigerating.

Herbs, Spices, and Other Flavorings

Herbs

Store fresh herbs loosely wrapped in plastic wrap in the refrigerator. Dried herbs are about three times as potent as fresh, but their quality diminishes over time. Buy in small quantities and store in a cool, dry place; heat and sunlight will ruin them.

Basil A slight anise flavor makes basil ideal for almost any Italian dish. The delicate fresh leaves should be added during the last few minutes of cooking. Dried basil can be added earlier.

Bay leaf Its potent flavor mellows with long cooking, so it is a good seasoning for soups and stews. Bay leaf also adds a new dimension to poached fruit. Break dried leaves in half before adding to a recipe to release extra flavor, but remove before serving.

Chervil Fresh chervil has a delicate taste somewhat like tarragon, but dried chervil has little flavor. Lacy leaves, which resemble parsley, make it a classic seasoning for fish or egg dishes.

Chives A member of the onion family, chives have far more flavor when fresh than when freeze-dried or frozen. Add chopped to egg, poultry, cheese, and fish recipes for color and taste.

Coriander Also called cilantro or Chinese parsley, this fresh herb looks like flat-leaf parsley, but its distinctive lemony flavor is essential as last-minute seasoning in many Oriental, Indian, and Mexican dishes such as salsas. Coriander seeds are available dried but have a totally different taste and use, chiefly in stews and soups.

Dill Fresh dill has beautiful feathery leaves and a delicate flavor. It especially complements fish and egg dishes and makes a good seasoning for cucumbers, carrots, potato salads, and cheese sauces. Dried dill is called dill weed and may be a little bitter. The more potent dill seeds are generally used in long-cooked recipes.

Marjoram The flavor of this herb is mildly reminiscent of oregano. It is popular in many meat or poultry dishes, bread stuffings, and potatoes.

Mint There are dozens of types of mint including peppermint, spearmint, and lemon mint. Most varieties have a sweet, cool, refreshing taste. Fresh mint is a standard garnish for iced tea or lemonade and is also popular as a dessert and jelly flavorings, and a classic seasoning for lamb. Dried mint is potent and should be used shortly after opening since it can change flavor.

Oregano A standard partner to basil, it is often used in Italian and Mexican dishes, especially with tomatoes. The dried herb has more flavor than most and thus can withstand long cooking. It's also good in salad dressings, marinades, and stuffings.

Parsley Both the flat- (also called Italian parsley) and curly-leaf varieties are available fresh so widely that it's usually unnecessary to purchase dried parsley. Though some cooks say that flat-leaf parsley is more flavorful, the two are interchangeable in recipes.

Rosemary Its slightly piny, bittersweet, distinctive taste is especially good with lamb but also complements poultry, steaks, potatoes, and tomato dishes.

Sage Its aromatic flavor is standard in poultry stuffing. Sage is also excellent with pork, liver, and cheese dishes. The plant is hardy even in cold climates, making it a favorite in a home herb garden.

Savory Both summer and winter savory have a mild but pleasant flavor that pairs well with other herbs such as oregano or thyme. It enhances many meat, egg, pasta, and rice dishes.

Tarragon Its pungent anise flavor is classic in many chicken, egg, and cheese dishes as well as sauces. Tarragon is also good with vegetables, especially carrots.

Thyme Its many varieties add pleasant flavoring to soups (especially chowders), stews, meat and poultry dishes, sauces, or stuffings. Fresh or dried, it is one of the most versatile herbs.

SPICES

Most spices are sold dried and should be stored tightly covered in a cool, dark place. Whole spices retain aroma and flavor for a year or more, but ground spices lose their potency after a few months.

Allspice Though the name indicates a blend, this berry is a spice all its own. Used in sweets and baking, it is also good in pickles, relishes, and meat dishes. It is also the predominant flavor in Jamaican jerk pork and chicken, and other Caribbean recipes.

Anise (fennel) Its distinctly licorice flavor is particularly good in tomato dishes, also in cakes and cookies.

Caraway These whole seeds are relatives of anise but have a slightly salty taste. They are particularly good in savory yeast breads, cheese dishes, cabbage, and other vegetable dishes and sweet pickles.

Cardamom Whole pods contain seeds that must be ground. A classic flavor in Scandinavian cooking, as well as cakes, breads, and cookies, it is also a pleasing seasoning for custards and sweet sauces.

Chili powder A blend of ground chili peppers, cumin, garlic, and oregano. The proportions and other additions vary according to brand.

Cinnamon Its sweet aroma is most commonly found in baked goods and desserts, some vegetables such as sweet potatoes, and certain Indian and Mexican savory classics. Whole cinnamon sticks can stir and flavor cider or coffee.

Clove Whole cloves are small unopened flower buds that are flavorful and attractive stuck in hams or floating in wine or cider. Ground clove is a potent seasoning in baked goods and candies.

Cumin Whole seeds are especially fragrant toasted for a few seconds in a hot skillet or in the oven before being ground for use in many Mexican and Indian dishes as well as in sauces and salad dressings. Cumin particularly complements chilis.

Curry A blend of many ground spices, its composition varies according to brand. The namesake seasoning in certain Indian lamb, chicken, beef, and vegetarian preparations, it is also good in yogurt.

Ginger Available as a fresh root, preserved, crystallized, and ground, ginger is used in Chinese stir-fries as well as in European cookies and all-American cakes. Various forms of ginger are not interchangeable, so use what is specifically called for.

Mace This is the dried casing surrounding whole nutmeg; it has a milder flavor and is used in many desserts and baked goods.

Mustard Mustard seed is sold whole or ground; its potency varies according to brand. Whole seeds are com-

(continued)

HERB TIPS

☛ Cilantro, dill, and basil sometimes come with roots attached. Immerse the roots in a glass of water or wrap them in wet paper towel to prolong freshness.

☛ Because most fresh herbs are more delicate than dried, add them near the end of lengthy cooking times.

☛ To enhance the flavor of dried herbs, rub them between your fingers for a few seconds or grind in a mortar and pestle before adding to a recipe.

(continued)

monly used in pickling mixtures. Ground mustard is used to add flavor and color to sauces, egg and cheese dishes, and such meats as veal or pork. The condiment includes other ingredients besides mustard. Whole and ground mustard are not interchangeable.

Nutmeg Used in much the same way as mace, its flavor is more distinctive, especially when freshly ground. Used in custards, fruit pies, and sweet vegetables such as yams.

Paprika A bright- to brick-red powder made by grinding the pods of mild sweet chilis or peppers. Its flavor ranges from mild and sweet to hot with a slight bite. Used in salad dressings, stews, and to lend color and tang.

Pepper The most common spice, it includes whole or ground black, red, white, and green peppercorns as well as paprika. Since ground pepper loses potency rapidly, buy whole peppercorns, which last indefinitely, and grind as needed. Cayenne or red pepper is among the strongest while white pepper is much milder. Along with salt, pepper is added to almost all savory dishes as an all-purpose seasoning.

Poppy seeds These little black seeds are commonly used in breads and cakes.

Saffron Dried crocus stamens used to flavor and give a golden color to rice, chicken, and fish dishes. Expensive.

Sesame seeds Also called benne seeds in the South, sesame seeds have a nutty flavor, especially when toasted. Good in crackers and breads, they also go well in many Asian dishes.

Turmeric Though its flavor is different, its golden color makes this spice a ready substitute for more expensive saffron.

Vanilla One of the most common and versatile of dessert and baked good flavorings, it is available as an extract or in whole beans. Use sparingly; its flavor is potent.

OTHER FLAVORINGS

Alcoholic beverages Wine, whiskey, liqueur, and beer are commonly used in cooking to add moisture and flavor. They need not be the very best quality, but they should be good enough to drink alone.

Aromatics Highly flavored vegetables such as carrots, onions, garlic, and celery are used to season many dishes, including most soups and stews.

Capers These buds from a small Mediterranean shrub are usually sold packed in brine. They are especially good with seafood, in sauces, and as a flavorful garnish.

Chocolate This is sold in unsweetened, semisweet, and sweet forms as

well as unsweetened cocoa powder. White chocolate is not really chocolate: It contains no cocoa solids. Note that various types of chocolate are not interchangeable in many recipes.

Garlic Widely used in Mediterranean and Asian cooking, garlic is also one of the most commonly used flavorings in the United States.

Horseradish This root can be purchased fresh, but is more commonly available prepared, either red or white. Unlike other condiments, prepared horseradish loses potency after a few months.

Hot-pepper liquid seasoning Brands on the market vary widely in potency,

so use lightly, then add more to taste.

Lemon Lemon juice and zest are added to many sweet and savory dishes to bring out natural flavor. The juice helps prevent discoloration of some fruits like apples and avocados.

Salt The world's most common seasoning, these crystals enhance the flavor of many foods. Though common table salt is specified for baked goods, Kosher and sea salt may be used interchangeably in general seasoning.

Soy sauce Made from soybeans, this is a basic salty flavoring for many Asian dishes. You can buy soy sauce in most supermarkets.

COOKING

Throughout history, traditional recipes and cooking techniques have been a constant that binds one generation to the next. In fact, mealtime is likely to be the most significant event in daily family life. Most important holidays and traditions involve specific food rituals.

PLANNING MEALS

One key to good meals is organization. Plan your meals ahead, bearing in mind taste, nutrition, and cost.

To save time and effort:

- Keep a grocery list in a handy place, perhaps on the refrigerator, with a pencil attached to a magnet. Noting needed supplies on an ongoing basis saves time and eliminates extra trips to the market.

- For optimum balanced nutrition, think in terms of a full day's menu. If you need help, develop meal plans on paper and balance them against a nutritional chart.

- Every week, plan to cook once for two meals. A large roast will yield enough meat for sandwiches or salads another night.

- Make one-dish meals such as casseroles, soups, and stews that require only a salad as accompaniment.

- Prepare foods in quantity. Bake extra potatoes expressly for another meal of potato cakes or hashed browns.

To provide variety within each meal, think about:

Color Variety: An all-white meal of chicken, cauliflower, and mashed potatoes has little appeal. Change the vegetable to green beans and the starch to mashed sweet potatoes, and the plate looks much more inviting.

Flavor: Mild tastes both tame and complement the heat of fiery dishes. That's why a dollop of sour cream is the usual garnish for a spicy chili and cool yogurt sauces generally accompany hot curries.

Richness: Follow creamed soup with a simple piece of grilled poultry or fish, then end the meal with fruit. Or balance a rich dessert with a light main course.

Taste Variety: If you use a strongly flavored food, such as garlic or cabbage, avoid repeating it in another dish in the meal.

Texture: Serve soft foods with crunchy ones. Try soups with crusty breads or crackers; meat loaf with carrot and celery sticks; applesauce with pork chops.

MAKING HEALTHIER MEALS

SIMPLE CHANGES IN your cooking and eating habits can improve nutrition without sacrificing taste or time.

- Reduce meat portions to about 3 ounces. Try to plan a meal so that meat is a supplement rather than the focus of a meal.

- Use lower-fat meats such as turkey or chicken. Ground turkey can often be substituted for ground beef in recipes.

- Sauté or sear meats in a nonstick skillet spritzed with cooking spray or coated with a light film of vegetable oil.

- Poach, broil, grill, or bake instead of frying whenever possible.

- Degrease all sauces, soups, and stocks by skimming off fat with a spoon, blotting with paper towels, or refrigerating and lifting off the cold hardened fat.

- Steam vegetables until just tender to retain maximum vitamins, minerals, fiber, and flavor.

- Learn to eat slowly. It is more enjoyable and you will feel satisfied with less food.

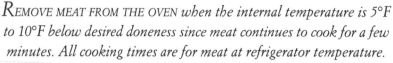

BEEF ROASTING TIMETABLE

REMOVE MEAT FROM THE OVEN when the internal temperature is 5°F to 10°F below desired doneness since meat continues to cook for a few minutes. All cooking times are for meat at refrigerator temperature.

APPROXIMATE COOKING TIME (MINUTES PER POUND)

WEIGHT (IN POUNDS)	RARE 140°F*	MEDIUM 160°F*	WELL DONE 170°F*	OVEN TEMPERATURE
Rib roast				
4-6	26-32	34-38	40-42	325°F
6-8	23-25	27-30	32-35	325°F
Rib eye roast				
4-6	18-20	20-22	22-24	350°F
**Rump roast boneless* (high quality)*				
4-6		25-30		325°F
**Tenderloin (whole)*				
4-6	45-60 (total time)			425°F (preheated)
**Tenderloin (half)*				
2-3	45-50 (total time)			425°F (preheated)
**Tip roast*				
3½-4	35		40	325°F
6-8	30		35	325°F
**Top round roast*				
4-6	23-25	23-25		325°F

* Temperature on meat thermometer. ** These meats are best when cooked at the temperatures indicated.

HOW TO PREPARE, COOK, AND STORE FOOD SAFELY

In addition to such commonsense practices as hand washing and general cleanliness, there are many other ways to ensure food safety:

Because raw meat can harbor bacteria, wash your hands and clean work surfaces regularly and thoroughly. Keep meat well refrigerated.

It is best to avoid raw meat dishes, such as beef tartare. Pork should be cooked thoroughly to avoid the potential (though now uncommon) threat of trichinosis.

Use raw poultry directly from the refrigerator after rinsing. Do not bring it to room temperature.

Beef

Beef has gained an undeservedly bad reputation in recent years because of its fat and cholesterol content. Like all red meat, beef is an excellent source of essential B vitamins and of complete protein. What matters is how much beef is eaten, both

Food and the Kitchen • COOKING

PORK ROASTING TIMETABLE

REMOVE MEAT FROM THE OVEN when the internal temperature is 5°F to 10°F below desired doneness since meat continues to cook for a few minutes. All cooking times are for meat at refrigerator temperature.

CUT	WEIGHT (IN POUNDS)	MEAT-THERMOMETER READING	APPROXIMATE COOKING TIME (MINUTES PER POUND)*
Crown roast	4-7	170°F	30-35
Leg (fresh ham)			
Half bone-in	7-8	170°F-185°F	35-40
Whole boneless	10-14	170°F	24-28
Whole bone-in	14-16	170°F-185°F	22-26
Loin roast			
Center rib or loin	3-5	160°F	20-25
Loin half	5-7	160°F	20-25
Loin blade or sirloin	3-4	160°F	30-35
Top loin, boneless	2-4	160°F	20-25
double	3-5	160°F	20-30
Shoulder arm picnic			
Bone-in	5-8	170°F-185°F	30-35
Boneless	3-5	170°F	35-40
Shoulder arm roast	4-6	170°F	40-45
Shoulder blade (Boston roast)	4-6	170°F	40-45
Tenderloin (roast at 425°F-450°F)	½-1½	160°F	20-30 (total time)

* Oven temperature: 325°F

in frequency and in quantity. Instead of an 8-ounce burger or a 10-ounce steak, cut the portion in half and eat it half as often. Trim off excess fat before cooking.

Well-marbled beef such as porterhouse steak contains more fat and is more tender and juicy than leaner cuts such as flank and round steaks, and skirt steak. However, leaner cuts can be equally, if not more, flavorful, when they are marinated or braised to tenderize and flavor them. Braised beef is done when it is fork tender.

Beef can be eaten rare, medium, or well done according to taste.

Rare: internal temperature of about 140°F. The color is brown on the exterior, with a pink-red interior and juices.

Medium: registers about 160°F, with a light pink interior and juices.

Well done: registers about 170°F and is brown throughout, with little juice.

Pork
Today's pork is bred to be much leaner than in the past, so older recipes that

GETTING READY

For good cooking follow these preliminary steps:
☛ Read a recipe all the way through in order to understand the complete procedure.
☛ Gather all ingredients and equipment before you begin.

LAMB ROASTING TIMETABLE

REMOVE MEAT FROM THE OVEN when the internal temperature is 5°F to 10°F below desired doneness since meat continues to cook for a few minutes. All cooking times are for meat at refrigerator temperature.

APPROXIMATE COOKING TIME (MINUTES PER POUND)*

WEIGHT (IN POUNDS)	RARE 140°F	MEDIUM 160°F	WELL DONE 170°F
Crown roast			
2-3 *(not stuffed)*	15-20	25-30	30-35
Leg roast (boneless)			
4-7	25-30	30-35	35-40
Leg (shank half)			
3-4	30-35	40-45	45-50
Leg (sirloin half)			
3-4	25-30	35-40	45-50
Leg (whole)			
5-7	20-25	25-30	30-35
7-9	15-20	20-25	25-30
Rib roast (rack), roast at 375°F			
1½-2	30-35	35-40	40-45
Shoulder roast (boneless)			
3½-5	30-35	35-40	40-45
Shoulder roast (square-cut, whole)			
4-6	20-25	25-30	30-35

* Oven temperature: 325°F

require long cooking times can result in dried-out meat. Some experts maintain that the new pork adapts well either to very quick cooking, such as stir-frying or sautéeing, for thin cuts, or to lengthy braising to tenderize the meat.

Pork tenderloin is a relatively expensive but extremely tender cut. It is low in fat and has absolutely no waste and cooks quickly and roasts, grills, slices, and sautés well.

Cook pork to the well-done stage, at least 160°F to 170°F, to avoid trichinosis; the meat should be uniformly pale gray throughout, with juices running clear.

Veal
Veal is the most delicate of all meats and has a subtle flavor and texture perfect for seasoning with herbs and other more distinctive ingredients.

WHOLE POULTRY ROASTING TIMETABLE

Raw poultry can carry salmonella bacteria, so be sure your bird is cooked through. Never return cooked poultry to an unwashed platter on which raw poultry has rested.

READY-TO-COOK WEIGHT (IN POUNDS)	OVEN TEMPERATURE	MEAT-THERMOMETER READING	TOTAL COOKING TIME (IN HOURS)
Capon (stuffed)			
5-6	325°F	180°F-185°F	2½-3
6-8	325°F	180°F-185°F	3-4
Capon (unstuffed)	325°F	180°F-185°F	Allow about ½ hour less
Chicken (stuffed or unstuffed)			
2½-3	350°F	175°F-180°F	1¼-1½
3-4	350°F	175°F-180°F	1½-1¾
4-6	350°F	175°F-180°F	1¾-2
Duckling (stuffed or unstuffed)			
4-5	350°F	180°F-185°F	2½-2¾
Goose (stuffed)			
9-11	350°F	180°F-185°F	3-3½
11-13	350°F	180°F-185°F	3½-4
Goose (unstuffed)	350°F	180°F-185°F	Allow about ½ hour less
Rock Cornish hen (stuffed or unstuffed)			
1-2	350°F	Rock Cornish hens are too small to take a meat thermometer.	1-1¼
Turkey (stuffed)			
8-12	325°F	180°F-185°F	3½-4
12-16	325°F	180°F-185°F	4-4½
16-20	325°F	180°F-185°F	4½-5
20-24	325°F	180°F-185°F	5-6
Turkey (unstuffed)	325°F	180°F-185°F	Allow about ½ hour less

☞ Keep a fire extinguisher handy and be sure everyone knows how to use it.

☞ Have a box of baking soda within reach to smother small fires.

☞ Keep emergency numbers, including the poison hotline, handy.

☞ Never immerse any plugged-in electric appliance in water.

☞ Make a habit of turning off burners and ovens as soon as you're finished using them.

☞ Cook hot liquids in pots and pans large enough that they won't boil over.

COOKING FISH

☞ To determine cooking time, place the fish on the kitchen counter and measure it with a ruler at the thickest part, even if it is stuffed, breaded, or rolled. Time the cooking as follows:

  10 minutes per inch if fresh

  15 minutes per inch if fresh and sauced

  20 minutes per inch if frozen

☞ Cook seafood with a little acid such as lemon or lime juice or wine to neutralize fishy-smelling enzymes.

Veal comes only from young animals. It is very lean with no marbling and only a thin external layer of fat. Like beef, better grades of veal carry federal grade stamps.

Cuts appropriate for roasting—rump, round, loin roast, rib and shoulder roasts—call for thorough cooking at low to moderate temperatures because of their lack of fat and the large proportion of connective tissue in the meat. Roast veal to an internal temperature of 170°F. The exterior will be reddish-brown and the interior a creamy white.

To test panfried veal for doneness, make a small slit in the center of the meat or near the bone to check that the color is creamy white throughout. Braised veal and veal cooked in liquid should be tender when pierced with a fork.

Lamb

With modern breeding and shipping, lamb is available year-round. Leg of lamb is a classic dish. Loin lamb chops and rack of lamb are expensive cuts. Try braised shoulder of lamb, stuffed lamb breast, and shoulder chops, which are less costly and just as flavorful.

Cook rare, medium, or well done, depending on individual preference.

Rare: registers about 140°F and has a reddish interior.

Medium: registers about 160°F and is a brownish-pink tinged with red.

Well done: registers about 170°F and is grayish.

Poultry

Chicken and turkey are excellent sources of iron, thiamine, riboflavin, and niacin, and lower in fat and calories than most other animal proteins, especially when eaten without the skin.

Despite strict processing standards, salmonella bacteria in raw poultry still pose a threat. Wash hands, surfaces, and knives carefully with hot, soapy water after handling raw poultry. Be sure to thaw frozen poultry slowly in the refrigerator, not at room temperature. If possible, reserve one cutting board just for poultry.

Cook chicken and turkey until it is well done. Good tests of doneness are an internal temperature of 180°F, juices that run clear when the poultry is pierced, and flesh that is no longer pink anywhere.

Tender boneless cuts cook in a few minutes while whole birds take many hours. Labels such as "old," "hen," or "stewing hen" indicate mature birds that may be on the tough side. These are better braised or stewed than roasted or fried.

When microwaved, poultry can cook unevenly. Test poultry for doneness with a meat thermometer in several spots to be sure it has reached the proper internal temperature throughout.

Refrigerate leftovers promptly. Put them in shallow dishes so they cool quickly to room temperature before refrigeration. Use in a few days.

Seafood

Fish and shellfish are generally low in calories. The so-called fat fish—salmon, mackerel, whitefish, bluefish, shad, lake trout—contain less fat than many meats, and much of that fat is unsaturated. "Lean" fish—ocean perch, cod, flounder, halibut, red snapper, haddock, hake, whiting—contain even less fat. All shellfish are lean.

If you're concerned about the cholesterol content of certain fatty fish and shellfish, consider this: Researchers have found that many fat fish (herring, mackerel, salmon, bluefish) contain a fatty acid that actually may help in *lowering* blood cholesterol. More good news: Shellfish such as scallops, clams, oysters, and mussels have lower cholesterol levels than originally believed.

In many recipes, different kinds of fish can usually be used interchangeably. Also, frozen fish and shellfish can replace fresh fish and shellfish; just thaw them first. Shellfish are rich in minerals, contain high-quality protein, are a good source of vitamins, and are low in calories. Except for shrimp and scallops, fresh, uncooked shellfish should be alive when bought, and cooked within 1 day. Like fish, shellfish cooks quickly. Shucked clams and oysters should be plump and shiny.

Eggs

Salmonella bacteria are present in eggs as well as poultry. Thorough cooking kills them.

- In the store, inspect the carton for any cracked or broken eggs. Discard any that were damaged on the way home.

- Check the expiration date on the carton to make sure it hasn't passed or isn't close.

- Store eggs in the original carton in the main section of the refrigerator. Do not remove and place them in the egg section on the door, where the temperature is higher and less constant.

- It's safest to avoid eating raw eggs in dessert mousses or meringues, homemade mayonnaises and sauces, Caesar salad, or eggnog.

- Cook eggs thoroughly. Scrambled eggs should be firm; poached and fried eggs should be set.

Dairy Products

Dairy products are highly perishable. Quality also depends upon shipping and handling en route to your store.

- Buy from a high-volume store that replenishes its stock frequently.

- Check expiration dates on containers before buying. When in doubt, look at several packages for the latest date. Later dates are usually at the back of the case. (It's also colder there.)

- Store in the refrigerator at all times.

- Discard all dairy products that have an off-odor or begin to develop mold—except hard cheeses (which can be eaten safely after mold is cut away) and mold-containing cheeses such as Roquefort.

HOW TO RESCUE A RECIPE

☛ To thicken a thin sauce, dissolve a teaspoon of cornstarch in a teaspoon of cold water, then whisk into a cup of hot sauce. Reintroduce as needed to the rest of the sauce. Simmer to thicken.

☛ For a curdled custard sauce, strain out the curds. Whisk in another egg and cook over very low heat or in a double boiler, stirring until the sauce thickens. Or blend briefly in a food processor.

☛ If a soufflé does not rise, serve it as a baked custard.

GRILLING

CHARCOAL USUALLY TAKES about 30 minutes to reach the proper temperature. Wait until the coals are covered with a light gray ash before cooking. Gas grills preheat in about 10 minutes.

For successful meals, note the following:

- To lower or raise heat during grilling, adjust the racks, vents, lid, or push coals apart or together.

- Most foods should be cooked over moderate heat several inches from the coals. Delicate items like bread should be placed near the edge of the grill farthest from the coals.

- Uniform thickness makes for easy timing when cooking several items together, such as burgers.

- Marinate foods in zipper-plastic storage bags for quick cleanup.

- Brush leftover marinade on foods while grilling. Before using as a table sauce, bring to a boil and simmer at least 5 minutes to destroy bacteria.

- Brush on thick marinades and sauces only during the last few minutes to prevent burning.

GRILLING SAFETY

To prevent fires and smoke inhalation, place grills in the open, not in an enclosed area such as a garage or next to the house. In addition:

- Always have water nearby in case of emergency.

- Never add starter fluid after the fire is going. This can cause a dangerous flash of flame. Keep flammable liquids well away from the grill when in use.

- Never allow children to play near a grill.

- Check coals several hours after cooking to be sure they are completely burned out.

METAL IN YOUR MICROWAVE

☞ It's possible to safely use some metal-containing cookware and some metals in your microwave. Always read the manufacturer's instructions before using metal in your microwave.

HOW TO MICROWAVE

Microwaves penetrate food up to a depth of 1½ inches, and heat is conducted from the outer edges toward the center. Therefore:

☞ Place denser, slower cooking foods near the edge and quicker cooking ones in the center.

☞ Stir foods from the outer (hotter) edge toward the center.

☞ Alternate the ends of unevenly shaped foods, such as corn on the cob, and rearrange halfway through cooking.

☞ Place foods of uniform size in a circle.

☞ Rotate casseroles or baked dishes for even cooking.

☞ Prick egg yolks, sausage casings, and skins of potatoes and other vegetables before cooking to prevent steam buildup.

Produce

It is difficult to know whether produce has been treated or sprayed with chemicals, so it is safest to assume that it has.

• In order to preserve the most nutrients and quality, wash all produce.

• Discard any fruit or vegetable showing signs of mold or other disease. The nutritional content will be severely diminished.

Canned Goods

Foods are canned according to strict government standards, but it is still important to inspect the food before consumption.

• Most commercially canned goods have a long shelf life. Once opened, the contents should be removed, treated like fresh food, and consumed quickly, with leftovers refrigerated.

• Never eat the contents of a dented or swollen can.

MICROWAVING

Microwave ovens vary primarily in size and extra features. Smaller ovens are ideal for small kitchens or single cooks, but they're often less powerful than large models. Extra features range from electronic touch controls to temperature probes that turn the oven off when the food is done.

ADAPTING RECIPES TO A MICROWAVE

YOU CAN PREPARE many of your favorite foods in your microwave if you follow these simple directions:

• Work only with recipes serving six or fewer.

• Reduce liquids in braised dishes, soups, or stews. Microwaving does not cause much evaporation.

• For even cooking, chop or slice ingredients to equal size.

• Shorter cooking time keeps the flavors sharper, so reduce seasonings and highly aromatic ingredients such as garlic.

• When baking, use only recipes developed for the microwave.

• Avoid recipes that call for crisply cooked or well-browned foods. They don't turn out well in microwave ovens.

• For best results, buy a microwave cookbook. When you wish to convert a conventional recipe, match it with a similar one in your microwave cookbook.

MICROWAVE COOKING TABLE

FOODS KEEP COOKING from internal heat after you remove them from the microwave, so take a temperature reading after the standing time to determine doneness. This is particularly important for roasted meats.

MEAT, POULTRY	TEMPERATURE WHEN REMOVED FROM OVEN	TEMPERATURE AFTER STANDING TIME
Chicken		
Whole (unstuffed)	180°F	Chicken should always
Whole (stuffed)	185°F	be cooked to doneness
Whole (cut up)	170°F	in the microwave oven.
Parts (bone in)	180°F	
Parts (boneless)	165°F	
Beef roast		
Medium rare	115°F-125°F	125°F-140°F
Medium	130°F-140°F	140°F-155°F
Well done	150°F-160°F	160°F-170°F
Pork roast	165°F	170°F

Programming features can allow you first to defrost, then cook the food to a predetermined degree. Some units also do double duty as conventional or convection ovens.

Each microwave oven is different, so read the instruction manual carefully and keep it handy for reference. Most microwave recipes were developed for use in ovens with 700 watts or more of cooking power. If yours is different, timing will vary.

You cannot double a microwave recipe without doubling the cooking time. Microwave cooking time is in direct proportion to the amount of food to be cooked. Two potatoes may take twice as long as one potato.

TIMING IS EVERYTHING

- Dense foods, such as lasagna, will cook or heat through more slowly than light porous foods, such as cakes and breads.

- As with any cooking method, foods at room temperature will take less time to cook than refrigerated or frozen foods.

- Microwave foods continue to cook by internal heat after removal from the microwave. After standing 1 to 2 minutes, they will be set.

MICROWAVES ARE ATTRACTED TO:

- Fats, so fatty meats such as bacon actually brown during cooking. Cheese and butter melt quickly.

- Moisture, so high water content foods such as fruits and vegetables cook quickly.

- Sugar, so syrups become hot quickly, and pastries with sugary fillings may become hotter on the inside than the outside.

SAFE MICROWAVING

☞ Never operate an empty microwave—you can damage your microwave.

☞ Supervise children when they operate the microwave.

☞ Cover liquid foods with plastic wrap or covers to hold in heat and to prevent splattering. Remove covers away from your face carefully to avoid steam burns. Plastic wraps should be vented to allow steam to escape.

☞ Be very careful with baby food and other foods you're giving children. There may be "hot spots." Stir before tasting; taste before serving.

A COOK'S TOUR OF COOKING TERMS

*MANY TERMS ARE USED EXCLUSIVELY in cooking. You need
to know what they mean in order to understand even basic recipes. Some
of the most common are defined here.*

Al dente Pasta cooked until just firm.

Bake To cook food in an oven, surrounded with dry heat; called roasting when applied to meat or poultry.

Baking powder is a combination of baking soda, an acid such as cream of tartar, and a starch or flour (moisture absorber). Most common type is double-acting baking powder, which acts when mixed with liquid and again when heated.

Baking soda The main ingredient in baking powder, baking soda is also used when there is acid (buttermilk or sour cream, for example) in a recipe. Always mix with other dry ingredients before adding any liquid, since leavening begins as soon as soda comes in contact with liquid.

Barbecue To cook foods on a rack or a spit over coals.

Baste To moisten food for added flavor and to prevent drying out while cooking.

Batter An uncooked pourable mixture usually made up of flour, a liquid, and other ingredients.

Beat To stir rapidly to make a mixture smooth, using a whisk, spoon, or mixer.

Blanch To cook briefly in boiling water to seal in flavor; usually used for vegetables or fruit, to prepare for canning, and to ease skin removal.

Blend To thoroughly combine two or more ingredients, either by hand with a whisk or spoon, or with a mixer.

Boil To cook in water that has reached 212°F and in which bubbles rise constantly to the surface.

Bone To remove bones from poultry, meat, or fish.

Bouquet garni A tied bundle of herbs, usually parsley, thyme, and bay leaves, that is added to flavor soups, stews, and sauces but removed before serving.

Braise To gently brown in a small amount of liquid over low heat in a covered pan until tender.

Bread To coat with crumbs or cornmeal before cooking.

Broil To cook on a rack or spit under or over direct heat, usually in an oven.

Caramelize To heat sugar until it liquefies and becomes a syrup ranging from golden to dark brown.

Cream The butterfat portion of milk. Also, to beat ingredients, usually sugar and a fat, until smooth and fluffy.

Cube To cut food into small even pieces, usually about ½ inch.

Cut in To distribute a solid fat in flour using a cutting motion, with two knives or a pastry blender, until divided evenly into tiny pieces. Usually refers to making pastry.

Deep-fry To cook by completely immersing food in hot fat.

Deglaze To loosen pan drippings by adding a liquid, then heating while stirring and scraping the pan.

Dollop A scoop-size blob of soft food, such as whipped cream or mashed potatoes.

Dot To scatter butter in bits over food.

Dredge To cover or coat uncooked food, usually with a flour or cornmeal mixture or bread crumbs.

Dress To coat foods, such as salad, with a sauce, or to clean fish, poultry, or game for cooking.

Drippings Juices and fats rendered by meat or poultry during cooking.

Fillet A flat piece of boneless meat, poultry, or fish. Also, to cut the bones from a piece of meat, poultry, or fish.

Fines herbes A mixture of herbs, traditionally parsley, chervil, chives, and tarragon, used to flavor fish, chicken, and eggs.

Flambé To ignite warmed alcoholic beverages, which are then poured over foods just before serving.

Flute To make decorative grooves. Usually refers to pastry.

Fold To combine light ingredients, such as whipped cream or beaten egg whites, with a heavier mixture, using a gentle over-and-under motion.

Glaze To coat foods with glossy mixtures, such as jellies or sauces.

Grate To rub foods against a serrated surface to produce shredded or fine bits.

Grease To rub the interior surface of a cooking dish or pan with grease, oil, or butter to prevent food from sticking to it.

Grill To cook food on a rack under or over direct heat, as on a barbecue or a broiler.

Grind To reduce food to tiny particles using a grinder or a food processor.

Julienne To cut in long, thin strips, matchsticklike in shape.

Knead To blend dough together with hands or in a mixer to form a pliable mass.

Macerate To soak in a flavored liquid; usually refers to fruit.

Marinate To soak in a flavored liquid; usually refers to meat, poultry, or fish.

Mince To cut in tiny pieces, usually with a knife.

Parboil To partially cook by boiling. Usually done to prepare food for final cooking by another method.

Poach To cook gently over very low heat in barely simmering liquid just to cover.

Reduce To thicken a liquid and concentrate its flavor by boiling.

Render To cook fatty meat or poultry, such as bacon or goose, over low heat to obtain drippings.

Roast To cook a large piece of meat or poultry uncovered in an oven.

Sauté or panfry To cook food in a small amount of fat over relatively high heat.

Scald To heat liquid almost to a boil until bubbles begin to form around the edge.

Sear To brown the surface of meat by quick cooking over high heat in order to seal in the meat's juices.

Shred To cut food into narrow strips with a knife or a grater.

Simmer To cook in liquid just below the boiling point; bubbles form but do not burst on the surface of the liquid.

Skim To remove surface foam or fat from a liquid.

Steam To cook food on a rack or in a steamer set over boiling or simmering water in a covered pan.

Steep To soak in a liquid just under the boiling point to extract the essence—e.g., tea.

Stew To cook covered over low heat in a liquid.

Stir-fry To quickly cook small pieces of food over high heat, stirring constantly.

Truss To tie whole poultry with string or skewers so it will hold its shape during cooking.

Whip To beat food with a whisk or mixer to incorporate air and produce volume.

Zest The outer colored part of the peel of citrus fruit.

KITCHEN EQUIVALENTS

MEASUREMENTS

1 tablespoon = 3 teaspoons
¼ cup = 4 tablespoons
⅓ cup = 5 tablespoons plus 1 teaspoon

1 cup dry = 16 tablespoons
1 cup liquid = 8 fluid ounces
1 pint = 2 cups

1 quart = 4 cups
1 pound = 16 ounces
4 quarts = 1 gallon

EQUIPMENT

8-by-1½-inch round cake pan = 4 cups
9-by-1½-inch round cake pan = 6 cups
8-by-1¼-inch pie pan = 3 cups
9-by-1½-inch pie pan = 4 cups
8-by-8-by-2-inch square pan = 6 cups
9-by-9-by-1½-inch square pan = 8 cups

9-by-9-by-2-inch square pan = 10 cups
11-by-7-by-1½-inch rectangular pan = 8 cups
13-by-9-by-2-inch rectangular pan = 14 cups
8½-by-4½-by-2½-inch loaf pan = 6 cups
9-by-5-by-3-inch loaf pan = 8 cups

INGREDIENTS

Apples 1 pound = 3 medium or 3 cups sliced

Bananas 1 pound = 3 medium or 1⅓ cups mashed

Barley 1 cup raw quick-cooking = about 3 cups cooked

Beans 1 cup dry = 2 to 2½ cups cooked

Blueberries 1 pint = 3 cups

Bread 1 pound loaf = 16 regular or 28 thin slices

Bread crumbs ½ cup fresh = 1 slice bread with crust

Bulgur 1 cup uncooked = 3 to 3½ cups cooked

Butter or margarine 1 stick = 8 tablespoons or 4 ounces

Cabbage 1 pound = 4 to 5 cups coarsely sliced

Celery 1 medium-size bunch = about 4 cups chopped

Cheese 4 ounces = 1 cup shredded

Cherries 1 pound = about 2 cups pitted

Chicken 1 2½- or 3-pound fryer = 2½ cups diced cooked meat

Chocolate 1 ounce unsweetened or semisweet = 1 square

Chocolate chips 6-ounce package = 1 cup

Cocoa 8-ounce can unsweetened = 2 cups

Cornmeal 1 cup raw = about 4 cups cooked

Cottage cheese 8 ounces = 1 cup

Couscous 1 cup raw = about 2½ cups cooked

Cranberries 12-ounce bag = 3 cups

Cream 1 cup heavy or whipping = 2 cups whipped

Cream cheese 8-ounce package = 1 cup; 3-ounce package = 6 tablespoons

Egg whites 1 large = about 2 tablespoons

Egg yolks 1 large = about 1½ tablespoons

Farina 1 cup regular or instant uncooked = 6 to 6½ cups cooked

Flour 1 pound all-purpose = about 3½ cups

Gelatin 1 envelope unflavored = 2½ teaspoons

Gingersnaps 15 cookies = about 1 cup crumbs

Graham crackers 7 whole crackers = 1 cup crumbs

Hominy grits 1 cup = about 4½ cups cooked

Honey 16 ounces = 1⅓ cups

Kasha 1 cup uncooked = about 3 cups cooked

Lemon 1 medium = about 3 tablespoons juice and 1 tablespoon grated zest

Lentils 1 cup = about 2½ cups cooked

Macaroni, elbow 1 cup = about 2 cups cooked

Milk, condensed 14-ounce can = 1¼ cups

Milk, evaporated 5-ounce can = ⅔ cup

Molasses 12 ounces = 1½ cups

Noodles 8 ounces uncooked medium = about 4 cups cooked

Nuts 1 cup chopped = 3 or 4 ounces

Oats 1 cup raw old-fashioned or quick = about 2 cups cooked

Onion 1 large = 1 cup chopped

Orange 1 medium = ⅓ to ½ cup juice and 2 tablespoons grated zest

Peaches 1 pound = about 3 medium or 2½ cups sliced

Pears 1 pound = about 3 medium or 2¼ cups sliced

Peppers 1 large bell = about 1 cup chopped

Pineapple 1 large = about 4 cups cubed

Popcorn ¼ cup unpopped = about 4 cups popped

Potatoes 1 pound all-purpose = about 3 medium or 3 cups sliced or 2 cups mashed

Raisins 15-ounce box = about 2 cups

Rice 1 cup uncooked regular = about 3 cups cooked; 1 cup uncooked instant = about 2 cups cooked

Saltine crackers 28 squares = about 1 cup crumbs

Shortening 1 pound = 2½ cups

Spaghetti 8 ounces uncooked = about 4 cups cooked

Split peas 1 cup raw = about 2½ cups cooked

Strawberries 1 pint = about 3¼ cups whole or 2¼ cups sliced

Sugar 1 pound confectioner's = 3¾ cups; 1 pound granulated = 2¼ to 2½ cups; 1 pound light or dark brown = 2¼ cups packed

Tomatoes 1 pound = 3 medium

Vanilla wafers 22 cookies = 1 cup crumbs

Yeast 1 package active dry = 2½ teaspoons

COMMON SUBSTITUTIONS

1 teaspoon baking powder = ½ teaspoon cream of tartar plus ¼ teaspoon baking soda

1 cup cake flour = 1 cup minus 2 tablespoons all-purpose flour

1 cup self-rising flour = 1 cup all-purpose flour plus ¼ teaspoon baking powder and a pinch of salt

2 tablespoons flour as a thickener = 1 tablespoon cornstarch or quick-cooking tapioca or arrowroot

1 ounce unsweetened chocolate = 3 tablespoons unsweetened cocoa powder plus 1 tablespoon butter, margarine, or oil

6 ounces semisweet chocolate = 1 cup chocolate chips, or 6 tablespoons unsweetened cocoa powder plus 7 tablespoons sugar and 4 tablespoons butter, margarine, or oil

1 cup whole milk = ½ cup evaporated milk plus ½ cup water

1 cup plain yogurt = 1 cup buttermilk

1 cup buttermilk = 1 tablespoon vinegar or lemon juice plus enough milk to make 1 cup. Let stand 5 minutes to thicken. Or 1 cup plain yogurt.

1 cup sour cream = 1 cup plain yogurt (in unheated recipe). To prevent yogurt from curdling in a cooked recipe, you will have to stabilize it with 1 egg white or 1 tablespoon of cornstarch or flour dissolved in a little cold water for every quart of yogurt.

1 cup chicken or beef broth = 1 bouillon cube or 1 envelope or 1 teaspoon instant bouillon plus 1 cup boiling water

15-ounce can tomato sauce = 6-ounce can tomato paste plus 1½ cans water

1 package active dry yeast = ½ ounce yeast cake or 1 package quick-rise yeast (allow half the rising time for quick rise)

KEEPING FOOD FRESH

WHEN THE LIGHTS GO OUT

☞ In a power failure, minimize refrigerator and freezer door openings. Protect food by placing blocks of dry ice on top of the packages or check with a local frozen foods locker plant about temporary storage. Frozen foods that have thawed completely should not be refrozen.

MINDING THE KITCHEN WHILE YOU ARE AWAY

☞ Check your smoke alarm and replace the battery, if necessary.

☞ Clean out the refrigerator and discard whatever may spoil.

☞ Leave your freezer almost full. If there is a power failure, the food will stay frozen longer.

☞ Unplug all small appliances.

☞ Check to be sure your stove and oven are turned off.

☞ Refrigerate opened boxes of cereal, pasta, and other dry foods if you will be away more than a month.

Most food purchased at the supermarket has already been stored for a considerable length of time. Transit and warehousing add days, and sometimes even weeks, to the time between harvest and purchase of fresh produce.

Dairy products and meats undergo similar transport delays. So it is a good practice to keep track of labels indicating the last day of sale or use. Even canned goods, which have long shelf lives, often have expiration dates printed (albeit sometimes very small) on the can.

REFRIGERATING

The best temperature range for refrigerator storage is 34°F to 40°F. Food spoils quickly above 40°F. Often the center shelf has the most even temperature, but read your owner's manual to determine where this is true in your model.

If you have any questions about the accuracy of your refrigerator's temperature, check it by placing a refrigerator thermometer in the center of one of the middle shelves. Always keep uncooked meat, fish, and poultry in the coldest part.

Try to minimize trips to the refrigerator since frequent opening and closing of the refrigerator door causes temperature shifts.

Refrigerators have bins, compartments, and shelves to save energy by preventing large shifts in temperature. They also help you organize what you store.

- Clean your refrigerator at least once a month.
- Periodically check your refrigerator temperature.
- Store milk and cream in original containers on the shelf that has the least shift in temperature.

- Store cheese tightly wrapped or covered in a cold part of the refrigerator or in the dairy drawer. Use promptly and check often, especially soft cheeses, which deteriorate within a few days.
- Store all uncooked meats well wrapped in the coldest part of the refrigerator.
- Store fruits and vegetables in the produce drawers or loosely wrapped on the center shelf of the refrigerator.
- Do not wash produce, except leafy greens, before storing, because it will spoil more quickly. Wash leafy greens, dry thoroughly, and store loosely wrapped in a paper, plastic, or cloth bag.
- Store condiments, soft drinks, and other foods not as susceptible to spoilage in the door, where they will be readily accessible.
- Label and date all leftovers. Store in a specific area or shelf where they will not be forgotten.

FREEZING

Freezing retards the growth of microorganisms and enzymes that cause food spoilage. For best flavor and texture, home-frozen foods should be used within 6 to 9 months.

Never store more than 2 or 3 pounds of food per cubic foot of freezer capacity at one time. Otherwise, you will overload the freezer, making it more difficult to maintain the necessary 0°F temperature. For accuracy, keep a freezer thermometer in the freezer and check the temperature about once a month.

An almost empty freezer is more expensive to operate than one that is nearly full. Frozen foods help keep their neighbors frozen, so keep your freezer well stocked. Place the newest packages in the bottom or near the back of the freezer, then move the older ones so they are next in line for use. Color code with different markers to help you identify foods in the freezer. Post a list of all frozen food (with dates) near the freezer and check off what is used. Thaw meats, fish, and poultry in the refrigerator. Thawing at room temperature encourages bacterial growth.

Partially thawed foods can be safely refrozen if the thawing has been brief and there are still ice crystals on the food. Never freeze or refreeze food on which you spot any indication of spoilage, such as off-odor or off-color.

Choosing a Container

If you're freezing food for a short time, high-quality plastic bags or containers are adequate. Wrap foods airtight to decrease the chance of "freezer burn," which occurs when air meets frozen food. Freezer burn is not harmful but adversely affects the food's texture and color.

For longer periods, use special wrappings such as heavy-duty aluminum foil, special freezer or boil-in plastic bags, or freezer wrap. You can also use heavy-duty plastic containers or jars. But never put glass containers in the freezer. Remember to leave head space in jars or containers because foods expand during freezing. In all cases, packages should be secure, airtight, and clearly labeled with contents and date.

Fruit

When freezing fruit, wash it well, then follow a specific freezing recipe. Sometimes ascorbic acid or another antidarkening agent is called for. These products are readily available in supermarkets and pharmacies. Fruit can be packed in syrup or sugar or be completely unsweetened.

Thaw frozen fruit in its freezer container, and use it as soon as it is thawed for best flavor and texture. When fruit is completely thawed, the texture will be a bit mushy, so plan on using frozen fruit in sauces, pies, or other recipes that don't require perfect texture.

Vegetables

When freezing vegetables, wash them thoroughly, then prepare according to individual freezing recipes. For optimal taste, color, and texture, most vegetables except peppers and onions are best blanched before freezing (see page 124).

Times vary for each vegetable and recipe. Frozen vegetables can be cooked from the frozen state or thawed first. Remember that cooking times will be shorter, since the vegetable was partially cooked during the blanching process.

DON'T FREEZE THESE FOODS:

- Salad greens and crisp raw vegetables to be used in salads and sandwiches, such as celery, onions, and sweet peppers, will lose their crispness and become limp after freezing.

- Eggs in the shell will expand and crack the shell. Hard-cooked egg whites will become tough and rubbery.

- Creamed cottage cheese will change texture, becoming grainy. Freeze only uncreamed or dry-curd cottage cheese.

- Sour cream will separate when frozen and thawed.

- Heavy or whipping cream will not whip high after freezing. If you like, whip it first, then freeze it. Thaw it in the refrigerator before using.

- Potatoes become mushy if frozen raw; watery and tough if boiled and then frozen.

FREEZING HINTS

☞ Freeze meatballs or cookies in a single layer on a baking sheet, then place in bags for long-term storage. That way they will freeze more quickly and won't stick together.

☞ Line a casserole with heavy-duty foil and allow enough to cover the top. After freezing, remove the foil-wrapped food to free the dish for other uses.

SAFEGUARDING GRAINS AND CEREALS

☞ If your refrigerator is large enough, move grains and cereals there (especially in the summer) so they'll last longer.

REFRIGERATOR STORAGE

EXCEPT AS NOTED, WRAP FOOD in foil or plastic wrap, or place it in bags or in airtight containers. This keeps food from drying out and odors from transferring from one food to another. Except for greens, do not wash food before storing it.

FRESH PRODUCE	STORAGE TIME	SPECIAL HANDLING
Fruit		
Apples	1 month	May also store at 60-70°F.
Apricots, avocados, bananas, melons, nectarines, peaches, pears	5 days	If necessary, allow to ripen at room temperature before refrigerating.
Berries, cherries	3 days	
Citrus fruit	2 weeks	May also store at 60-70°F.
Pineapples	4 days	
Plums	5 days	Let ripen at room temperature, then refrigerate.
Vegetables		
Asparagus	3 days	
Beets, carrots, parsnips, radishes, turnips	2 weeks	Remove any leafy tops before refrigerating.
Broccoli, brussels sprouts, green onions, soft-skinned squash	5 days	
Cabbage, cauliflower, celery, cucumber, eggplant, green beans, peppers	1 week	
Corn	1 day	Leave in husk.
Lettuce, spinach, all leafy greens	5 days	Rinse, drain before refrigerating.
Lima beans, peas	2 days	Leave in shell.
Tomatoes	1 week	If necessary, ripen tomatoes at room temperature, away from light, before refrigerating.

DAIRY PRODUCTS	STORAGE TIME	SPECIAL HANDLING
Butter	2 to 3 weeks	
Buttermilk, sour cream, yogurt	2 weeks	
Cheese		
Cottage, ricotta	5 days	
Cream, Neufchâtel	2 weeks	
Slices	2 weeks	
Whole pieces	1 month	Cut off mold if it forms on surface of cheese.
Cream	1 week	
Eggs		
In shell	1 month	
Whites, yolks	4 days	Cover yolks with water.
Margarine	1 month	
Milk		
Whole, skimmed	1 week	Do not return unused milk to original container; this spreads bacteria to remaining milk.

MEAT, FISH, AND POULTRY BEFORE COOKING	STORAGE TIME	SPECIAL HANDLING
Fresh meat (beef, lamb, pork, veal)		Leave in plastic wrap. Or if not prepackaged in plastic, wrap loosely in waxed paper so surface can dry slightly.
Chops, steaks	3 days	
Ground, stew meat	2 days	
Roasts	3 days	
Sausage, fresh	2 days	
Variety meats	2 days	
Processed meats		Times are for opened packages of sliced meat. Check date on unopened vacuum-packed meat.
Bacon, frankfurters	2 weeks	
Ham		
canned (unopened)	6 months	
slices	3 days	
whole	1 week	
Luncheon meats	5 days	
Sausage, dry, semidry	3 weeks	
Fish, shellfish (all kinds)	1 day	
Poultry (all kinds)		Keep wrapped.
fresh, thawed, frozen	2 days	If not in plastic wrap, wrap loosely.

PACKAGED AND PREPARED FOODS—LEFTOVERS OR AFTER OPENING		
Cakes, pies		
Cream, custard	2 days	
Coffee		
Ground	2 weeks	After opening.
Cooked or canned foods		
Broths, gravy, soup	2 days	
Casseroles, stews	3 days	
Fruit, vegetables	3 days	
Juices, drinks	6 days	
Meat, fish, poultry	2 days	
Stuffings	2 days	Remove stuffings from poultry and refrigerate separately.
Flour		
White, rye, whole wheat	1 year	
Nuts (shelled)	6 months	
Pickles, olives	1 month	
Refrigerated biscuits, cookies, rolls		See expiration date on label.
Salad dressings	3 months	
Salads		
Potato, coleslaw	2 days	
Wine		
Table	3 days	
Cooking	3 months	

THE COLD FACTS

PROPERLY WRAPPED (SEE PAGE 129) and frozen, food will hold its full flavor and nutrients for the times listed below; after that, flavors may fade but the food will still be safe to eat. It's safe to refreeze foods if they still contain ice crystals. NEVER REFREEZE OR EAT ANY FOOD WITH AN OFF-ODOR OR OFF-COLOR.

STORE-BOUGHT FROZEN FOODS

FOOD	STORAGE TIME
Breads	
baked, unbaked dough	3 months
Cakes	
angel-food	2 months
layer cake, frosted	4 months
pound, yellow cake	6 months
Doughnuts, pastries	3 months
Fish	
"fatty" fish—mackerel, trout, etc.	3 months
"lean" fish—cod, flounder, etc.	6 months
Fruit	1 year
Ice cream, sherbet	1 month
Juices, drinks	1 year
Meat	
beef	
roasts, steaks	1 year
ground beef	4 months
lamb, veal	
roasts, steaks	9 months
pork	
chops	4 months
roasts	8 months
Pancake, waffle batter	3 months
Pies	8 months
Poultry	
chicken, turkey (parts)	6 months
chicken, turkey (whole)	1 year
duckling	6 months
goose	6 months
turkey rolls, roasts	6 months
Shellfish	
Alaska King crab	10 months
breaded, cooked	3 months
lobster, scallops	3 months
shrimp (unbreaded)	1 year
Vegetables	8 months

FROZEN FOOD TIPS

- Pick up frozen foods immediately before going to the checkout counter.

- Buy only foods frozen solid and with no dribbles on the package, odor, or other signs of being thawed.

- Put all frozen foods together in one bag so they'll stay as cold as possible for the trip home.

- Store frozen foods in their original wrapping. Place in your freezer as soon as possible.

- Cook or thaw as the label directs.

- Do not freeze eggs in the shell, creamed cottage cheese or cream cheese, or custard pies.

HOME-FROZEN FOODS

FOOD	STORAGE TIME	SPECIAL HANDLING
Bread		
baked	3 months	
unbaked dough	1 month	Use only in special recipes.
Butter, margarine	9 months	
Cakes	3 months	
Cheese		
dry-curd cottage cheese, ricotta	not recommended	
natural, processed	3 months	Cut and wrap cheese in small pieces.
Cookies		
baked	3 months	
dough	1 month	
Cream		
heavy	2 months	Thawed cream may not whip.
whipped	1 month	
Egg whites, yolks	1 year	To each cup yolks, add 1 teaspoon sugar for use in sweet, or 1 teaspoon salt for nonsweet, dishes.
Fish, shellfish		Wrap all fish and shellfish tightly in heavy-duty foil or freezer wrap.
"fatty" fish—bluefish, trout, etc.	3 months	
"lean" fish—cod, flounder, etc.	6 months	
shellfish	3 months	
Fruit pies	8 months	Freeze baked or unbaked.
Ice cream, sherbet	1 month	
Meat		Keep in vacuum packages. If meat is purchased fresh and wrapped in plastic wrap, check for holes. If none, freeze in this wrap up to 2 weeks. For longer storage overwrap tightly with freezer wrap or heavy-duty foil.
bacon	1 month	
cooked roasts		
beef, lamb	1 year	
pork, veal	8 months	
frankfurters	2 weeks	
ground, stew meat	3 months	
ham	2 months	
steaks, chops		
beef	1 year	
lamb, veal	9 months	
pork	4 months	
Nuts	3 months	
Poultry		Wrap in heavy-duty foil or freezer wrap as airtight as possible.
cooked, with gravy	6 months	
cooked, no gravy	1 month	
uncooked, (whole)		Thaw uncooked poultry in refrigerator or under cool running water. Cook within two days of thawing.
chicken, turkey	1 year	
duckling, goose	6 months	
uncooked (parts)		
chicken	9 months	
turkey	6 months	
Vegetables	1 year	

GOOD FOODS FOR CANNING

☛ Applesauce
☛ Fruit preserves
☛ Peaches
☛ Pickles
☛ Relishes
☛ Tomatoes

SHELF STORAGE

Unopened commercially canned and jarred foods can be stored safely for periods up to one year. Once opened, check the label to see if refrigeration is necessary. Many products have expiration dates, which should be noted. Organize your pantry so that all foods are rotated and used within a year or less.

Make a plan of how to use available storage space. When building a pantry, shallow shelves are best; food is less likely to be "lost" when it can be seen easily. Lazy Susans or hinged shelves that swing out from the cupboard allow you to see and retrieve food from several angles.

- Store similar foods together with labels facing front.

- After purchasing new items, place them behind older ones of the same type.

- At least once a year, clean the cupboard and discard any rusted, damaged, or bloated cans.

- Store flour, rice, cereals, and other dry foods tightly covered to keep out moisture and prevent the spread of mealworms.

HOW LONG IS THE SHELF LIFE?

TIMES REFER TO unopened products. Always check expiration dates on packages. Use promptly after opening. Refrigerate when indicated.

Baking powder and soda 1 year

Cake, frosting, and cookie mixes 1 year

Canned meats, vegetables, fruits, soups, milks, gravies 1 year; refrigerate after opening

Cereals 6 months

Chocolate (chips and baking) 1 year

Coffee 1 year; refrigerate after opening

Flour 1 year

Frosting (canned) 8 months

Fruit (dried) 6 months

Gelatin (unflavored) 18 months

Herbs and spices (ground) 1 year; keep in a cool place; refrigerate red spices such as paprika

Honey, molasses, syrups 1 year

Jelly and jam 1 year

Milk (nonfat dry) 6 months

Oils 3 months; refrigerate if not using promptly after opening

Packaged crackers, cookies, bread crumbs 2 to 4 months

Pancake and piecrust mixes 6 months

Pasta and macaroni 1 year; store airtight after opening

Pickles and olives 1 year; refrigerate after opening

Puddings and gelatin mixes 6 months

Rice (white) 2 years

Root vegetables such as white and sweet potatoes, onions, squash 1 week at room temperature; store with plenty of air circulation in a dry, dark place

Shortening (solid) 8 months

Spices (whole) 1 year

Sugar (granulated) 2 years

Tea (instant) 1 year

Tea (loose and bags) 6 months

Vinegars 1 year

Yeast (active dry) follow package date

CANNING

Canning preserves food by heating it hot and long enough to destroy microorganisms and enzymes that may cause spoilage and changes in color, texture, flavor, and nutritive values. It is critical that the canning process be done correctly to prevent toxicity. Use only tempered glass jars with specially designed caps for canning.

Always follow the recipe and directions that come with canning equipment, jars, and lids. The consumer information service provided by the Department of Agriculture also gives advice on safe canning practices. Consult these sources before beginning to can.

Techniques

There are two methods of canning, depending upon the type of food to be preserved.

Acid Foods: These contain natural acid, though with different degrees of acidity. Acid foods include all fruits and fruit juices, tomatoes, jams, and preserves. Also in this category are foods to which acid has been added, including some pickles, relishes, and sauerkraut.

These foods can be canned safely at 212°F using a boiling-water bath. Special equipment is available, but preserving can also be done in any deep kettle with a rack and a tight-fitting lid. The rack should keep the jars at least 1 to 2 inches below the surface of the water. The jars must be placed so they do not touch each other during processing.

Low-Acid Foods: Almost all vegetables, meats, poultry, seafood, mushrooms, and soups are low in acid and need a temperature higher than 212°F for safe processing. Use a special steam-pressure canner, which heats to 240°F, a tight seal, and a lid with a safety valve, a vent, and a dial or weighted pressure gauge.

EQUIPMENT

Having the right kitchen equipment saves time and effort and is often essential to producing the right results from a recipe. High-quality kitchen equipment will give you many years of valuable service and will more than repay your investment. Start with the basics, then gradually build your kitchen around them.

POTS AND PANS

Cookware is made in a variety of materials; each has different characteristics and it is important to understand them before you buy. Many cooks purchase individual pots and pans in different materials to suit specific uses, rather than a full set in one material.

Aluminum: (moderate cost; recommended for all-purpose cooking): This versatile material is the most commonly used for cookware. It is made in different "gauges," which refer to the thickness of the metal—the lower the gauge number, the thicker the aluminum. Cast aluminum is extra thick and heavy.

Most aluminum cookware has a nonstick finish; some has anodized coatings to strengthen the aluminum, making it scratch and stick resistant and easier to clean.

ADVANTAGES: excellent heat conductor; relatively light to handle; easy to clean.

BASIC POTS AND PANS

If you are a beginning cook or stocking a kitchen for the first time, consider these essential pieces. Keep in mind your style of cooking, the amount of food you cook, and your storage space. Pots and pans are not the same thing. A pot has two small side handles while a pan has one long handle. The terms skillet and frypan are used interchangeably.

UTENSIL	USES
1-quart pan with lid	For heating canned soups, convenience foods; melting butter; cooking eggs; sauces
2- to 2½-quart pan with lid	For cooking fresh or frozen vegetables; heating canned foods, leftovers; cooking rice, hot cereals
5- or 6-quart pan/ Dutch oven	For pasta, stews, soups; braising; sauces; stir-frying
8- or 9-inch skillet with lid	For eggs, omelets; small-scale sautéing; grilling
10- to 12-inch skillet with lid	For most sautéing, braising, shallow panfrying
14- by 11-inch roasting pan	For roasting meats and poultry

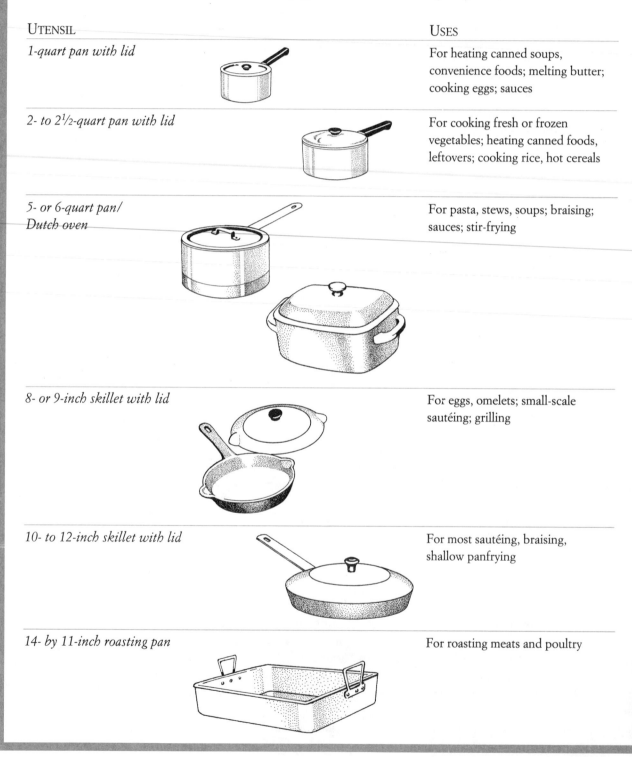

DISADVANTAGES: Unfinished aluminum can streak if put in the dishwasher, or pit from acidic foods; can discolor foods.

Stainless steel: (moderate to high cost; recommended for all-purpose cooking): Look for cookware that is a combination of stainless steel and other materials, such as aluminum, copper, and carbon steel; avoid imports made only of stainless steel, which by itself is not a good heat conductor. 18/10 is a high-quality grade in stainless steel combination cookware, which is available with a nonstick finish.

ADVANTAGES: exceptionally durable; smooth; scratch resistant; easy to clean.

DISADVANTAGES: possible high cost; needs to be combined with other metals for good heat conduction.

Copper: (high cost; recommended for browning and sauces): This is a superior cookware material. It reacts with certain foods, so must be lined with tin or stainless steel. Never cook or serve in unlined copper pots or pans.

ADVANTAGES: exceptionally good-looking; excellent heat conductor; durable.

DISADVANTAGES: needs frequent polishing; any cracks or scrapes in the lining mean the cookware must be relined.

Cast iron: (low to moderate cost; recommended for even browning, especially at high heat, and for long, low simmering): Cast iron needs an initial "seasoning"—a light, even coating of vegetable oil heated in a moderate oven for two hours, then wiped out. It should not be scoured or washed with strong detergents (see page 55).

Cast iron is available with a porcelain enamel coating inside and out for rust protection and easy care.

ADVANTAGES: retains and conducts heat evenly; strong; durable. Cooking in unlined cast iron adds iron to the diet.

DISADVANTAGES: heavy; rusts if not thoroughly dried; porcelain enamel is expensive and can chip or crack.

Heat-resistant glass and ceramic: (moderate cost; recommended for baking and microwaving): As this material heats slowly and unevenly, low to medium heat is best for top-of-the-range cooking.

ADVANTAGES: easy to clean; can be used directly from the refrigerator or freezer to the range top, in the oven or microwave, or for serving/storing.

DISADVANTAGES: hot spots at high heat; can be cumbersome; breakable.

Enamel on steel: (low to moderate cost; recommended for all-purpose cooking): Steel with porcelain enamel inside and out is used for both thin, low-cost cookware and high-quality pieces. Stainless steel rims prevent chipping. The material performs best on low to medium heat.

ADVANTAGES: attractive; easy to clean; stain resistant; doesn't react with foods or absorb odors or flavors.

DISADVANTAGES: thinner cookware may get hot spots and cook unevenly; can chip or crack.

KNIVES

No tool is more important in the kitchen than a good, sharp knife. Better quality knives are made of high-carbon no-stain steel. They have a keen and durable edge, can be sharpened easily, and won't rust or discolor. They are moderate to high in cost and should last a lifetime.

Stainless steel is typically used for less expensive knives. It is shiny and easy to clean, but because of its hardness, the blade is difficult to resharpen once dull.

Because good knives require maintenance to keep them sharp, some consumers like the convenience of serrated knives that never need sharpening.

These have little teeth that saw through food rather than cut. These knives *cannot* be sharpened. Although they stay sharp for a long time, once they are dull, they must be discarded. Never-need-sharpening knives are low to moderate in cost.

NONSTICK COOKWARE

Nonstick finishes on cookware are popular because they are easy to clean and allow you to cook with little or no fat.

New nonstick finishes are longer lasting and more durable than in the past. All kinds of cookware are available with nonstick finishes. The coatings may differ in formulation and thickness as well as in the way they are applied to cookware. They will not melt into foods or liquids; they are nontoxic and would not be harmful even if swallowed.

Before using nonstick cookware for the first time, season it by lightly rubbing the cooking surface with vegetable oil. Avoid putting nonstick cookware in the dishwasher as this removes the seasoning.

Most manufacturers recommend using plastic or wooden utensils on their nonstick cookware although some can be used with metal utensils.

☞ A forged blade rather than a stamped one.

☞ A full tang—the better the knife, the longer the tang (the part of the blade that extends into the handle). The knife should be triple riveted or permanently bonded to the handle.

☞ A sculpted handle designed for comfort and control during use. The knife should feel well balanced in your hand.

☞ A lifetime warranty—a quality knife is an investment.

"MAID" SERVICE

☞ Buy a coffeemaker with a timer, and wake up to fresh-brewed coffee.

GRINDING TIME

☞ Serious coffee lovers grind their favorite blend of beans at least once a day. A good grinder will grind beans ultrafine and will not leave large fragments.

How to Sharpen Knives

Keep knives sharp—dull ones can be both difficult and unsafe to use. You can maintain the sharp edge on a fine knife by giving it a few strokes at a 20-degree angle across a sharpening stone lubricated with a bit of vegetable oil or water, or across a sharpening steel at a 30-degree angle.

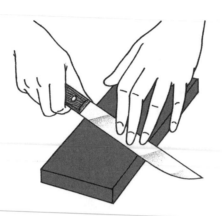

Once a knife edge is dull, it is best to have it professionally resharpened by a grinding service or at a cutlery store.

There is now a moderately priced three-stage electric sharpener that makes it easy to sharpen knives at home. Avoid using knife sharpeners attached to electric can openers.

BASIC SMALL APPLIANCES

Small electrical appliances offer convenient ways to prepare foods and save time. Here's a list of some basic small appliances.

Coffeemakers: While automatic drip coffeemakers are very popular, percolators are also used. Drip models come with cupcake or cone-shaped filter baskets in 8- to 12-cup capacities and compact 1-, 2-, and 4-cup models.

Look for these features in a coffeemaker:

- Automatic shutoff.
- Drip stop to interrupt the coffee flow when the carafe is removed (so you can pour a cup during the brew cycle).
- Programmable timer.
- Special cycle for making just a few cups.
- Coffee bean grinder.

Toaster and toaster oven: In addition to toasting bread, some wide-slot toasters also handle bagels and other breakfast foods. Cool touch exteriors protect against burns, and models with electronic controls ensure consistent toast color cycle after cycle.

Toaster ovens do not toast bread quite as well, but operate as miniovens for baking, broiling, and top browning. They are energy efficient and ideal for small cooking jobs.

Can opener: Some models are taller than standard size, or adjust to accommodate tall cans. A cutting assembly that removes for easy cleaning is important.

Blender: This is the best machine for blending liquids, pureeing, mixing drinks, and crushing ice. They are available with glass, plastic, or metal containers. Although many models have 12 to 14 speeds, 3 to 5 speeds are all that are necessary. More costly models with touch-pad controls are easier to clean than push-buttons.

Food processor: This machine can chop, slice, shred, grind, mix, and knead dough. Gourmet cooks and large families will need a full-size heavy-duty unit while a compact model or minichopper that handles small amounts might satisfy those with small families or limited cooking needs.

Mixer: Hand-held and stand mixers are the two choices. Hand mixers are portable and easy to store. They are perfect for light mixing jobs like cakes and whipped cream; some heavy-duty models can handle cookie dough.

Stand mixers are more powerful and can do all kinds of heavy mixing jobs, even knead bread dough. Because of their size and weight, stand mixers usually sit out on the counter.

Slow cooker: The bottom and sides of this cooker, also known as a crock pot, help to maintain a low, even temperature. The pots are ideal for stews, soups, and anything that requires long cooking times.

ESSENTIAL KNIVES

When buying a knife, always get the best quality you can afford. A few well-chosen knives will serve you well and prove a worthwhile investment. The knives shown below are standard equipment in most well-stocked kitchens.

TYPE	USES
8- or 10-inch chef's knife	For chopping and cutting—the most commonly used kitchen knife
paring knife	For peeling and small cutting jobs
serrated or bread knife	For slicing bread, delicate cake, and tomatoes
boning knife	For boning meats, poultry, and some seafood
carving or slicing knife	For carving cooked meats and poultry
cleaver	For large chopping jobs

THE CUTTING EDGE

☞ To keep knives sharp and prevent accidents, store knives in a wooden knife block, on a magnetic rack, or in a partitioned drawer.

☞ Hand wash knives and dry them immediately. Avoid washing knives in the dishwasher.

☞ Cut only on a wooden or plastic cutting board.

☞ Never use a knife for nonfood purposes like opening a box or prying off a jar lid.

SHARPER SCISSORS AND SHEARS

☞ To hone a dull scissors edge, use an aluminum oxide bench stone (available at hardware stores). Put a little household lubricating oil on the stone, then place the open scissors blade on the stone's coarsest face. Slant the blade slightly so that it tips back toward the stone at a 10° angle. Draw the scissors blade firmly from end to end on the stone until the edge has been sharpened. Turn the scissors and repeat with the other blade. If the scissors still do not cut smoothly, tighten the screw that holds the blades together.

USEFUL COOKING UTENSILS

*THERE ARE SO MANY DIFFERENT cooking utensils that not even
the largest kitchen could hold them all. It is best to outfit your kitchen slowly
with high-quality durable items as your needs and cooking interests
develop. Consider the following:*

CUTTING, PEELING, AND GRATING

6- to 7-inch chef's knife	serrated bread knife	boning knife	poultry shears	4-sided grater
serrated utility knife	paring knife	knife sharpener or sharpening steel	swivel vegetable peeler	cutting board
	carving knife	kitchen shears	can opener	

MICROWAVE EQUIPMENT AND UTENSILS

glass-ceramic cookware	microwave-safe cooking rack	microwave-safe glass or plastic storage containers	microwave-safe plastic colander	plastic wrap
microwave-safe dinnerware	microwave-safe glass bakeware, bowls, casseroles, custard cups, measures	microwave-safe plastic bowls, casseroles, bakeware, measures, spoons	microwave thermometer	waxed paper
microwave browning dish			paper plates	wooden spoons
			paper towels	

MIXING AND MEASURING

blender	graduated measuring cups for dry ingredients	ladle	slotted metal cooking spoon	wire whisk
electric mixer		rubber spatula	measuring spoons	mixing bowls
food processor	liquid measuring cups (1, 2, 4 cups)	ruler	wooden spoon	
		large metal cooking spoon		

OTHER USEFUL COOKWARE

2-tined fork	Dutch oven (5- to 8-quart)	strainer or sieve	potato masher	steamer
large and small metal spatula	saucepot (5- to 8-quart)	colander	meat thermometer	wire rack
skillets (10", 12")	13" by 9" glass and metal baking pans	salad spinner	omelet pan	metal tongs
saucepans (1, 2, 3 quarts)	steamer rack	heat-and-serve covered casseroles (2, 3-quarts)	ramekins	custard cups
		large roasting pan	soufflé dish	
			springform pan	

BASICS FOR BAKERS

Baking (cooking with dry heat) is a delicate art, and not one that can be successfully undertaken without the proper equipment. The following tools will allow you to create and embellish dishes both from scratch and from mixes.

Cake pans A set of two 8-inch round pans, a set of two 9-inch round pans, two 8-inch rectangular pans, a 10-inch tube pan, and a 9-inch springform pan with bundt insert, all in sturdy aluminum

Cake tester Metal with plastic handle

Cookie cutters Metal or plastic, in assorted sizes

Cookie press With several cutter shapes

Cookie sheets At least 2 large, flat, in aluminum, shiny, insulated, or with a nonstick finish

Cooling wire rack Large, stainless steel or aluminum

Decorating tubes and pastry bag

Flour sifter Stainless steel or heavy plastic, with rotary crank

Jelly roll pan Sturdy aluminum, 15½ by 10½ by 1 inch

Loaf pans Two in aluminum or glass, preferably with nonstick finish, 8¼ by 4½ by 2½ inches or 9 by 5 by 3 inches

Muffin pan Aluminum, shiny or with nonstick finish, in 12-mold size

Offset spatula For icing

Pastry blender Sturdy handle, steel wires

Pastry board Marble or wood

Pastry brush

Pastry cloth Canvas

Pastry cutter

Pastry wheel Plain edge for trimming; fluted for decorative strips

Pie bird Ceramic

Pie pans 8- or 9-inch, glass or aluminum

Pie weights Small; metal or ceramic

Pizza pan Aluminum or nonstick finish

Rolling pin Hardwood, marble, or ceramic

Spatula Metal

BAKING TIP

☞ When using a glass baking dish, lower the oven temperature by 25°F, because glass retains heat longer than metal.

HANDLE WITH CARE

- Read and follow all manufacturers' instructions for cookware and appliances.

- Do not use electrical appliances when floor or counters are wet.

- Unplug small appliances when you're not using them. Disconnect from the wall outlet before unplugging the cord from the appliance.

- Use a separate grounded electrical circuit for each major appliance.

- Never allow small children to touch or operate kitchen appliances.

- Keep a working fire extinguisher and smoke detector in the kitchen (see page 287).

☞ Put pots and pans on similar size burners. Small pots on big burners waste energy and are a safety hazard.

☞ Choose the right size; pots that are too big take an unnecessarily long time to heat.

APPLIANCE TIPS

☞ Never inspect or work on an appliance until it is unplugged.

☞ Keep all appliances clean.

☞ Do not allow grease buildup on range burners.

☞ Periodically clean the condenser coils of your refrigerator.

☞ Read the manufacturer's directions for all appliances, and keep them in one accessible place.

☞ If an appliance doesn't work, check to make sure it is plugged in and all controls are properly set before calling for service.

**MICROWAVE FEATURES
TO CONSIDER**

☞ Automatic defrost system.

☞ Programming control: an automatic sequence of different power levels and cooking times.

☞ Temperature probe: works like a thermometer. When the desired temperature is reached, the oven turns off.

☞ Preprogrammed or sensor cooking for automatic cooking/reheating of many foods, even popcorn and pizza.

APPLIANCES

One of the most important purchases you make for your home is a major appliance. Here are some tips:

- Do your research ahead of time. You generally know in advance when an appliance needs replacing, so don't buy in a hurry.

- Talk to friends about their experiences, with various brands, good or bad.

- Check the space available for the appliance as well as door and hallway clearances for delivery.

- Decide what capacity or size you need.

- Decide what special features you want and will really use.

- Ask the dealer to show you the use and care manual for the appliance you are interested in. Look it over *before* making your purchase.

- Ask about the warranty. What is covered and for how long?

- Ask about delivery charges and servicing availability.

Once the appliance is in your home, try each feature and control. Most defects show up during the first few uses and you want to know of any problems before the warranty expires.

Ranges, Ovens, and Cook Tops

There have been many technological developments reflected in the design of cooking appliances.

Ranges: A range is a freestanding unit that combines a cooking surface with an oven. Models that drop in and slide into a countertop provide a built-in look. Some ranges have an additional oven above the cooking surface. Ranges are now available with a gas cooking surface and an electric oven. New ranges are now easier to clean. All but the least expensive models have self-cleaning ovens.

Electronic controls offer temperature-setting accuracy. There is a big choice in surface cooking options (see opposite).

Wall ovens: These come in single- and double-oven models. Electronic controls and self-cleaning ovens are available. Some models offer conventional/convection cooking. Convection ovens use a fan to circulate hot air in the oven for faster, more even cooking.

Cooking surfaces: Built into the kitchen counter, they offer a great deal of flexibility in kitchen design. Cook tops are available with a variety of surface-cooking options (see opposite).

Microwave Ovens

A microwave's cooking power is measured in output wattage, which ranges from 500 watts to 1,050 watts. Higher-wattage ovens cook foods faster than lower-wattage ovens. Low-wattage ovens (under 700 watts) are suitable for defrosting and reheating foods. Microwaves range in size from compact (with interiors of .4 cubic feet) to full size (with 1.6 cubic feet).

If you intend to cook with your microwave oven, choose a high-power full- or midsize oven.

A convection/microwave oven can be used as a microwave oven alone, convection oven alone, or as a combination oven. It offers the speed of microwave cooking and the browning and crisping of convection.

Microwave ovens are also available in units that take the place of a range hood, as part of a double-wall oven, and as the upper oven in a double-oven range.

Refrigerators

Some top- and bottom-mount refrigerators are equipped with doors and handles whose swing can be reversed with a few basic tools. This is particularly useful if you plan to move and take the refrigerator with you. Look for these other items:

Energy efficiency: Look for the yellow-and-black Energy-Guide label on the refrigerator. The Guide will give you the estimated average annual operating cost. Compare these with costs for models of the same size and

SURFACE-COOKING OPTIONS

Given below are some of the pluses and minuses of various cook-top features, which you should keep in mind before choosing a unit.

TYPE	ADVANTAGES	DISADVANTAGES
GAS		
Conventional Burner	Generally inexpensive to buy. Easy to control heat. Any type of cookware can be used.	Difficult to clean.
Sealed Burner	Prevents food from spilling beneath range top for easy cleaning. Any type of cookware can be used.	Only one burner may be designed for cooking on low heat.
ELECTRIC		
Coil Element	Least expensive to buy. Any type of cookware can be used.	Less responsive than gas. Difficult to clean.
Solid Disk Element (Cast Iron)	Provides very even heat. Easy to clean.	Can discolor. Very slowest to heat up and cool down. Must be used with flat-bottomed cookware.
Glass Ceramic (Smooth Top)	Very easy to clean.	Must be used with flat-bottomed cookware.
Radiant Element	Least expensive.	More expensive than electric elements to purchase.
Halogen Element	Glows brightly. Heats quickly.	Expensive to purchase.
Induction	Coils create a magnetic field with cookware so food gets hot but the surface stays cool. Fastest type of cooking surface. Very responsive. Safe. Energy efficient.	Very expensive. Works only with magnetic metal cookware (iron and steel). Currently available only on cook tops.
Modular (Changeable Plug-In Modules)	Easy to change cooking modes such as coil element, smooth-top grill, griddle.	Modules must be stored when not in use.

type. Today's refrigerators are the most energy efficient ever built. A refrigerator that costs less to run, but has a higher purchase price may be the better buy.

Features:

- Adjustable shelves/bins for maximum storage flexibility.
- Automatic ice makers.
- Clear plastic or "crystal" bins.
- Dispensers for crushed ice, cubes, and water.
- Electronic systems to monitor functions.
- Extra-deep door shelves.
- Humidity controls on crispers.
- Rollers allow the refrigerator to be moved easily for cleaning.
- Tempered glass shelves that hold spills (in full or split width).

These are the choices in refrigerator styles:

Top mount: This model has two doors with the freezer on top. Available in a wide range of models and sizes. Available with manual defrost, cycle defrost (which means the freezer must be manually defrosted), and no-frost.

Side-by-side: This style has two doors with full-length refrigerator and freezer sections. It also comes in built-in models that fit flush to cabinets. It has more total freezer space than other styles and more up-front visibility of food. The doors require less aisle space for opening.

The style costs more to buy and operate than a top-mount and narrow shelves in the smaller capacity sizes may limit storage of bulky or wide items. All are no-frost.

Bottom mount: This model has two doors with a freezer at the bottom. It is convenient as more of the fresh food space is at eye level, but requires stooping to get at the freezer. All are no-frost.

Single door: This has one outside door with a small inner freezer compartment for short-term storage only. It is the least costly to buy and operate and has limited capacity. All must be manually defrosted.

OVEN EFFICIENCY

☞ Cook more than one food at once, such as a roast and baked potatoes.

☞ Preheat only when necessary and for no longer than needed.

☞ There's no need to preheat the oven for large roasts and other long-cooking foods.

☞ Avoid frequent door openings. They waste energy, allow heat to escape, and result in longer cooking times.

☞ Turn off the oven a few minutes before the cooking time is over. Residual heat will allow the food to continue cooking.

Freezers

Freezers are fairly simple units designed to keep food at 0°F or below. For maximum cooling efficiency, keep a freezer close to full but avoid overloading (see pages 128–129). Choose a model that does not greatly exceed your storage needs.

Upright freezers permit more food to be visible, but they are less efficient as cold air is lost each time the door is opened. They are available with manual defrost and no-frost.

Chest freezers with several bins and shelves can be almost as convenient as upright models, but they take up more floor space. All must be manually defrosted.

No-frost freezers are more expensive to buy and operate, but they are much more convenient. A hidden advantage of manual defrost is that it forces you to take an inventory of freezer contents.

Automatic Dishwashers

When it comes to convenience and saving time, it is hard to beat a dishwasher. Prerinsing is not necessary with today's dishwashers due to better technology.

When shopping, check the Energy-Guide label on the dishwasher for the estimated annual operating cost. Look for an energy-efficient model.

Features:

- Adjustable racks with flexible loading.
- Delay start.
- Electronic control for cycle readout.
- Electronic system to diagnose problems.
- Flush control panels that blend with your kitchen cabinetry.
- Hot-water temperature booster.
- No-heat drying option.
- Special cycles for pots and pans, light wash, or rinse and hold.
- Special insulation for quiet operation.

TABLEWARE

To make the most of your tableware, choose patterns that look good together and that are versatile enough to be dressed up or down according to the occasion. Always look at tableware together in a place setting before you buy it.

CHINA

The word "china" is used as a convenient shorthand for any ceramic dinnerware. It's common to choose a set of good china, usually bone china or porcelain, and a set of everyday dinnerware, usually in stoneware or earthenware. All are generally dishwasher safe except those with decorations over the glazing that are not fired on. Check with the manufacturer or test-wash a piece (see pages 55–56).

Bone china: This fine china, made with bone ash, is prized for its translucency and whiteness; it is usually expensive.

Porcelain: This is a hard, translucent china similar to bone china, known for its richness of pattern. It's usually safe to put porcelain in dishwashers, but confirm this with the manufacturer.

Stoneware: Less expensive than bone china and porcelain, this hard, opaque china holds heat well, so it makes good serving and dinnerware. Colors tend to be earthy. Stoneware is safe in dishwashers and microwave ovens. It can go from oven to table to refrigerator and is usually inexpensive.

Ironstone: This is a hard, heavy white pottery similar to stoneware, and moderately priced.

Earthenware: This inexpensive pottery is not as strong as other types of china. Its lower firing temperature permits more brilliantly colored glazes, making unusual patterns possible.

FLATWARE

Sterling, silver plate, and stainless-steel flatware (in descending order of cost) are all beautiful and durable.

Serving pieces needn't match flatware in either pattern or material. You can mix ornate place settings and simple serving pieces, or the other way around.

Sterling

Solid sterling silver offers luxury plus the value of a precious commodity. Prices vary depending on the pattern's detailing, complexity of handwork, and silver content.

Sterling won't wear out. If you use it regularly, you will have to polish it only rarely, and it is dishwasher-safe. But load the basket carefully so the silver isn't crowded. Be sure to remove the flatware before the dry cycle and dry by hand if hard water spotting is a problem. The intense heat can loosen the blades from some older hollow-handle knives.

Silver Plate

Silver plate has the look of solid sterling, and is an economical alternative when you don't want to pay sterling prices.

Some brands have a very thick coating of silver, measured in microns, over the undermetal (usually nickel and steel). Others have a thinner coat. The thicker coating looks better and lasts longer.

Look for a manufacturer's warranty that utensils are dishwasher-safe. Avoid putting silver plate with worn spots where the base metal is exposed in dishwashers. This intensifies the deterioration of the silver coating. Contact between silver and stainless steel items in the dishwasher can cause pitting. Make sure these materials do not touch especially in the flatware basket.

METAL DETECTOR

☞ Overglazed metallic-trim china can't go into a microwave oven or dishwasher, so it isn't as versatile as other china.

CARING FOR BREAKABLES

☞ To avoid chipping precious china and crystal, place a kitchen towel in the bottom of the sink before hand-washing them.

Stainless Steel

Prices range widely for stainless-steel flatware. Better pieces usually have more chromium for stain resistance and more nickel for luster and strength. Utensils with a numerical rating of 18/8, for example, have 18 percent chromium and 8 percent nickel and are considered durable. Stainless-steel flatware is dish-washer-safe, and good-quality brands last many years.

Recent innovations have introduced color in stainless-steel flatware. Anodizing, lacquer, cloisonné, or semiprecious stones often adorn handles.

GLASSWARE

Clarity and flawlessness are marks of high-quality glassware. Both attributes are enhanced when lead is added to the formula—up to a maximum of about 32 percent. If you opt for a cut-glass pattern, hand cutting is preferred to machine cutting, though it is more costly.

While all kinds of glasses are available for all kinds of drinks, the only necessary types are tall and short tumblers and stemmed wineglasses. In general, choose glasses with a graceful shape that are comfortable to hold.

TRADITIONAL PLACE SETTING

THE STANDARD FORMAL FIVE-PIECE place setting consists of a dinner plate, a salad/dessert plate, a bread and butter plate, and a cup and saucer. A table setting, however, can have many variations. The one below is a traditional formal arrangement, including a service plate, wine- and water glasses, and utensils for several courses.

SALAD PLATE · DESSERT FORK · DESSERT SPOON · WATER GLASS · WINEGLASS · NAPKIN · SALAD FORK · PLACE FORK · SOUP BOWL · SERVICE PLATE · DINNER PLATE · PLACE KNIFE · SOUP SPOON · TEA SPOON

TABLEWARE GLOSSARY

*F*ROM SIMPLE TO SPECIALIZED, HERE *is a range of table and serving pieces.*

PLACE FORK   SALAD FORK   PLACE KNIFE   PLACE SPOON   SOUP SPOON   TEA SPOON   BUTTER SPREADER   BUTTER KNIFE   FISH FORK   FISH KNIFE   COCKTAIL FORK

SERVING FORK   GRAVY LADLE   CAKE KNIFE   PIE SERVER   PASTA SERVER   LASAGNA SERVER

DESSERT FORK   DESSERT SPOON   ICED-TEA SPOON   DEMITASSE SPOON   CARVING KNIFE   CARVING FORK   CHEESE KNIFE

Glassware Glossary

The following are the most common types of glasses and are fine for a range of drinks.

SHORT TUMBLER

A 5- or 6-ounce capacity with straight or slightly sloping sides. Used for fruit juices, water, old-fashioneds, whiskey on the rocks, and soft drinks.

TALL TUMBLER

A 10- to 12-ounce capacity with straight or slightly sloping sides. Used for drinks mixed with fruit juices, exotic tropical drinks, highballs, soft drinks, iced tea, and other drinks that require lots of ice cubes.

WINEGLASS (WHITE)

About 4-ounce capacity on a stemmed base. The typical white wineglass has a smaller bowl and taller stem, so the warmth of your hand won't reach the bowl and destroy the wine's crisp flavor.

WINEGLASS (RED)

Should be large enough to be filled only one-third full, so the wine can be swirled to bring out its full flavor.

COCKTAIL GLASS

About 4-ounce capacity, with a wide-rimmed top and a stemmed base. Used for martinis, Manhattans, and other mixed cocktails.

TALL FLUTE OR TULIP GLASS

About 4-ounce capacity, with a tall, narrow bowl on a stemmed base. Used for Champagne, sparkling wines, and Champagne cocktails.

LIQUEUR GLASS

About 1½-ounce capacity on a short-stemmed base. Used for small amounts of liqueurs and cordials.

BRANDY SNIFTER

Varying capacity with large, round, wide-bottom bowl that narrows to a slightly inverted rim and a short-stemmed base. Made to be cradled in the hand so that the brandy may be warmed and swirled to release its bouquet.

THE ART OF NAPKIN FOLDING

FOLLOW THESE STEPS for an elegant "butterfly."

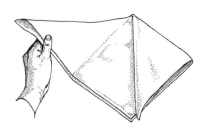 

1. Form a triangle from an open square napkin. Fold the right corner to the center. Take the left corner to the center, making a diamond.

2. Keeping the loose points at the bottom, turn the napkin over. Then fold downward in half to form a triangle.

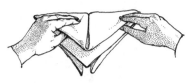 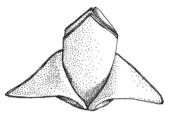

3. Tuck the right corner into the left. Stand the napkin up; turn it around, then turn the petals down.

4 You now have a butterfly.

Stemmed glasses vary in size and shape according to the type of drink to be served. An all-purpose glass for red and white wine, a Champagne flute, and a water goblet are the three most useful types.

You may want to opt for at least two wineglasses: one for red and one for white wine.

Caring for Fine Crystal

Hand washing is best for all crystal, especially for uncut and gold-trimmed glasses. Rinse glasses thoroughly to remove soap. Although you can wash heavy crystal in a dishwasher, place it only in the top section and make sure glasses don't touch.

Since long-standing moisture may encourage mold or bacterial growth, dry each glass thoroughly.

When wine has left sediment in a decanter, fill it with a room-temperature solution of half water/half vinegar and allow it to soak. A bit of rice can be added to provide mild abrasion. If you gently swish it around, it won't scratch the crystal.

Avoid drastic temperature changes when handling crystal. Extreme changes may cause cracks.

MIX AND MATCH

☞ Barware and stemware don't have to match. Cordial glasses and brandy snifters also do not have to match your stemware pattern.

PERFECT SETTINGS

☞ Use ornate silver with contemporary linens and china for unusual settings.

☞ Try a Victorian cookie box or bonbon dish to hold cheese sticks or vegetables on the dinner table.

☞ For a child's birthday, cover the table with Sunday comics. Use Chinese newspapers for a Chinese feast.

☞ Make a tablecloth out of a designer sheet or a folk-art rug. Stitch napkins from sheeting.

☞ Make a centerpiece of dimestore toys or small collectibles like a group of circus animals or glass balls.

ENTERTAINING

The key to throwing a successful party is planning. Whether the party is large or small, casual or formal, you must plan in advance:

- Invitations, whether issued by hand, mail, or telephone, should always be specific about time, date, and dress.

- To keep track of numbers, request an R.S.V.P. by a specific date.

- Concentrate on planning food and beverages. Be realistic as to your time, cooking ability, and budget. Unless you're hosting a kitchen party with a few close friends, it is best to go with reliable favorites. Don't attempt complicated new recipes for guests.

- Decorations set the stage, but they need not be elaborate. Candles and fresh flowers are always reliable.

- Plan music, lighting, and games. Conceptualize the party from beginning to end. Details often make the difference between a good party and a great one.

PARTIES FOR ADULTS

There are myriad occasions for adult parties from anniversaries to holidays. Each calls for different plans, but there are some general guidelines:

- For a cocktail party, be sure to provide plenty of food for nibbling.

- For large groups, if possible, set up two bars so guests don't jam one area.

- Always offer nonalcoholic beverages in addition to alcohol.

- Allow about 30 minutes to 1 hour for drinks if a full meal is to be served.

PARTY EXTRAS THAT MAKE A DIFFERENCE

- ☞ Use real linen, china, and flatware.
- ☞ Make personal place cards for seated meals.
- ☞ Spend time with each and every guest. Plan potential topics of conversation if guests don't know each other well.
- ☞ Be sure to introduce newcomers to at least two guests before leaving them alone.
- ☞ Send guests home with a tiny party favor such as a mini-box of home-baked cookies or a single flower.
- ☞ Ask a good friend to listen to your party plans and to help you, if necessary. Offer to return the favor.
- ☞ Don't work so hard that you can't be a guest at your own party.

PARTIES FOR TEENAGERS

Planned independence guarantees successful teenage parties. Plan carefully with your teen, then be home and occasionally in evidence, but let the teen be the host.

- Provide lots of things to do: music, games, dancing, yard sports, videos. It's hard to know which will be the hit of the party.

- Make plenty of food, especially food guests can put together themselves. Try sandwich fixings and oversize rolls, chili with a dozen condiments, or top-your-own pizzas.

- Be creative with beverages. Fruity, highly garnished punches are festive, but also have an array of soft drinks on hand. Be firm on the rule for no alcohol.

- Warn neighbors ahead of time that music may be loud, particularly if the party is outdoors.

PARTIES FOR CHILDREN

Include the guest of honor or "host" in the planning. Listen carefully to his or her wishes, but know the child. A shy child may love the idea of a big birthday bash but will probably be happier with a smaller party with a few good friends.

- Have the host draw the invitations.

- Childproof the party area. Roll up rugs or move furniture as needed.

- Kids love to participate. Supply a sturdy white paper tablecloth, lots of glitter, and washable paints, then have the guests make the table decor. Leave the cupcakes unfrosted, and set out an array of icings and sprinkles. Provide cups full of ice cream, then let the guests garnish their own.

- Make sure at least one adult is in the party room at all times. Accidents or mishaps can occur very quickly.

- Set firm time limits. Attention spans are short, and it's better to end before guests get cranky.

- Have inexpensive party favors for guests to take home.

- Take photographs.

PLANNING A BIG PARTY

At one time or another, everyone hosts a big party, whether it's a wedding reception, anniversary party, or holiday open house for the office. This kind of party may be intimidating, but careful planning makes it easier to pull off.

- Think the party through, and invite only as many as can be accommodated by

PARTY FAVORS

☛ Good favors include inexpensive balloons, small flowering plants and, in the autumn, tiny pumpkin jack-o'-lanterns.

PARTY TIMETABLE

Use this timetable as a checklist to plan a big party.

FOUR WEEKS AHEAD

- Mail or deliver the invitations. Do not rely on the telephone or word of mouth.

- Keep a written guest list.

- Plan the menu.

- Check on cooking and serving equipment. Rent or buy what may be needed.

- If needed, arrange for help with parking and rent coat racks.

THREE WEEKS AHEAD

- Shop for nonperishables and disposable items.

- Buy liquor, nonalcoholic beverages, and mixers.

- Make a mental plan for traffic flow and table service.

- Check to make sure linens are clean and ironed.

- Order any special grocery or butcher items.

TWO WEEKS AHEAD

- Cook and freeze foods such as desserts, breads, and casseroles.

- Check the condition of the garden if the party is to be outdoors.

- Do any major housecleaning.

- Polish silver if needed.

- Begin storing ice in the freezer (if not planning to purchase).

- Order flowers.

TWO DAYS AHEAD

- Set the buffet table.

- Set up the bar.

- Set up the music.

- Clean the rooms where the party will be held, and rearrange furniture as necessary.

- Begin making food or portions of recipes such as pasta or potato salads, crudité dips, and some desserts.

- Post a last-minute itemized checklist in a central kitchen location.

ONE DAY AHEAD

- Shop for perishable foods.

- Do bulk of cooking.

- Pick up and arrange flowers.

- Call all helpers and give explicit instructions.

- Make the punch base.

- Draw a timetable of what needs to be cooked and served when.

DAY OF THE PARTY

- Finish cooking.

- Arrange ice and fruit for the bar.

To prevent over- or underbuying, use these estimates for the typical adult-size portions:

- Bone-in meat, poultry, or fish: 6 to 8 ounces.

- Boneless meat, poultry, or fish: 3 to 4 ounces.

- Cheese: 1½ ounces.

- Cooked rice or pasta: ½ to ¾ cup.

- Cooked vegetables: ½ to ¾ cup.

- Raw vegetables or salad greens: 1 cup.

- Raw fruit: 1 cup.

- Salad dressing: 2 to 3 teaspoons.

your budget—and space. You don't want to jam 30 people into a 15' x 12' living room.

- Consider parking, restrooms, coat storage, and other needs of a large group. Arrange for some chairs, but you needn't have one for every guest.

- Keep food and drink simple.

- Plan for enough food. It's better to have too much food than too little.

- If necessary, hire help (teenagers or professionals) for kitchen preparation, serving, and cleanup. Include this in the budget. Only those of legal drinking age can bartend.

- Rent any necessary glasses, tableware, and serving equipment.

- Shop at outlet stores for paper goods.

- Choose appropriate music at a listening level to enhance but not dominate conversation.

- If absolutely necessary, have a separate well-vented area for die-hard smokers.

- Take photographs.

Menu Planning

For a large party, buffet service is easiest. Foods can be prepared ahead and served with minimum last-minute fussing. Consider foods that can be served at room temperature. These are easiest to handle and they stay at peak flavor. Avoid delicate hot sauces and soufflés. Opt for roasts, hams, and turkeys that serve large numbers and are attractive, appealing, and easy to manage. If guests are going to have to eat standing up or with plates on their laps, precut meats so knives won't be necessary.

- Make several salads ahead of time. If the budget allows, you can buy salads at a high-quality take-out store or delicatessen. These are also good items for friends to bring if they offer.

- Put out rolls and an array of condiments, such as relishes, and pickles and olives.

- Self-serve finger desserts are easiest to manage. Cookies, petit fours, tartlets, and brownies are good choices, as is fresh fruit such as grapes, apples, and orange slices. Avoid frozen desserts.

PLANNING A SMALL
DINNER PARTY

These days, most people host small dinner parties without professional help, so simple preparation and presentation are essential. Invite only as many as can be seated comfortably at a single table. Usually, six or eight is a manageable number.

- Plan 1 or 2 hors d'oeuvres to be served with drinks. One should be simple and light.

- Plan the menu for ease of preparation, minimum last-minute work, and general appeal. Serve dishes you know you do well. Avoid delicate sauces and tricky garnishing.

- Be sure there is enough oven and stovetop space for cooking.

- Plan the seating arrangement in advance and direct guests to their places or have place cards.

UNCORKING CHAMPAGNE

1. Hold the bottle in one hand and remove the wire muzzle with the other.

2. Tilt the bottle slightly and hold the cork firmly while rotating the bottle.

3. Pull the bottle down gently and slowly to reduce internal pressure. The cork will come out with a soft "pop." There should not be a loud explosion at uncorking.

- Keep the first course simple, such as a salad or soup that can be prepared in advance.
- For an outdoor grilling or a kitchen party, let guests participate in some food preparation.
- Assemble plates in the kitchen or serve food family-style at the table.

PARTY IDEAS ON A BUDGET

Breakfast: An easy inexpensive meal for entertaining small groups of early risers. Offer a selection of cereals, fresh muffins, and fruits as well as juices and coffee.

Brunch: An informal meal for groups of mixed ages and interests; good for a buffet with make-ahead casseroles, breads, and fruits. Try organizing it around a theme, such as Creole.

Tea: An old-fashioned custom enjoying a revival and an easy meal to make ahead and serve. Small sandwiches are simple to prepare, and finger desserts can be purchased from a bakery. Concentrate on quality tea service and attractive presentation. Use good linens and silver. Try a Victorian theme with lots of ribbons and lace.

Cocktail party: An occasion for plenty of attractive finger food to be passed around and laid out on tables. Use a bartender to control alcohol consumption and offer nonalcohol alternatives. Enlist someone to monitor cleanup of glasses and plates if it's a large party. Indicate definite beginning and ending hours.

Picnic: An occasion for easily transportable foods such as salads and cold meats. Take plenty of ice or coolers to keep food fresh. Remember to pack trash bags for cleanup.

Potluck: An easy meal; the host organizes the menu and assigns dishes to each guest. Noncooks can bring beverages, flowers, or bakery desserts. The host provides all serving and eating utensils. Service should be buffet-style.

After-event supper: A meal to follow the theater, Christmas caroling, or a game.

Keep it informal and relaxed. Casseroles or sandwiches and salads are appropriate. Serve family- or buffet-style.

SETTING UP A BAR

Bar needs vary greatly according to the size, makeup, and budget of a party. The general rule of thumb is 1½ ounces (1 jigger) hard liquor and 3 or 4 ounces of wine equal one cocktail serving. Most quality liquor stores allow returns of unopened bottles, providing wine has not been refrigerated, so open a bottle only when needed.

If you are serving only wine, have red, white, sparkling, and perhaps blush. If wine is part of a more complete bar set-up, white wine is the most commonly requested.

Every bar should have an interesting supply of soft drinks, bottled and flavored waters, and fruit or vegetable juices.

Liqueurs are usually served after dinner. Brandy and cognac are the most common types. Fruit, coffee, and herbal flavors are also popular. The best-quality liqueurs can be expensive but have almost unlimited shelf life.

Wine: Tradition says that white wine goes with white meats such as poultry, fish, and seafood, that red wine accompanies meats and richly sauced dishes, and that blush and sparkling wines are served with anything. These days, the rules are less strict. The best guide is your own taste.

- In general, light wines, both white and red, best complement light and delicate foods. Bolder wines of both colors stand up better to richer, more assertive foods.

- Red wines are generally best when uncorked and allowed to "breathe" for about fifteen minutes before serving at room temperature. The older the wine, the less breathing time it needs.

BAR TIPS

☞ If possible, chill cocktail and beer glasses ahead of time.

☞ Handle glasses by the stem to avoid leaving fingermarks and warming the contents.

☞ Add carbonated beverages at the last minute, even to punches.

☞ To avoid spills, don't fill glasses to the brim.

☞ Keep a kitchen towel handy. Making drinks can be messy.

☞ Don't overserve.

☞ Never allow an inebriated guest to drive a car.

THE WELL-STOCKED BAR

THERE ARE NO rules when it comes to stocking a bar. Follow your preferences and those of your most frequent guests. Stock your bar with the following items and you should be able to handle any occasion.

WINE TIPS

☞ Acidic foods such as salad with vinaigrette dressing are best served between wine courses. The acids may fight—rather than complement—the wine.

☞ When cooking with wine, use one you would also enjoy drinking.

☞ When pouring red wine into another container, be sure to leave any sediment in the bottom of the bottle.

☞ White, blush, and sparkling wines should generally be served chilled soon after uncorking.

☞ Blush wines are considered to be rather light.

☞ Champagne goes with almost anything. It's also served as an aperitif and a dessert wine.

ALCOHOL

Beer	Gin	Sherry (dry and sweet)	Vermouth (dry and sweet)
Blended whiskey	Liqueurs: coffee, orange, herbal	Sour mash whiskey	Vodka
Bourbon	Rum	Tequila	Wine (red, white, blush, and sparkling)
Brandy	Scotch		
Champagne			

MIXERS

Club soda	Sparkling and still waters (flavored and plain)	Tomato or seasoned vegetable juice
Fruit juice		
Soft drinks		Tonic water

GARNISHES AND FLAVORINGS

Angostura bitters, for Manhattans and Old-fashioneds	Ice (preferably coarsely crushed)
Citrus, whole, slices, wedges, or peels (lemon, lime, and orange)	Maraschino cherries, for Manhattans and Old-fashioneds
Coarse salt, for Margaritas	Olives, for Martinis
Cocktail onions, for Gibsons	Simple syrup, for sweet cocktails and punches
Cream of coconut, for Piña Coladas	Worcestershire, for Bloody Marys
Hot-pepper sauce, for Bloody Marys	

EQUIPMENT

Blender	Cocktail napkins	Cutting board	Jigger
Bottle opener	Cocktail shaker or pitcher	Dish towel	Paring knife, for fruit zests
Citrus squeezer		Drink stirrers	Strainer
Coasters	Corkscrew	Ice bucket	

CHAPTER 5

DECORATING AND DESIGN

*Front-Wheel-Dri... ...ools, Upholstered Furniture, Your C... ...How to Turn Bed Sheets into Curt... ...HANDY TIPS: For Buffing Wood Flo... ...king Rooms Look Larger, Ironing P... ...ating a ☞MONEY-SAVING HINTS: How to Turn Bed Sheets into Curtains, Save on Car Repairs, Buy Produce, Choose Carpeting ☞HANDY TIPS: For Buffing Wood Floors, Preventing Carpet Dents, Unsticking Stacked Glasses, Making Rooms Look Larger, Ironing Pleated Skirts, Arranging Flowers, Jump-Starting a Car, Cleaning Tile Grout, Creating a Home Office, Fixing a Leaky Faucet ☞STEP-BY-STEP GUIDES: To Checkbook Security ☞*DOING IT YOURSELF: *Learning the basics: all about color, style, and furniture arrangement. Four steps to success. Home decorating checklist: What to ask before you start. How to make a floor plan. Where to put light fixtures. Classic lamp-shade styles. How to hire professional help.* ☞PAINTING: *All about paint: How to choose a color. Preparing a room. Buying the best brushes, pads, and rollers. Step-by-step stenciling. Easy touch-ups and cleanup tips.* ☞WALL COVERINGS: *All about wallpaper, from vinyl to Mylar. Hanging prepasted paper step by step. Decorating tips: creating decorative effects and enhancing space.* ☞WINDOW TREATMENTS: *How to choose fabrics and linings. The ups and downs of window shades. Classic curtains.* ☞FLOORS: *How to shop for carpeting. Pile variations. How to judge quality. Buying a pad. The facts on wood flooring, from style to grade. Shopping for stone, brick, and tile.* ☞FURNITURE: *Shopping on a budget. How to buy antiques. The inside facts on upholstery. Slipcovers. How to buy the right mattress.* ☞THE KITCHEN: *What to know about cabinets, countertops, sinks, and appliances. The work triangle explained. Storage ideas: making the most of tight spaces.* ☞THE BATHROOM: *All about fixtures, tubs, showers, toilets, and bidets. Bathroom checklist: What you need for safety and efficiency.* ☞THE HOME OFFICE: *Making the most of a small space. Lighting and electronics. Furniture and storage.* ☞STORAGE: *How to minimize clutter and maximize space. Organizing kids' rooms. How to take control of your closets. Bedroom storage for adults and children.* ☞EVERYTHING YOU NEED TO KNOW: *About Choosing Pots and Pans, Front-Wheel-Drive Cars, Making Healthier Meals, Vacuum Cleaners, Garden Tools, Upholstered Furniture, Your Credit Card Statement, Curtain Styles* ☞MONEY-SAVING HINTS: *How to Turn Bed Sheets into Curtains, Save on Car Repairs, Buy Produce, Choose Carpeting* ☞HANDY TIPS: *For Buffing Wood Floors, Preventing Carpet Dents, Unsticking Stacked*

DOING IT
YOURSELF

DECORATING FOR EASY CARE

☛ Minimize clutter: The fewer decorative objects, rugs, and "layers" in your decor, the easier it is to clean and keep tidy.

☛ Choose soil-camouflaging patterns rather than solids, which tend to show spots more easily.

☛ Use washable slipcovers to help protect good upholstery and keep cleaning bills down.

☛ Place washable area rugs in front of your easy chairs, in the entry hall, and in other heavy-traffic spots to protect carpets from wear and soil; then stash them out of sight when company comes.

☛ Hang sheer liner curtains at windows; these help filter out airborne soil while letting in light.

☛ Use semigloss paint for door and window frames; the smooth surface makes it easy to clean away fingerprints.

Decorating is one of the most satisfying aspects of caring for your home. Choosing paint colors, fabrics, and new furnishings is not only enjoyable and creative, but it also helps you learn how to make the most of what you already have.

If you are new to decorating, try starting with some simple changes. Even small touches—new lamp shades or colorful throw pillows, for example—can make a surprising difference in a room.

Then move on to more ambitious schemes. To start, familiarize yourself with the decorating basics: color, style, furniture arrangement, and lighting.

COLOR

Color is probably the single most powerful element in a decor. It can set a mood, provide interest and accents, and even compensate for architectural problems by actually altering the perception of depth and space.

Because color has specific attributes, it is easy to make it work for you. For example, warm colors—red, orange, yellow, and their various tints and shades—attract attention, increase the apparent size of objects, and tend to soften their outlines. Walls painted in warm colors appear to move forward and make a room seem smaller.

By contrast, cool colors—blue, green, and their various tints and shades—are soothing, decrease the apparent size of

FOUR STEPS TO SUCCESS

To save time and money in any decorating project, plan ahead by following these simple hints from the pros:

1. Take inventory: Make a list of your existing furnishings. Note what you want (or need) to keep and what you'd like to replace. Then plan to add any new pieces in order of priority.

2. Keep a loose-leaf notebook: Give each room or project its own section and insert an envelope behind each divider to hold product literature, clippings from magazines, paint chips, and fabric swatches. Jot

down the names of recommended professionals and craftspeople and tips from friends.

3. Window-shop: Spend time in decorating, fabric, and department stores. Note what you like and what things cost so you can plan a budget.

4. Develop a floor plan: Sketch a plan of the room or rooms you want to decorate and experiment with furniture arrangements (see pages 160–161).

THE COLOR WHEEL

*To ANALYZE COLOR relationships, decorators
often refer to the color wheel, a universal device based on the
way colors fall in the spectrum. The wheel is divided
into three color types—primary, secondary, and tertiary—
located in specific places at equal intervals.*

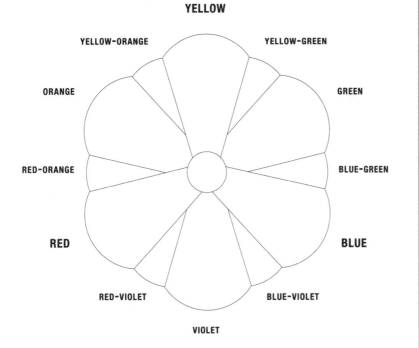

- There are **three primary colors**—red, yellow, and blue. These are the pure colors in the spectrum; they cannot be made by mixing any other colors.

- There are also **three secondary colors**—orange, green, and violet—made by mixing equal amounts of two primary colors.

- The **six tertiary colors**—yellow-orange, red-orange, red-violet, blue-violet, blue-green, and yellow-green—result when a primary color is mixed in equal parts with an adjacent secondary color on the color wheel.

Here are three basic decorating schemes based on these color relationships:

Analogous or monochromatic scheme: This is an approach that is nearly always successful, using colors that are adjacent on the color wheel (for example, blue-green, blue, and blue-violet).

Different shades of the same color (pastel green and forest green) also work well together.

Triadic scheme: This incorporates three colors equidistant from each other on the wheel, such as yellow, red, and blue.

Contrasting scheme: This focuses on colors opposite each other on the wheel, known as complementary colors. When used together, complementary colors (red and green, for example) appear to vibrate, so it is a good idea to use one as a main color and the other as an accent.

☞ Emphasize interesting architectural features, such as Victorian moldings, by painting them a contrasting color to the wall.

☞ Camouflage unattractive features, such as old radiators, by painting them the same color as their background.

☞ Fool the eye: Make a long narrow room appear wider by painting the end walls a warm color or the side walls a cool color. In a small house or apartment, paint or carpet all the floors in the same color (a medium or light shade) to make the floor area seem larger.

COLOR CONTROL

☞ Unless you are really sure of yourself, avoid extremes; too much of one color can be distracting, and you may tire of it sooner than a subtler mix.

DECORATING CHECKLIST

*KEEP IN MIND THAT SPACE can be flexible. Think about
how room use might change over time; two young children who share a room
might want separate bedrooms as teens. Age and health problems are
also factors. If you anticipate that climbing stairs will become a problem, you may
wish to consider shifting room use so that you can primarily use one floor.*

*To focus on your needs, ask yourself the questions given below;
if you are using a decorator, this information will be particularly useful to him or her.*

☐ How old is each household member, and how long will he or she live in the house?

☐ Where will each person sleep?

☐ Where will each person spend time alone?

☐ Where will the family gather for leisure activities?

☐ Where do household members like to eat—in the kitchen, in the dining room, in front of the TV?

☐ Do you need an all-purpose family room, including a kitchen, dining area, and sitting area? Or a media center? The family room might include a media center, a laundry area, a play space, and a home office.

☐ Do you need specialized rooms—a home office, a workshop, an exercise area, or a playroom?

☐ Do you need specialized storage for books, collectibles, music, videotapes, or sports equipment?

☐ Which entry doors get used the most?

☐ Which part of the house receives the most sun and natural warmth?

☐ How do you usually entertain—with sit-down dinners, buffets, living-room get-togethers?

INVOLVING THE FAMILY

☛ Get the whole household in on planning your decor: Furnishings should work for everyone's needs.

objects, and make their outlines appear crisp. Walls painted in cool colors appear to recede and make a room seem larger.

Colors also react to other colors in very specific ways. Against a dark background, light shades appear darker. Against a light background, dark colors are more intense. A medium tone appears light when placed against a dark background, and looks dark against a light background.

How to Choose Colors

Choose colors that you know you like instead of risking an untried combination.

As a rule of thumb, restrict the main colors in a room to three or fewer; these will be most noticeable on the walls, fabrics, and floor coverings. Then introduce accent colors with accessories, flowers, and artwork.

If you aren't decorating from scratch, start with the elements you are not planning to change—the carpet or wallpaper, perhaps—and select new accent colors to go with them.

If you are decorating your entire house, select one color scheme, then vary the individual colors from room to room. If your scheme is a mix of yellow, blue, rose, and white, for example, the yellow could dominate in the bedroom, the blue in the living room, and both rooms would incorporate smaller touches of rose and white.

Neutrals

Neutrals, which include white, tan, gray, brown, and black, are not found on the color wheel (see page 157) and are technically not colors. They do, however, have a marked effect on colors. A neutral scheme makes an effective backdrop because it helps the color stand out. Neutrals also make good accents.

STYLE

There is an enormous range of decorating styles—from traditional to ultracontemporary—and choosing one is entirely a matter of your personal taste. Consult books, magazines, and even museums to get an idea of different styles and find one that you really like.

You can select one style for your whole house, or do some rooms one way, some rooms another. The key is common sense. If you have young children, for example, you would logically want to use washable fabrics and sturdy furniture in rooms where kids roam.

Whatever the style, it will likely fall into one of two categories: formal or casual.

As a rule, a formal decor is elegant and reserved. It is best suited to rooms that have less traffic, or that you use for special occasions.

In a casual decor, where styles and pieces tend to be mixed, there is more room for flexibility; any element will work as long as it contributes to the overall effect.

A casual decor with comfortable hard-wearing furniture suits the rooms that you use the most for leisure activities, such as the TV or family room.

ARRANGEMENT

Good furniture arrangement relies on three basic elements: scale, balance, and placement.

Scale and balance: These affect how furniture pieces relate to each other and to the room they are in. In general, it is best to select smaller pieces for small rooms and large pieces for large rooms.

Do not mix furnishings that are dramatically different in size. If you have a three-seat sofa and oversized armchairs, for example, pair them with a substantial coffee table; a small table or chest would work better for a love seat.

TRAFFIC LANES

For easy access and an uncluttered look, leave:

☛ At least 3 feet of open space to allow adequate walking room.

☛ At least 3 feet of space behind dining and desk chairs.

☛ Two to 3 feet of space between furniture pieces; 1½ feet between a sofa or chair and a coffee table.

☛ Two feet of open space around a bed.

☛ Three feet in front of a bureau or cabinet to open drawers.

☛ A 3-foot arc of space around a door.

HOW LONG WILL IT LAST?

WHAT	HOW LONG
Carpet, rugs	With care, at least 10 years.
Interior paint	5 years.
Upholstery	With care, if upholstery is made of tightly woven fabric in a long-wearing fiber, at least 10 years.
Wallpaper	10 years.
Wood furniture (tables, dressers, desks, etc.)	With care, generations.

HOW TO MAKE A FLOOR PLAN

A FLOOR PLAN IS A simple diagram of a room drawn to scale. Making one is an easy and effective way to try different arrangements for furniture and large appliances—without having to move the pieces themselves. To make a plan, follow these easy steps and transfer the dimensions to a piece of graph paper, using one (or more) graph square(s) to represent one foot of actual space.

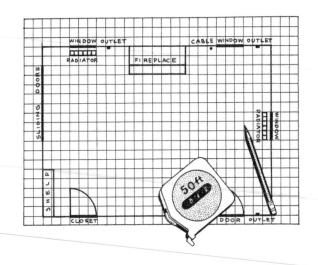

1. Using a retractable tape, measure the perimeter of the room at floor level, indicating door, window, and fireplace size and placement, and mark the dimensions to scale on graph paper. Be sure to measure and mark the direction and distance of door swings.

2. Measure and mark the location of built-ins, radiators, and heat registers, as well as any outlets, switches, phone jacks, and antenna connections.

3. Photocopy your completed plan.

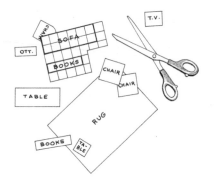

4. Measure your furniture (or large appliances) to the same scale on a separate piece of graph paper and make cutouts.

Place the cutouts on the photocopied plan according to the arrangement you want. Check to see whether the outlets, switches, and any hookups are located conveniently (and not blocked) and adjust your layout accordingly.

5. When you are pleased with a layout (or layouts) trace around the cutouts. You may want to keep a scheme or two on file, especially if you'd like to rearrange a room for a change of season.

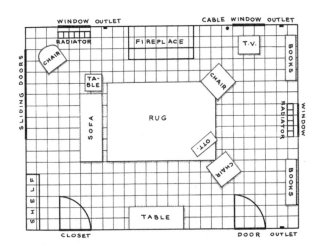

HOW TO WORK WITH A PROFESSIONAL

While you can solve many decorating problems on your own, a professional can also provide valuable expertise.

Usually, an interior designer or a decorator (the terms are interchangeable) begins by spending time in your home to determine your preferences, budget, and space and lighting needs.

Based on this information, he or she will then make a preliminary selection of fabrics, paint colors, carpet, fixtures, and furniture, and bring you samples to review in your home.

This can help enormously in narrowing the choices; moreover, since many items are available "to the trade only" (through a design professional), a designer can show you samples you would not be able to purchase on your own. (Usually, the designer takes a percentage of the cost of the items purchased.)

Designers are also trained to make floor plans, suggest renovations, oversee workers, design custom furnishings, and provide advice on color schemes and furniture placement.

Typically, they charge a fee or a percentage of the cost of goods they order for you. However, many will tailor services; for example, charging an hourly rate for a preliminary consultation.

To work effectively with a designer, you need a good rapport and a sense of trust, since you will be making many personal decisions with him or her.

Ask your friends for recommendations. Interview several designers before choosing one. Ask for references; be sure to check if the designer stayed within budget.

Many home design stores have in-house designers who often come at a discount if you are buying a certain amount of merchandise from the store. Chances are, if you like and trust the store, you can rely on its designer.

SAFE PASSAGE

☛ When placing your furniture, always watch for potential hazards, like dangling lamp cords, which can cause tripping. Be sure that small area rugs are secured to the floor (with nonskid pads or strips of adhesive tape) and that vases and other fragile items are in safe spots, away from high-traffic areas.

Through the telephone directory, you can also contact your local chapter of the following organizations for recommendations. Membership indicates a certified level of expertise.

American Society of Interior Designers (A.S.I.D.) Designers who have passed the group's written test and have given proof of their experience and skills in decorating.

Certified Kitchen Designer (C.K.D.) Professional members of the National Kitchen & Bath Association.
Designers Lighting Forum (D.L.F.) Professional members of a group interested in promoting better residential lighting.
Interior Design Society (I.D.S.) Interior designers who work in retail stores.

To determine whether furnishings are balanced, try to think in terms of size and weight. Two same-sized sofas placed opposite each other will appear balanced. Or place one sofa opposite two armchairs if they appear to have the same weight.

You can also use smaller elements, such as a side table, grandfather clock, or even tall potted plants to fill in and build up weight. Built-in features, such as a wall of bookshelves, can also function as part of the balance equation.

Placement: Evaluate traffic patterns and arrange furnishings so there is a clear pathway in and out of each room, and from one area to another (see page 159). Don't crowd a small room with big pieces of furniture that make it difficult to move around in and are visually overwhelming.

Do, however, consider the special features or attributes of a room. For example, you might wish to plan groupings that will make it easy for people to draw close to a fireplace, to enjoy the view from a picture window, or have conversations.

You can also place furniture to "manipulate" space: Three small groupings instead of one large one will make a big room seem more inviting and comfortable and will help define smaller spaces within it.

LIGHT AND LIVELY

☛ Because colors look different under different light conditions, always bring home fabric swatches and paint chips and check them—during both day and night—under typical lighting conditions in your house. (Remember that pastels look best in sunlight and tend to fade at night).

☛ Similarly, when you shop for light fixtures, take swatches with you to see how they look when they are lit by different bulb types.

BRIGHT IDEA

☛ Use a rheostat, or dimmer, to brighten or subdue light in a room as the occasion may suggest.

WHICH BULB IS BEST?

DIFFERENT BULBS CAN dramatically change the look of a room, affect the quality and brightness of the light, and even influence your mood. Some light fixtures take only one of the three basic types described here; others can take any (this should be specified on the fixture).

Incandescent: These are the most common all-purpose type. Flattering light; easy on the eyes. Relatively inexpensive, easy to find in stores, and easy to install, but can be short-lived and hot to the touch. Come in long-life, energy-saving, and pastel models, and in all sorts of shapes (see box page 163).

Halogen: There are two types: screw in (similar to incandescent) and special shapes (double-ended, bayonet, miniature thread). Produce a bright white flattering light that casts a sparkle; are good for accent and track lighting. Focused, intense beam. Relatively expensive. About one fourth more light than incandescents for the energy they consume.

Fluorescent: Both compact screw-in and tubular fluorescents are now available for the home in bulbs that give warm soft light (different from the harsh light associated with the tubular fluorescent bulbs typically used in schools and offices). Good for high levels of general lighting in the kitchen, bath, and family room.

Long-lasting and very energy efficient; about five times more light for the amount of energy they consume than incandescent bulbs (and can last ten times longer).

Come in as many as ten distinct nuances of white; "warm" or "soft white" light is complementary to many colors and complexions. "Full spectrum" bulb is most similar to natural light.

LIGHTING

There are two basic types of home lighting:

Ambient: This general lighting provides overall illumination (often a ceiling light).

Task: This puts a concentrated pool of light where you need it for close work, such as reading, stove-top cooking, or sewing.

In most rooms, you will want a combination of both, although there is no one way to do it. In a dining room, for example, many people prefer an overhead fixture on a dimmer (rheostat), supplemented only by candles.

However, if you have enough individual lights placed around a room, you may not need a ceiling light; several standing and table lamps set by sofas and chairs in a living room can work together to create the ambient lighting.

Keep in mind the nature of the room and its function, and choose your lighting accordingly. Follow these guidelines:

Entrance halls and stairways: direct light, so that people can see where they are going.

Public spaces, such as living and dining rooms: overall ambient lighting combined with softly lit areas for comfortable living and entertaining.

Kitchen: bright overall lighting and direct task lighting.

Bedrooms: soft, intimate lighting.

Libraries, studies, and work spaces: good task lighting that will enable maximum comfort and efficiency.

Bathrooms: good lighting around the mirror.

Making Lighting Work for You

To determine where you want to place your lights, experiment with different schemes with a clip-on work light and a long extension cord; move the light around the room and observe the effects.

The following placement suggestions will also help ensure a successful lighting scheme:

SEEING THE LIGHT

☞ A three-way bulb gives you flexibility if more than one person will use a lamp at various times. Some household members might want more light for an activity or task than others.

☞ Try separate fixtures and controls in an eat-in kitchen so you can dim the light over the work area and hide any mess while you eat.

LIGHT READING

☞ Table lamp: 20" to 25" from where you hold your book.

☞ Floor lamp: 20" from where you hold your book.

☞ Wall lamp: 15" from where you hold your book.

BASIC BULBS

INCANDESCENT BULBS COME in a range of shapes for different fixtures. A reflector bulb works for track lighting, for example, while decorative shapes are used in sconces and chandeliers.

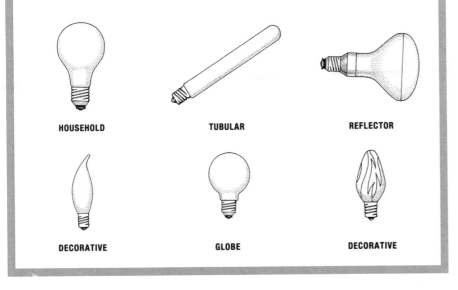

HOUSEHOLD   TUBULAR   REFLECTOR

DECORATIVE   GLOBE   DECORATIVE

SHADY BUSINESS

☞ A dark lamp shade may work best for a certain lamp style, but will let out less light; a light neutral lets out the most light.

- Place table lamps at or below eye level so they don't shine in people's eyes.

- To augment a ceiling fixture, put an additional fixture on top of a high cabinet or shelf and angle in at the ceiling for additional ambient light.

- Use a strip of small bulbs hidden behind a valance to provide a soft, suffused light; this can be a pleasing effect for floor-length draperies.

- Light a work area from more than one direction to prevent distracting shadows.

- Place a ceiling fixture in the center of a room or over a major piece of furniture, such as a dining table or piano.

SIX CLASSIC LAMP SHADES

ALWAYS TRY TO TAKE YOUR lamp with you when you are shopping for a shade. If that isn't possible, measure the height of the base and of the metal harp that holds the shade. As a rule of thumb, the shade should measure about half the total height of a table lamp.

Here are six classic styles:

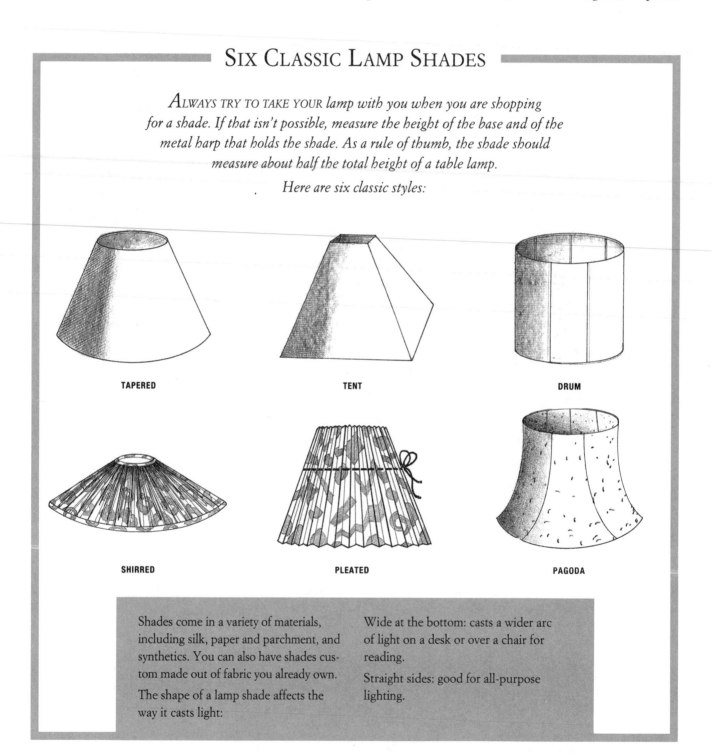

TAPERED　　　　　**TENT**　　　　　**DRUM**

SHIRRED　　　　　**PLEATED**　　　　　**PAGODA**

Shades come in a variety of materials, including silk, paper and parchment, and synthetics. You can also have shades custom made out of fabric you already own.

The shape of a lamp shade affects the way it casts light:

Wide at the bottom: casts a wider arc of light on a desk or over a chair for reading.

Straight sides: good for all-purpose lighting.

PAINTING

Painting is one of the easiest and least expensive ways to bring new life to a room. Even if you've never painted, you will have good results if you understand the basic paint types and finishes, and prepare your room properly.

CHOOSING COLORS

Any reliable paint or hardware store displays racks of free color samples called paint chips. These chips are arranged in strips of similar colors and related tones to show you the range of a particular shade.

After selecting some chips, take them home and look at them with your fabrics, furnishings, and flooring materials in the room that you plan to paint during the day and at night under artifical light.

Once you've narrowed the choices, buy a pint of the color you like and try it out on a sizable section of the wall. Evaluate it with your fabric, furnishings, and flooring materials in both daylight and at night under artificial light.

PAINT AND PRIMER

There are two types of paint: primer and finish paint. Use primer to prepare a surface so it holds the finish coat well. This is especially important for new drywall, plaster, and wood.

Primer also seals cracks, stains, and wood knots that might otherwise show through, and inhibits rust on metal surfaces.

Priming is always a good idea, but it is essential if you have done any patching or scraping. You should also use primer if you are applying a light color over a dark color or a matte finish over a glossy coat.`

Latex Versus Alkyd

Both primer and finish paint, which is more opaque than primer, come in two basic types:

Latex: This is an easy-to-use water-based paint that is generally less expensive than alkyd. It produces a slightly rough finish and dries in a few hours. Relatively odor free, this paint emits nontoxic fumes and needs only soap and water for cleanup.

Alkyd: This is an oil-based solvent-thinned paint that takes about 24 hours to dry. Alkyd resists moisture better than latex. However, it has strong-smelling fumes that can be toxic if inhaled over a sustained period, so it is important to wear a face mask and work in a well-ventilated area when using it.

Cleanup also requires time and patience as you must use mineral solvents like turpentine to get the paint off you and your brushes. Because these solvents are flammable, you must separate your rags from other refuse. Ask your garbage collector about disposing of them properly (see page 291).

How Much Paint to Buy?

A gallon of paint covers about 450 square feet. To figure how much you need for a wall, multiply the length and height; for a ceiling or floor multiply two adjacent sides. Be sure to subtract the area taken up by doors, windows, fireplace, or other spaces that won't be painted. When applying two coats, just double the figure.

For example, consider a 12' × 18' room with an 8' ceiling, with two windows each on one long wall and one short wall, and a doorway on the second long wall.

1. The two long walls measure 144 square feet each (8' × 18') for a total of 288 square feet. The two short walls

HOW LONG WILL IT TAKE?

☛ To paint a 12' x 18' room with 8' ceilings: 6 to 7 hours of actual painting time for primer, paint, and a finish coat of latex paint; more for alkyd.

measure 96 square feet each (8' × 12') for a total of 192 square feet.

2. Add these sums for a total of 480 square feet.

3. Now subtract the windows (3' × 4' each) and the doorway (3' × 6½'), a total of 68 square feet (rounded up from 67½).

4. The result is 412 square feet. Therefore, the walls can be covered by 1 gallon of paint per coat. For the ceiling area calculate the corresponding floor area.

THE RIGHT EQUIPMENT

Using a good applicator will help your job go faster and smoother. The better the quality, the better the results. Don't cut corners; cheap brushes and rollers can cause your paint to smudge and streak.

Brushes: These are typically used for trim and for "cutting in" (painting edges around windows, doors, and wall and ceiling joints that a roller can't reach).

A good brush has flagged (split) ends for even spreading and dense bristles that bounce back to shape when you tap them against your hand. Natural bristles are traditionally used for alkyd paint because they hold the paint better but swell when used with latex; nylon and polyester are fine for latex.

Use the largest brush possible for the job to avoid streaking. A 1- or 2-inch angle-cut sash brush is recommended for window frames and moldings, a 3- or 4-inch brush for cupboards, doors, and cutting in.

PAINT POINTERS

☞ As different batches of paint can vary slightly in color, it is best to buy more than you need, allowing a little extra for spills and touch-ups. Many paint and hardware stores take back unopened cans of paint—ask first. Store extra paint in pint jars and label them by room for quick touch-ups.

WHICH PAINT FINISH WHERE?

INTERIOR PAINT (LATEX AND ALKYD) comes in a variety of finishes from flat to a shiny high gloss. Each has its uses:

FINISH	RECOMMENDED FOR	APPEARANCE	CHARACTERISTICS
Flat	Little-used rooms like dining rooms and guest bedrooms	Soft matte; slightly porous and soft	Absorbs grease and moisture; not easily washable
Eggshell	Hallways, family rooms	Soft matte with a slight sheen	Absorbs grease and moisture
Satin	Hard-wear rooms like children's bedrooms, kitchens, bathrooms, hallways	Slight sheen; reflects light	Scuff and scratch resistant; sponges clean easily
Semigloss	Woodwork, trim	Somewhat shiny; reflects light	Highly scuff and scratch resistant; sponges clean very easily
Pearl	Cabinets, woodwork, trim	Glossy sheen	Highly scuff and scratch resistant; sponges clean easily
High gloss	Cabinets, woodwork, trim	Very glossy sheen	Highly scuff and scratch resistant; sponges clean easily

Pads: These edging tools are used to apply paint to hard-to-reach places such as corners or for intricate work such as railings and window frames. They combine the speed and smoothness of a roller with the precision of a brush, but without the brush marks. They come in a variety of shapes for different uses and in an array of materials for different finishes. Foam, for example, is good for flat surfaces while mohair will smoothly cover walls with a rougher texture such as stucco. A long handle can be attached to a pad to reach high surfaces.

Rollers: The workhorses for painting interior walls, rollers are the best tools for covering an area smoothly. Sizes range from about 2 inches wide, for flat woodwork, to 18 inches wide. A 9- or 10-inch roller is customary for walls, ceilings, and floors.

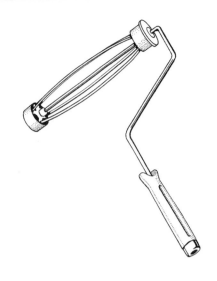

Roller sleeves: Purchased separately, these are slipped on the roller, then discarded after the painting is done. The best rollers hold the sleeve securely without requiring a wing nut.

A short nap, or pile, is good for smooth surfaces or a soft matte finish.

A thick pile works best for rough surfaces like stucco and brick.

Lamb's wool sleeves are recommended for alkyd paint, but synthetic nap is fine for latex.

SEEING SPOTS

☞ If you wear glasses, wipe them right away with a clean cloth if they get paint on them so that it will not dry on the lenses and damage them.

PAINTING DOS AND DON'TS

DO:

- Wait until you are ready to start painting before mixing the paint, since it will separate as it stands.

- Line your roller tray with aluminum foil or a disposable plastic liner to give it a longer life.

- Thoroughly clean brushes and put them in a plastic bag and store them in the freezer after you are done painting for the day. This will keep them soft and ready for painting the next day.

- Put a rubber band over the open paint can when you are painting to wipe excess paint off the brush. This will prevent drips on the can and give you just the right amount of paint on your brush.

DON'T:

- Assume machine-mixed paint will stay mixed until you get it home. Pour a third of the paint into another container, and mix the remainder. Pour back the reserved third, continuing to stir.

- Leave brushes in a paint container during breaks. Lay the brush flat on a wire grid, over the open can. Or wrap the brush in a plastic bag or aluminum foil.

- Leave the roller in the tray when you're finished, or it may get stuck for good.

SPECIAL PAINTS

IN ADDITION TO STANDARD WALL and ceiling paint, there are a number of paints and finishes for specific situations. Some are practical; some are decorative.

FINISH	WHAT TO USE IT ON	WHAT IT DOES
Aluminum paint	Metal, painted wood, masonry	Gives surfaces a silvery aluminum color. Reflects heat on radiators.
Epoxy paint	Plaster, masonry, concrete, cinder block, wood, metal, porcelain	Gives surfaces such as refrigerators, sinks, and bathtubs a hard, ceramic appearance.
Glaze (clear or tinted)	Wood	Produces a rich, semitransparent finish. Adds depth to wood grain and solid colors underneath.
Masking stain	Wood	Provides an even color on mismatched woods.
Penetrating stain	Wood, concrete	Helps floors and stairwells withstand heavy traffic.
Porch and floor paints	Wood	Brings out color gradations and markings.
Textured paint (white or tinted)	Plaster, wood	Creates a sandy (finely grained), rough (pebbly, randomly grained) or stuccolike (heavily grained) finish that adds texture and masks imperfections on a surface.
Waterproofing paint	Unpainted concrete, cement, brick, stone, stucco (especially good for basement walls)	Helps prevent moisture from seeping through.

Pans: A heavy-duty metal pan is recommended; lightweight trays may tip or lose their shape. Make sure the pan is the right size for the roller.

GETTING READY

Careful preparation is crucial to a good paint job. First, you need to get the room itself ready. Remove as much furniture as possible. Roll up the rugs. (This is a good time to send them out for cleaning and refurbishing.)

Cover the floor with plastic drop cloths and make a path on top with old newspapers to help soak up wet paint. Place any remaining furniture in the middle of the room and cover it with drop cloths tied down with clothesline.

Remove any hardware you don't want painted, including switch plates, doorknobs, latches and locks, curtain rods and brackets, picture hooks, and light fixtures. Use masking tape to cover anything you can't remove, such as thermostats.

Then get yourself ready for painting. Paint spatters everywhere. It is a good idea to wear old clothes, old shoes or sneakers, a head covering, and surgeon's rubber gloves.

How to Prepare a Surface
No matter how great your paint job may look, it won't last if you haven't prepared the surfaces before you start.

If the walls and ceiling are grimy, wash them. This is especially important in the kitchen or bathroom, where film from grease or soap residue can build up, making it difficult for new paint to adhere.

Use a powdered floor cleaner or trisodium phosphate (TSP) and work

from the bottom up to avoid streaks. Special fungicides are available for washing off mildew and preventing it from returning to mar your new paint job. Allow all surfaces to dry thoroughly before painting.

You also need to clean out cracks, holes, and nail pops (where nails have risen and become visible) and fill them with spackle or plaster (see page 214) and scrape away any loose paint. You can use a standard scraper or try one of these specialized tools:

A hook scraper: takes paint off windowsills and door frames.

A triangular shave hook: gets at paint and dirt embedded in woodwork.

A razor scraper: takes paint off moldings and window muntins.

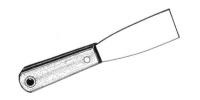

A putty knife: handily separates softened paint and wallpaper from a surface.

PLEASANT DREAMS

☞ If you are painting a bedroom, you will want to sleep somewhere else so that you can avoid fumes until the paint dries.

SAFETY STEPS

☞ Keep ladders away from closed doors so others can't hurt themselves or you by barging in (see page 207 for information on ladder safety).

HOW TO PAINT

To avoid drip spots, paint the ceiling first, then the walls, beginning at one corner and working your way around the room.

Do your cutting in first, brushing a narrow strip of paint where the walls and ceiling meet, along door and window frames and trim, and anywhere else a roller will not reach.

Then fill in the large areas with a roller, working in one 3-foot-square area at a time. Make several zigzag strokes upward and downward in the shape of a W, then smooth them out with horizontal strokes. Finish with the windows, doors, moldings, and trim, doing the baseboards last.

DROP CLOTHS

☞ Canvas drop cloths absorb paint and are less slippery than plastic. Although they are more expensive, they can be reused.

GOLDEN TOUCH

☞ A touch of gold on darkly painted walls adds a feeling of luxury and richness. Try it on crown moldings, around doors, or on chair rails.

Drying Time

Drying time varies depending on humidity levels. Even though latex paint is formulated to dry almost on contact, it's generally better to paint on a dry, mild, windless day, so that the paint will dry more quickly, and you can leave the windows or doors open wide for good ventilation.

DECORATIVE TECHNIQUES

Decorative finishes create unusual, often textural, effects that provide interest and dimension to a surface. Many are called *faux* finishes because they imitate the look of a specific material, such as the mottled colors and distinctive graining of marble.

Most specialty finishes involve applying a base coat color, then a glaze or opaque finish on top to make an interesting pattern. These methods include sponging, ragging, stippling, spattering, and marbleizing. They are fun to do but can be rather complicated.

Follow the directions in a book, video, or the pamphlets that paint companies offer free at paint stores, and experiment on a sample board or a section of the wall before you actually begin painting a surface.

STEP-BY-STEP STENCILING

Stenciling, which involves creating a repeated paint design with a cutout pattern, is a simple, inexpensive way to transform a room with distinctive decoration.

Favored for both borders and overall designs, this fail-safe method, which requires no freehand work, has a long tradition in this country, where it was originally used to imitate more expensive printed wallpapers.

You can use it for an all-over pattern, or try a border around a door or window, near the ceiling or baseboard on a wall, or at the edge of a floor.

Buy ready-made stencils (and complete stencil kits) in craft stores, or make your own from stencil card—a heavy treated paper also available in craft stores—cutting the design out with a sharp utility knife.

To create a pattern with more than one color, you will need a stencil for each color. Clean the cards periodically with a damp sponge to prevent paint buildup on them.

Paint stores sell stenciling brushes with stiff, tight bristles and flat heads, but you can use any brush that produces an effect you like.

Fast-drying Japan paints are recommended for the stencil colors.

1. Prepare the surface with flat finish paint (latex or alkyd).

2. If you have more than one stencil, start with the largest. Begin in a corner—or wherever the design starts—lightly penciling the position for the stencil on both the horizontal and the vertical.

3. Tape the card to the surface, following the pencil marks.

4. Dip the brush into a stenciling color, wiping off excess paint with a paper towel so that the brush is almost dry.

5. Apply the paint in a circular motion, or use a dabbing, pouncing motion for more interesting mottled effects within the stenciled design.

6. Repeat the process, moving across the surface to continue the pattern.

7. Let the paint dry thoroughly and repeat for additional colors.

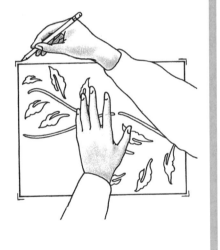

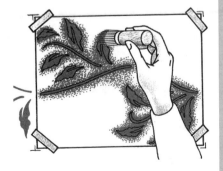

STENCIL STRATEGIES

☛ When working with an intricate stencil pattern, glue a sheet of fine dressmakers' netting onto the back to hold it together while you paint.

☛ Use waterproof drafting tape to repair stencils that become damaged.

☛ Use a stenciled design over a textured paint finish for an interesting effect.

☛ Spray stencil designs lightly with gold or silver paint for added luster.

WALL COVERINGS

Wall coverings can make a strong decorative impact in a room, adding pattern, texture, and color. They can also be useful problem solvers, disguising uneven plaster or an old paint job.

Next to paint, wallpaper is probably the most common and economical wall decoration. Other popular choices include fabric, tile, paneling, and stucco.

ALL ABOUT WALLPAPER

This versatile covering comes in standard paper as well as washable synthetics, great for baths, kitchens, and children's rooms. Most home decorating stores supply sample books; you can order from these, or buy ready-stocked rolls right off the shelf.

Designer patterns are also available through decorators. Rolls range in price from about $10 to $100 a roll (the more specialized the paper, the more costly).

Many coverings come with coordinating fabrics, window treatments, and even lamp shades.

You may also want to consider a wallpaper border. Placed along the top of a plain painted or papered wall, borders add detail to rooms and hallways. They generally come in strip form, but are also available as part of the wallpaper itself.

Here are some popular types of wallpaper:

Machine printed: the most economical and durable.

Hand printed: more individual and distinctive designs, but take more care and skill to hang because they are more fragile. Can be quite costly.

Washable: has a thin vinyl coating so it can be wiped down. (Don't scrub or you may wear away the coating.)

Solid vinyl: waterproof and scrubbable; a good choice for kitchens, baths, and children's rooms. Vinyls must be pasted to the wall with a fungicidal adhesive to prevent mold from forming underneath.

Flocked: has a velvetlike raised pattern that stands out in relief. Fragile and should be used in low-traffic areas. Paste ruins pile, so these papers require special care in hanging. Vinyl flocks are less delicate.

Foil and Mylar: shiny covering with a metallic plastic film or Mylar coating on a paper base. Some also have a printed pattern. Not recommended for walls with imperfections, which the shiny surface exaggerates. The metallic finish can conduct electricity, so it's important to cut around light switches and sockets and to avoid tucking the wall covering under face plates.

Grass cloths: made of natural grasses woven into a mat and glued onto a paper backing. Adds texture, but is delicate and hard to hang. Synthetic lookalikes are less fragile and cheaper.

Decide what kind of effect you want to achieve before you go to the store or showroom; that way you won't be overwhelmed by the variety once you get there. When you decide on a pattern, order all you'll need at once. If you don't, discrepancies between different batches may show up on your walls.

HANGING PAPER

Hanging your own wallpaper is a challenge; unless you are experienced, it is probably best to turn the job over to a professional.

If you are a beginner and want to give it a go, try a prepasted, pretrimmed medium-weight covering with an all-over pattern so you don't have to worry about matching from strip to strip; you can also avoid the trimming often necessary to make matched patterns fit a room (see pages 174–175).

Papers used in a moist environment like the bathroom need an especially tight fit so that mildew won't creep in behind the paper.

Preparing Your Walls

Whether you're wallpapering yourself or hiring a professional, you will save time and money—and ensure good results—by preparing your walls properly.

Most experts recommend removing old paper before applying new, but if the existing covering is very smooth and tight, you can put a new one over it.

Be sure to secure loose seams in an existing covering using vinyl glue, and use a razor to cut a small X over any bubbles. Smooth over any uneven places with spackle (see page 214) and apply a primer/sealer.

Removing Old Paper

To remove a strippable wall covering, grip a corner of the paper from the base-board and pull until the entire strip comes off. Some vinyl coverings leave a paper backing behind; if it is tight, you can leave it on and hang the new paper right on top of it without using a sealer or primer. Otherwise, use a scraper, available at paint and hardware stores, to take off the backing.

You can also use scrapers to take off stubborn papers; remove any residue with an abrasive pad or steel wool dipped in warm water. Be sure to rinse the wall thoroughly to remove all the tiny steel wool particles. If there is glue residue, remove it with a special solvent, also available at your paint or hardware store. Then apply a primer or sealer.

Really stubborn wall coverings require moisture to remove them. First, cover the floors with a drop cloth. Sponge the wall totally with a commercial wallpaper remover, allowing it to

PAPER POWER

- Create interest by pairing two different wallpaper patterns in the same room. At the bottom of a wall, place one pattern to chair-rail height and put a paper with another pattern in the same color family above it (try stripes and a floral); paste a border where the two coverings meet.

- Reserve bold prints for the foyer or a room where you don't spend much time; otherwise, you may tire of the pattern.

- Choose large geometrics for punch in a large room; use small geometrics to create the illusion of subtle textures in a small room.

- Use vertical stripes to make a ceiling seem higher.

- Paper the ceiling of a large room to make it seem smaller and cozier; leave the ceiling of a small room unpapered to create a sense of height.

- If you find a wallpaper you especially like, but can't afford to buy it in quantity, use it for a small room such as a bathroom or powder room. Or buy one or two rolls of the paper to use as panels against a solid background.

soak into the paper for the time indicated on the package label.

Resoak one strip of paper at a time and remove it with a scraper. If the liquid does not penetrate, score the wall covering with sandpaper or a scraper. Remove any residue as above.

If the wall covering still won't come off, you may need a steamer or sprayer to saturate the paper; you can rent one at a hardware or home decorating store.

Paint ceiling and moldings before applying new paper.

HOW TO HANG PREPASTED WALLPAPER

*FOR BEST RESULTS, FIRST REMOVE all wall accessories and hardware,
including light switches, plates, and wallpaper that you can. Paper the walls,
then put the wall accessories back. Cut your paper to fit angles; if there are
too many odd-shaped surfaces, don't try the job yourself.
A standard roll of wallpaper will cover about 36 square feet of wall surface. (Measure
the surfaces in the same way you measure for painting [see pages 165–166].)*

YOU'LL NEED THIS BASIC EQUIPMENT:

• A long table to measure, cut, trim,
and book (or fold) wallpaper strips
(see step 5, opposite). Improvise
with sawhorses and boards, or rent
a table if necessary.

• Stepladder

• Measuring tape

• Spirit level to align paper

• Water tray

• Wallboard taping knife

• Utility knife

• Smoothing brush

• Sponge

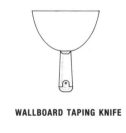

WALLBOARD TAPING KNIFE

SMOOTHING BRUSH

UTILITY KNIFE

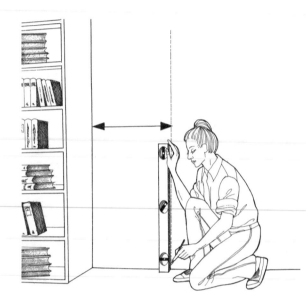

ESTABLISHING A PLUMB LINE

1. Decide where to start and stop. It is almost
inevitable that the pattern will mismatch at your stop-
ping/starting point, so choose an inconspicuous place
(behind a door, for example). If there is a floor-to-ceil-
ing breaking place, such as a bookcase, start there.

2. Measure out from the stopping/starting point
to the width of your wallpaper, and mark with
a pencil. Draw a vertical plumb line at this point,
establishing a true vertical with a spirit level.

If you are starting at a corner move your plumb
line ½ inch closer to the corner.

3. Measure the wall height, then add 2 inches to
the top and to the bottom. Cut a strip to this length.

4. Loosely reroll your strip inside out. Soak
the strip in water, according to the manufacturer's
directions.

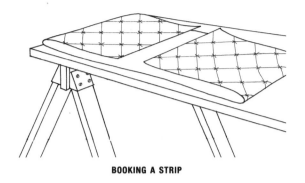

BOOKING A STRIP

5. Pull the strip slowly from the water and fold it loosely on the table, glue side to glue side, so the two ends meet in the middle of the strip—known as "booking" the strip. Wait for the paste to activate, according to the time indicated in the manufacturer's instructions.

SMOOTHING ON THE PAPER

6. Unfold the top part of the strip and place it glue side down on the wall alongside your starting line, letting the top overlap 2 inches on the ceiling. If starting in a corner, fold the extra ½ inch of paper in or around that corner.

7. Unfold the bottom and smooth the strip onto the wall with a smoothing brush, working out large air bubbles from the center angling down to the sides. Avoid horizontal strokes except at the ceiling line.

TRIMMING WALLPAPER

8. Trim off any excess paper at the top and bottom of the strip by running a utility knife along the edge of a wallboard taping knife.

9. Cut the next strip, adding one pattern repeat to the length for matching. Repeat the soaking and application process, butting strip edges together without overlapping them. Align the pattern of the old strip to the new.

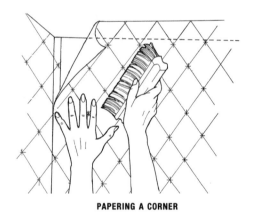

PAPERING A CORNER

10. Repeat for all remaining strips. When you come to a corner, measure the distance from the edge of the last strip to the corner and add ½ inch to it. Cut your next strip to this width. Hang the strip, wrapping the ½ inch around the corner; it will cover any bare wall that might have shown from turning the corner. Hang the remaining strip on the next wall butting the corner and covering the overlap.

11. When you are done, wipe the paper down with a damp sponge to remove any glue residue.

SHEET CHIC

☞ You can turn flat bed sheets—which come in a wide range of patterns—into curtains with almost no sewing. Just remove the stitches at the side of the top border and insert a curtain rod; hem if the panel is too long. If a sheet has a decorative border, you can cut it off and turn it into a tieback.

OPEN WIDE

☞ For sliding or French glass doors use a curtain rod wider than the window. When fully open, the curtains will have space to pull all the way back and not cover the doors.

Depending on their fabric and style, window treatments can block out unwanted light, provide privacy or enhance a view, insulate drafty windows, and make a room look and feel warmer. You can also use window coverings to unify windows of different size or to make small windows seem more impressive.

CURTAINS AND DRAPERIES

Curtains and draperies are the most common types of decorative window coverings. The terms are interchangeable; however, "curtain" is sometimes used to describe an informal treatment in which fabric is gathered or tied onto a rod or pole. "Drapery" suggests a more formal cover.

Traditional or highly decorated rooms will probably call for curtains or drapes, whereas more contemporary or streamlined rooms might benefit from blinds or shades.

If you buy curtains: The most economical option, ready-made curtains come in standard stock sizes that most windows (also standard in size) conform to.

If you have curtains custom made (or make them yourself): Full floor-length curtains can use a surprisingly large amount of fabric—as much as 22 yards for a pair of very full, gathered curtains.

As the fabric is usually a significant portion of the total cost of curtains, shop for closeouts to find yardage at a bargain price. But don't compromise the look of the curtain by skimping on fabric.

Allow enough yardage so the window treatment looks as full as possible. Double the fabric width for each curtain or drapery panel, and triple it for very lightweight fabrics.

Lining

Lining lengthens the life of curtains and draperies by protecting them from fading. Lining also reduces street noise, helps block sunlight, and increases insulation. Lined curtains also have more body, so they hang better.

Line a moderately priced silky cotton fabric, and it will look almost as luxurious as more expensive silk taffeta.

You can also use interlining, a layer of padding between lining and curtain that gives curtains extra body. Thermal fabric is a good idea for unusually drafty windows.

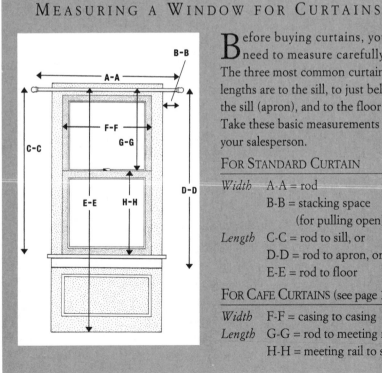

MEASURING A WINDOW FOR CURTAINS

Before buying curtains, you need to measure carefully. The three most common curtain lengths are to the sill, to just below the sill (apron), and to the floor. Take these basic measurements to your salesperson.

FOR STANDARD CURTAIN

Width	A-A = rod	
	B-B = stacking space (for pulling open)	
Length	C-C = rod to sill, or	
	D-D = rod to apron, or	
	E-E = rod to floor	

FOR CAFE CURTAINS (see page 179)

Width	F-F = casing to casing	
Length	G-G = rod to meeting rail	
	H-H = meeting rail to sill	

WINDOW SHADES

Simple, inexpensive, and versatile, shades let in maximum light when open and cover the entire window neatly when closed. They are available in stock sizes and can also be custom made. Here are some classic types:

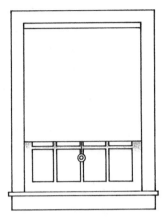

ROLLER SHADES: pull down from a tensioned roll and hold their places automatically; a light downward snap makes them roll up again. Typically come in a durable material known as shade cloth, sometimes with a vinyl coating; they may also be made of canvas or other fabric.

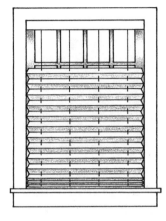

BOTTOM-UP SHADES: mounted on the windowsill instead of at the top. Good for privacy without totally eliminating light.

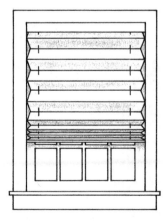

PLEATED SHADES: combine the softness of curtains with the clean lines of a shade. Available for skylights, arched, and circular windows. Usually made of permanently pleated polyester fabric and can be sheer or opaque. Come in double- and triple-cell thicknesses for insulation.

BALLOON (OR AUSTRIAN) SHADES: fabric shades that pull up by means of tapes or cords threaded through rings sewn into the fabric. When the shade is raised, horizontal folds or bellows form, one on top of the other.

IN THE SHADE

☞ Shade materials can include fiberglass, cotton, linen, rattan, bamboo, and natural grasses. Optional metallic backings for window shades offer energy savings by cutting heat in summer and reducing heat loss in winter.

☞ You can have fabric laminated to shade cloth for a custom treatment or use a do-it-yourself kit available in fabric stores.

ALL THE TRIMMINGS

☞ If you are making curtains and using washable fabric such as polished cotton, make sure your trims are also washable; many trims, such as satin and lace, must be dry-cleaned.

BLINDS AND SHUTTERS

BLINDS AND SHUTTERS, AVAILABLE IN stock sizes, are slatted window coverings that offer insulation, superior light control, ventilation, and excellent privacy when they are tightly closed. The slats can be tilted at a range of angles to provide ventilation and minimize glare while letting you enjoy the view.

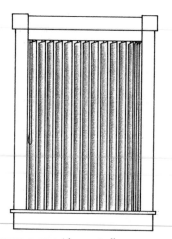

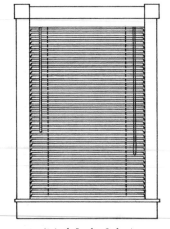

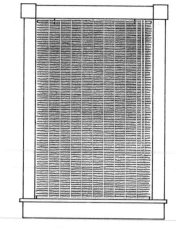

VERTICAL BLINDS (slats typically measure 4 inches wide):

made of vinyl, aluminum, wood, and fabric; draw completely to one side and are a good choice for sliding glass doors or large picture windows. Some accommodate wallpaper or fabric inserts; two-toned treatments available.

MINIBLINDS (1-inch [or less] slats): offer unobtrusive alternatives to wider slats; come in metal or metal-look vinyl.

MATCHSTICK BLINDS: inexpensive natural fiber, usually reed, roll up.

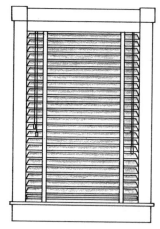

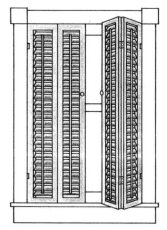

VENETIAN BLINDS (2-inch slats): wood, metal, or vinyl (available in colors; also in natural finish wood); tapes can contrast or blend with the slats.

SHUTTERS: wood; hinged to the window frame. Open and close easily and fold up, so they take little room. Offer privacy and ventilation.

CLASSIC CURTAIN STYLES

SELECT CURTAINS ACCORDING TO THE amount of privacy you need.
Sheer fabrics filter daylight, but are see-through from the outside at night, when
your lights are on. If this concerns you, opt for a medium to heavy fabric.
Or try using heavier curtains with sheer, unattached liners.

SIDE DRAPES AND VALANCE

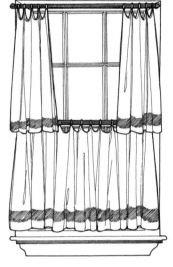

DOUBLE-TIER CAFÉ

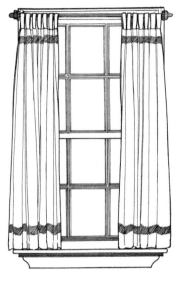

TAB

PRISCILLA WITH RUFFLE

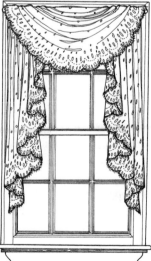

SWAG AND CASCADE

SHEET SMARTS

If you make curtains from sheets, note the following:

- Twin sheets measure approximately 44 square feet
- Full sheets: 54 square feet
- Queen-size: 63¾ square feet
- King-size: 76½ square feet

Therefore, twin sheets are a bargain when they sell for half or less the price of king-size; full sheets for two-thirds or less the price of king-size; and queen-size sheets for three-quarters or less the price of king-size.

FLOORS

BEST BACKING

☛ Carpet backing is typically made of a natural fiber, like jute, which should not be used on damp areas, or a synthetic, which is less expensive. Ask what type it is before you buy; a latex coating increases durability.

REDUCING COSTS

☛ When shopping for carpet, see if you can find remnants; these can be bound and made into area rugs.

Floors are often overlooked, but because they are the single largest expanse in a room, they actually have a powerful effect on the decor.

A single floor or covering is rarely suitable for every room in your house, so it is especially important to do good research. If possible, visit showrooms so that you can compare different materials in person as opposed to using catalogs.

Looks are only one consideration; comfort underfoot, noise and energy insulation, and washability and durability are equally important.

Be sure to bring your floor measurements to a salesperson so you can get a cost estimate; most materials are sold by the square foot or the square yard, which can add up fast. (For example: a 12' x 18' room measures 216 square feet, or 24 square yards.)

CARPETING

Carpeting is a wall-to-wall floor covering that is tacked down to a floor or subfloor. Soft underfoot, it is usually easy to care for, and helps unify and bring warmth to a room. (For advice on carpet cleaning see pages 42–43.)

Carpet is a serious investment, but it will last a long time if you select a good-quality, soil-resistant brand. When shopping for carpet, bring along fabric samples and paint chips so that you can coordinate colors and designs. After making a preliminary selection, take a large sample—at least 1 or 2 square feet—and live with it a few days.

Try walking on it, test to see if your doors swing over the pile easily (don't forget to include the depth of padding), and check the texture and color during daylight, and at night under different types of artificial lighting.

How to Measure
Carpet is sold by the square yard in standard widths (9, 12, 15, and occasionally 18 feet). Most stores will do your measuring for you. If the carpet has a pattern, you need to order extra to match the pattern at the seams.

Avoiding Hidden Costs
Always check with a salesperson to see if installation is included in the price. Ask about the underlay pad, too. Check to see if the dealer will remove old carpet and move furniture for you. They may also need to remove doors; are they going to charge extra for this?

UNDERSTANDING YOUR OPTIONS

Carpet is available in both wool and synthetic fibers: One isn't necessarily better than the other; it's the quality of the specific brand that counts. Wool is natural, warm, and strong but can be significantly more expensive than synthetic fibers.

Nylon is the most common synthetic carpet fiber; it is the strongest and holds its color well. It can also be cleaned easily. Other synthetics include acrylic, which looks and feels like wool; polyester, which tends to mat unless it is blended with nylon; and polypropylene, which resists mildew and is often used in indoor-outdoor settings.

Most carpeting comes with a stain-resistant finish. Premium-brand wool also offers resistance to crushing and matting.

Tufted and Woven
Most carpet is either tufted or woven. Tufted carpet accounts for more than 90 percent of home carpet sales. In tufted

carpet, adhesive-sealed primary and secondary backings hold the tufts in place.

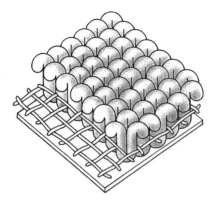

Tufted carpet

On woven carpet, the pile is woven with the backing to form a single fabric; there may or may not be a second backing. Good quality is available in both types. A good tufted carpet may last many years and come in many colors and patterns. Woven carpet, while much more expensive (up to twice the price of tufted carpet), can hold more detailed patterns.

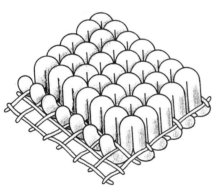

Woven carpet

Tufted and woven carpets come in a variety of surface textures created by cutting, looping, or twisting the fibers, or a combination of these processes. Salespeople refer to the surface texture with the following standard terms:

Plush: has an evenly sheared, smooth, lush surface that has the appearance of a new-mown lawn. It is luxurious, but it shows footprints and vacuum marks easily. It is best in lower-traffic areas.

Textured: has tightly twisted yarns that produce a crinkly surface. It is hard wearing and doesn't show dirt as much as plush or sculptured carpets do.

Sculptured: is made with a cut-and-loop technique that produces a multi-level surface pattern. It looks elegant and is more hard wearing than plush carpet.

Berber: has nubbier, bigger loops than textured carpet. In traditional Berber carpets, the loops are all the same size. In new, nontraditional Berbers, multi-level loops form patterns. Berber carpets now come in a wide range of shades.

Patterns and Solids

A color pattern may be woven into the carpet, or printed on the carpet's surface. Small patterns—florals, pin dots, and geometrics—are a safe choice because they don't compete with other patterns in

CARPET QUALITY

☛ When shopping for carpet, fold a sample back on itself. If the backing is visible, the weave may be too loose. The pile should be dense with tight twists and the sample hard to fold. Check, too, for loose strands, snags, and any uneven coloring.

STANDARD AREA RUG SIZES:

- ☛ 2' x 3'
- ☛ 3' x 5'
- ☛ 4' x 6'
- ☛ 9' x 12'
- ☛ 12' x 15'

PILE POSSIBILITES

BOTH TUFTED AND woven carpets are available with different piles, which create different looks, depending on how the loops are treated.

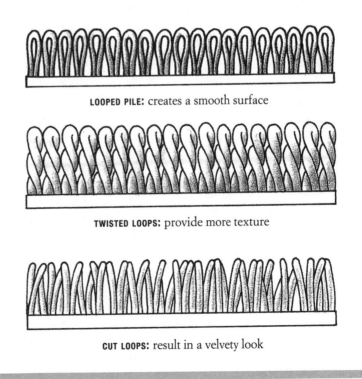

LOOPED PILE: creates a smooth surface

TWISTED LOOPS: provide more texture

CUT LOOPS: result in a velvety look

TRADITIONAL ORIENTAL RUGS

☞ Oriental rugs are made up of a series of knots; the more knots per square inch, the better the quality. A good rug has 800 knots per square inch ; a better rug has more than 1,000. Besides the number of knots per inch, the vibrancy of color and clarity of pattern determine the quality of the rug.

☞ Characteristic regional patterns once were produced only in that region. Today copies, which can be almost as good as the real thing, are likely to be made almost anywhere. For example, Belgium produces very fine copies of Oriental rugs.

a room. If you choose a large pattern, consider whether the motifs will look odd if they get cut off by a corner or door.

Patterns tend to camouflage dirt and are good for areas subject to food stains, such as dining rooms, or traffic, such as the foyer. They also don't show footprints or vacuum marks as clearly as solid colors do. If you prefer a solid, consider a medium tone, which will hide dirt and lint better than a very light or dark shade.

Buying a Pad

All carpeting except foam backed needs a good-quality underlay pad. A pad helps carpet look and feel better underfoot and protects it from wear, in addition to providing heat and sound insulation.

There are several types of padding. Most common, prime urethane padding is a good insulator and usually used for residential carpeting. This springy material comes in various thicknesses and densities. Bonded urethane (made from pieces of prime urethane) is less expensive and of lower quality.

Hair and jute (felt) padding, another good insulator, is also used for wall-to-wall carpeting. It is especially durable, and more expensive than urethane.

A less expensive alternative is waffle-pattern rubber padding, generally used for area rugs. It can disintegrate quickly.

To test the feel of the padding, place a large carpet sample on top of each pad sample and try them out, preferably in stocking feet.

AREA RUGS

An area rug is a rug that doesn't reach wall to wall and that has finished edges— hemmed or trimmed. Unlike carpeting, area rugs can be rolled up and moved, so they offer more flexibility. They can warm a room while still showing off a beautiful floor; you can also layer them over carpeting to break up a large space, tie together a furniture grouping, or add more pattern. A room-sized rug can give the appearance of carpeting.

Here are some common types:

Aubusson: ornately patterned from France with decorative floral, scenic, or scroll designs, made in a flat tapestry weave.

Braided: reversible rug made from braids of narrow fabric strips.

Dhurrie: loosely woven handmade flat reversible Indian wool or cotton rug; often pastel colored with geometric patterns.

Kilim: tightly woven wool rug with geometric patterns traditionally made in the Middle East. Colored with natural dyes.

Needlepoint: hand-stitched wool rug with decorative floral patterns or scenes. Portugal is known for its fine needle-point rugs.

Oriental: knotted rug in colorful designs made of hundreds of knots per square inch. Traditionally handwoven in the Middle East, but many Oriental-design rugs are now machine made. Genuine Oriental rugs are natural fibers; others may be synthetic.

Rya: shaggy Scandinavian wool rug; hand-woven in bright abstract patterns.

Sisal: rug of sisal hemp fabric, tightly woven, and displaying geometric or herringbone designs. Sisal-look rugs are now being made in wool.

WOOD FLOORING

Wood is a classic floor covering that complements virtually any decorating style. It is versatile, relatively inexpensive, and takes well to refinishing when it gets old and worn looking. Stained or polished to a new shine, many a beautiful floor has emerged from underneath a layer of old carpet or vinyl.

Hardwoods, including oak, maple, beech, birch, hickory, walnut, mahogany, and teak, offer rich colors and durability, but are more expensive. Softwoods, typically pine, are less expensive, but more prone to scratches and denting. (See pages 224–227 for care of wood floors.)

Wood floors come in three types:

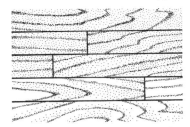

Strip: the most common type of wood flooring; is made up of 2- to 3-inch wide boards usually laid lengthwise, crosswise, or on a diagonal. It gives linear perspective to a room and shows off the natural beauty of wood.

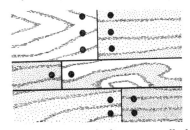

Plank: composed of strips installed in random widths. It is reminiscent of Colonial-era design, and can be ordered with wooden plugs at the end of each board to simulate the pegged floors of that time.

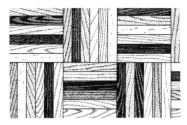

Parquet blocks: squares of wood strips, typically measuring 12" × 12". They are more decorative than strip or plank flooring and create strong patterns underfoot.

Wood Grades

Wood flooring is graded according to its appearance. The highest grades have the fewest knots and surface variations in color and grain. Strength and durability do not diminish in lower grades of the same wood. You may prefer a lower grade with more surface variations and knots, which can add interest to the grain pattern. There are three basic grades.

Clear: the highest grade; indicates heartwood (the best-quality wood from the tree heart), generally free of defects.

Select: the next highest grade; also high quality but has some knots and color variations.

Common: the lowest grades; have more knots, burls, and streaks than the above grades, but are sometimes chosen for this very reason to add character.

Costs vary depending on the type and grade of wood, the finish, and the region of the country in which you live, but you can generally count on spending about $4 to $10 per square foot for wood floors.

RESILIENT FLOORING

There are several types of resilient floor coverings available including vinyl sheet goods, vinyl composition tile, solid vinyl tile, and rubber floors.

Vinyl sheet goods are available in a vast array of colors and patterns. The best consist of a durable wear layer over a printed or inlaid pattern and cushion backing. Depending on construction, vinyl sheet goods feature varying degrees of stain resistance, care requirements, and cost.

Vinyl composition tile made of vinyl resins, fillers, and color pigments, is generally less expensive than vinyl sheet goods. It is available in many colors and patterns. The self-stick variety is well suited for do-it-yourselfers.

Both solid vinyl tile and rubber flooring are generally very durable. However, colors and patterns can be limited and cost is usually high.

There are two basic forms of resilient floors: tiles and sheet goods. Sheet goods have fewer seams to attract dirt than tiles do, but their installation is difficult and best left to a professional.

Both types can be laid directly over a smooth concrete or wood subfloor or an existing floor that is properly prepared.

LOW UPKEEP

☞ Light-colored vinyl tends to show scuff marks. If you are using vinyl in a heavy-traffic area, select a pattern that will camouflage scuffs and dirt.

TILE AND ERROR

☞ Always buy extra tiles for repairs since stock colors and styles change frequently. If you are making a repair and don't have any of the original tile, be creative. Choose a different kind—for instance, glazed with a decoration—to set next to and complement unglazed terra-cotta tiles.

NONRESILIENT FLOORING

Floor materials that are hard and do not give underfoot, such as slate, marble, granite, brick, and tile, are called nonresilient.

While these materials do not offer the comfort of wood and vinyl, they are extremely durable. In temperate climates, most nonresilient materials can be laid outdoors as well as indoors and are, therefore, ideal for extending indoor-outdoor living and entertaining areas.

Nonresilient flooring can be relatively expensive due to both the cost of the material and the cost of labor to install them properly. (It is possible to install these types of flooring yourself, but it is difficult and time consuming, and the margin for error is very high.) If you find the look appealing, you can bring costs down by limiting such materials to a small area, such as a foyer.

Stone and Brick

Stone flooring comes in a remarkable range of colors, so you can find one to go with virtually any color scheme. It can be laid in irregular patterns, which tend to look casual, or regular patterns, which establish a more formal ambience.

Marble and granite, which come in tile form, are the most elegant; you can also use slate. While some experts recommend sealing stone floors for protection, the sealant can cause marble to discolor.

Brick, which can be laid in a variety of graphic patterns, needs a polyurethane sealer so it doesn't stain.

Ceramic Tile

Since ceramic floor tile, typically laid directly on a subfloor with adhesive and finished with grout, is impervious to water, it makes a particularly good choice for bathrooms, entry halls, and sun rooms. Unglazed tile is a good choice for patios, because it is not slippery like glazed tile.

In general, the more expensive the tile, the better the quality. Grout is available in a wide variety of colors to match any color or pattern of tile.

Glazed ceramic tile cleans easily and does not need to be sealed, but grout does.

Quarry Tile

This is usually unglazed with a matte finish. It comes in the various earthy tones of clay as well as with decorative finishes in a wide range of colors. Unglazed quarry tile must be finished with a sealer after it is laid or it will stain. It too is secured with grout.

Terra-cotta: plain ceramic tile that comes decorated with relief or inlaid designs. Be aware that it can stain.

Color-glazed floor tile: useful for bathrooms if small tiles are specified; the small size keeps the floor from being slippery, and the glazing keeps water from seeping into the tile.

FURNITURE

There is no single rule for choosing furniture. Some people prefer using old family pieces, adding new items as needs or tastes change.

Others prefer to start from scratch, buying all the pieces for a room at one time to make sure that everything is coordinated precisely. Your choices depend entirely on your personal taste, budget, and decor.

If you decide to buy a new piece, it pays to invest in the best quality you can afford. A cheap upholstered piece will probably lose its shape and pop its springs in a few years, whereas a better version can last for generations.

Opt for classic styles and durable fabrics, and avoid fad styles that soon look dated. If the structure is sound, you can always revitalize a chair or sofa with new upholstery or a slipcover when the upholstery wears out.

SHOPPING ON A BUDGET

You don't have to buy cheap furniture to buy furniture cheaply. There are lots of ways to get the pieces you want—from high-style designs to antiques—at prices you can afford.

Familiarize yourself with good-quality pieces: Browse in better stores, even if your budget is tight, a sale may bring the price of a better piece down to one you can afford. Some department stores have special plans to delay or spread out your payments without charging you interest.

Shop for floor samples: Most stores hold regular sample sales. Even if a sale isn't on, a lower price is often available for the asking.

Try making kit furniture: A full range of pieces, from tables to sofas, is available in kit form. Most styles are contemporary, but, mixed with antiques, they can create a warm and inviting decor.

Shop for used furniture and antique pieces at flea markets and estate sales: Don't fool yourself; choose pieces that don't need repairing and refinishing if you will be unhappy undertaking those projects. Check for wear and scratches.

Buy from a decorator show house at the end of its run: You get high style at a fraction of the usual cost.

ANTIQUES

Any piece of furniture that is over 100 years old is considered an antique. It takes considerable expertise to make serious investments in antiques, but not all purchases have to be major. You can still find bargains at auctions and flea markets. Many moderately priced antiques are cheaper than a similar new piece bought off the showroom floor.

When buying an old piece, check to see whether it is stable. Doors should swing smoothly and quietly, hang evenly, and close and remain closed. Drawers should slide freely. Look for interlocking dovetail joinery and a uniform finish. Even hard-to-reach areas near joints or in carvings should be evenly stained and free of glue.

Alterations reduce the value of an antique, so it is wise to check for repairs and patching if you consider your purchase an investment.

Otherwise, choose an old piece for the same reason you would a new one: because you love it.

CARING FOR WOOD FURNITURE

Wood furniture benefits from moderate humidity and a steady temperature.

- Draw curtains whenever possible to avoid overexposure to direct sunlight, which causes fading and dryness.

- Store table leaves as close as possible to the table itself so all are exposed to the same humidity levels.

- Dust with a lint-free cloth.

- Use a humidifier in the winter if your house is very dry.

- Avoid placing furniture in front of sources of direct heat, such as radiators, registers, and fireplaces.

ANATOMY OF AN UPHOLSTERED CHAIR

*EVERY ASPECT OF upholstered furniture is important—
especially parts you cannot see.*

CREDIT OR CON?

☛ Avoid so-called easy credit deals for large furniture purchases. Reputable stores don't even offer them and they are sure to add a considerable sum to the list price, often with hidden interest charges and penalties.

SAVING A SEAT

☛ To save money, you can update old-fashioned porch or den furniture. If you are buying it used, rather than refurbishing a piece you already own, look for structural soundness and original cushions with springs. Foam rubber deteriorates and may have to be replaced.

CHECK THE CUSHIONS

Before you buy an upholstered chair or sofa, make sure the cushions:

☛ Have the same firmness.
☛ Are identical on both sides so you can reverse them.
☛ Have zippers.
☛ Are covered under the upholstery with durable fabric.

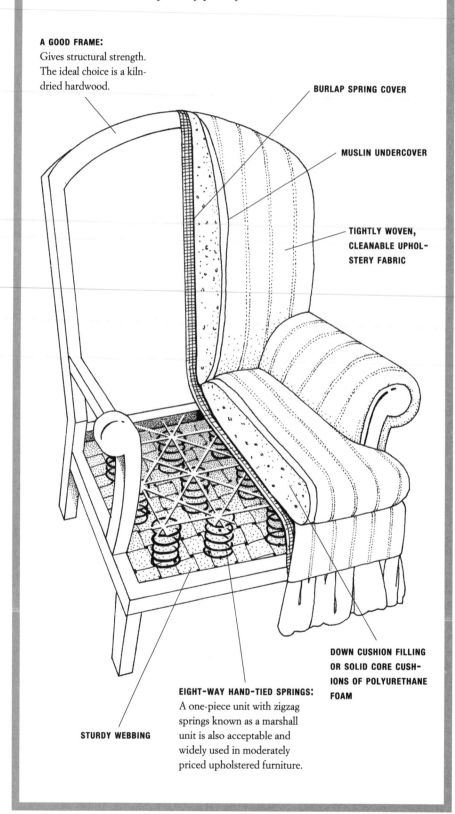

A GOOD FRAME:
Gives structural strength. The ideal choice is a kiln-dried hardwood.

BURLAP SPRING COVER

MUSLIN UNDERCOVER

TIGHTLY WOVEN, CLEANABLE UPHOLSTERY FABRIC

DOWN CUSHION FILLING OR SOLID CORE CUSHIONS OF POLYURETHANE FOAM

EIGHT-WAY HAND-TIED SPRINGS:
A one-piece unit with zigzag springs known as a marshall unit is also acceptable and widely used in moderately priced upholstered furniture.

STURDY WEBBING

SLIPCOVERS

Slipcovers expand your decorating options for upholstered furniture. Use them to cover a threadbare sofa or chair, for a seasonal change, or to protect pieces from heavy use.

CHAIR WITHOUT A SLIPCOVER

SAME CHAIR WITH A SLIPCOVER

- Consider buying an upholstered sofa that also comes with a set of slipcovers; you'll get twice the longevity out of the upholstery.

- Slipcovers can be custom made or bought ready made. Custom-made covers fit best and cost the most. You can save money if you're handy with a sewing machine by stitching your own custom covers. Look for patterns in fabric stores.

- Ready-made covers are sold in chain stores. Or try draping a piece with sheets or remnants and tuck and tie the fabric into place. Use double-faced tape to secure the material.

SPACE STATIONS

☞ Multipurpose pieces such as drop-leaf and extension tables, nesting side tables, sleep sofas, and futons all provide convenience and can be tucked into place when not in use.

CUSHION COMFORT

☞ Avoid shredded foam cushions; the foam mats eventually and the cushions become lumpy.

STURDY FURNITURE

☞ To test for quality, lift an upholstered piece from one end; you shouldn't hear any creaking sounds. Check for reinforcement blocks at points of structural stress, such as corners, and ask your salesperson what type of wood the frame is. It should be made of a hardwood, such as oak or maple.

UNFINISHED FINISH

☞ Check to see if the back of a large case piece—such as a hutch, bookcase, or bureau—is finished. Some manufacturers use low grade wood for the back to reduce the price. This is okay if you plan to place a piece against a wall.

BUYING A MATTRESS

Always buy a mattress and a box spring together. The only way to determine comfort and firmness is to lie down and try the bed in the showroom. If you are going to share it, be sure to shop with your partner.

Innerspring mattress on a box-spring foundation: the most popular choice. Both units have tempered-steel wire coils covered with layers of padding.

The standard number of coils varies depending on the bed size; at least 200 coils for a twin bed, 300 coils for a double, 375 coils for a queen, and 450 for a king are recommended.

Foam mattress (without coils): differs from innerspring in "feel." The polyurethane foam should have a minimum density of 2 pounds per cubic foot.

Top-of-the-line mattresses generally offer the best durability and lasting support.

THE WELL-DRESSED BED

Bedclothes, which come in numerous variations, can dramatically change the look of your bed—and your bedroom. The set here has all the essentials, plus some popular decorative touches. Instead of a floor-length bedspread, many people prefer a dust ruffle, which fits under the mattress, topped by a comforter or duvet (with a removable cover for easy washing).

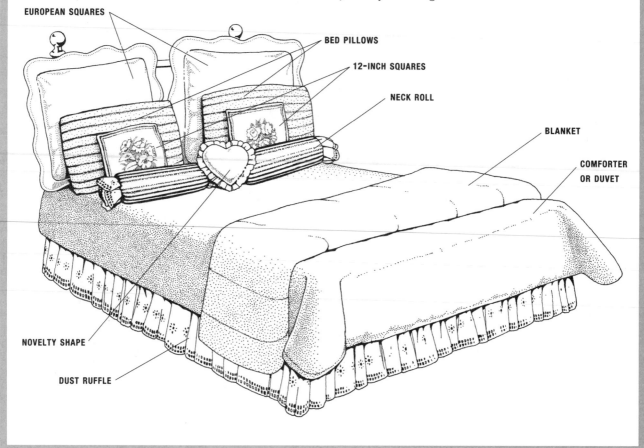

EUROPEAN SQUARES

BED PILLOWS

12-INCH SQUARES

NECK ROLL

BLANKET

COMFORTER OR DUVET

NOVELTY SHAPE

DUST RUFFLE

MATTRESS STANDARDS

☞ Mattresses and box springs come in these standard lengths and widths:
daybed (33" x 76")
twin (39" x 76")
double (54" x 76")
queen (60" x 80")
king (76" x 80")
You can also have mattresses and custom sheets made to fit odd-sized beds and headboards.

PILLOW TALK

Fine pillows are usually closed by a hand-sewn seam rather than with a zipper; under the outer covering, a muslin ticking usually covers the stuffing. The stuffing itself might be one of the following:

- Down: tiny feathers; very soft and plush.
- Down/feather mixture: soft, but not as soft as pure down.
- Down with polyester fiberfill: similar to down and feathers but less expensive.
- Foam rubber: firm; typically less expensive than other types.

WALL DECORATIONS

Few rooms seem complete without wall decorations. Paintings, prints, posters, photographs, textiles, and drawings are obvious choices, but you can also use autographs, maps, children's artwork, awards, diplomas, and old advertising art and decorative plates to great effect.

Before hanging a group of wall decorations, lay it out on the floor or draw it to scale on a piece of graph paper. You can also get an idea of how it will look by tracing the framed artwork on paper, then making cutouts and taping them to the wall.

If you want to assemble a composition slowly over a period of time, start with the largest picture you have in the center and fill in around it as you go.

FRAMING

The best way to try out different frames and mats for a work of art is to bring the piece to a frame shop.

Deciding on mat size and color is usually a matter of eyeing the art, mat, and frame together. Put different combinations in each corner and stand back to judge the effect. Some people prefer a mat that is slightly wider on the bottom to add substance and weight. Art dealers and collectors recommend:

THE BIG PICTURE

☛ A mix of pictures and other items mounted in a group can substitute for a single large picture.

GETTING FRAMED

☛ Custom framing can be surprisingly expensive. You can save money by using ready-made frames, available in art-supply stores and through catalogs, and following simple instructions. Some frame-shop outlets also offer a do-it-yourself service. You do the simpler tasks like fitting the pieces together; then the store takes over, cutting the mat and assembling the glass and frame.

CARING FOR FRAMED ART

NEVER:

- Spray cleaner directly onto the glass. It can stain the mat or art if it drips behind. Instead, spray the cleaner onto a cloth before dusting.

- Hang or store art over a radiator or heat register. If you hang a piece over a fireplace, there should be a mantel to deflect heat, soot, and smoke, which can damage a work rapidly.

- Hang valuable art in a bathroom or kitchen where moisture or grease can harm it.

- Direct a bright light onto a piece of art. If you are using a picture light, make sure it is not stronger than 25 watts.

- Expose art to direct sunlight, which can badly fade prints and paintings.

ALWAYS:

- Inspect your framed artwork periodically. If you notice deterioration, stains, or other changes, have a custom framer check them.

HOW TO HANG PICTURES AND MIRRORS

KEEP THESE TIPS in mind when hanging pictures and mirrors:

- Hang pieces so they are at eye level. A foot or so above the average furniture piece is typical.

- If you are hanging small works, such as a group of family photos, make sure people can see them.

- A busy background, such as strongly patterned wallpaper, needs strong pictures. However, avoid highly ornate frames for walls with very busy wallpaper. Such a frame looks much better against a simpler background or a solid color.

- Experiment with shapes. A circle, oval, or diamond introduced among the usual squares and rectangles of picture frames will make a dramatic statement.

HANGING A MIRROR

☞ To hang a mirror, use hardware made specifically for that purpose (see pages 216–217). Make sure that the fastener is securely attached to both the wall and the mirror. Check the package's instructions or with the retailer to be certain that it is adequate for the weight it will bear.

FLOWER POWER

☞ A shadow-box frame has a very deep interior so three-dimensional items such as dried flowers can be displayed in it.

Acid-free matting and museum-quality adhesives: ordinary paper and adhesives can cause discoloring.

Museum-type frames: these separate artwork and glass so they do not touch.

Ultraviolet-resistant glass if exposure to excessive sunlight is anticipated: too much sun can fade pigments under ordinary glass.

Glare-free glass: if you are hanging a picture in a very sunny area.

Since needlework and textiles are particularly fragile, have them mounted so they can be unmounted without harm. Have your frame shop do this or ask them for guidelines.

Mirrors

A beautifully framed mirror can have as much decorative effect in a room as a painting and is often a less expensive alternative. It will also add sparkle and make the most of natural light by reflecting it.

There are as many different types of mirror frames as there are picture frames. You can also use picture molding—wood or plaster framing usually used for posters or art—to hold a mirror. Glass-framed Venetian mirrors and mirrors with carved baroque frames are such powerful decorative elements that they can be used as focal points. Also consider stars, sunbursts, tiny mirrors in very large frames, round bull's-eye mirrors, and mirrors in unusual shapes or made of smoked glass.

You can add mirrors to a mixed group of wall decorations or hang several framed mirrors in various sizes and shapes together for an unusual display.

FLOWERS

Cut flowers enliven any room with their color and beauty, and those with a strong scent, such as hyacinths, lilies of the valley, and paperwhite narcissus, also impart a lovely aroma to the air.

Like potted plants, however, cut flowers need special care:

- Cut garden flowers early in the morning or after sundown, rather than in the midday heat. Bring a bucket with a few inches of lukewarm water with you and place each stem in it as soon as you cut it. When you return to the house, refill the bucket with cold water and leave it in a cool, dark place overnight, or at least for several hours. This conditions the flowers and provides needed moisture. (Purchased flowers also need a water bath for a few hours before they are arranged.)

- Flowers with woody stems, such as roses, chrysanthemums, and lilacs, last longer if you scrape and split the stem ends with a knife, so they can absorb more water. If a stem exudes a milky substance, as poppies and poinsettias do, seal the end by dipping it in boiling water or singe it with a candle.

- Recut the stems of cut flowers and strip the bottom leaves before placing them in water so they can drink.

HOW TO ARRANGE FLOWERS

IF YOU ARE USING A shallow container to arrange flowers, you need a holder, such as a wire frog or the spongy material called oasis (which should be soaked in water for 15 minutes before use). Anchor the frog with tape or wedge the oasis in place. You can also use marbles or crumpled chicken wire for support.

Professional flower designers offer these secrets to success:

- Build the arrangement so that it echoes the shape of the container or roughly follows the form of a circle, sphere, or triangle.

- Use larger foliage and flowers to form the basic shape. Place the tallest items first. Then place additional items to make the outline of your design. Fill in with more flowers and foliage.

- Dark colors often look best at the base or center of the arrangement, with lighter colors near the edges.

- For the best effect, floral centerpieces should be 2 inches lower than eye level of seated guests.

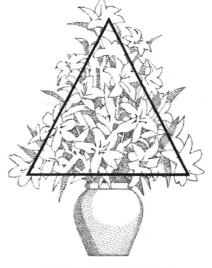

FOLLOWING A TRIANGLE SHAPE

FROG

OASIS

THE KITCHEN

While the design guidelines on pages 156-191 apply to any room in the house, some rooms need special consideration. First and foremost is the kitchen. You can improve an existing kitchen plan or design a new one by following these simple rules for space usage.

- Store the utensils and appliances you use the most so they are easily accessible.

- Keep your work areas clear and reserve plenty of room to put away utensils, tableware, cleaning supplies, and food.

- Designate a snack preparation area—perhaps with a microwave oven—to help keep traffic out of the main work space. If you cook or entertain a lot, consider a 6-burner stove top and an extra sink. Many families also like to have a place for informal meals in the kitchen.

FREE KITCHEN DESIGN

☞ Many home store chains offer free computer-aided kitchen design. Take advantage of this service.

CABINETS

Cabinets are the main design element in a kitchen and usually the biggest expense. To save money, you might simply refinish the cabinets you have; painting or replacing the fronts or even the hardware can also give them a brand-new look.

Replacement choices include factory-made stock units and custom-made woodwork. Stock cabinets offer a huge range of colors, finishes, and door designs, as well as storage options, such as pull-out doors and divided tray racks, and are usually available faster than custom designs (in about six to eight weeks).

Custom designs generally take longer and cost more, but not always. If you want a simple design, a contractor or carpenter may build cabinets for less than the price of stock models, so it is worth looking into.

Inspect your cabinets thoroughly before you have them installed to be sure

SPACE-STRATEGY

TO SAVE SPACE:

- In a narrow corridor kitchen, group all the appliances on one side and keep the counter depth to 24 inches. Keep the counter depth on the opposite side to 18 inches and gain 6 inches of floor space for easier movement around the room.

- Install a fold-down work surface.

- Use top cabinets that extend to the ceiling for more storage space.

- Lay flooring on a diagonal to make the room seem wider.

- Hang pots and utensils from an iron rack or use a pegboard.

FOR ENOUGH SPACE:

- Reserve 2 to 3 feet of counter area for food preparation in a small kitchen, and 3 to 4 feet of counter area in a large kitchen. Three feet of counter space in the cooking area is also recommended.

- Standard counter height is 3 feet.

- Do not make service or cooking islands closer than 3 feet from any wall cabinets.

- Reserve 3 feet of counter space for dishwashing and drying.

they have arrived as ordered and are in perfect condition. Look for consistency of paint color or wood grain. Professional installation is recommended; if you don't want to use your architect, designer, or a carpenter, local home stores now offer the services of a professional to install cabinets at a cheaper price. After the cabinets are installed, make sure the drawers ride smoothly, the doors hang evenly, and clearances are adequate.

COUNTERTOPS

The ideal countertop is impervious to stains, scratches, and moisture, won't scorch, and is easy to clean. Unfortunately no single material offers all of these attributes, so you need to weigh the drawbacks and advantages of each type. The following materials are the most commonly used; if possible, bring samples home and test them for durability yourself.

Ceramic tile: available in a wide selection of colors and patterns in an equally wide price range. Tiles are somewhat prone to chipping and cracking and can cause china and glass to break on impact. The tiles themselves are heat resistant and easy to clean, but the grout tends to collect soil and food. The surface is expensive, but lasts a long time.

Granite: notable for its beautiful colors and markings, which can create an especially sophisticated look. Granite comes as a solid-surface material or in tiles. It is durable and heat resistant, but it can stain. China and glass will break on impact. The cost is generally high, but it lasts a long time.

Hardwood and butcher block: natural maple or oak surfaces that take little care, and are very durable. They do, however, burn easily. To avoid marks, don't use for cutting.

Laminate: a synthetic material sold under various brand names. It offers the broadest range of colors, including solid and patterns, such as *faux* granite and marble finishes, and is among the more economical counter surfaces. It is highly stain and scratch resistant, but it is not heatproof and it is hard to repair.

Color-through laminate: more expensive than regular laminate but the seam lines disappear, scratches are less noticeable, and repairs are easier to make.

Marble: an elegant stone, with interesting graining patterns; it is durable and makes a cool, smooth surface for rolling and kneading pastry dough. It is heat resistant, but it stains. China and glass will break on impact. It is expensive, but lasts a long time.

Solid surfacing: a manufactured material that mimics natural stone, and comes in white, neutrals, some pastels, and *faux* marble and granite patterns. It is very durable and, unlike other counter materials, can be carved and shaped for various effects. For example, a long sweep of counter can have a sink carved out of it, or a bull nose or bevel can be created on the edge. You pay for these advantages, however; the material is expensive.

Stainless steel: favored for its sleek high-tech look. This shiny material is heatproof, easy to clean, and stain resistant; it is prone to scratching.

Terrazzo: a mosaic of marble chips set in a concrete base. It is very durable and heat and water resistant, but it stains. China and glass will break on impact. It is expensive, but lasts a long time.

You may wish to design your counters with a combination of materials. A ceramic-tile or stainless-steel surface adjacent to the stove top is handy for resting hot pots and pans; a slab of butcher block will provide you with a built-in chopping area. When combining materials on the same counter, make sure the two will abut with flush seams at the same level; check with the manufacturer or your contractor.

SINKS

The location of your sink depends on the placement of the refrigerator and stove (see pages 194–195); in all cases, however,

A ROOM WITH A VIEW

☛ Windowless kitchens are a common feature of modern apartments—even expensive ones. And they can be depressing! Cheer them up by putting a window-sized poster or painting where you would ordinarily expect a window. Or, if you can, consider a 3' x 4' tile picture for the spot.

THE WORK TRIANGLE

A TRADITIONAL KITCHEN PLANNING DEVICE, the work triangle is an invisible triangle connecting the refrigerator, sink, and stove so that there is the shortest walking distance between them. If the stove and refrigerator are side by side, use extra insulation for energy conservation. The complete triangle perimeter should total less than 26 feet, measured from the center front of each appliance. No single leg of the triangle should be shorter than 4 feet or longer than 9 feet. Here are four classic plans:

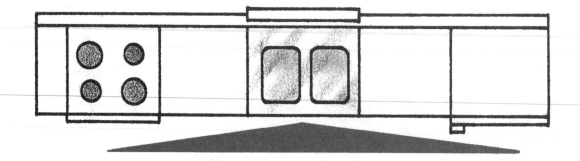

GALLEY: most efficent in long, narrow spaces

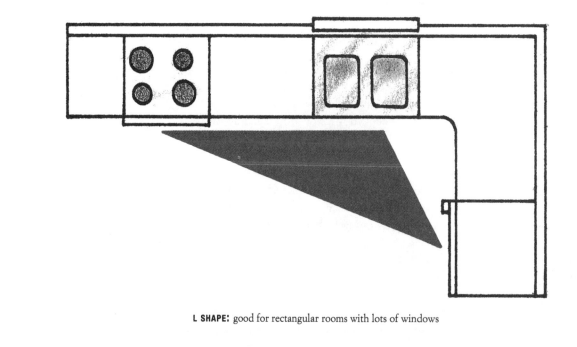

L SHAPE: good for rectangular rooms with lots of windows

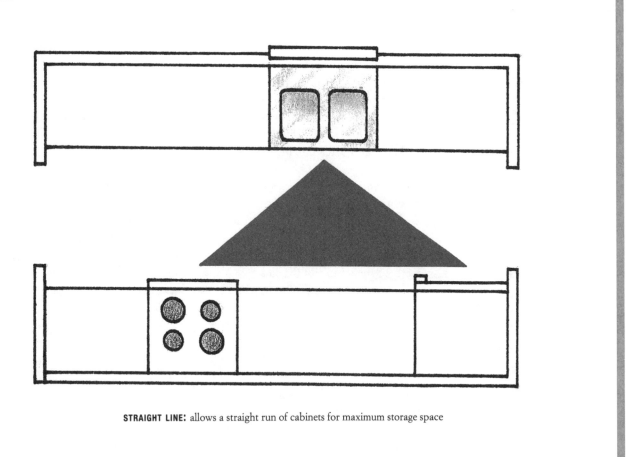

STRAIGHT LINE: allows a straight run of cabinets for maximum storage space

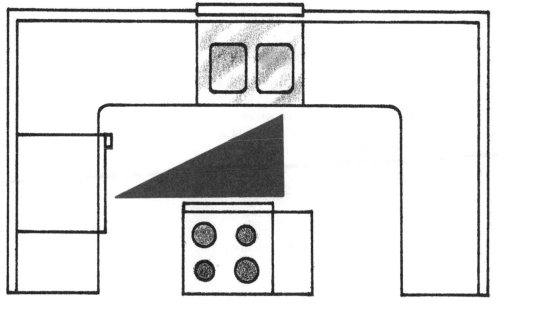

U SHAPE WITH ISLAND: makes distances shorter in large kitchens

SELECTING STAINLESS STEEL

☛ Of the two types of stainless steel, nickel and nonnickel bearing, nickel bearing is preferred because it resists stains better.

APPLIANCE INSTALLATION

☛ Professional installation of appliances is generally required. Your home center may have professionals who will install appliances for you at a lower cost than that charged by independent professionals.

SIZING UP YOUR REFRIGERATOR

☛ As a rule of thumb, two people need a minimum of 12 cubic feet of food storage; add 2 cubic feet for every additional household member. Thus, the ideal refrigerator for a household of four would have a storage capacity of 16 cubic feet. For more information about popular refrigerator-freezer combinations, see pages 142 and 144.

EASY CLEANING

☛ Put your refrigerator on casters so you can easily move it when you want to clean behind it.

it is important to have ample counter space on either side.

Faucets

The best kitchen faucets are made with an inner casing of cast or forged brass, which resists corrosion. Most new faucets are washerless, with a cartridge or ceramic disc that helps prevent dripping (see page 239). Other new features include temperature controls that can be set to save energy and prevent scalding. There is even a model that senses the presence of your hands and turns on and off automatically. Test faucets at a showroom for feel and aim; ideally they should direct water to the middle of the sink.

Faucets come in the following finishes:

Chrome: Polished chrome is the most popular finish for kitchen faucets because it is bright, durable, and does not need to be polished.

Brass: This finish will last forever, but needs to be polished periodically. Antique brass is popular for traditional looks, but it is not as durable as most other brass finishes.

Gold plate: A truly stunning finish, it is highly durable, but expensive.

SINK MATERIALS

Stainless steel: solid; cannot wear off, chip, or crack but can scratch. Easiest to keep clean; no special cleansers are required. Light and easy to install; lasts indefinitely.

Enameled steel: less expensive than stainless steel, but chips easily.

Porcelain: available in many colors. Heavy and more difficult to install. Can cause dishes to chip.

Colored coating: This is very practical, and provides the option of many different colors to match the kitchen design. It is easy to clean, but may chip.

APPLIANCES

When choosing your refrigerator, cook top, oven, or dishwasher, it is a good idea to visit many showrooms or dealers as the range of styles and types is constantly expanding. Increasingly, manufacturers design appliances that are not only hardworking, but also good-looking. Appliances now come with sleek new profiles and a variety of finishes, including glass, enamel, and stainless steel. It is also possible to fit new appliances with panels to match your countertop or cabinets.

Major appliances come in standard sizes; your choice depends on your specific space allowances. Get help from a knowledgeable salesperson. Some appliances must be operated on 220 volts instead of the more common 120 volts. Check your home's voltage capacity before making a purchase. (See pages 142–144 for more on kitchen appliances.)

Decorating and Design • THE KITCHEN

SINK TYPES

In SMALL KITCHENS (LESS THAN 150 square feet), single-bowl sinks measuring 24" x 21" are recommended. Larger kitchens can accommodate double- or triple-bowl sinks, which are ideal for the dual purposes of preparing food and depositing dirty dishes as you put together a meal. Here are some options:

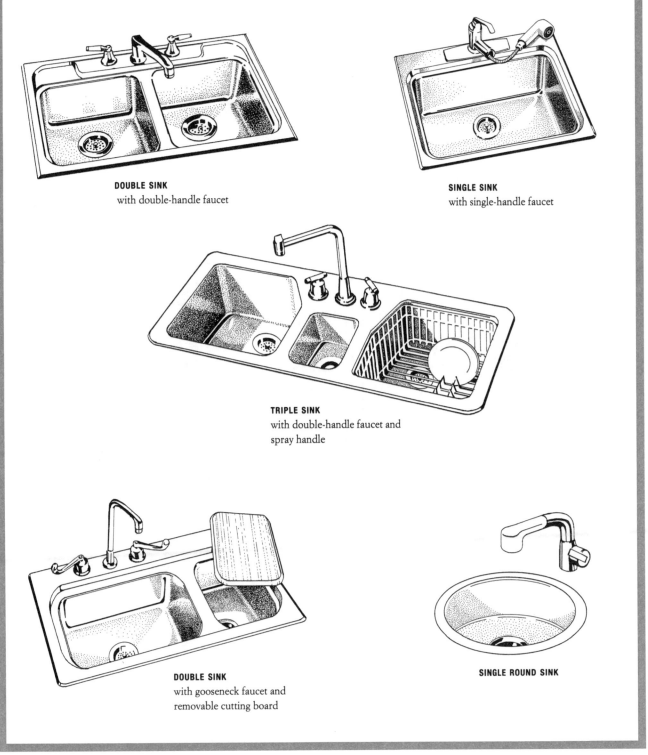

DOUBLE SINK
with double-handle faucet

SINGLE SINK
with single-handle faucet

TRIPLE SINK
with double-handle faucet and
spray handle

DOUBLE SINK
with gooseneck faucet and
removable cutting board

SINGLE ROUND SINK

KITCHEN STORAGE

Good storage can dramatically increase kitchen efficiency. Consider good-looking pots and pans part of the decor, and hang them in the open on a ceiling rack; a rolling cabinet can tuck into a corner and double as counter space or a cutting board. Use inexpensive trays and racks to organize cabinets, or try a custom pull-out door to make use of otherwise wasted space.

POT RACK

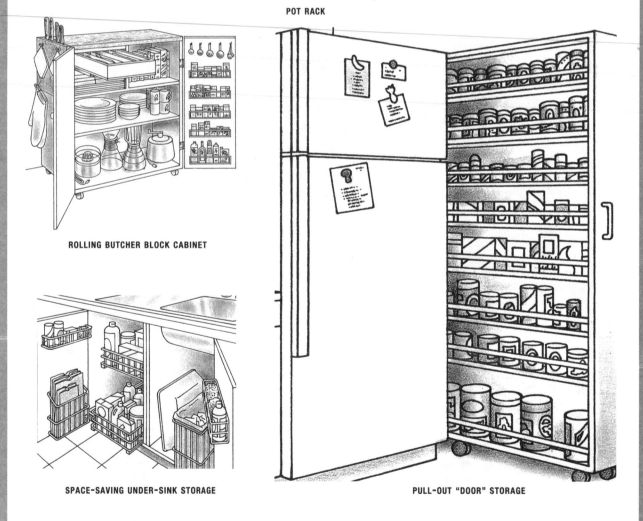

ROLLING BUTCHER BLOCK CABINET

SPACE-SAVING UNDER-SINK STORAGE

PULL-OUT "DOOR" STORAGE

THE BATHROOM

Bathrooms are often small and cramped, but they can still be attractive. Even a few inexpensive touches, like a new shower curtain or towels, can make a difference. Improving the lighting, faucets, and fixtures constitutes a bigger investment, of course, but repays you with efficiency and good looks.

Moistureproof, easy-care surfaces are best for bathrooms. Ceramic tile can be coordinated with ceramic fixtures; marble and granite tiles are also popular choices because they, too, hold up well to moisture. While these are generally more expensive than ceramic tile, they can still be relatively economical in small areas. If you are using wallpaper, choose a good-quality vinyl or coated paper and have it installed professionally so it won't peel.

FIXTURES

Like kitchen appliances, bathroom fixtures now have attractive designs, and can be chosen as much for style as for efficiency and durability. Consult your local building department before installing a new fixture to make sure it meets local regulations. Recently manufacturers have begun making easy-to-install fixtures, so you don't necessarily need to call in a professional. As a rule of thumb, white fixtures are the least expensive.

Tubs
The most common materials for tubs are vitreous china and enameled cast iron, which are durable and keep a good shine. Lighter-weight fiberglass and acrylic tubs are also gaining popularity. Molded in one piece, these are relatively easy to install. (Be sure to measure first, however, to make sure you can get the all-in-one piece through the door to your bathroom.)

Many tubs are also set into a surround, which can be finished with ceramic or stone tile that is made without sharp edges for such purposes. Tubs come in standard lengths and depths. Ask a salesperson to let you get into a tub you are considering and test it for comfort; the way the back is sloped can make a big difference.

If your bathroom is odd shaped or small, you may want to consider a square or round tub. Always check the water capacity and weight of a tub to make sure that your house framing can support it.

Greater water demand will place a burden on your water heater and pressure, so you may need to upgrade these systems. Ask your plumbing contractor.

Showers
Most tubs can be fitted with a shower head so you have both fixtures in one, but a stall shower is more common in a small bathroom. The flat floor minimizes slipping. Some stall showers come with a seat; you can also install a waterproof ceiling light for safety and convenience.

The key to a good shower is a good-quality shower head that can be adjusted for angle, jet power, and stream. You can also install water jets at waist level to help you direct water to tired muscles, much as a whirlpool jet does.

Sinks
There are three basic types of bathroom sinks: pedestal, wall mounted, and vanity. Some wall-mounted models are made to fit in corners, which helps make the most of tight space. Vanities provide useful counter space and can often accommodate more than one sink.

Hardware
Tub, shower, and sink faucets are usually a separate purchase. Some are installed in

BATHROOM CHECKLIST

For a safe, efficient bathroom, be sure you have:
☛ A low water use toilet and washerless faucets.
☛ Durable, moistureproof, stain-resistant surfaces.
☛ Good ventilation.
☛ Adequate light, especially over the sink.
☛ Nonslip floors, grab bars in the tub and shower, and no obstructions to trip you in the dark.
☛ Plastic, rather than glass, bottles.

TALL TALE

☛ The comfortable sink height for most adults is from 34 to 38 inches. You can mount a wall sink wherever you want it; vanity sinks can be made tall.

☞ If possible, light both the sides and the top of the mirror.

☞ Don't overlight: 120 to 180 watts total are adequate in a small bathroom. Shiny surfaces cause stronger light to glare.

☞ Opt for incandescent bulbs, which flatter skin tones.

BATHROOM SPACE SAVERS

- Consider buying the small-sized fixtures used on boats; you can shop for them through boating supply catalogs.

- Hang a triangular cabinet or shelves to take advantage of corner space.

- To minimize clutter, give each household member his or her own shelf or basket and label it.

- Keep individual blow dryers, toiletries, and grooming supplies in family members' bedrooms.

- Use hooks for towels. Four towels fit in the space needed to hang two towels on a towel bar.

- Hang a vinyl-coated shower caddy from the shower head to store shampoo bottles and soap neatly.

the fixture itself, some in the wall above. Typical materials are chrome, ceramic, plastic, and enamel; choose the best quality that your budget allows.

Toilets and Bidets

While toilets come in a variety of styles and colors, the most important factors to consider are how they flush and how much water they use. Check with your salesperson about the flushing system; many models now offer more efficient alternatives to the old-fashioned water guzzlers, which flush water down the sides. A 1.5-gallon flush toilet is a much better choice than older 5-gallon flush models.

A good option is siphon flushing, which is quiet, traps odors, and uses less water than side flushing. Another, less costly choice is the reverse-trap type.

Although they are more common in Europe, bidets are gaining popularity in this country. A typical bidet fills like a sink, and has adjustable water temperature and a water flush around the rim that serves as a cleaning aid. A new type has an upward spray mechanism in the center so that all washing is done with clean running water.

Bidets are generally sold in colors and designs that coordinate with toilet fixtures, so you can buy the two as a pair. Most models are oval so they can be straddled; some come in chair designs. Locate a bidet next to the toilet with plenty of room for access.

THE HOME OFFICE

Many people find it useful to have a home office, either for paying bills and writing letters, or for conducting business. An extra bedroom is an ideal space to set up an office, but if you don't have that option, you can create one in part of a room.

Find an out-of-the-way area such as an alcove in the living room or the corner of a large foyer. Set up a desk (a table works just as well) and file cabinets, and partition off the area with bookshelves.

Your basic need is enough space; then improvise. Square baskets make great ad hoc file cabinets and can tuck easily under your work area. Keep pencils and pens neat with a catchall caddy and supplement your file system with a bulletin board.

FURNITURE

You can take advantage of recent innovations in office furniture. All-in-one office units save space and often offer options such as camouflaging doors that close over your work area to hide paper files and electronics when they are not being used. File stacks fit into 12" x 12" spaces.

- Take computer measurements along when you buy furniture so you don't buy the wrong size. For example, printers vary in dimensions, so some may need more space than others.

- Ergonomic chairs (designed for people performing specific tasks) are crucial for prolonged computer or desk work.

- If you have room, consider a small round table, which is great for office meetings.

- If you don't want to invest in a desk, create one that you can easily take apart.

LIGHTING AND ELECTRONICS

Pay attention to lighting. It is one of the most important elements of office design. Lighting on the computer screen should be indirect to prevent glare. To illuminate working materials, however, you may want to consider a direct lighting source such as a gooseneck or swivel lamp.

- Be sure you have enough electronic outlets and jacks for phones, faxes, etc. This is the electronic age and you always need more than you think.

- Invest in a surge suppressor to protect your equipment from electrical glitches. Even when there isn't a storm, elec-trical surges can harm your computer; always unplug your computer when it isn't being used.

- If your computer screen is near a wall, don't select a bright print wall covering. Choose low-glare wall coverings and desk surfaces and matte-textured fabrics in medium tones to avoid added glare. Persistent glare can be reduced by antiglare filters that attach directly to computer monitors.

- Working on a computer for prolonged periods can lead to visual and muscular fatigue. Much of this stress can be avoided by using a chair with adequate back and shoulder support, arranging the computer monitor so that it is 18 to 24 inches away and slightly below eye level, placing the keyboard for comfortable typing, and by taking occasional breaks (every two hours or so).

THE IDEAL OFFICE

A GOOD HOME OFFICE IS both comfortable and functional. Make sure that the chair and desk heights are suitable and that the lighting is good.

WINDOW:
Should be at right angle to display screen face. Pull curtains if the terminal is less than 20 feet away.

DISPLAY SCREEN:
Top should be slightly below eye level. Adjusts for height and angle.

CHAIR:
Backrest should support lower back.

SEAT HEIGHT:
Should be adjustable for comfortable posture.

DOCUMENT HOLDER:
Should be at same height and distance from the user as the display screen.

WALL:
Use matte paint finish to prevent glare.

DESK TOP:
Should leave enough leg room and space for posture adjustments.

STORAGE

(To learn how to cut clutter, see page 22.)

The good news is almost any storage area can be better organized. With a little planning, any closet, cupboard, or shelf can hold more and be more convenient.

The bad news is that everyone has too much stuff for too little space and clutter—the inevitable result of too many things left out in the open—is a constant problem. (To learn how to cut clutter, see page 22.)

Increase storage space by adding storage extenders. For instance, a shoe rack mounted on the wall of a closet will free the floor for a wheeled unit holding half a dozen bulky sweaters. Consider using a drop shelf that flips up to become a table or desk in a tight space, or a pullout TV shelf that makes your television less obtrusive when not in use.

Minimize clutter by assigning a place for all the objects you own. Have an attractive box on a bureau to catch spare change, notes, bills, receipts, paper clips, loose buttons, and jewelry. Hang a rack near the door for keys, and have a table at the entryway for gloves, hats, mail, and kids' backpacks and school bags.

WALL SYSTEMS

An arrangement of cupboards and shelves known as a wall system can be one of the most efficient solutions to your storage problems.

Most storage system units have optional fittings to accommodate different storage needs, including record dividers, drawers for audio- and videocassettes, drop-leaf panels for use as a desk or bar, and display lights. Most of these can be added as you like, which minimizes expenses.

In general, stacking systems offer more flexibility than tall all-in-one pieces. Since stacking modules are usually smaller, they can be rearranged into a variety of configurations and built up to different heights. They are also easy to move. Look for units with a leveling device in the base so that they can be lined up exactly.

BOOKCASES

Books are collectively heavy, so it is important to make sure your shelves are well supported. Sturdy shelving has a tight-fitting back panel, cross bracing, and corner blocks. Stationary shelves that are structurally locked into the side panels are the most stable, but adjustable shelves are more flexible; these are fine for paperbacks.

Standard-size hardcovers need 10 to 12 inches of shelf depth. Oversized art books, reference volumes, and manuals require a depth of 15 to 18 inches.

KID STUFF

☞ In a child's room where new toys and paraphernalia seem to materialize almost daily, toy chests, under-bed boxes, clothes bags, and child-sized hangers are especially handy.

TRUNK SPACE

☞ A big steamer or camp trunk can serve as a sideboard in the dining area and can hold dishes, silverware, serving pieces, table linens, and even out-of-season blankets and quilts. Top it with an unusual piece of fabric to add visual interest.

☞ For more storage space, use small trunks or chests as coffee tables and side tables in the living room and den, and as tables in the bedroom.

SHELF STORAGE

- When shopping for a wall system, check to see if the shelves are structurally attached to the cabinet, rather than resting on movable pins; the unit will support more weight.

- If you own freestanding bookcases and storage units, but would prefer a built-in look, you can add decorative moldings at the top and bottom and paint or stain the units to match the walls. Or you can refinish the wall to match the storage units.

Children's Storage

*Kids like to keep their belongings out on display;
ample shelf space, pegs, and a roller toy chest help them do it neatly.*

Bedroom Storage

*Built-ins can go a long way to maximizing space in a bedroom.
This simple but efficient design lets you show off your books while neatly
stowing clothes and bedding in drawers and cupboards.*

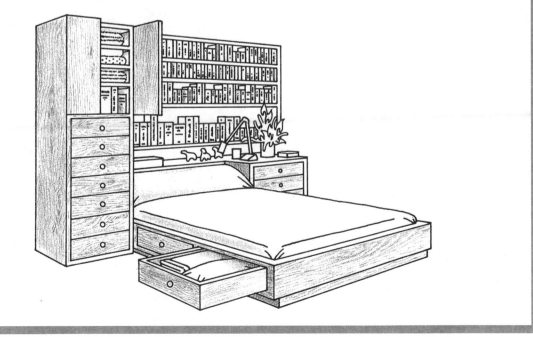

Organizing Your Closets

To organize a closet or wardrobe, consider ready-made storage extenders such as shelves, shoe holders, and hanging bars, available in home decorating stores and easily installed.

Tidy Tips

You can also try these space-saving ideas:

- Replace a single hanging bar with several bars at different heights. Jackets, blouses, trousers, and skirts can be hung in tiers.

- Hang high shelves to store items that are used only occasionally or seasonally (such as ice skates), leaving lower shelves and storage areas for more frequently used items.

- Build shelves or cubbyholes to accommodate shoes, sweaters, bulky clothing, and sports equipment.

- Fit children's closets with adjustable rods to "grow" with the child.

- Think creatively. If there isn't enough room for bed linens in a hall or bedroom closet, put them in an empty dining-room sideboard. Or place Christmas items on the top shelf in the pantry.

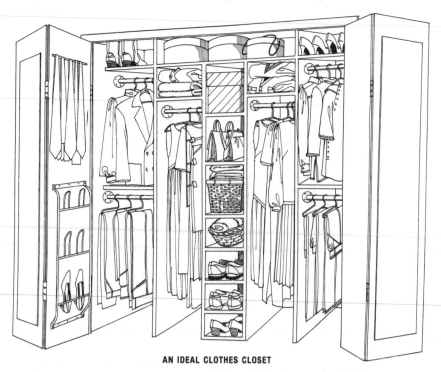

AN IDEAL CLOTHES CLOSET

AN IDEAL LINEN CLOSET

CHAPTER 6

MAINTENANCE AND REPAIR

Front-Wheel-Dri... ...ools, Upholstered Furniture, Your C... ...How to Turn Bed Sheets into Curt... ...☛HANDY TIPS: For Buffing Wood Flo... ...king Rooms Look Larger, Ironing ... ...ning Tile Grout, Creating a ☛MONEY-SAVING HINTS: How to Turn Bed Sheets into Curtains, Save on Car Repairs, *Buy Produce, Choose Carpeting* ☛HANDY TIPS: *For Buffing Wood Floors, Preventing Carpet Dents, Unsticking Stacked Glasses, Making Rooms Look Larger, Ironing Pleated Skirts, Arranging Flowers* ☛THE HOME WORKSHOP: *When to use nails, screws, bolts, and hooks. Stepladder and extension ladder ratings and safety tips.* ☛MENDING CHINA AND GLASS: *Choosing the right glue.* ☛RESTORING WOOD FURNITURE: *Camouflaging scratches, dents, and stains. Strengthen aging chairs by refitting rungs and spindles. Pros and cons of varnish, paint, and stain finishes.* ☛WALL AND CEILING REPAIRS: *Patching plaster and plasterboard. Applying spackle smoothly.* ☛HOW TO HANG ANYTHING: *Picking the right hanger. Putting hangers into wall studs for better support.* ☛DOORS: *Truing misaligned hinges. Silencing squeaky doors and rattling doorknobs. Step-by-step lock installation.* ☛WINDOWS AND SCREENS: *Opening a jammed window. Patching and replacing screens. Replacing broken glass.* ☛FLOORS: *Reviving wood floor finishes. How to put in new parquet, vinyl, and ceramic tiles. A guide to wood floor treatment options.* ☛HEATING SYSTEMS: *Thermostats, furnaces, boilers, and heaters. Hints for a warmer home. Using your fireplace safely.* ☛COOLING SYSTEMS: *Air conditioners and fans.* ☛WEATHERPROOFING: *Weather stripping and insulated windows. Proper insulation placement.* ☛PLUMBING: *Thawing frozen pipes. Short-term pipe repair. Fixing leaky faucets. Unblocking clogged drains and toilets.* ☛ELECTRICITY: *Repairing tripped circuits and blown fuses. Replacing old cords and switches. How to install a new outlet.* ☛ROOF REPAIRS: *Following water flow to discover leaks.* ☛GUTTERS: *Combating rust and wear. Cleaning out dirt and leaves. Patching leaky gutters.* ☛THE YARD: *Growing healthy grass. Maintaining a lawn mower. Stocking a garden toolshed. Weed killers. Using lawn chemicals safely. Seasonal lawn care guide. Identifying and combating insect and animal pests. Tips for snow removal.* ☛EVERYTHING YOU NEED TO KNOW: *About Choosing Pots and Pans, Front-Wheel-Drive Cars, Making Healthier Meals, Vacuum Cleaners, Garden Tools, Upholstered Furniture, Your Credit Card Statement, Curtain Styles* ☛MONEY-SAVING HINTS: *How to Turn Bed Sheets into Curtains, Save on Car Repairs, Buy*

THE HOME WORKSHOP

Even if you don't think of yourself as handy, you can take care of a surprising number of tasks—assembling toys, hanging pictures and shelves, repairing dripping faucets—if you have the right tools on hand (see pages 208–209).

SAFETY

If used without proper safety precautions, any tool—no matter how basic—can be dangerous. To avoid problems follow these safety rules:

- Always ask for help when you need it.
- Never pick up a tool unless you are comfortable handling it.
- Never work with children nearby and never let children handle tools.
- Never draw any cutting tool toward your body, and always stand to one side as you work (if you're right-handed, stand to the left of your work as you saw and vice versa).
- When setting or removing a screw or nail, keep your free hand away from it.

NAILS, SCREWS, BOLTS, AND A HOOK

THE FASTENER YOU USE DEPENDS on the job; if you are in doubt, ask advice at your hardware store. Keep some of these basic types, which come in many sizes, on hand:

BOLT:
all purpose for wood and metal; strong hold yet easily removed

DRYWALL SCREW:
threaded whole length; angled head sinks into drywall; can also be used in wood

PENNY NAIL:
all purpose; good for general wood carpentry

SCREW HOOK:
wood screw with hook for hanging

SHEET METAL SCREW:
threaded whole length; creates own hole in wood; needs starter hole in metal

WOOD SCREW:
partially threaded; extra holding power for general wood carpentry

WHAT YOU SHOULD KNOW ABOUT LADDERS

LADDERS COME IN fiberglass, wood, and aluminum. Safe and strong, fiberglass ladders are used by professional workers, but are more expensive; wood and aluminum are fine for home use. Wood ladders are cheaper than aluminum and are preferred because they feel stable underfoot. Aluminum is a good choice for an extension ladder, however, because the lightweight material makes the bulky ladder easier to handle.

STEPLADDER

Stepladders, which fold open (and stand on their own), are the most stable.

They come in standard sizes. The smaller, 2- or 3-foot height is good for most indoor tasks, such as reaching shelves or replacing light bulbs. You will need the 6' 6" size for painting ceilings or pruning tall shrubs.

Extension ladders, which slide open (to double or triple size), are more cumbersome and less stable because they have to lean on something to stand up. They can, however, extend much longer than a stepladder, from 16 feet to 40 feet, and may be necessary for jobs like house painting or cleaning gutters.

SAFETY TIPS

- Be sure the ladder is stable and level before climbing it.

- Always face the ladder when climbing.

- Never stand higher than the second step from the top. To reach something above your head, get someone taller to help or get a higher step ladder.

- Stand straight and stretch no more than an arm's length right or left. If you can't reach what you want, climb down and adjust the ladder.

- Don't climb and carry. Put your tools in your pocket or a tool belt, or rest them on the swing-down shelf—if you are using a stepladder—before you climb.

- Never use an aluminum ladder where it might touch power lines.

LADDER RATINGS

☞ All ladders come with a load-rating label indicating how much weight they can carry:
Type 1 (industrial): up to 250 lbs
Type 2 (commercial): up to 225 lbs
Type 3 (household): up to 200 lbs
Types 2 and 3 are fine for most households.

EXTENSION LADDER

THE BASIC TOOLBOX...

A GOOD SET of tools is a worthwhile investment that will save you money in the long run. Start with the following basics and invest in the best quality that you can afford.

TOOL TIPS

☛ Use a tool only for the job it's intended to do and follow the manufacturer's instructions carefully. For example, don't use a screwdriver as a pry bar or a wrench as a hammer. A misused tool is often damaged and may later slip, jam, or bend, which could lead to an injury.

☛ Any power tool you use in the yard should be equipped with heavy-duty cords approved for outdoor use. If your yard work requires an extension cord, make sure that it, too, is intended for outdoor use.

☛ If a power tool jams, turn it off and unplug it before you look for the problem. Lawn mowers and snow blowers can be especially dangerous—never try to unclog the blades or tinker with the motor unless they are switched off.

☛ Never leave tools, nails, and other sharp objects lying around the yard or on the floor of your garage or workshop. Even a rake can be dangerous if someone steps on it. Lean yard tools safely against a wall or fence with sharp edges pointed inward when they aren't in use.

CLAW HAMMER (16 oz.)

DUCT TAPE

GLUE (all-purpose white, epoxy, silicone, cellulose)

HAND DRILL AND ASSORTED BITS (ranging in size from $\frac{1}{16}$ inch to $\frac{1}{4}$ inch; for frequent use, consider an electric drill)

LUBRICANT (lightweight household oil)

NAILS AND SCREWS (assorted)

PAINTBRUSHES (4- or 8-inch for walls; 2-inch for corners and edges)

PICTURE-HANGING WIRE

PLIERS

PLUNGER

SANDPAPER (fine to coarse grades)

SCISSORS

PHILLIPS SCREWDRIVER

SLOTTED SCREWDRIVER

SCREWDRIVERS (slotted and Phillips head; various sizes)

SPIRIT LEVEL

STAPLE GUN AND STAPLES

STEEL WOOL (fine to coarse grades)

STRAIGHTEDGE

TAPE MEASURE

UTILITY KNIFE

WIRE (assorted gauges)

WIRE CUTTERS

WORK GLOVES

WRENCH (adjustable)

…AND MORE

Consider adding these tools to your collection as you become more adept at home repairs and know what you need.

ALLEN WRENCH: to tighten bolts with sunken hexagonal heads.

AWL: to make a starter hole.

C-CLAMPS (assorted sizes): to hold objects in place while you work on them.

CAULKING GUN: to weatherproof doors and windows.

CHISELS: (cold): to tackle heavy-duty jobs. (Wood): assorted sizes up to 1 inch.

CROSSCUT SAW (small): to cut smoothly across the grain of wood or to make a clean cut through plywood.

DUST MASK: to filter out fumes and dust.

FILES (wood and metal; round, flat, and needle): to shape and smooth.

HACKSAW: to cut metal—a protruding nail, for example.

JACK PLANE (12" to 15"): to shave wood—a sticking drawer, for example.

KEYHOLE SAW: to make a straight cut through a bored hole and to fit tight spaces where a crosscut saw won't go.

MONKEY WRENCH: to tighten or loosen nuts on joints.

NAIL SET: to drive the head of a finishing nail below a wood surface.

ALLEN WRENCH

AWL

HACKSAW

JACK PLANE

MONKEY WRENCH

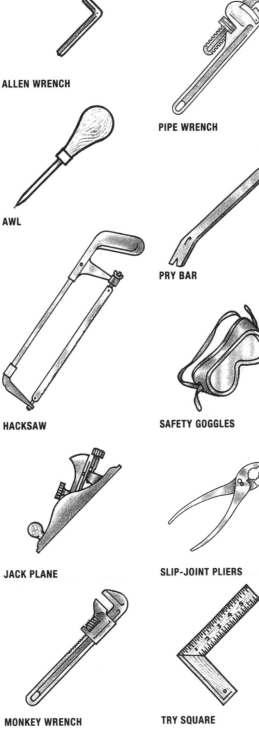

PIPE WRENCH

PRY BAR

SAFETY GOGGLES

SLIP-JOINT PLIERS

TRY SQUARE

NEEDLE-NOSE PLIERS: for gripping in a tight spot.

NOTCHED TROWEL: to apply tile adhesive.

PIPE WRENCH: to loosen or grasp pipe and pipe fittings.

PRY BAR: to pull things apart, usually wood.

PUTTY KNIFE: to apply various patching compounds.

SABER SAW: to power-cut through metal and wood.

SAFETY GOGGLES: to protect eyes from dust and debris.

SLIP-JOINT PLIERS: to grip pipes and other fittings; these pliers have a movable pivot that increases the jaw space.

SOCKET-WRENCH SET: to loosen inset nuts and bolts; versatile and easy to handle.

TACK RAG: to pick up particles, such as dust or paint shavings.

TOOL BELT: to carry a few tools; ideal when working on a ladder.

TRY SQUARE: to mark a perfect right angle or check a square corner.

VISE (metal or wood): to secure pieces of wood or metal when working on them.

MENDING CHINA AND GLASS

GLUE CLEANUP

☞ Wipe up spilled adhesive with a rag dipped in nail-polish remover.

Repairing china or glass is never foolproof; any piece with great sentimental or dollar value is best repaired by a professional.

When you mend simple breaks yourself, remember that the holding power of glue is weaker at stress points. Use any pieces with repaired knobs, handles, and stems carefully, if at all, as the break may recur.

APPLYING GLUE

Before gluing, lay out all the broken pieces in the exact pattern and order for reassembly. Work with two pieces at a time. Coat one edge of a piece, then press it gently to its mate and firmly secure the two parts until the adhesive cures (firm to the touch), using masking tape, rubber bands, or a weight, such as a book, if appropriate.

To keep pressure on a difficult patch—on the base of a goblet, for example—you may need to build a small frame to hold the item securely (ask for suggestions at the shop where you purchase the glue). You can also use sand (see below), or prop the broken piece with books or other items, angling it so gravity holds the mended section in place.

After gluing, take a single-edge razor blade and scrape away beads of hardened adhesive squeezed out of the mended joint.

WHAT KIND OF GLUE?

For REPAIRING MOST glass, porcelain, and earthenware, you can use one of three basic types of glue, available at craft or hardware stores. Always follow the manufacturer's instructions and use a newspaper or cloth to protect your work surface.

TYPE	PURPOSE
Household cement (clear and amber)	For earthenware and porous crockery. Not as strong as silicone. Don't use for stressed areas or on objects in contact with water. Highly flammable. Dries in 24 hours.
Epoxy	
gel	For earthenware and stress points (handles, knobs). Seeps into pores of surface to make very strong bond. Dries in 1 to 5 minutes.
putty	Can be used to build up a missing piece as if modeling clay for porcelain or earthenware. Dries in 20 minutes.
Silicone adhesive	For nonporous glass and porcelain. Will permanently seal stress cracks and breaks and holds up to dishwasher heat and freezer cold. Impervious to water and soap. Dries in 24 hours.

To hold a broken object at the necessary angle for gluing, work it gently into a container of play sand (available at craft shops) or cat litter. Set in the broken piece and let gravity hold it in place.

RESTORING WOOD FURNITURE

Before you consign a damaged or worn piece of furniture to the trash heap, consider whether you might be able to fix it at home. Many pieces require nothing more than cleaning or regluing.

DENTS, SCRATCHES, AND STAINS

Any valuable piece of furniture, or one with major breaks, scratches, dents, or stains, should be repaired by a professional.

You can, however, take care of many minor repairs with such basic supplies as reconstituted wood filler, stick shellac, and wax sticks. Most of these products come in colors to match different wood finishes and are generally available at paint or hardware stores. Carefully follow the manufacturer's instructions.

Shallow dents where the finish is undamaged: Raise the grain with steam heat. Heat your iron to a high setting. Dampen three or four layers of cotton cloth and lay them over the dent. Press the hot iron over the cloth until it stops sizzling. Repeat if the first application doesn't raise the grain.

Light scratches and blemishes: Rub using a thick paste of boiled linseed oil with pumice or rottenstone (see page 36). If the scratch is still noticeable, rub gently with 0000 steel wool moistened with paste wax or pure lemon oil. If that doesn't work, rub the scratch with a wax stick in a matching color.

Deep scratches: Fill with stick shellac in a matching color.

Deep dents and gouges: Pack with a reconstituted wood filler. Use a light shade of filler so that you can stain it to match your furniture. When the filler is dry, fine-sand it smooth with 150- to 180-grade sandpaper. Stain and finish it to match the rest of the piece.

Burns: For deep burns, scrape away the charred wood with a knife blade and lightly sand the area with 150- or higher sandpaper. Retouch with stick shellac.

For less serious surface burns, make a paste from rottenstone and linseed oil. Rub it in with a soft cloth (apply to the burn only) and polish with a clean cloth.

Water stains: If available, rub with a mixture of fireplace ashes and vegetable oil. Or, rub gently with 000 steel wool and a few drops of motor oil. Wipe clean with a dry cloth.

LOOSE CHAIR RUNGS

When a chair rung or spindle has come loose and doesn't fit in its socket again, the problem may be old glue.

To soften and remove the old glue, daub it with a cotton swab soaked in warm white vinegar. Use a dull-bladed knife to scrape it away down to the bare, clean wood.

As you scrape, try not to shave any wood from the joint, because this will make the fit even looser.

If, after cleaning, the rung or spindle fits too loosely in its socket, wrap the end with thread until it fits snugly, then coat with white glue. Let the glue dry, coat the socket sides with glue, and insert the threaded end. Hold it in place using a piece of clothesline and a dowel (see box page 212).

SANDING AND POLISHING

Sandpaper and steel wool come in standard grades. The coarsest grades are for heavy-duty jobs, such as removing varnish or peeling paint; fine grades are for polishing and reaching into detailed areas.

SANDPAPER GUIDE

600	Ultrafine
400–500	Superfine
320–360	Extrafine
220–280	Very fine
120–180	Fine
60–100	Medium
40–50	Coarse
25–50	Extracoarse

STEEL WOOL GUIDE

0000	Superfine
000	Extrafine
00	Very fine
0	Fine
1	Medium
2	Medium coarse
3	Coarse
4	Extracoarse

HOW TO MEND CHAIR RUNGS

*MEND UNSTRESSED BROKEN, split, or loose furniture
parts with any of three different types of glue: liquid hide
glue (slightly amber in color), aliphatic adhesive (creamy), or
polyvinyl acetate (known widely as white glue).*

To repair a split rung, apply white glue, wipe off excess, then wrap tightly with masking tape. Remove the tape after the glue has set and within 24 hours. Otherwise, it will be difficult to peel off.

To hold rungs in leg sockets while glue dries, tightly wrap a piece of clothesline around the two legs just below the rung and tie. Insert a dowel and twist to tighten.

STRIP EASE

☛ Electric hand sanders, which you can rent, save time and effort, and are great for removing finishes from flat surfaces (but don't try using them on detailed areas as they can cause damage). Choose a machine with orbital (circular) movement; for big jobs, try one with a two-hand grip. A palm sander—a small orbital sander that you can hold in one hand—speeds your work on small areas and even helps around furniture legs and spindles.

☛ Fit the sanders with fine sandpaper in the 180- or 220-grade range. Be sure to work carefully to avoid gouging the wood. Go with, not against, the grain.

RESTORING A WOOD FINISH

When you rescue furniture from the attic or buy flea market bargains, the finish may be worn or scratched. Such pieces are often ideal for refinishing.

Sometimes, however, cleaning by gently and quickly washing it with soap and water is enough to restore the old finish to solid wood. Dissolve a few chips of mild bar soap in a bucket of warm water.

Dip a soft, clean rag in the water, squeeze it out, and test a small corner of the piece to see if dirt comes off. If so, continue to wash the surface carefully and quickly dry with a soft cloth.

You can also remove the dirt with special cleaning solvent or denatured alcohol, which can generally be found at paint or hardware stores. When cleaning a wood veneer, always use a solvent; warm water may cause buckling.

Stripping Old Finishes

Stripping involves using a chemical solvent to soften paint or varnish so it's easy to scrape off. If you have never done stripping, start with a small piece of furniture that has a simple shape and flat surfaces; elaborate carving and turnings make it much more difficult to get off the old finish.

Chemicals in many removers are toxic and can burn your skin and clothing. If you apply solvents indoors, do it only in a well-ventilated space. Better yet, work outdoors—in your driveway, for example.

For protection, wear old clothes—long pants, long-sleeved shirt, protective gloves, eye goggles, and tie your hair back.

Scraping: Apply the remover following the manufacturer's instructions. Use an inexpensive throw-away paint brush, chemicals ruin a good brush.

When the finish has softened, scrape it away with a putty knife or a piece of wood; scrapers can gouge the wood.

Use a metal scrub brush, a toothbrush, or a cotton swab in details and crevices, and burlap or steel wool on leg turnings, rubbing back and forth.

As you scrape, deposit the material in a large juice or coffee can. Dispose of it with other household hazardous waste as your community directs (see page 291).

The final steps: After scraping, rub 00 or 000 steel wool (see page 211) over the entire surface to pick up any residue. Before refinishing, fine-sand the surface with 150- or finer sandpaper and vacuum away the sawdust.

Wipe the surface with a tack rag (a varnish-impregnated sticky cloth) to pick up specks the vacuum missed.

Choose a finish from the chart below.

TAKE A SHINE TO

☛ To get an extra-glossy finish, first apply a primer to a stripped or unfinished piece of furniture and let it dry. Apply a coat of alkyd enamel in a shade slightly lighter than the desired color. Let that dry, and lightly sand with 220- or higher-grade sandpaper. Add a second coat, if necessary. Finally, coat the piece with a clear polyurethane varnish, which will darken the color slightly.

FURNITURE FINISHES

CHOOSE AMONG THESE TREATMENTS TO refinish a stripped furniture piece or to finish a new untreated piece. Clear finishes and wax are best for enhancing wood grains while opaque paints help camouflage flaws or inferior woods. Always try a test patch on a hidden area to be sure of the final effect. Follow the manufacturer's directions carefully, and be sure to work in a well-ventilated area.

TYPE	APPEARANCE	DRYING TIME	HOW MANY COATS?	PROS AND CONS
Enamel paint	Opaque; creates high gloss.	24 hours	You may want 2 coats; check after applying first coat. Prime first for best results.	Wide color choices. Moderately expensive.
Natural-resin varnish	Clear; enhances wood grain; creates high or low gloss.	24 hours, perhaps more	Several. Between coats rub with 000 steel wool; finish with 0000 for high gloss.	Water and alcohol resistant. Resists scratches. Inexpensive.
Polyurethane varnish	Clear; enhances the wood grain; creates high or low gloss.	12 hours between coats	At least 2. Between coats rub with 000 steel wool; finish with 0000 for high gloss.	Water and alcohol resistant. Tough finish. Expensive.
Shellac	Creates clear finish with white shellac; darker with orange shellac.	2 hours between coats	Four to 6. Between coats, sand with 400-grade open-grained sandpaper. Finish with wax.	Poor resistance to heat, alcohol, water. Not for table surfaces. Will stain, melt with heat. Inexpensive.
Wood stain	Darkens color while highlighting grain. (Use penetrating oil stain for best results.)	24 hours	One. Fine-sand with 150-grade sandpaper and finish with varnish or shellac.	Can alter tone and color. Low to moderate cost.

WALL AND CEILING REPAIRS

With a little know-how and the right materials, you can tackle minor wall and ceiling repairs, such as patching plaster and plasterboard.

For small holes and cracks use spackle, a puttylike vinyl or acrylic compound that is easy to work with. Plaster, less forgiving but stronger, is necessary for large holes.

PATCHING PLASTER

Small Hole

To repair a small hole in plaster, such as one made by a picture hanger, begin by brushing away any loose material.

1. Wet the area with a sponge. Apply ready-mix spackle, pressing it in with a putty knife or your finger. Let it dry for two hours.

2. Using 150-grade sandpaper, sand the patch smooth.

3. Wipe clean. Apply primer before painting.

Hairline Cracks

1. Using a screwdriver, dig out beneath the lines of the crack, then brush away any loose material. Wet the area with a sponge.

2. Press ready-mix spackle into the crack with your finger and smooth over with a putty knife. When dry, use 150-grade sandpaper to sand the patch smooth.

3. Wipe clean. Apply primer before painting.

Large Hole

1. Clean plaster dust from the hole, and check to see if plasterboard, wire, or wood lath is visible. If so, use it as backing for your patch. If not, cut a piece of heavy screening an inch larger all around than the hole.

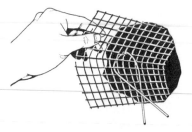

2. Loop a wire through the center of the screen; bend the screen through the hole and with the wire, pull it taut against the back of the plaster surface.

3. Fasten the two ends of the wire around a ballpoint pen or ⅜-inch dowel longer than the hole is wide. Turn the pen or dowel (like winding the key for a toy) until the twisted wire holds the screen firmly in place.

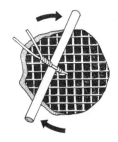

4. Apply plaster or spackle coat with a putty knife over the screen, working it under the dowel, and smooth out.

5. Allow the plaster or spackle to dry according to the manufacturer's instructions. Then remove the pen

SMART SPACKLING

☞ Do not paint new plaster immediately. Let it dry for at least two hours or a powdery substance will form.

☞ Spackle shrinks as it dries. When the spackle dries, sand the surface with 150- to 220-grade sandpaper until the surface is smooth and flush with the wall. If necessary, apply more spackle, let dry, and resand.

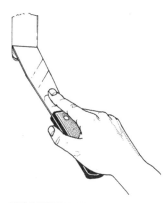

USE A PUTTY KNIFE TO SMOOTH SPACKLE INTO A SMALL HOLE.

CRACKED OR DAMAGED CERAMIC TILES, such as in a kitchen or bathroom, are simple to replace. Be sure to wear goggles to protect your eyes and work gloves for your hands. Spread a drop cloth below your work area to catch tile shards. Follow the manufacturer's instructions for using adhesive and grout.

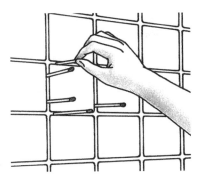

2. Position the chisel blade at an angle and tap the blade between the tile and backing to force out the fragments.

3. Clean the opening with a paint scraper and rough sandpaper (60 or 80 grade).

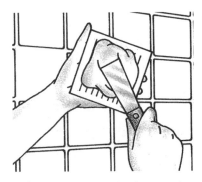

1. Using a screwdriver, awl, or nail set, scrape out the grout surrounding the broken tile. Fit the blade of a cold chisel into a crack in the tile and tap it with a hammer until tile pieces break away.

If there are no visible cracks, hold the chisel perpendicular to the tile at the center and tap. Don't use a heavy hand; you don't want to puncture the material behind the tile.

4. Using a putty knife, spread ceramic tile adhesive evenly over the back of a new tile. Press the tile in place.

5. Insert matches or pins (2 or 3 per side) into the grout space around the new tile so it stays centered until the adhesive cures.

6. When the adhesive has set, remove the matches or pins and use your fingers to press new grout into grooves. Wait 10 minutes. Wipe away excess grout with a clean, damp sponge.

---

or dowel and snip the wire even with the surface.

6. Apply a second coat so the patch will be flush with the wall and smooth it out. When this dries, sand the area smooth with 150-grade sandpaper and apply primer before painting.

PLASTERBOARD HOLES

Plasterboard, also called gypsum board and drywall, is a solid dry board surfaced on both sides with a special paper. It is commonly used in new construction or over old plaster walls that are in poor shape.

Small Holes and Dents
Patch a tiny hole not much larger than a nail with spackle, as you would for a plaster surface (see page 214).

Large Holes
Patching large holes requires special joint compound, drywall tape, and extra plasterboard for making patches. If you've never worked with these materials, call a professional.

TOGGLE BOLTS

☞ A toggle bolt has spiderlike expansion legs that spread against the back of the wall or ceiling, forming a brace that locks the bolt in place. The toggle drops when you remove the bolt and can't be reused.

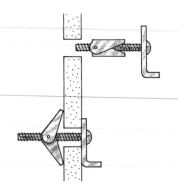

EXPANSION BOLTS

☞ Often called a Molly for the brand that made it popular, this hanger has a sleeve around the screw. As the screw and sleeve are tightened in a predrilled hole, the sleeve expands, wedging itself against the wall material. If you remove the bolt, the sleeve stays in place.

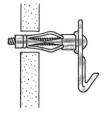

HOW TO HANG ANYTHING

The key to hanging anything properly, be it a mirror, a plant, or bookshelves, is in using the right hanger for the job.

First, match the hanger to your wall material. Toggle and expansion bolts (see left) are good for plasterboard, drywall, and wood paneling. Special hardened-steel masonry nails are available for concrete. You can also buy special anchors to prevent chipping plaster and concrete and to provide a "grip" for the hanger.

Second, make sure your hanger can carry the weight of the item. Commercially packaged hooks and other hangers give recommendations.

To determine the best position for a picture or a mirror see the suggestions on page 190.

LIGHTWEIGHT OBJECTS

You can use a regular picture hook to hang an item of five pounds or less on a plaster or plasterboard wall.

For an item weighing more than five pounds use two hooks, which distribute the weight, putting less strain on each nail point.

1. With a spirit level, mark two perfectly level points on the wall about one quarter of the way in from both sides of the object.

2. Cover the nail marks with a small piece of clear plastic tape so the nails won't start hairline cracks.

3. Nail the hooks to the wall, making certain the hooks fall directly over your marks.

SUSPENDED OBJECTS

A screw eye or screw hook (see page 206) is best for hanging a lightweight item from the ceiling. Drill a hole to the same diameter as the screw shaft. Lightly tap an anchor (see page 217)

STUD FINDERS

Studs are the vertical framing timbers in walls. Whenever possible, fasten your hanger into a stud when you are hanging a heavy object to give it extra support.

With your knuckles or a light hammer, rap the wall continuously, moving horizontally. When you reach a stud, the rap should sound a pitch higher and less hollow.

The baseboard should be nailed to the studs (although sometimes it isn't). The nail heads may be visible.

If you live in a modern high rise, the studs are probably steel. In that case, you will need metal screws and a drill bit strong enough to penetrate steel. Electronic and magnetic stud finders, available at most hardware stores, will help you locate steel studs.

PUTTING UP SHELVES

*T*HE SIMPLEST AND MOST INEXPENSIVE *form of shelves uses slotted metal standards (also called channels), metal brackets and wood, plywood, or particleboard for shelves. For best results, attach the standards to wall studs and paint the standards and brackets to match the wall color before you start.*

 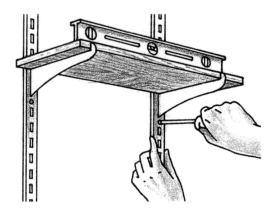

1. Drill a starter hole and lightly screw one standard into the wall at the top. Hold it straight and with a spirit level check the true vertical. Mark for the bottom screw. Drill starter holes for all the screws. Drive in wood screws at least 1¼" long.

2. To align the holes in the second standard with those in the installed standard, first loosely attach the standard to the wall with a nail so there is some up and down movement. Then lightly fasten the brackets, place a shelf board on the brackets, and lay a spirit level on the board.

3. Gently move the standard up and down; when the spirit bubble is dead center, drive a single screw through one hole in the second standard to hold it in place.

4. Remove the nail, shelf, and brackets. Check the true vertical with a spirit level, adjust if necessary, and fasten the standard with wood screws.

5. Insert the brackets and lay on the shelf boards.

---

into the hole. Insert the screw into the anchor and twist until firmly set.

SHELVES AND OTHER HEAVY OBJECTS

Putting up shelf brackets or hanging a clay pot of geraniums calls for a fastener that can support up to 50 pounds; consider toggle or expansion bolts.

Drill a hole the same diameter as the fastener shaft into the wall or ceiling and insert the fastener.

For objects that weigh 25 to 50 pounds, divide the load between two fasteners.

Place the hangers so you can make your drill hole in a stud (see opposite). The strength of any hanger is at its maximum when hung at a right angle to the support.

Do not hang heavy objects from a wood joist in the ceiling; that could cause it to bow, resulting in a bad crack.

ANCHOR ALERT

☛ Use an anchor to provide a "grip" for a picture hanger, and to prevent damage to the wall surface. Anchors come in different sizes. Be sure to use the recommended drill size for the anchor you have chosen.

DOORS

Squeaking, scraping, and sticking doors are all relatively simple to rectify. It is even easy to remove and replace a faulty lock set. For exterior doors, however, you may want to hire a locksmith to ensure security.

FIXING SCRAPING AND SQUEAKS

Straightening, or truing, a door not only stops scraping and squeaking, but also prevents damage to the floor, carpet, and door frame.

Tightening the Hinges
More often than not, a problem occurs when the top hinge has worked loose. This causes the door to tilt slightly down from the jamb. If one or both of the top hinge halves (called leaves) are loose, remove the screws and the leaves.

For a quick repair, replace the screws with screws that are one and a half times longer. These will bite a little more deeply.

For a longer-lasting repair, reinforce the original screw holes with wood dowels.

1. Clean out any dirt or wood shavings and measure the diameter of the hole. You will need a dowel that's a fraction smaller in diameter so it will fit tightly.

2. Insert the dowel in the hole and mark it for length. Remove and cut the dowel on the mark.

3. Dip a small brush in white glue and daub it inside the hole and on the dowel.

4. Insert the dowel so that the end is flush. Clean off any glue that squeezes out and wait until it dries.

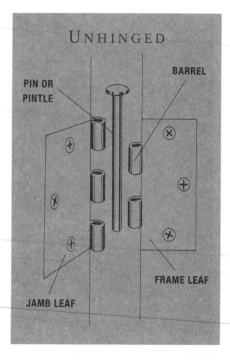

5. Drill a pilot hole in the dowel for the screw. Repeat for all the screw holes and reinsert the screws.

Shimming the Hinges
If the door scrapes along the floor or jamb, one hinge leaf may be set too deeply.

1. Place a spirit level on the door top to check that it is truly horizontal. If the level indicates a sag toward the floor, the lower jamb leaf is set back too far. A tilt toward the ceiling means the top jamb leaf needs adjustment.

2. Wedge a magazine under the outside corner of the door to prop it up. Remove the offending jamb leaf (see above). Place one or two sheets of cardboard (depending how much the door sags), cut to fit the leaf, between the leaf and jamb cutout.

3. Puncture the cardboard to meet the screw holes and reattach the leaf.

HOW TO SILENCE DOOR SQUEAKS

Most squeaks are caused by hinges. To get rid of them:
☞ Support the door and remove one hinge pin at a time. Clean all parts with steel wool.
☞ Lubricate the pin and barrels with a petroleum-based product. Replace the pins.
☞ Sometimes squeaks occur inside the lock or in the latch as it slides past the strike-plate opening. Remove the lock from the door (see page 220). (If your door lock differs substantially, refer to the manufacturer's literature or get help from a locksmith.) Lubricate the lock with an all-purpose oil and replace.

ANATOMY OF A DOOR

While doors vary slightly, most will have the basic parts illustrated here.

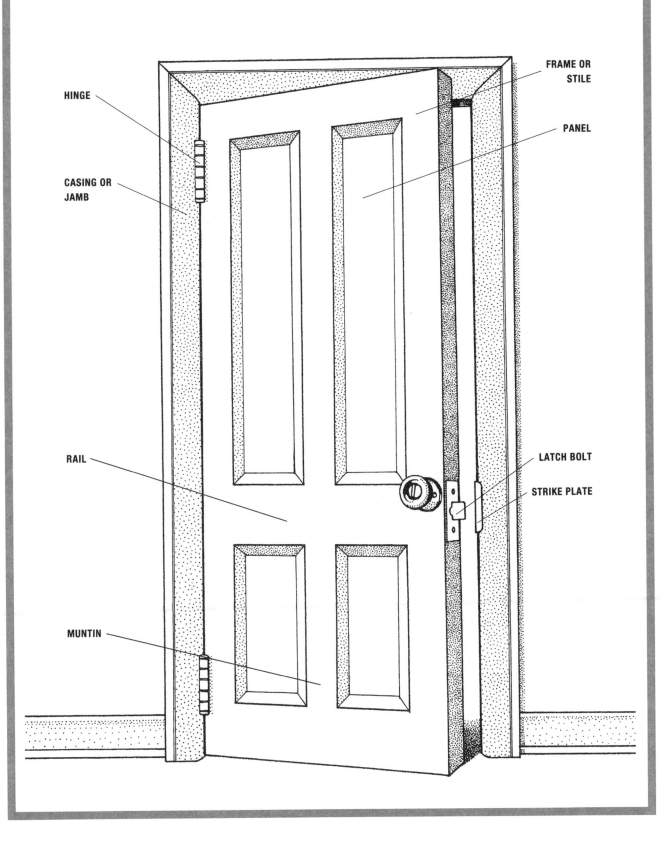

HINGE

CASING OR
JAMB

RAIL

MUNTIN

FRAME OR
STILE

PANEL

LATCH BOLT

STRIKE PLATE

HOW TO INSTALL A LOCK SET

EXTERIOR DOORS NEED sturdy locks; check them often to make sure they're in good working order. If you need to install a new lock set on any door, here's how:

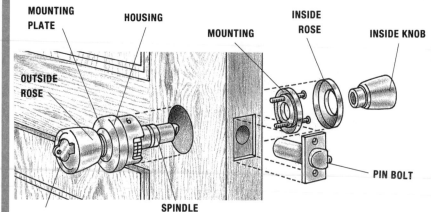

1. Using the manufacturer's template, mark on the door the areas to be cut.

2. Using a hole cutter attachment on a drill, cut the lock-set hole through the door. Adjust the hole cutter and drill a hole into the edge of the door for the latch.

3. Match the faceplate hole and the latch hole and, with a pencil, mark the faceplate outline. With a hammer and chisel, cut out this area to the depth of the faceplate.

4. Push through the outside knob assembly.

5. Push the latch through the door-edge hole until its assembly engages with the lock mechanism.

6. Slip the faceplate over the latch and insert screws.

7. Slip the mounting plate over the spindle and tighten bolts through the locking mechanism cylinder.

8. Place the inside rose over the mounting plate and attach the inside knob to the spindle (it connects with a spring catch).

RATTLING DOORKNOBS

☛ Doorknobs often rattle because the tiny screw holding the knob to the shaft is loose. Tighten the screw with a small-blade screwdriver, or with the round end of a nail file. A loose knob may also be caused by a bent center spindle—the metal pin through the lock that holds indoor and outdoor knobs. You can take apart the lock set (see box at right), remove the spindle, and try straightening it in a metal vise. If that fails, invest in a new lock set.

Planing Wooden Doors

If after checking the hinges and alignment the door still sticks, you may need to plane it.

1. Make a pencil mark where it sticks. If the door scrapes at the top, stand on a ladder and plane the top, working inward from the outer corners.

2. Using a jack plane, shave only a small amount at a time, checking the fit as you work. Planing too much could leave an unsightly gap.

3. If the door scrapes at the bottom or side, you need to unhinge it. Plane, then sand the planed areas.

4. Wipe up the dust with a tack rag and apply one or two coats of clear wood sealer. This helps keep out moisture, which swells and warps wood.

WINDOWS AND SCREENS

When windows and screens aren't snug and tight in cold weather, warm air will escape; in hot weather, mosquitoes can find their way indoors. You can take care of minor repairs yourself.

UNJAMMING A STUCK WINDOW

When you try to loosen a tight window take care not to chip the frame or paint. Never hammer directly on the sash or frame. Instead, hold a small block of wood against the sash and tap it with a hammer. Repeat at intervals around all sides.

If the window is still stuck, work a putty knife between the sash and the stop (the fixed wood molding holding the sash in place). Gently rock the knife back and forth and repeat up and down on both sides and along the sill.

If that doesn't work, from outside the window, insert a pry bar between the sash and sill at midpoint to lever the sash open.

SCREENS

Patching Holes
Most hardware stores carry two types of patches to repair small screen holes or tears: aluminum mesh and plastic sheet with printed cross-hatching. Either is fine. Although many new screens are made of fiberglass, there are no fiberglass patches—either the plastic or the aluminum patch will work. Clean the screens before patching (see page 45).

1. Using scissors, trim the loose mesh ends around the edge of the hole in your screen.

2. Cut a square patch about one inch larger than the hole on all sides.

2a. For an aluminum patch, remove two or three outside wires on all four sides of the patch. Bend down

ANATOMY OF A WINDOW

WHILE THERE ARE various window types—casement, pivot, louvered, and sash—the double-hung sash window illustrated here is most common.

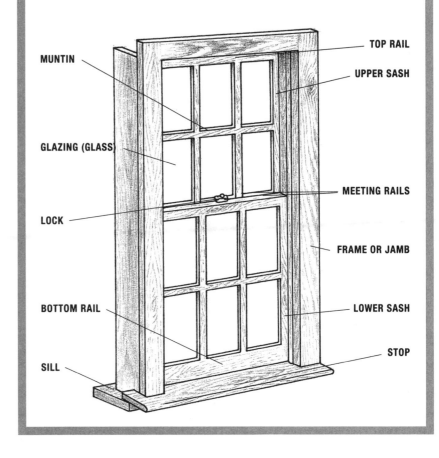

MUNTIN

GLAZING (GLASS)

LOCK

BOTTOM RAIL

SILL

TOP RAIL

UPPER SASH

MEETING RAILS

FRAME OR JAMB

LOWER SASH

STOP

the protruding wires around the patch over the edge of a small block of wood so that these strands are at right angles to the patch itself. The patch should look like a short-legged spider.

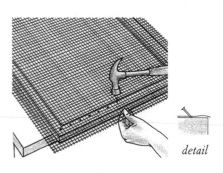

Placing an aluminum patch

Center the patch over the hole and push the bent wire ends through the screen. While pressing the patch against the screen, bend down the wire ends on the opposite side of the mesh, toward the center of the patch.

2b. For a plastic patch, strip off the protective cover on the adhesive-backed patch and place it over the hole, pressing to seal.

Replacing Screening

1. Pull out the old screening from the frame. On a wood-frame screen, pry off the molding and remove the tacks or staples using a slotted screwdriver. On an aluminum or vinyl frame, pry off the narrow strips called splines.

2. Cut the replacement screen to measure one inch wider than the frame on all sides. In this way, it will reach beneath the moldings on a wood frame and into the grooves on a vinyl or aluminum frame.

2a. On a wood frame, fasten the replacement screen on one side with tacks and pull it taut and smooth over the opening.

Still holding the screen tight, drive the tacks in at a 45-degree angle with the heads toward the screen center. Repeat for the final two sides. Replace the molding and tack into place.

2b. On an aluminum or vinyl frame, place the screening over the opening and clamp one end. Pull the screening taut over to the opposite groove and holding the screen taut, press in the spline. Remove the clamps on the opposite end, and holding the screen taut, press in the spline. Repeat for the final two sides.

3. With a sharp utility knife, trim away excess screening beyond the molding or splines.

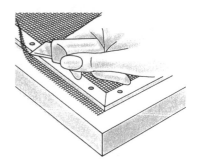

Trimming the edges around wood molding

HOW TO REPLACE WINDOW GLASS

MOST WINDOWS MADE BEFORE ABOUT 1970 use putty. To replace window glass in new windows, consult the manufacturers. Measure the opening exactly, show a piece of the glass to a salesperson, and buy glass cut to size. Use putty (glazing compound) or caulk and glazier points to secure the new glass. Work on the outside of the window. To replace glass in older windows, see below.

REPLACING GLASS IN OLD WOOD SASH WINDOWS

glazier point (enlarged)

1. Using pliers, pull out any remaining glass slivers from the frame and remove the triangular metal glazier points that hold the pane in place.

2. Scrape away the old putty (glazing compound) from the frame with a putty knife or the tip of a slotted screwdriver.

3. Spread a thin layer of new glazing compound around the frame—just enough to "grab" a newly inserted

glass pane. Position the glass in the opening and press it in.

4. Reinsert the glazier points and gently press them into the wood with the edge of a putty knife blade until they hold. (There's no need to sink them deeply into the wood.) For a typical 10"x 10" or 12"x 12" pane, two points per side are plenty.

5. Using your fingers, roll a ⅜-inch-diameter "rope" of glazing com-

pound and press it all around the glass perimeter next to the frame.

6. Smooth the compound by drawing the putty knife along the rope at a 45-degree angle between the frame and pane. Clean off any excess.

If the compound doesn't form smoothly, dip the putty blade in linseed oil and try again.

REPLACING GLASS IN OLD METAL SASH WINDOWS

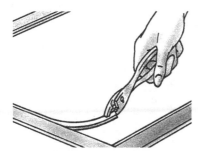

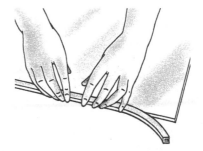

1. Glass in a metal sash—particularly a storm sash—is almost always held in place with a flexible vinyl spline that wraps around the glass edge. Remove the broken glass following the instructions above and lever out the spline with a slotted screwdriver blade.

2. Once you have one end of a spline out, grab and pull it with your hands or pliers. The rest will come right out.

3. Wrap the new glass with the vinyl splines. Reassemble the window in the order you took it apart.

FLOORS

The most commonly used household floor coverings—wood, vinyl, tile, and stone—don't require much special attention, but they shouldn't be ignored.

Treat your floors kindly—use doormats and protect good wood floors with throw rugs—to lengthen their life.

Many materials also benefit from a protective sealer or wax. Don't leave chipped, peeling, or broken surfaces unattended as floor traffic will only make problems worse.

RESTORING WOOD FLOORS

Wood floors treated with a penetrating sealer and still in reasonably good condition may be restored with a sealer or a reconditioning agent. A sealer won't flake when scratched, as varnish will, because it sinks below the wood surface rather than coating the top.

A floor finished with polyurethane may be lightly sanded and recoated. If possible, use the same brand and type of polyurethane as before. Mismatched finishes may show discoloration.

REFINISHING

If you are going to refinish(which can be a substantial undertaking), you must sand away all traces of the old finish. You will need to rent an upright sander (for the main area) and a disc sander (for the floor edges). Both machines should have dust-collecting bags.

You'll also need sandpaper in coarse, medium, and fine grades. Wear a paper breathing mask and ventilate the space when you begin sanding.

Board Floors

1. Remove all rugs and furnishings, including window dressings. Thoroughly vacuum the floor, window sills, and any shelves. Clean off any wax with a solvent remover.

2. Look for nail heads showing above the wood surface. Use a nail set and hammer to tap them back. An exposed nail will rip up the sandpaper.

3. Carefully remove the quarter-round wood moldings between the floor and baseboard with a pry bar or chisel. If there are no moldings, remove the baseboard. (This also gives you a chance to redo the moldings if desired.)

4. Carefully lower the sanding drum, fitted with your coarsest sandpaper, to the floor and begin guiding the machine across it. Don't stop until you reach the other end of the room. Overlap your sanding runs. Sand with the grain, which always runs the length of each board. At the beginning and end

BURN OUT

☛ For small cigarette burns on carpets, try carefully clipping out the burned surface fibers with curved fingernail scissors.

HOW TO TREAT A NEW WOOD FLOOR

If not pretreated by the manufacturer, a new wood floor needs to be sanded and finished. Sand new floors with an upright machine fitted progressively with coarse, medium, and fine sandpaper. When you finish, thoroughly vacuum the floor, and wipe with a tack rag.

After sanding, use a paste wood filler to treat oak, mahogany, walnut, and chestnut boards, which tend to have open pores. After the filler dries, sand lightly. To make new pine floors glow, seal the surface with shellac before applying varnish.

Three coats of any finish are recommended. After the first and second coats dry, sand the floor. After the third coat, buff the floor. To protect the finish and make the floor shine, apply paste wax and buff again.

of every run, tip the sander back on its wheel to lift the drum off the floor to prevent gouges.

Sanding a board floor

5. Following the same procedure, make a second pass with medium-grit paper and a final run with fine-grit paper.

6. Use the hand-held disc sander to finish the edges. For hard-to-reach corners, wrap sandpaper around a wood block and finish the job by hand.

7. Vacuum the floor and any other dirty surfaces. Pick up any dust with a tack rag.

8. If you're going to stain or bleach the wood floor (see page 227), do it now.

Parquet Floors

1. Follow steps 1 through 3 for board floors. Then run the upright drum sander, fitted with medium-grit paper, on a diagonal across the full width of the room.

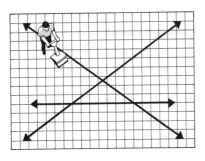

Sanding a parquet floor

2. On your second pass, run the sander along the opposite diagonal, across the full width of the room using fine-grit paper.

3. Run a floor polisher fitted with a screen disc up and down the longest dimension of the room.

4. Finish the process by following steps 6 through 8 for board floors.

DAMAGED FLOORS

Damaged flooring is unattractive and can cause structural problems in the long run. A broken ceramic tile or a curled vinyl tile allows water to infiltrate, undermining the subfloor.

You can replace parquet tiles and vinyl tiles with a few simple supplies—a hammer, chisel, adhesive, and grout. Replacement tiles are available where flooring is sold.

Wood Parquet

Wood parquet, laid in squares, or blocks, adheres to a subfloor with mastic. Most blocks are connected to one another with tongue-and-groove edges.

1. To replace a damaged block, work from the center out . With a sharp chisel at least an inch wide, cut away the center, then slide the chisel underneath.

2. Tap the chisel beneath the block from the opened center toward the edges until the mastic bond is broken and the block is forced up.

   Don't be concerned about breaking the tongues. You'll be cutting them off anyway.

3. With a paint scraper, clean up the square of sticky subfloor. Cut off the tongues from the blocks surrounding the open square with a keyhole saw.

4. Lightly sand the subfloor so that the surface of the new parquet block will be flush with the existing flooring. Vacuum the square and rub a tack rag over the surface to pick up dust particles.

How to Repair Wood Floor Scratches

HAIRLINE SCRATCHES	**DEEP SCRATCHES**
Unsealed wood: Dip a very fine-grade steel wool pad in pure lemon oil or paste wax. Rub the scratches gently, working with the grain. Polish with a soft cloth. *Polyurethane finish:* Hand sand the scratches with 150- to 180-grade sandpaper. Vacuum the dust and touch up the area with a new coat of polyurethane. For best results, use the same brand of polyurethane as originally applied.	Hand sand scratches with 150-grade sandpaper. Coat the scratch with a paste wood filler matching the wood tone, following the product instructions. Just before the filler sets, wipe up any excess. Let the filler dry for 24 hours. Sand the surface with 150-grade sandpaper. When the surface is smooth, switch to a finer grade paper (180- to 220-grade). Apply a finish to match the existing color.

GOING THE EXTRA YARD

☛ Whenever you have a new floor or covering installed, always ask for at least a dozen extra tiles, and a yard or two of extra carpeting or vinyl for future patching and repairs.

NAILING IT DOWN

☛ Firmly nailed (tacked) tight-pile carpet is the safest stair covering. If you prefer a natural finish or paint on stair treads, avoid high-gloss finishes. They can be slippery.

5. Make certain the new parquet block precisely fits the open square. The new block will have two tongues and two grooves. Cut off one of the tongues with a keyhole saw.

6. Apply a new coat of mastic to the subfloor. Brush a thin coat of white glue over the three tongueless edges. Carefully fit the one remaining tongue into its groove and lower the block into place.

7. Clean off any excess glue and weight the block with several books for at least 12 hours.

Ceramic Tiles

When chipping at ceramic tiles, wear goggles and work gloves (see page 215).

1. Smash the tile's center with a cold chisel and hammer. Clear away the loose fragments and pry up any remaining tile by tapping the chisel beneath each piece.

2. Using a paint scraper and sandpaper, remove the old adhesive. Drop in the replacement tile, dry, to make certain it fits.

3. Remove the tile and coat the back with ceramic tile adhesive; set it into the floor space and, with toothpicks, center it. Allow the adhesive to dry overnight.

4. Remove the toothpicks and fill the cracks with grout.

Vinyl Tile

1. To lift a broken or peeling tile, place a cloth over it and warm it with an iron on medium heat to soften the adhesive. Using a wide-blade putty knife, pry up the tile and scrape up the remaining adhesive. Lightly sand the subfloor and vacuum.

2. Set in the new tile, dry, to test the fit. If it is slightly large, remove and rub the edges with 120-grade sandpaper, turning the tile so all four sides are evenly shaved.

3. Using a notched trowel, spread new adhesive on the subfloor. Press in the new tile and weight it with books or bricks for at least 6 hours.

WOOD FLOOR TREATMENT GUIDE

To protect a new wood floor, you need to finish it (see page 224). You may also want to refinish an older floor for a new, fresh look. Oil-based finishes require 2 coats; water-based treatments need at least 3 coats. On pine and other soft woods, use a sealer (of the same brand) before varnishing.

Finish	Effect	Useful Information	Cost	Durability
Oil-modified polyurethane (solvent-base)	Available in high gloss and satin finishes.	Easy to apply. Buff first coat with fine steel wool, then wait 14 hours before applying second coat.	Moderate	Toughest of finishes, but will scratch. Will last 3 to 5 years.
Water-base polyurethane	Clear in color. Available in moderate gloss to satin finishes.	Available in two basic types (both require 3 to 4 coats): high acrylic—easy to apply, dries fast; and high urethane—also fast-drying, but harder to apply. Some require sanding between coats; check product label.	Moderate	Both basic types wear well. High urethane slightly more difficult to repair. Will last 2 to 3 years.
Lacquer	Produces a high gloss or matte finish in clear, black, or white.	Very difficult to apply. Hire a professional. Not popularly used today.	Moderate	Wears well but will scratch. Will last 3 to 5 years.
Shellac	Creates a protective sheen; maintains the wood's natural look without darkening.	Easy to apply. Don't allow to puddle; brush out smoothly. Sand lightly between each of 3 coats. Tends to chip; not very resistant to water or alcohol spills, but is easily repaired. Can yellow.	Inexpensive	Wears well but will scratch. Will last 1 to 2 years.
Penetrating sealer	Creates a subtle sheen; maintains the wood's natural look.	Easy to apply. Penetrates rather than coats wood. Easily repaired.	Moderate	Wears well. May dull in hard-wear areas; easy to repair and may not need resanding. Lasts 1 to 3 years.
Paste wax	Polishes and protects floor finishes.	Easy to apply; must remove old paste wax with solvent-base cleaner before applying new. Buff with a soft cloth or electric polisher once dry.	Moderate	Hard-wear areas need retouching in 3 to 5 months. Will last 6 months.
Bleach (oxalic acid)	Removes stains and discolorations. Will lighten a dark color.	Easy to apply. Available at hardware stores in crystals, which are mixed with water. Mop, allow to dry, rinse. Poisonous; follow label directions. Work in a well-ventilated area. Wear gloves.	Inexpensive	

HEATING SYSTEMS

A few simple preventive measures will help keep your heating system in top working order and can save you an emergency house call from a heating contractor.

Get to know the parts of your heating system and whether it's a furnace, boiler, heat pump, or space heater. Read the manufacturer's literature if it's available.

THERMOSTATS

All central warm-air and hot-water heating systems are controlled by thermostats, which you set to the temperature you want your house to be. When the temperature reaches the setting, the heating system automatically shuts off, then restarts when the temperature drops below the setting.

The thermostat should be located in a room where the temperature is stable and that reflects the average conditions in your house.

Setting the temperature is a matter of personal preference, but 68°F is considered a good norm. If you go away for an extended period, turn down the thermostat to save fuel, but not lower than 55°F to prevent pipe freezes.

FURNACES

There are two basic types of furnaces—gas- or oil-fired and electric. In each, a duct system carries warm air to registers in the rooms being heated.

Each fall, ask your heating contractor for an annual furnace checkup to make sure it is in good operating order. If you have a gas- or oil-fired furnace, also ask the contractor to examine the flue for leaks, which can send carbon monoxide gas into your house.

If you have a gas-fired furnace, at various times through the heating season open the fire door when the gas flames are visible. The flames should be blue. If they are yellow tipped or streaked with yellow, tell your contractor. It's likely the air/gas mix is incorrect and needs adjustment.

HOT-WATER BOILERS

A hot-water boiler (also called a hydronic heater) heats water, which is sent by a pump through pipes to radiators or fin-tube convectors that release heat into the rooms.

- Before the cold season, have your boiler serviced to make sure that it's running efficiently and there are no air pockets.

- Excessive clanking soon after the boiler is turned on indicates there are air blocks in the water lines running to the radiator or convectors.

Release the air by opening the petcocks (small faucets or valves) on each radiator or convector. Hold a glass beneath each petcock. When air stops and water flows evenly, close the petcock.

On newer boilers, an air-eliminator valve is located on the boiler itself. When you have the boiler serviced, ask the contractor to open the valve to release the air.

STEAM BOILERS

A steam boiler heats water until it turns to steam, which travels through pipes to radiators throughout the house.

Though this system is rarely specified in new construction, it is often found in older homes. It requires annual maintenance.

- Dirt, lime deposits, and rust in the water tend to make the boiler sluggish, increase fuel use, and can eventually clog piping. Ask a heating contractor to check the system before the heating season.

- Air blocks can also impede the flow of steam to radiators; open radiator vents with a key that should accompany the system, and allow the air to escape.

Be sure to do this when the system is not in use or has been shut down for several hours. Be careful; steam can cause serious burns.

HEAT PUMPS

A heat pump, also called a reverse-cycle air conditioner, cools air in hot weather and automatically reverses itself in cold weather to heat.

A fan draws air into the unit, where it is cooled or heated, depending on the season, and blown through vents to rooms in the house.

Follow these simple maintenance steps twice a year—before warm weather and at the beginning of the cold season:

- Change the filter.

- Call a contractor to clean the outside coils; they should be free of dirt, dust, leaves, and grass clippings.

PORTABLE SPACE HEATERS

Portable space heaters are small units that you can move from room to room to help direct extra heat where it's needed.

There are two basic types: electric and kerosene.

Electric: Electric units include the newer fan heaters, which generate warmth throughout a room.

The more old-fashioned models with electric resistance elements only direct heat to spot areas.

Kerosene: While new kerosene space heaters are safe, old ones can be dangerous because they produce carbon monoxide. If you use an old model at all, do so in a well-ventilated area. Always pay strict attention to the instructions and safety rules provided by the manufacturer.

Always open a window before lighting the heater.

FIREPLACES

A fireplace has five basic parts: firebox, hearth, damper, flue, and chimney (see page 230).

The firebox is where the fire is set and its floor is the hearth.

The damper is the metal gate between the firebox and the chimney. Open it before lighting a fire. When a fire is lit, smoke travels through the damper and the flue-lined chimney out into the open air.

Before cold weather begins, take the following steps to be sure your fireplace operates properly and safely.

- Check the flue for leaves or birds' nests. On a sunny day, use a mirror and a powerful flashlight to look up the chimney through the open damper. If you see blockage, call a chimney sweep for help.

- Once a year, hire a chimney sweep to clean soot from the flue and inspect it for cracks. You want to be assured that no flame will find its way to your house's framing through a crack and that caked soot, which can cause a chimney fire, is cleaned away.

DON'T BLOCK THE HEAT

☞ Enjoy the full benefit of your heating system by making sure there are clear paths in front of all registers and radiators. Carpets and furniture can block heat, creating cold spots in a room.

DAMPER CONTROL

☞ Fires draw in cold air as they burn, while the heat escapes up the chimney. Fireplace inserts with glass doors help prevent this, circulating warm air back into the room. If you don't intend to make a fire in the fireplace, close the damper.

ANATOMY OF A FIREPLACE

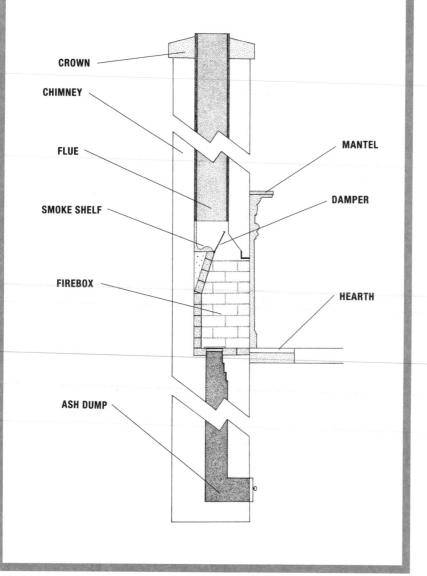

CROWN

CHIMNEY

FLUE

SMOKE SHELF

FIREBOX

ASH DUMP

MANTEL

DAMPER

HEARTH

place two or three crumpled newspaper sheets, a layer of thinly cut kindling, and one small dry log. Light; when the log catches fire, add another.

Follow these safety tips:

- Do not put colored newspaper (or any paper with dyes), plastic, or laminated items into the fire. They will emit toxic gases when burned.

- Build a well-tended small fire. This is safer than a three- or four-log blaze, which may send sparks and embers up and out the chimney.

- Keep a screen in front of the fireplace to prevent sparks and embers from shooting beyond the hearth.

- Always use fireplace tools to move a log. A basic set includes a poker, tongs, brush, and bellows.

- Do not leave a fire untended overnight. Douse it by shoveling ashes over the flames.

How to Buy and Store Firewood

Invest in dense hardwood logs for firewood; oak, hickory, and beech are all prime. These burn more cleanly than softwoods, such as pine and cedar, which leave a sticky residue that clogs flue linings. Avoid painted scrap lumber which can give off fumes.

Most firewood should be aged for at least one year in a dry place. Pine needs two years to dry the sap. The drier the wood, the easier it will be to ignite.

Since logs burn more efficiently when dry, shelter outdoor stacks under a waterproof cover that allows air to reach the sides.

Firewood is sometimes sold by the cord (8 x 4 x 4 feet, or 128 cubic feet, or between 350–400 logs), but more often by the "face" cord, which can run anywhere from 32 cubic feet to 96 cubic feet. When comparing rival prices, make sure measurements are identical.

PREFAB LOGS

☞ Ready-to-burn, prefabricated logs offer an alternative to cordwood. These paper-wrapped "logs" are more expensive, but burn longer. They're also clean, light, easy-to-store, and relatively smoke-free.

- If your fireplace has warm-air circulators embedded in the firebox walls, vacuum the ducts at the beginning of each heating season.

- Have any cracks in the firebox and hearth repaired.

Lighting a Safe Fire

Before you lay a fire, check to see that the damper is open. Start with a bed of ashes about one inch thick. Over it

COOLING SYSTEMS

Cooling and ventilation are as important as heating, and there are many systems available, from fans to air conditioners. Choose carefully, according to your needs and the local climate so you can regulate your home's temperature for both comfort and energy efficiency.

Energy Ratings

The more efficient the cooling equipment, the less power required, which saves energy and money.

All room air conditioners have energy-efficiency ratings (EER). To check a unit's efficiency, always note this rating. A rating of 9 or more is quite good.

Central units are measured differently because they generally stay on for far longer periods than room units. They are rated over the entire season.

A central air conditioner or heat pump has a SEER number, which stands for seasonal energy-efficiency rating. A SEER of 10 or more is excellent.

ALL ABOUT AIR CONDITIONING

There are two types of air conditioners: room units and central systems.

A central system circulates cool air throughout the entire house by means of vents.

A room air conditioner installed in a window cools only the room it is in.

Buying one or two individual room units just to cool spaces used most often is far less expensive than installing a central system.

Before working on either type, turn off the power or unplug the unit.

Room Unit Maintenance

- Change the filter several times during the cooling season. If the filter is permanent, soak it in warm, soapy water and rinse.

- At the beginning of the cooling season, vacuum the evaporator coils, which lie behind the filter (immediately behind the front grille).

- Using a spirit level, check to see that the unit slants slightly toward the ground, so that condensed water flows out.

- Off-season, cover the outside of the unit to prevent rusting.

Central System Maintenance

- Change a disposable filter or wash a permanent one several times during the cooling season. If the filter is permanent, soak it in warm, soapy water and rinse.

- Once a year, have a professional wash the condensing coils, oil the fan motor with motor oil, if required, and vacuum the evaporator coils located in the ducting above the furnace.

- Check regularly to make sure that leaves or fallen branches aren't covering the fan grille on the outdoor condensing unit.

- During cold months, cover the outdoor condensing unit with a waterproof tarp.

EIGHT COOL WAYS TO SAVE MONEY

1. If you have central air conditioning, keep the thermostat at 78°F. Estimated energy savings range up to 25 percent over a more typical setting of 72°F.

2. Install the central air-conditioner's condenser on the north side of your home, out of direct sunlight.

3. Install awnings over windows not shaded by a roof overhang.

4. Draw draperies and blinds during hot days.

5. Minimize use of heat-generating appliances, such as the range or clothes dryer, during hot weather. Use the microwave and sun-dry your clothes, if possible.

6. Take advantage of cool summer days: Open windows and turn off the air conditioner.

7. Make sure your cooling system has a SEER or EER rating above 9.

8. Replace inefficient gable vents in your attic with vents along the roof ridge and underneath the eaves.

SMOOTH START-UPS

☛ Switch on the power for the outside unit of a central air conditioner at least 24 hours before turning on the whole system. In that time, a small resistance element warms up the refrigerant, making it flow smoothly when given the first call for cooling.

MADE IN THE SHADE

☛ For long-term energy efficiency, plant trees or tall shrubs to provide afternoon shade on the south and west sides of your home.

BUILT-IN FANS

A few strategically located fans can effectively circulate air, distributing heat in the winter and cool air in the summer. Fans also curb mildew growth in damp areas like bathrooms.

Attic Fans

Attic fans—installed face up in the attic floor in some newer homes—can provide comfort during hot months.

The same attic fan can work in two ways. You can run it during the day so the fan blades draw warm house air up into the attic, which then flows out through existing attic venting, or operate the fan only at night, so it draws cool air through open house windows. If no one is at home, turn it off during the day and keep your windows closed and shades pulled.

For best results establish the right ratio between fan speed (in cubic feet per minute, or CFM) and square footage of the living spaces. Your fan dealer can help you compute this ratio.

HOW TO MAINTAIN AN ATTIC FAN

- Clear bugs and dirt from the screening over attic vents (generally located either in the gable ends or along the roof ridge), so exhaust air can exit freely.

- Lubricate the fan motor and bearings once each season.

Ceiling Fans

Ceiling fans can help make your house energy efficient throughout the year. In hot weather, the fan blades draw up cool air and recirculate it around the room. In cold weather, the fan gently forces down warm air. (A single switch reverses the direction.) To maintain a ceiling fan:

- Lubricate the motor once a year.

- Clean the blades and motor housing, which are located directly above the fan-blade shaft, monthly with a dry cloth.

- Call for service if the blades begin to wobble on the stem or if short-circuiting recurs frequently.

Exhaust Fans

Fans are particularly important for bathrooms and kitchens to dispel both odors and moisture, which can cause mold and, over time, structural rot.

Simple window units are available; you can also have a wall-mount unit professionally installed.

Be certain the fan vents directly outdoors. If it vents into attic space, the attic insulation may become soggy.

To maintain an exhaust fan:

- Most new exhaust fans do not need lubrication, but a few older fans do, and should be oiled once a year.

- About once a year, with a dry cloth, clean the grille, the blades, the shaft, and the motor housing above the blades.

- If the stem wobbles or the fan starts making a loud noise, call for service.

PIPE INSULATION

☛ To prevent freezing, insulate any pipes running through the unheated areas of your house with adhesive-backed insulating tape (check with your plumber). Insulation also stops "sweating" in hot weather and in time pays for itself by saving energy.

WEATHERPROOFING

If your home isn't weathertight, it can leak as much as a month's worth of heated or cooled air in a year. Check for leaks, especially around windows and doors. Weather stripping and insulated windows are the key to energy efficiency.

WEATHER STRIPPING

Weather stripping seals leaks around exterior doors and windows. It is found in nearly all houses built after World War II.

Old weather stripping is usually made of felt or aluminum, and if it is more than twenty-five years old, it needs to be replaced.

There are two basic replacement types: rubber and plastic V-shaped. As a rule, rubber stripping is installed (with tacks, staples, or adhesive) to the top

WINDOWS

To make a window airtight, use rubber weather stripping on the top and bottom rails and plastic between the sash and jambs.

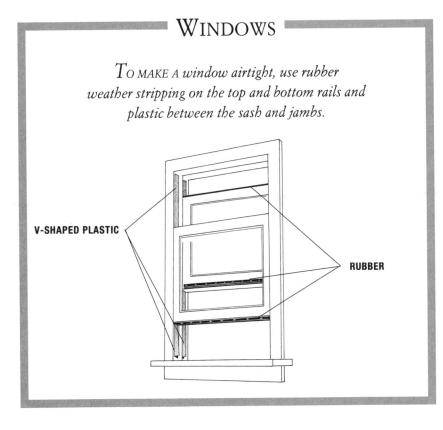

V-SHAPED PLASTIC

RUBBER

Draft leaks often occur from behind electrical outlets and light switches. You can seal them with foamed plastic, which comes in a spray can.

1. Turn off the current to the outlet or switch plate (see page 241). Remove the outer plate and the receptacle or switch (see page 243).

2. Squirt the foamed plastic around the junction box cutouts, located behind the outlet or switch plate, and openings around incoming and outgoing wiring.

3. Let it dry for 45 minutes.

4. Replace the parts and turn on the current.

and bottom rails of the windows, while plastic stripping goes between the sash and jambs and at the meeting rails.

It is also used on the header and jambs of exterior doors.

You can also seal the door by attaching a door sweep over the threshold. Choose a brushlike sweep that attaches to the door bottom or a vinyl sweep that compresses against the door bottom.

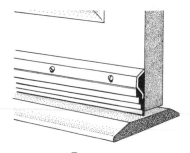

Door sweep

INSULATED WINDOWS

Tight, well-insulated windows are extremely important. Among the many energy-efficient options available are:

Storm windows: A well-installed storm window raises the insulating value of a single-glazed (one layer of glass) window between 80 percent and 100 percent.

As window insulating values rise, the need for storm windows decreases. Storm windows may increase insulating values of double- or triple-glazed windows by only 20 percent.

Double-glazed: In this type, two panes of window glass sandwich an air pocket, doubling the insulating value of a single-glazed window.

Triple-glazed: Three panes of glass sandwich two air pockets, which increases the insulating value by 60 percent over double-glazed windows. Triple-glazed windows cost more, but they also reduce sound transmission.

Low-emissivity glazed: These double- or triple-glazed windows are treated with an almost invisible film. They allow visible light to enter all year but keep reflected heat out during the summer and in during the winter. They are most effective if awnings or roof overhangs block the entry of direct sunlight in the summer.

Low-emissivity windows cost about 10 percent more than the others.

CAULKING AIR LEAKS

CAULKS ARE SOLD IN 11-OUNCE cartridges with a pointed nozzle at one end. The cartridges fit into a caulking "gun" that presses caulk through the nozzle when you pull the trigger. For best results, use at a 45-degree angle.

Many types of caulk are produced in a variety of colors. If you can't find the right color, use a transparent formula. Silicone caulks are recommended, although less expensive butyl and acrylic types also work well.

Some caulks cannot be painted over, so read the label before purchasing.

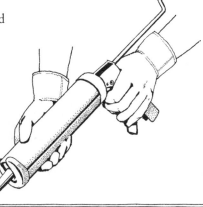

Caulk in the following places:

- Cracks between exterior siding and window and door frames.

- Thin cracks between wallboard and floors; remove the baseboard first.

- Slivers of air space at the point where piping passes through a wall.

- Along the joint between the wood sill plate and the top of the concrete foundation wall in the basement.

WHERE TO PUT INSULATION

*W*HETHER YOU LIVE IN THE *north or south, your home will benefit from insulation, which keeps warm air in and cool air out, or vice versa, depending on the season and climate. Good insulation can help you save significantly on fuel costs; here are some areas that typically need it.*

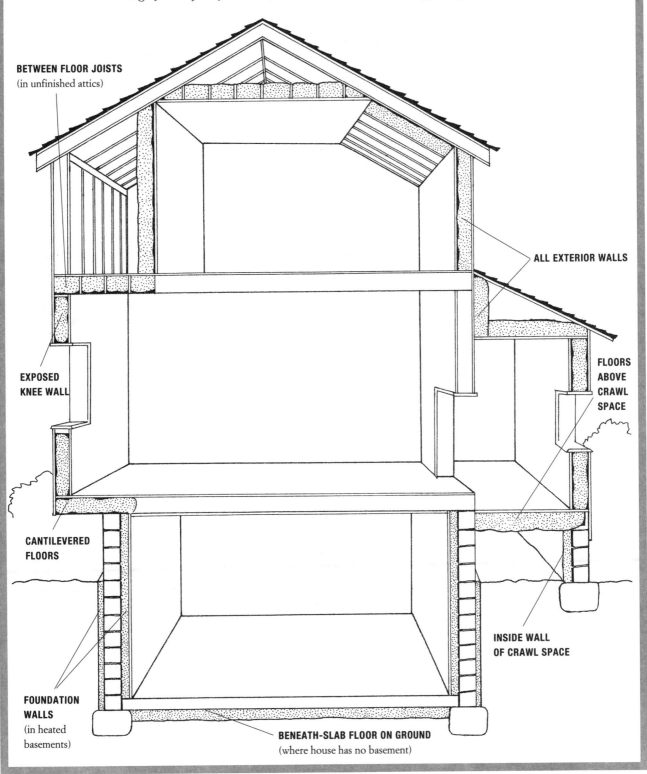

BETWEEN FLOOR JOISTS
(in unfinished attics)

ALL EXTERIOR WALLS

EXPOSED KNEE WALL

FLOORS ABOVE CRAWL SPACE

CANTILEVERED FLOORS

INSIDE WALL OF CRAWL SPACE

FOUNDATION WALLS
(in heated basements)

BENEATH-SLAB FLOOR ON GROUND
(where house has no basement)

Plumbing

If you familiarize yourself with your system, you can tackle many repairs, such as fixing leaky faucets and clearing blocked drains.

THE BASIC SYSTEM

Simply explained, plumbing delivers freshwater—usually from a community reservoir, a spring, or a private well—and takes away wastewater. You'll find a main cutoff valve that turns the water on and off inside the house near the point where freshwater piping enters.

From the main cutoff, a pipeline branches off to a water heater (the tank is almost always located near the main cutoff valve). Cold water continues on in the original pipe. Hot and cold water travel through these separate pipes to every plumbing fixture in the house.

Each fixture also has its own cutoff valve. Beneath a sink, for instance, there is one for the cold-water line and another for the hot water. Toilets, which don't require hot water, have only one. With these valves you stop or start the flow of water to the fixture.

Wastewater flows through a main soil pipe either to a septic tank or to a city sewage system.

A trap, a U-shaped bend in wastewater piping, is always located immediately below the point where water drains from a fixture.

THAWING ICE IN PIPING

Ice can build up inside an exposed, uninsulated, cold-water supply pipe during subfreezing weather, causing the pipe to burst.

ONE DROP LEADS TO ANOTHER

☞ Although a leaky faucet may seem like an insignificant problem, one drop every second adds up to more than six gallons of water daily—a good reason to make quick repairs.

PLUMBING DOS AND DON'TS

MOST COMMON PLUMBING problems result from careless housekeeping. Even the newest systems need to be treated kindly. Follow these pointers to avoid clogs and overflows.

DO:

- Know the location of all cutoff valves before an emergency arises.
- Protect drains with hair strainers or clean periodically with a bent coat hanger or long-shaft screwdriver.
- Keep drains clear of food.

DON'T:

- Pour liquid fat, which coagulates and clogs, down a kitchen drain. Let it solidify, and dispose of it with the garbage.
- Send anything but food scraps down an automatic food disposer.
- Flush anything down the toilet except bathroom tissue and human waste.

The first indication of a frozen pipe is a dwindling supply of water from faucets. If you can, check any areas where the freshwater supply piping is exposed to cold weather such as near an exterior wall.

If there's ice inside the piping, the metal will be extremely cold. To prevent freeze burns, cover the piping with a cloth before checking the pipe.

If the pipe has burst, shut off the water supply using the cutoff valve and call a plumber.

If the pipe has not burst, move quickly to thaw the ice.

- Do not use a blow torch or heat gun to thaw the pipe.

- Wrap the icy area with cloths soaked in boiling water. Repeat until the ice thaws and water runs freely from the faucets.

- If you have electric heat tape, wrap the frozen area with it, and plug the tape into a nearby outlet.

HOW TO FIX LEAKY FAUCETS

There are two types of faucets: older models requiring a washer and newer models that have a washerless cartridge within the faucet throat. The latter are designed to eliminate drips, but may eventually wear out.

Repairing either kind is usually easy and should take no more than 20 minutes.

If you have difficulties and time isn't a problem, you could photograph the faucet, show the picture to a clerk at a plumbing supply shop, and ask for help.

To fix a faucet with a washer
1. Close the cutoff valve so that no water spurts out when you begin disassembling the parts (see page 238). As you disassemble the faucet, lay out the parts in order. Then when you're ready for reassembly, simply reverse the order.

PATCHING PINHOLE LEAKS

*W*HEN A PIPE *springs a leak, turn off the water at the cutoff valve. Have a professional make the repair. For small leaks, make these temporary patches while you wait for help. Dry the pipe surface first.*

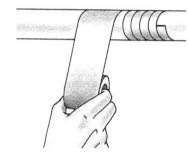 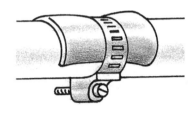

Wrap the leak with electrician's or duct tape. Replace that section of piping as soon as possible.

Cover the area around the leak with a section of garden hose held tightly with worm-drive clamps, available at most hardware stores.

2. Remove the screw holding the handle (sometimes beneath a Cold or Hot cap).

3. Remove the stem on a sink faucet, unscrew the nut beneath the handle with pliers or a small wrench, and lift out the stem (the working portion of the faucet beneath the handle). On a tub faucet, remove the first nut on the stem, and then with a socket wrench, loosen the larger nut that holds the bonnet (the cuplike metal cover to the tub stem).

4. At the bottom of the stem, you'll find the washer. Pry off the washer (or if it's held by a screw or a bolt, use a screwdriver or pliers). See the illustration on page 238.

5. Take the washer to a plumbing supply shop. Buy a half dozen replacements exactly like it. (Next time the faucet leaks, you'll have a washer on hand.)

FAUCET WITH A WASHER

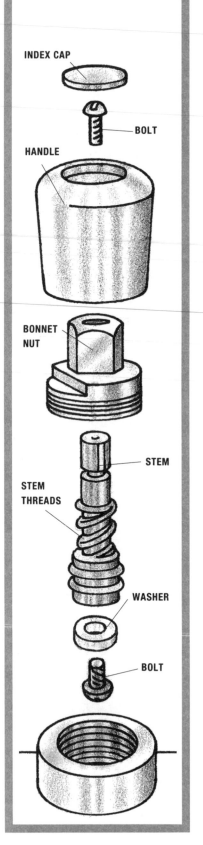

INDEX CAP

BOLT

HANDLE

BONNET NUT

STEM

STEM THREADS

WASHER

BOLT

6. Attach the new washer, and reassemble the parts. Close the faucet to prevent water from spurting through the piping when the water is turned on.

7. Open the cutoff valve. Turn on the water faucet, let it run for a few seconds, then close it. If there's still a leak, call a licensed plumber.

To fix a cartridge faucet

1. If you kept the repair instructions, follow the steps outlined. If not, begin by closing the cutoff valve (see page 236).

2. Pry off the handle or lever cap. If the cap is permanently connected to the lever, remove the screw holding the lever. In some cases, the lever and cap are held in place with a set screw immediately below the lever. Use an Allen wrench to turn the set screw.

3. If you see a nut, remove it, and lift off the threaded sleeve. The cartridge is below the sleeve. Slip off the clip holding the cartridge in place; it lies at the base of the faucet housing.

  If you don't see a nut, your faucet has another fastening system. To unseat it, remove the two long screws that go through the cartridge.

4. Slip in a new cartridge, available at hardware stores, designed for that faucet, and replace the parts in reverse order. If you run into trouble, call a plumber.

CLOGGED DRAINS

If your sink or tub drains slowly or if it is completely plugged, try pouring a quart of boiling water mixed with ¼ cup of ammonia into the drain. If that doesn't work, try these suggestions in the following order:

1. If the sink or tub is full of water, bail it out. If your drain has a strainer, remove the screw and lift it off. Pour hot water over the drain to a depth

of at least 3 inches in the sink or tub.

  Cover the drain tightly with the cup of a plunger, or "plumber's helper," and force the cup down hard three or four times. Lift the plunger to see if the water is draining. If not, plunge again.

2. If the drain is still blocked, the clog is probably in the trap—the U-shaped pipe just below the drain—which often has a clean-out plug at the bottom. This method applies to only some sinks and toilets. (The trap isn't visible on a tub, so you'll need to call a plumber.)

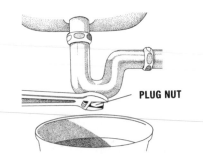

PLUG NUT

  Place a bucket beneath the trap. Fit a wrench snugly around the plug nut, and with a steady pull—not a yank—remove the plug. If you need to remove the blockage in the trap, use the hook end of a wire clothes hanger.

3. If the U trap has no clean-out plug or the blockage doesn't budge, remove the trap.

  First, measure the pipe diameter and buy several new gaskets (rubber rings) to fit the joints.

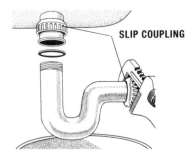

SLIP COUPLING

  Place a bucket under the trap. You'll see two large nuts, one at either end of the trap pipe. These are

CARTRIDGE FAUCET

THE CARTRIDGE FAUCET VARIES ONLY slightly from one with a washer.

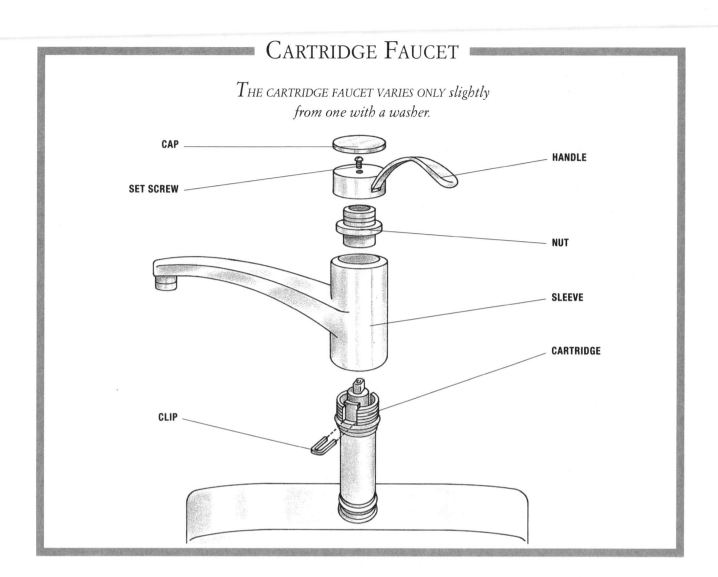

CAP

SET SCREW

HANDLE

NUT

SLEEVE

CARTRIDGE

CLIP

slip couplings. Remove both using steady pressure with a large-jaw wrench so as not to strip the threads, and remove the old rubber gaskets.

Clean out the trap and the drain pipe ends with a coat hanger bent into a coil to fit the pipe diameter. If it's still clogged, you can use a plumber's auger—a cylinder-shaped "pusher"—but if this is necessary, it is best to call a plumber.

When the trap is clear, place new gaskets on the trap joints and refasten the slip couplings.

4. If none of these solutions works, the clog is beyond the trap and probably lies somewhere in the pipes beneath the basement floor or underground beyond your house. Call a drain-cleaning service.

TOILET PROBLEMS

Clogs

You can usually open a clogged toilet drain with a plunger. Fit the rubber cup completely over the toilet bowl passage before plunging. Pump several times. If that fails, call a drain-cleaning service.

Continuous Running

Continuous running can frequently be traced to a tank ball or flapper that isn't seated properly in the discharge opening.

Remove the tank top and jiggle the lift wire. The ball or flapper usually falls into place.

If the ball doesn't fall properly, buy a replacement, which is inexpensive

HOW TO SOFTEN YOUR WATER

If you find that soap doesn't lather well in the shower, white clothing takes on a gray cast after laundering, and bathing always leaves a tub ring, your water is probably too hard.

This happens when minerals like calcium and magnesium leach into ground water. Water softeners simply reverse the process by exchanging hard-water mineral ions for gentle sodium or potassium ions.

Water-softening equipment consists of either a single tank or two tanks, one for softening water and one for storing salt, which must be replaced periodically.

Purchasing the equipment and replacing the salt on your own is fairly simple and cost effective in the long run. (You will need to have the unit professionally installed.)

You can also rent from a water-softening service company, which will provide the unit, salt, and regular maintenance.

The treated water need be directed only to faucets serving tubs, showers, and washing machines. A piping bypass installed by a plumber will send untreated water to toilets, outdoor faucets, and at least one supply of drinking water, if you wish.

WHETHER REPAIRING A running toilet or replacing a tank ball, it helps to know the ins and outs of your toilet's interior.

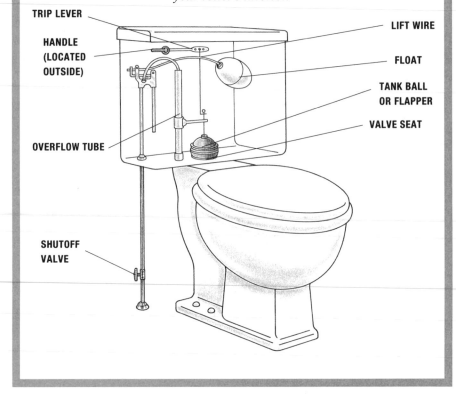

and easy to install; follow the manufacturer's instructions.

Less often, the discharge valve seat is corroded, permitting water to seep between the valve seat and the ball.

Close the shutoff valve (usually located on the wall beneath the tank), flush the toilet, and clean the valve seat with a steel wool pad until the parts work properly.

If water still leaks into the bowl, you may need a new tank, a job for a professional.

Another possibility is that the tank float has sprung a leak. With water inside, the metal float is too heavy to rest on top of the water.

Stuck in a sinking position, the float continues to signal the supply valve for more water.

If this is the case, buy a replacement and install following the manufacturer's instructions.

If the water level inside the tank is above the overflow tube and nothing else seems out of place, the problem may be the result of a faulty supply valve.

Close the shutoff valve. Replace the entire tank mechanism. Home centers, hardware stores, and plumbing supply outlets sell complete tank kits with detailed installation instructions. This task is not as daunting as it may seem, but it does take patience and the ability to follow instructions closely. If you lose heart, call a licensed plumber.

ELECTRICITY

Most of us take electricity for granted until it fails. Then the mystery and danger we associate with it often keep us from attempting repairs. There is danger, but if you approach problems with an understanding of the basic elements, it's possible to do many small electrical repairs and improvements in complete safety.

The first rule for working on the electrical system in your house is to cut off power at the entry panel by turning off the main disconnect.

UNDERSTANDING BREAKERS AND FUSES

The entry panel—which holds the circuit breakers and fuse box—is a permanent guard against two possibilities:

- the danger of attaching too many appliances to a circuit

- an unwanted surge of electrical power entering your house lines.

In either case, the power is cut off. A circuit breaker "trips" the connection, or a fuse "blows," meaning the electrical connection burns out.

1. Before resetting a breaker or replacing a fuse, try to determine what triggered the power cutoff. Most often, a power overload is the cause. For example, you may have plugged an iron into a circuit already taxed to its limit with lights, a TV, and a toaster.

2. Turn off switches and appliances on that circuit (see above right), and unplug at least one of the offending appliances. If you don't, when you reset the breaker or replace a fuse, you'll overload the circuit again.

3. Reset the circuit breaker by flipping the tripped switch all the way off and then all the way on.

4. To replace a fuse safely, switch on a flashlight, and turn off the house power by pulling down the handle on the outside of the fuse box, or by pulling out the cartridge marked "MAIN" on the panel. Remove the blown fuse (its glass top will probably be clouded and the metallic connection immediately below the glass broken). Replace with one of proper amperage.

5. Turn on the house power.

EASY IDENTIFICATION

☞ Label your circuit breakers and fuses to show what house appliances and switches are served by which fuses. Trip each breaker and loosen each fuse one at a time. Have a partner locate the corresponding appliances and switches that are without power. Write the information on a label next to the switch or fuse. Repeat for all circuits. Keep a flashlight and spare fuses handy to the box.

ANATOMY OF A LAMP

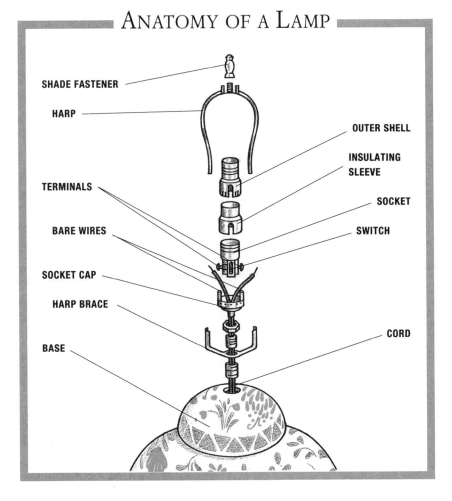

SHADE FASTENER
HARP
TERMINALS
BARE WIRES
SOCKET CAP
HARP BRACE
BASE
OUTER SHELL
INSULATING SLEEVE
SOCKET
SWITCH
CORD

☞ Always replace a blown fuse with one of the same amperage (current strength).

If you screw a 15-amp fuse into a 30-amp circuit, for instance, it will blow very quickly.

If you put a 30-amp fuse into a 15-amp circuit, you cancel the protection the fuse is meant to provide. It is supposed to blow at 15 amps.

REWIRING A LAMP

Rewiring a lamp is a straightforward process. Follow the instructions provided here using anatomy of a lamp (see page 241) as a guide.

1. Unplug the lamp. Remove the shade fastener and lift off the shade.

2. To remove the harp, squeeze the base and pull up.

3. Pull off the outer shell and insulating sleeve by working them back and forth.

4. Loosen the terminals. Untie the knot and straighten the bare wires.

5. Cut off the old plug and at the base of the lamp splice the end of the

new cord to the old cord. Pull the old wiring through the lamp and discard it. (As you pull the old wiring through the lamp, the new wiring will be pulled into place.)

Underwriter's knot

6. Split the new wire and tie an underwriter's knot to relieve strain on the wire. Make certain enough wire

HOW TO REPLACE AN OUTLET

Most new homes are built with three-blade grounded outlets or ground-fault circuit interrupters (GFCI). A GFCI will quickly cut off misdirected electricity. It is recommended to replace old two-blade outlets, which aren't grounded. It is especially important to do so in the kitchen, pantry, laundry, and bathrooms—wherever water is nearby—to reduce the chance of electrical shock.

JUNCTION BOX

COLORED CURRENT WIRES

GROUND WIRE

NEW RECEPTACLE

HERE'S HOW:

1. Turn off your house power (see page 241).

2. Unscrew and remove the wall plate.

3. Unscrew and pull out the ceramic receptacle.

4. Is a green or bare wire in the metal junction box? If no, stop here: Ask an electrician to run a ground wire to the box or install a GFCI receptacle.

5. If yes: That is the ground wire. It should be locked beneath a nut on both the junction box and on either the top or bottom of the new, three-hole receptacle.

6. Observe where the colored wires carrying current are attached. Make a note of their location, and attach wires to the new receptacle in the same way.

7. Replace the parts in reverse order.

8. Turn on your house power.

remains above the knot to attach firmly to the terminals.

7. Remove insulation from the wire ends and hook wires around the terminals in a clockwise direction one at a time.

8. Attach a new plug.

9. Replace the socket.

10. Slip the insulating sleeve and outer shell over the socket; reattach the harp and screw down the shade.

SWITCHES

Replacing Switches

Replacing a switch is simply a matter of disconnecting the old switch, then rewiring the new switch exactly as the old switch was done.

1. Turn off your house power (see page 241).

2. Unscrew and remove the switch plate.

3. Unscrew and pull out the old switch.

4. Replace the wires on the new switch exactly as they were located on the old switch.

5. Replace the parts in reverse order.

6. Turn on your house power.

ROOF REPAIRS

Keep your roof in good condition in order to prevent expensive repairs that can result from leaks. All roof materials have limited lives, on the average of twenty to forty years, but it's a good practice to check the roof annually and to contact a reputable roofing contractor when repairs are needed.

A typical roof consists of rafters (or roof trusses), sheathing (usually plywood), underlayment (tar paper), and tiles or shingles, which form the outermost layer.

The joints between the roof covering and chimneys, vent pipes, dormers, or skylights are closed with sheet metal or asphalt mats called flashing. Flashing is sealed with roof cement.

HOW TO LOCATE LEAKS

Many leaks are not located directly above the wet spot they cause. Rain or melting snow usually sneaks in through a crack drop by drop. Instead of falling immediately, droplets tend to run down the underside of sheathing or a rafter. When they hit a protruding nail or a knot, they fall.

Attic Leaks

Locating a roof leak is next to impossible if the attic is finished. Show the wet mark to a roofing contractor.

If your attic is unfinished, you can check for leaks yourself. On a rainy day, use a strong-beamed flashlight to locate the spot where water is dripping,

CHILDPROOF OUTLETS

☞ To protect children from shocks, insert plastic outlet protectors in unused wall outlets. Or replace an existing outlet with a special safety outlet. (To operate, you must insert the plug prongs into the openings and twist the plug ¼ turn so that the prongs make contact with the electrical source.)

FOUR SIMPLE ENERGY SAVERS

☞ Use screw-in fluorescent or high-intensity-discharge (HID) bulbs for freestanding and table lamps.
☞ Use dimmer switches.
☞ Turn off lights when you leave a room.
☞ Use a ceiling fan instead of your air conditioner.

ANATOMY OF A ROOF

The typical roof consists of these basic parts:

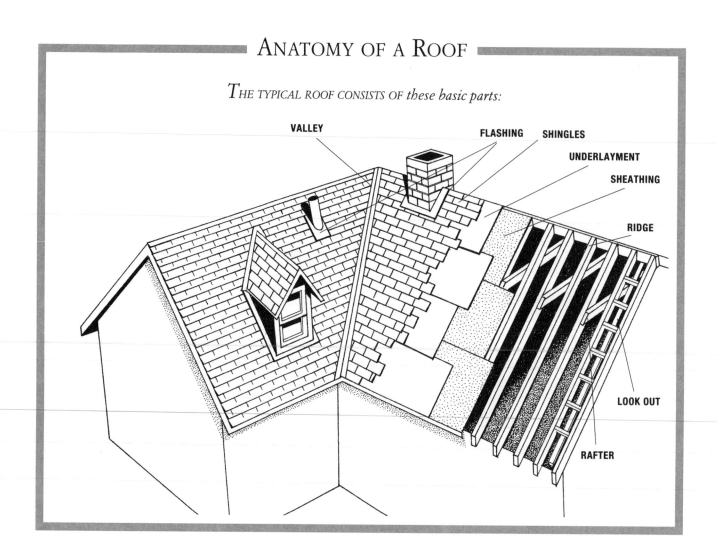

VALLEY · FLASHING · SHINGLES · UNDERLAYMENT · SHEATHING · RIDGE · LOOK OUT · RAFTER

ROOF SAFETY

If repairing or replacing the roof yourself, follow basic ladder safety rules:

☞ Work only in mild weather

☞ Never work in rain or high winds.

☞ For a better grip wear soft-soled shoes such as sneakers if you have to step on the roof.

and carefully trace the wet water track to the leak. Mark the spot with chalk or spray paint.

On a bright sunny day, turn off all lights and look over the entire roof for a pinhole beam of sunlight. Mark the spot. Once you find the leak, from the attic side of the roof, generously fill the crack or hole with silicone caulk (see page 234).

Then cut a ³/₈-inch-thick plywood patch three times as large as the hole. Coat one side of the plywood with white glue; from the ceiling side press it over the hole and fasten it to the ceiling with ¹/₂-inch nails so that it stays put while the glue dries.

This should stop the leak, but keep in mind that a leak is usually a signal that a new roof will soon be necessary.

TROUBLESHOOTING ROOF PROBLEMS

Leaks aren't always a result of broken shingles. They also occur when a new roof is improperly flashed or when roofing is incorrectly installed, particularly in awkward spaces, such as in a valley.

To keep track of the condition of your roof, check it over once a year by looking through binoculars from the ground. If you spot any broken, bent, or missing shingles or tiles, or spots of mold, call a repairperson.

GUTTERS

utters help protect your house by collecting rainwater at the roof edge and draining it out a downspout. Without them, runoff can erode the soil around your foundation and eventually cause basement leaks.

Gutters are typically made of aluminum, copper, steel, or vinyl. All materials perform well, but because vinyl gutters don't rust, peel, or corrode, they require less maintenance. Washed and painted as needed, a metal gutter can last for several decades.

At least twice a year, clear blockages.

Scrub all gutter and downspout surfaces with a stiff scrub brush and water. Inspect the inside of the gutter for signs of wear. Patch the smallest pinhole before it grows. If a painted gutter is peeling, scrape it and repaint it using a latex paint specifically recommended for use on exterior metal. There's no need to paint copper or stainless steel. For unpainted gutters, apply two coats of a waterproofing sealer.

CLEARING BLOCKAGES

Wet, decaying leaves packed in a gutter or a downspout not only cause blockages, but also are a particular problem as their weight may cause lightweight metals like aluminum to bend or break.

Moreover, when evergreen needles and oak leaves rot, they can produce metal-eating acid.

Here are two ways to clear blockages:

- Climb an extension ladder and remove the decay by hand.

- Stay on the ground and use a special gutter cleaner, which you can attach to your garden hose. You can then aim a powerful spray at the blockage.

Gutter Guards

A good way to reduce gutter cleaning is by using gutter guards. Buy them at hardware stores and home centers; install according to the manufacturer's directions.

Or make your own:

1. Cut heavy screening 6 inches wide in lengths determined by the screening

---

FIXING A LEAKY GUTTER

IF YOUR GUTTERS leak, the water could cause damage to your house's foundation. Look for signs of leaks (rust stains on house sidewall, for instance) at least twice a year. Always clean and dry the area around a hole before making repairs.

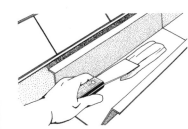

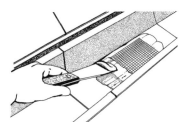

PATCHING A SMALL HOLE

- Aluminum gutter: Follow the manufacturer's instructions. Apply plasticized aluminum and spread evenly.

  Over a large hole, stretch fine aluminum screening or heavy aluminum foil into a thin bed of plasticized aluminum around the hole. Then apply a second coat over the screening or foil.

- Steel gutter: Patch a small hole with roofing cement.

  Close a large hole by embedding a patch of galvanized steel flashing in a bed of roofing

PATCHING A LARGE HOLE

cement, followed by a layer of roofing cement over the patch.

- Vinyl gutter: Close small holes with silicone caulk.

  Cover a large hole with a vinyl patch embedded in plastic adhesive.

- Copper gutter: Plug a small hole with silicone caulk.

  Embed a new patch of copper in roofing cement to close a large hole. Solder leaks at gutter joints.

ANATOMY OF A GUTTER

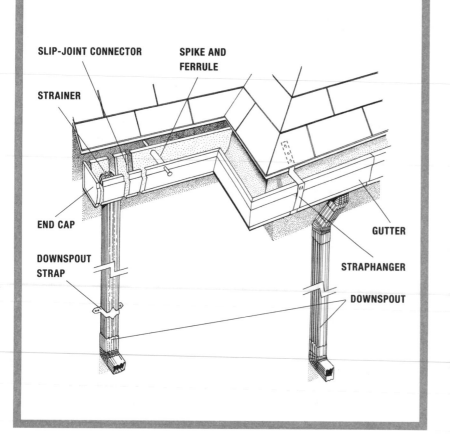

SLIP-JOINT CONNECTOR

SPIKE AND FERRULE

STRAINER

END CAP

DOWNSPOUT STRAP

GUTTER

STRAPHANGER

DOWNSPOUT

(see pages 165–168)

EXTERIOR PAINTING

A good exterior paint job should last five to seven years. Unless you are experienced, you should leave repainting to a professional, but you can do minor touch-ups if you use the right paint and equipment:

- For wood exteriors, choose a good-quality exterior alkyd for the primer coat and a good-quality exterior latex for the finish coat (see pages 165–168). One coat of each should be enough.

- Buy enough paint. Read the label to find out how much a can covers.

- Use good-quality brushes and rollers.

- Never paint in rain, drizzle, mist, or fog. This could lock moisture into the paint film and later cause flaking. Nor should you paint in direct sunlight. Paint spreads poorly on a heated surface.

HOW TO PAINT

1. Scrape off all paint that has blistered or flaked. Fresh paint fails quickly when you apply it over a loose old coat.

2. Wash the surface due for new paint; dirt prevents paint from clinging firmly.

   Remove mildew (dark-green or black stains; often found on the north wall of a house near the ground) by scrubbing with a solution of 1 cup of household bleach to 1 gallon of water.

   Allow the surface to dry thoroughly before painting.

3. Lightly sand away any old, hardened paint drips.

4. Mask with tape areas you don't want painted.

5. Paint from the top down.

size. (Or buy 12-foot lengths of heavy screening already cut to a width of 6 inches for use as gutter guards.)

2. Wedge a screening piece lengthwise between the outer edges of the gutter (normal width 5 inches), so that the screening bows upward.

3. Repeat for the next piece of screening, meshing the cut ends of both sections so that leaves don't fall in between.

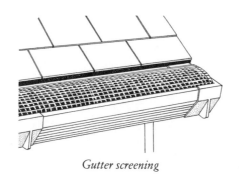

Gutter screening

TAPE TIP

☛ When painting, remove tape from masked areas as soon as possible. Tape left overnight may be difficult to peel off. When painting window trim, many find it easier to scrape dried paint from window glass with a razor scraper rather than bother with masking tape.

HOME REPAIR CHECKLIST

IF YOU ARE at all uncertain about how to fix something, hire a professional. However, do so with care:

Complaints about home-improvement contractors and professional repair people are near the top of the list of problems reported to the Better Business Bureau and the U.S. Council of Consumer Affairs.

Most are linked to miscommunication: What you wanted or expected was not what you received. These suggestions will help increase the likelihood that you'll be satisfied with the people you hire.

☐ Spend time getting the right person for your job. Ask your local builders' association or your friends for recommendations. When you have a list, ask your local Better Business Bureau or consumer-affairs office for information about their reputations.

☐ Get estimates from at least three contractors. Then ask the following information:
- Do they have a current license? (Not all states require licensing.)
- Do they have workman's compensation and liability insurance? (The contractor may sue you if he or she is injured on the job.)
- What is their business and/or home phone number or address? (In case there's an emergency or disagreement about the bill.)

☐ Ask to see projects the contractor has recently completed that are comparable to yours—especially if you're planning a major project like remodeling a kitchen or adding a bathroom.

☐ Review the work-order form or contract to make sure you both understand what's expected. It should include:
- A job definition
- Starting and completion dates
- A detailed list of services and/or materials (size, color, weight, brand name of parts)
- The total price or an itemized estimate.
- A cancellation penalty, if applicable.
- The payment schedule (ideally, one third at the beginning, one third when half done, and one third when the job is satisfactorily completed).

☐ If the job includes replacing any parts, make sure you keep the old ones. Label them and put them where you can find them in case you have problems later and need to find out whether the part actually needed replacing.

☐ Don't pay cash.

THE YARD

There are two hard and fast safety rules:

☞ Always wear safety goggles. Goggles offer much-needed protection when you prune and trim, spray pesticides, chip away at stone, chop wood, use power tools, or perform any other task that could put your eyes at risk.

☞ Always wear work gloves. Gloves help prevent scratches and blisters and will protect you from tetanus and other bacteria that thrive in soil.

Yard and garden work can be a relaxing hobby. Here are some basic techniques and a few handy tools that will keep yard work under control.

MOWING

There are two basic mowers: power rotary and reel. Power rotary mowers come in two basic styles—walk behind and rider. The manual reel mowers slice with a scissorslike action and give a smooth cut. While quiet and non-polluting, they require substantial effort and are only suitable for small lawns.

Improper mowing can gradually ruin a lawn. These rules will keep you out of trouble:

- Mow when the grass is dry. A mower may crush wet grass.
- Mow before you use fertilizer, seed, or pesticides.
- Rake and bag clippings, or use a mulching mower designed to chop blades of grass into bits small enough to reenter the soil as a nutrient.

FERTILIZING

If you want to keep your lawn lush and green, you will need to fertilize it. In particular, grass needs nitrogen, phosphorous, and potassium, contained in commercially sold fertilizers.

Contrary to popular belief, lime, or calcium oxide, is not a grass food. It's used to neutralize soil that is too acidic.

If you planted a warm-season grass, wait until summer to fertilize. Otherwise, spread fertilizer after the first spring mowing.

Follow the instructions on the bag to determine how much fertilizer to apply on a specific area. The amount you'll need depends on the dominant grass species and the area to be covered. You also need to check the nitrogen ratio in your fertilizer. Nitrogen promotes growth and greenness, but too much can make your lawn susceptible to disease and insects. Consult the grass seed chart (see page 250 or a chart in your local garden shop).

SEEDING

To prepare an uncultivated area for new seed, lightly till the soil, removing any rocks. Rake it until the soil particles are no larger than peas.

Spread the seed on a windless day in early spring. Stroke the soil gently

---

MOWING SAFELY

POWER MOWERS HAVE a number of built-in safety features. Even so, you should take these added precautions.

DO:
- Mow across a slope rather than up and down when using a walk-behind machine. On a riding mower, up and down is fine.
- Turn off the motor if you need to inspect or work on it. Unfasten the spark plug to double your safety.
- Turn off the motor when you stop to empty the grass bag or unclog the discharge chute.
- Make sure grass is cleared of toys, large sticks, and stones.

DON'T:
- Permit anyone to stand in the line of the discharge chute. Flying stones and sticks can do serious injury.
- Add gasoline to the tank of a running mower. Turn off the machine, let it cool, and then add fuel.
- Carry youngsters on a riding mower.

---

and only once with the back of a bamboo rake.

Fertilize and lightly water for two weeks, two or three times a day.

Do not begin to mow until the new grass is taller than two inches.

RESEEDING

The best time to reseed thinning grass is in early fall, except in southern regions, where you reseed in spring.

If water use is restricted, try a seed mix with a high content of tall fescues, fine fescues, and perennial ryegrasses. Otherwise, use the same seed variety you have been using.

Groove the soil by drawing a rake across the area to be seeded. (New seed germinates better inside grooves.)

Spread the seed on a clear windless day, and cover it with a light layer of rich soil or peat moss.

Soak the area with water every two or three days for about three weeks.

SPRING MOWING

☛ After the first spring cut, mow no more than ⅓ of the grass height; sun may weaken the roots of grass clipped too low.

MOWER MAINTENANCE

WHILE THE SETUP MAY VARY slightly, your power rotary lawn mower will likely have all the basic parts illustrated here. Use the diagram and instructions as a guide when caring for your mower. If any of the directions require further explanation, refer to the owner's manual.

CONTROLS
GAS CAP
GAS TANK
AIR FILTER
DRIVE BELT HOUSING
SPARK PLUG
BLADE

At the beginning of the season:

1. Change the oil (use only oil recommended by the mower manufacturer).

2. Fill the gas tank with fresh, unleaded gasoline.

At the end of the season:

1. Disconnect the spark plug. With a screwdriver or putty knife, scrape away hard-packed dirt and grass from the blade, wheels, and mower housing.

2. Clean the motor housing with a rag slightly dampened in kerosene.

3. Check the drive belt for tears and wear. Replace a faulty belt.

4. Check the blade. If the edges are nicked and dull in places (which is likely), have a professional sharpen it.

5. Reconnect the spark plug, and let the engine run until all gasoline is gone. Gasoline left in the tank over winter may clog the motor.

6. Store the mower in a clean, dry location.

GRASS SEED

All grasses grow well in a balanced soil with a low clay content.
To determine the balance of your soil get it tested by calling your agricultural
extension agent listed in the phone book under "Government Agencies." Then
choose a seed or mixture of seeds to suit your needs.

Variety	Needs	Mowing Height	Fertilizer Ratio*	Good For	What You Should Know
Bahia	Warm nights, hot days	1½" to 2"	1 to 4	Sunny or partly shady areas	Easy to grow, but coarse and not as tight as Bermuda or St. Augustine; adapts to sun or moderate shade.
Bermuda	Warm nights, hot days	½" to 1½"	1 to 5	Sunny or shady areas	Hardy for southern climates; plant in sunny areas; attractive texture and deep color.
Fine fescue	Cool nights, warm days	1" to 2"	1 to 3	Shady areas	Attractive dark-green color; easily adaptable to different soils; excellent shade grass.
Kentucky bluegrass	Cool nights, warm days	1" to 2"	2 to 6	Sunny areas	Most popular; hardy; pretty dark-green color; good in sun or light shade in north; shade in south.
Merion Kentucky bluegrass	Cool nights, warm days	½" to 1"	3 to 6	Sunny areas	Has the same qualities as Kentucky bluegrass, but also forms a denser growth, as on a golf course.
Perennial ryegrass	Cool nights, warm days	1" to 2"	1 to 4	Sunny or partly shady areas	Easily grown; coarser than bluegrass; may require reseeding after 2 years. Bright green.
Red fescue	Cool nights, warm days	1½" to 2"	1 to 3	Partly shaded areas	Very adaptable and undemanding; grows in sun, light shade; tends to be somewhat coarse.
St. Augustine	Warm nights, hot days	2" to 3"	1 to 5	Sunny or shady areas	For southern climates; dark green and coarser than Bermuda, but adaptable to sun or shade.
Tall fescue	Cool nights, warm days	1" to 3"	1 to 3	Sunny or shady areas	Not for fine lawns, but good for areas where growing other grasses is a problem. Does best in sunny areas; coarse.
Zoysia	Warm nights, hot days	1" to 2"	1 to 4½	Sunny or partly shady areas	Slow grower, but one of the most attractive varieties of southern grasses; requires little attention; adapts to sun, light shade. Tough; best cut with a reel mower.

* Lbs. nitrogen in fertilizer/1000 sq. ft. (see page 248)

BASIC GARDENING TOOLS

START WITH A few basic tools that will help with the most simple garden chores. The best tools have wooden handles and one-piece solid-socket steel attachments. Handle tools safely. Clean, dry, and put them away after use. Store them indoors to avoid rust.

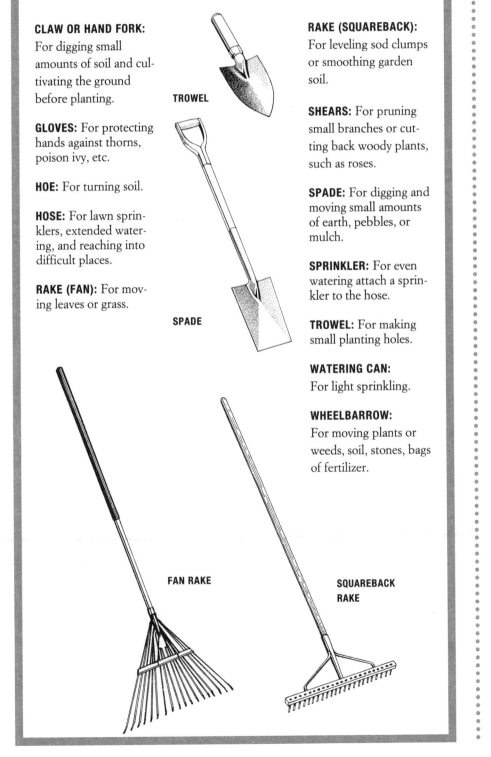

CLAW OR HAND FORK: For digging small amounts of soil and cultivating the ground before planting.

GLOVES: For protecting hands against thorns, poison ivy, etc.

HOE: For turning soil.

HOSE: For lawn sprinklers, extended watering, and reaching into difficult places.

RAKE (FAN): For moving leaves or grass.

TROWEL

SPADE

FAN RAKE

SQUAREBACK RAKE

RAKE (SQUAREBACK): For leveling sod clumps or smoothing garden soil.

SHEARS: For pruning small branches or cutting back woody plants, such as roses.

SPADE: For digging and moving small amounts of earth, pebbles, or mulch.

SPRINKLER: For even watering attach a sprinkler to the hose.

TROWEL: For making small planting holes.

WATERING CAN: For light sprinkling.

WHEELBARROW: For moving plants or weeds, soil, stones, bags of fertilizer.

DEEP BREATHING

☞ If water pools on your lawn after a normal rain, your soil may be too dense, preventing grass roots from getting enough water and air. Spike the soil with a pitchfork or rent a soil aerator to loosen it.

SPRINKLER SAVVY

☞ There are two basic types of sprinklers, underground and impulse. To thoroughly soak the soil, allow water to penetrate well below the grass root systems. That may take hours. A mere surface-wetting sprinkle can force grass roots to turn up for water.

- Wear a hat, gloves with long cuffs, a long-sleeved shirt, work pants, long socks, and sneakers.

- Work on a windless day. Use a spade or trowel to loosen dirt around the plants; then pull the plant stem up from the base. Carefully pack the uprooted plants in a plastic bag, seal tightly, and dispose with your trash.

- Remove and wash your clothes, including the sneakers. Take a shower and use plenty of soap.

- Never burn poison ivy. Smoke from the fire will absorb and carry itch-inducing chemicals. A person passing through the smoke may be seriously affected.

WEED KILLERS

If weeds such as crabgrass crowd out your grass, attack the next spring. Wait until the dandelions bloom; then spread a "weed-and-feed" mix, available at garden shops. Most of these weed killers are inorganic, but some organic mixes are now available as well.

There are two types—wet and dry mix. Both work well.

Apply a wet mix with a hose-end sprayer on a windless day. Hold the hose end at knee level and point it toward the grass. Avoid overspraying, which can kill flowers and shrubs.

Spread a dry mix on a windless day, and soak the mix into the soil with a good watering.

Do not apply weed-and-feed mixes when there is no apparent threat of weeds. The weed killer is potent and repeated applications could kill the lawn.

USING CHEMICALS AND PESTICIDES

Many home owners worry about using weed killers, fertilizers, pesticides, and other chemically based concoctions on the lawn and in the garden because these products contain toxins. To avoid them altogether, you can use organic nonchemical weed killers and fertilizers. New grass varieties, more resistant to weeds and insects, also lessen the need for weed killers.

If you do use chemical products in your yard, do so sensibly:

- Wear goggles and a nose and mouth mask while spraying or spreading fertilizers or pesticides.

- Read labels carefully and follow instructions exactly.

- Keep pets and children away while you are working with any chemical.

HARDY GRASS THE NATURAL WAY

YOU CAN GROW a rich, verdant lawn without spreading a single processed chemical.

1. Begin by having the soil tested for nutrients and acidity, then select organic fertilizers to correct any imbalances.

2. In areas where drought is a persistent problem, buy grass seed that is tolerant of dry weather.

Cut no more than ⅓ off the grass blade height at any one time. Let the clippings (which are rich in nitrogen) remain on the soil. In a few days, they'll be absorbed into the soil, acting as a natural fertilizer.

3. To get rid of crabgrass without chemical de-weeders, overseed (spread seed over) your lawn. Let your cultivated grass grow to 4 inches, at which point it will soon suffocate the crabgrass. Then mow.

A SEASONAL GUIDE TO LAWN MAINTENANCE

DIFFERENT WEATHER MEANS different treatment for
your lawn, which logically demands the most attention during
warm months. Always have a sharp mower blade. (A dull blade damages
the grass.) Both rotary and reel mower blades are tricky to sharpen;
get a mower-repair shop to do the job. Check the mower instructions
if you're not sure how to raise and lower the blade.

SPRING

Dethatch: If you haven't dethatched your lawn within the last three years, do so now. Thatch is made up primarily of dead grass clippings that over time have become packed tightly between new blades of grass. A layer more than ½-inch deep impedes water and nutrients from reaching grass roots, and is the cause of the vast majority of lawn problems.

You can rent a power dethatcher, buy a dethatching blade for your rotary power mower, or use a dethatching rake. Gather all loosened thatch and deposit it in the trash or on a compost pile.

Roll: Take one pass with a roller to help press the crowns back into the soil.

If the ground is wet, rolling also smooths out frost bumps.

Mow lower: For the first spring cut, set the mower blade low but not so low that new plants are damaged. Cut from ½ to ⅔ of the new grass blade. A low cut makes the first spread of fertilizer and weed killer more effective.

Test the soil: Before fertilizing, which should be done after the first spring mowing, get a soil test. Do not overfertilize. This can "burn" out the root system. Add lime if the soil is in need of higher alkalinity, which the soil test will determine.

Water: Begin watering the lawn regularly immediately after the last frost. Do so between late morning and early afternoon. Watering in the evening encourages the growth of fungi. Soak the lawn.

Reseed: Spread new seed and weed killers after fertilizing.

SUMMER

Mow regularly: When the grass grows quickly, mow every few days. Mow grass in shaded and slower-growing areas every week or two.

If water use is restricted in your community, let the grass grow taller for better protection from the heat.

If the grass turns brown, don't mow, but get rid of all weeds. (Sun-browned grass is often dormant, not dead.)

AUTUMN

Final mowing: Cut low on the last mowing of the growing season, and rake up the cuttings. This discourages insects and bacteria that thrive in the tall blades during the winter.

Reseed: If you intend to reseed, try to do so in the fall (for exceptions see page 249).

*PESTS BOTH INDOORS AND OUT can do real damage; inspect
periodically to catch problems before it's too late. The following remedies are
alternatives to chemical treatments. Most are essentially nontoxic and have
minimal environmental impact. If pest problems persist, however,
call in a reliable exterminator.*

INSECTS

PEST		NASTY HABITS	WHAT TO DO
Ants		Invade kitchen cabinets, counters.	Set out traps or bait containing boric acid. Pour boiling water into nest.
Carpenter ants		Bore into moist wood.	Treat holes with boric acid. Check for structural damage and repair.
Carpet beetles		Larvae eat wool, fur.	Have rugs professionally cleaned once a year. Dry-clean wools, furs; store with moth crystals.
Cockroaches		Invade kitchens and bathrooms; eat paste in book bindings.	Spread pyrethrum (chrysanthemum blossoms); or use mix of ⅓ borax, ⅓ cornmeal, ⅓ flour, dash of powdered sugar.
Houseflies		Buzz annoyingly and bite. Can transmit disease.	Secure screening; swat flies where they land and disinfect spot; use fly traps.
Mosquitoes		Buzz annoyingly and bite. Can transmit disease.	Secure screening; hang insect pest strips; use hair spray to stiffen wings; then kill.
Moths		Eat wool, fur, any clothes with stains	Have rugs professionally cleaned once a year. Dry-clean wools, furs; clothes before storage; store in cedar cupboard or with moth crystals.
Silverfish		Eat paste in book bindings; invade damp areas, such as basements and bathrooms.	Keep a dry basement; spread out pyrethrum (see Cockroaches).
Termites		Eat wood. Can weaken house frame to point of collapse.	Look for ½-inch wide mud tunnels along foundation; scrape them off. Fill with fresh dirt. Check for structural damage and repair.

ANIMALS

THE FOLLOWING PRECAUTIONS should help keep out pesky animals. If any do get in your home, call a professional game warden or exterminator for help.

PEST	NASTY HABITS	WHAT TO DO
Birds	Leave droppings; bring in fleas, other insects.	Close all attic and basement access with strong screening after birds have gone.
Deer	Raid gardens; carry ticks, rabies.	Secure garbage containers; place netting over plants.
Mice	Eat food scraps; travel through wall cavities. Can bite if cornered.	Set traps.
Raccoons	Nest in fireplaces; steal food; carry rabies.	Close all attic, basement, and chimney access with strong screening after raccoons have gone.
Squirrels	May nest in attic insulation; leave droppings. Can bite if cornered.	Close all attic and basement access with strong screening after squirrels have gone.

LYME DISEASE

☞ Ticks transmit Lyme disease, which usually begins with an enlarged bite or rash, fever, tiredness, headache, and stiff, achy joints. If you have any of these symptoms, particularly if you live in a wooded area where deer and ticks thrive, contact your doctor. Antibiotics can be an effective treatment. For information call the Centers for Disease Control and Prevention (404) 332-4555.

SNOW BLOWERS

You MAY WANT to consider investing in a snow blower if you live in a part of the country where snowfalls are heavy or frequent. Snow blowers make snow removal quick and easy and reduce the risk of back and shoulder injury.

Two kinds of snow blowers are available: walk-behind units and snow-blower attachments for lawn or garden tractors. Walk-behind units can be used on both sidewalks and driveways; tractor blowers are for driveways only.

SAFETY RULES

Snow blowers can cause accidents, so it's important to use them properly. Read the manufacturer's instructions carefully before using your snow blower for the first time.

Always turn the snow blower off before cleaning blockages from the discharge chute.

When clearing snow from a hill with a walk-behind snow blower, always work from side to side, never up and down. You have better control of the machine that way and, if you do lose control, it won't fall on you or drag you down the hill.

DON'T GET SNOWED

☞ Just before an expected snowfall, spread a little sand, rock salt, or cat litter on steps, sidewalks, and driveway to help prevent snow from sticking.

☞ Use a rubber-tipped floor squeegee to remove light snow from porches and stairs. It's quicker than sweeping or shoveling and won't scratch paint surfaces.

☞ To keep snow from sticking to your shovel, coat both sides with salad oil, cooking spray, or any household wax.

☞ To avoid pulling a back or shoulder muscle, use a small shovel or fill only half of a large one. Instead of trying to lift heavy wet snow with a shovel, move it with a garden rake.

PREPARING FOR WINTER

Taking care of your house is a year-round process. Obviously, you should solve problems as they occur. Cold weather, however, calls for special jobs:

• Service your furnace (see pages 228–229).

• Weather-strip leaky windows and doors (see page 233).

• Check chimney flues (see pages 229–230).

• Insulate water pipes against freeze-ups, as needed (see sidebar on page 233).

• Stock firewood (see page 230).

CHAPTER 7

CAR CARE

Sheets into Curt... ...HANDY TIPS: For Buffing Wood Flo... ...king Rooms Look Larger, Ironing ... ...ning Tile Grout, Creating a ☛ Mo... ...e on Car Repairs, Buy Produce, C... ...reventing Carpet Dents, Unsticking Stacked Glasses, Making Rooms Look Larger, Ironing Pleated Skirts, Arranging Flowers, Jump-Starting a Car, Cleaning Tile Grout, Creating a Home Office, Fixing a Leaky Faucet ☛ STEP-BY-STEP GUIDES: To Checkbook Security, Unblocking a Sink, Buying a Home, Successful Decorating, Performing CPR, Changing Flat Tires, Refinishing Furniture, Hanging Shelves, Lawn Mower Maintenance ☛ PREVENTIVE MAINTENANCE: Servicing a car safely. Anatomy of a car. Checklist: maintenance tips for a healthy car. How to gauge oil, coolant, tire wear, vital fluids, filters, and belts. Comparing drive systems. The facts about gas grades. Tools, supplies, and documents to keep handy. Manual and automatic transmissions explained. Special seasonal maintenance. Replacing worn air filters. ☛ COMMON PROBLEMS: Checking a battery. What to do when your car won't start: checking fuel, transmission, battery and spark-plug cables. Engine stall answers for hot and cold weather. Step-by-step jump-starting instructions. How to cope with an overheated engine. Transmission: What can go wrong. The meaning of noisy or misaligned brakes and the brake warning light. What to check if steering is difficult. Replacing exterior bulbs and electric fuses. Money saving tips for car care. Different tires for different conditions. Changing a tire in twelve simple steps. ☛ ROAD EMERGENCIES: Handling an accident properly. How to cool an overheated car. Regaining traction in snow, ice, sand, and mud. Steps for safe foul-weather driving. Minimizing the hazards of brake failure. All about child safety seats. ☛ KEEPING UP APPEARANCES: How to wash your car. Waterproofing with wax. Touch-up tips: fixing paint damage and torn vinyl. ☛ EVERYTHING YOU NEED TO KNOW: About Choosing Pots and Pans, Front-Wheel-Drive Cars, Making Healthier Meals, Vacuum Cleaners, Garden Tools, Upholstered Furniture, Your Credit Card Statement, Curtain Styles . . . and much more ☛ MONEY-SAVING HINTS: How to Turn Bed Sheets into Curtains, Save on Car Repairs, Buy Produce, Choose Carpeting ☛ HANDY TIPS: For Buffing Wood Floors, Preventing Carpet Dents, Unsticking Stacked Glasses, Making Rooms Look Larger, Ironing Pleated Skirts, Arranging Flowers, Jump-Starting a Car, Cleaning Tile Grout, Creating a Home Office, Fixing a Leaky Faucet ☛ STEP-BY-STEP GUIDES: To Checkbook Security, Unblocking a Sink, Buying a Home,

PREVENTIVE MAINTENANCE

Regular servicing is an essential part of owning a car. If you change the oil, check other fluids at required intervals, and arrange for timely inspections, you should be able to avoid unexpected breakdowns.

The information here covers what you can inspect and service yourself and when it's wise to seek professional help.

It is not, however, intended to replace the specific information in your owner's manual. To keep your warranty in effect, you must follow that manual scrupulously.

SAFETY PRECAUTIONS

Working on your car can be dangerous, so follow these commonsense rules:

- Never run an engine in an enclosed space.

- Never work on a car if you are tired, ill, or have been drinking alcohol or taking medication.

- Do not wear a necktie or loose clothing. Tie back hair, so it won't catch in moving parts. Take off jewelry; metal can cause electrical shorts that may give you a shock or burn you.

- If you smell gasoline, do not light a match, smoke, use a heater, turn on a light switch, or run a power tool, fan, or electric motor—all of which can cause sparks and lead to an explosion.

- Never work under a raised car unless it's supported by jack stands or ramps (cars can roll or fall off jacks). Make sure it's on level ground. Block the wheels with rocks or pieces of wood, and set the parking brake. Put an automatic transmission in Park and a manual transmission in Reverse.

ON THE READY

For easy maintenance, stock these supplies in your garage:
- ☞ Air filter
- ☞ Brake fluid
- ☞ Funnel with a flexible neck
- ☞ Motor oil
- ☞ Oil filter
- ☞ Power-steering fluid
- ☞ Transmission fluid

BOUGHT A USED CAR?

☞ Write to the manufacturer for an owner's manual for your year and model.

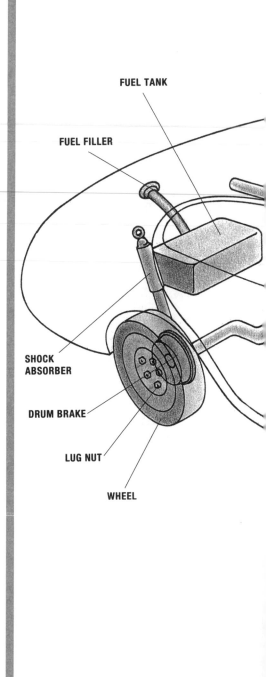

FUEL TANK

FUEL FILLER

SHOCK ABSORBER

DRUM BRAKE

LUG NUT

WHEEL

ANATOMY OF A CAR

While the setup may vary slightly, a front-wheel-drive car has all the basic parts shown below. Familiarizing yourself with these will help you keep your car in top running order.

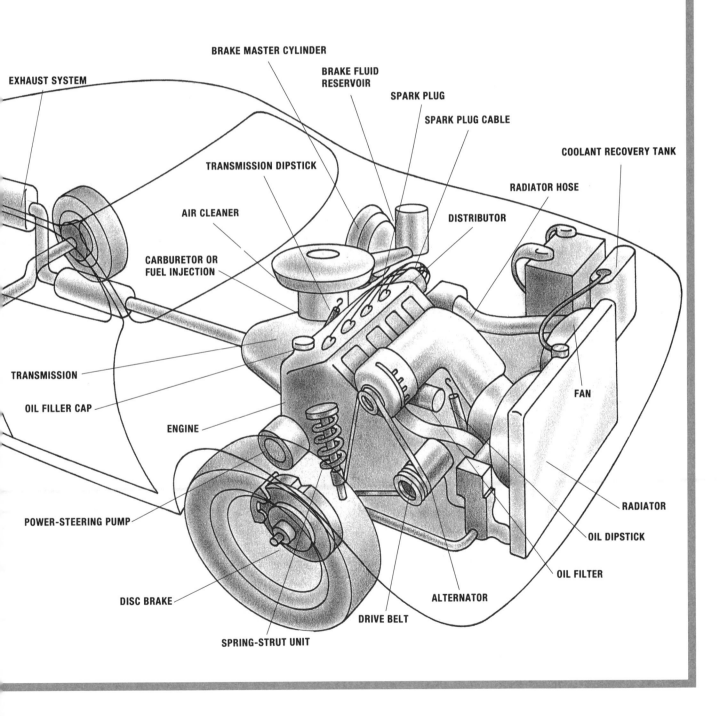

BRAKE MASTER CYLINDER

BRAKE FLUID RESERVOIR

SPARK PLUG

SPARK PLUG CABLE

EXHAUST SYSTEM

COOLANT RECOVERY TANK

TRANSMISSION DIPSTICK

RADIATOR HOSE

DISTRIBUTOR

AIR CLEANER

CARBURETOR OR FUEL INJECTION

TRANSMISSION

FAN

OIL FILLER CAP

ENGINE

POWER-STEERING PUMP

RADIATOR

OIL DIPSTICK

OIL FILTER

DISC BRAKE

ALTERNATOR

DRIVE BELT

SPRING-STRUT UNIT

Car-Care Calendar

Follow this schedule of regular maintenance checks to prevent car trouble. This is a general timetable; for best results, refer to the specific maintenance recommendations and schedule in your owner's manual. If you're not comfortable doing a particular task yourself, consult a professional.

Every Time You Buy Gas

- Check the engine oil level.
- Check the coolant level in the radiator recovery tank.
- Check the windshield washer fluid level.

Every Month or 1,000 Miles

- Check tire pressures.
- Examine the tires for tread wear or damage.
- Check the surface under a parked car for leaks.
- Check the lights.
- Check the brake, transmission, and power-steering fluid levels.

Every 3 Months or 3,000 Miles

- Change the engine oil and oil filter.
- Have the chassis lubricated (if it has lube points).
- Check the flashlight batteries in your emergency kit.

Every 6 Months or 6,000 Miles

- Check all fluid levels.
- Check all drive belts. Adjust any that are loose; replace any that are damaged.
- Check all radiator and coolant hoses. Replace any that are damaged or leaking.
- Check the battery.
- Check the exhaust system for rustouts and leaks. Have defective parts replaced immediately.

Once a Year or 15,000 Miles

- Have the brakes inspected for damage and wear (twice a year if you do mostly stop-and-go driving).
- Check the shock absorbers. Replace any that are leaking or ineffective.
- Have the headlight aim checked and adjusted.
- Check the air filter.
- Have the wheel alignment checked.
- Rotate the tires.
- Lubricate all hinges and locks.

Every 2 Years or 24,000 Miles

- Replace the antifreeze. Have the cooling system flushed if the drained coolant is brown, rusty, or gummy.
- Have the timing belt checked (on cars so equipped). Replace it, if necessary.

Every 3 Years or 36,000 Miles

- Inspect the spark plugs and cables. Replace cables if they are cracked, brittle, oil soaked, or have soft spots.
- Replace worn plugs.

Every 4 Years or 48,000 Miles

- Replace all drive belts and hoses that haven't previously been replaced.

SELF-SERVICE CHECKS

Because many gas stations are now self-service, an experienced mechanic no longer looks under the hood each time you buy gas.

If you don't get full service regularly, you need to perform these simple safety checks yourself. Refer to your manual to find out what types of oil and other fluids you should use.

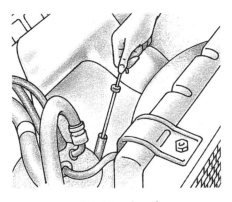

Checking the oil

Oil Level

Check the oil level every time you buy gas. The amount of oil clinging to the dipstick tells you how much is in the crankcase.

To read the oil level, park on flat ground, shut off the engine, and wait a few minutes for all the oil to drain back into the crankcase. Open the hood and find the dipstick, which is yellow or labeled "Oil" on many new cars.

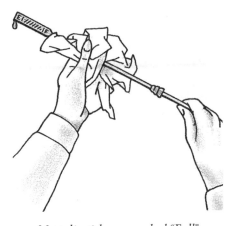

Most dipsticks are marked "Full" and "Add." The correct oil level is between those two lines.

Remove the dipstick, wipe it clean with a paper towel, and insert it all the way back into its tube. Pull the dipstick out again and note the level of the oil clinging to it.

If the oil is at or below the Add mark, unscrew the oil filler cap, and add one quart; be sure to use the correct oil weight for your car (see page 264). Pour the oil into the filler, then screw the cap on tightly, and recheck the level.

Antifreeze

Cars need antifreeze in both winter and summer. This coolant not only lowers the freezing temperature of the water in the radiator, but also raises its boiling point so the car does not overheat in hot weather. The coolant mixture in your radiator should be a 50/50 mixture of antifreeze and water.

Check the coolant level in the transparent plastic recovery tank alongside the radiator every time you get gas and check the oil. Most tanks are marked "Hot" and "Cold."

The coolant inside the tank should be above the appropriate mark according to whether the engine is hot (after driving) or cold (before it's first started).

If your car has no recovery tank, remove the radiator cap to check the coolant level. Do this only when the engine is cold—after the car has been sitting several hours or overnight. If the engine is hot, scalding water will boil out.

Push down on the cap and turn it counterclockwise to open it. There should be enough coolant in the radiator to cover the core tubes inside. (Replace the cap if its rubber gaskets are brittle or cracked.)

If the coolant level is low, add a 50/50 mixture of antifreeze and water to the recovery tank or radiator. Check the coolant level several days later. If it continues to drop, there's a leak in the system.

At least once every two years, have the coolant drained entirely and replaced with a fresh mixture of antifreeze and water.

The Driving Force

☞ *Front-wheel-drive:*
This compact system concentrates the mechanical elements at the front of the car, allowing more seating room. Most common in new cars, it gives you good traction on slippery roads, but can result in a nose-heavy car that causes extra wear on front tires. It is relatively complex and more difficult to service than rear-wheel-drive.

☞ *Rear-wheel-drive:*
Simple, sturdy, and relatively inexpensive, this system is preferred for easier handling in high-performance cars. However, it is heavy and gives you poor traction on slippery roads.

☞ *Four-wheel-drive:*
Sometimes called all-wheel-drive or 4x4, this system provides the best traction on slippery roads and unpaved surfaces (and most can be switched to 2-wheel-drive when road conditions improve). However, it's relatively heavy, complex, and expensive. It also consumes more fuel than a 2-wheel-drive car.

Tire Pressure

Incorrect pressure is the most common cause of tire wear. Tires with too little air increase fuel consumption, reduce corner turning power, and may squeal when you round a corner at normal speed. Tires with too much air give a harsh ride and wear out first at the center. Uneven pressure in the tires may cause a car to pull to one side or shimmy.

Check tire pressures at least once a month and before long trips. You will find the desired pressure on a label on the driver's door, on the tire itself, or in your owner's manual. Be sure to check all tires (including the spare) when they are cold (not driven for at least 3 hours).

To check tire pressure, use a tire pressure gauge. To operate, unscrew the cap on the end of the tire valve on the wheel, and press the gauge firmly onto the valve stem so that no air leaks out. Then remove the gauge and read the pressure on the scale.

To use a gas station air pump, turn the handle on the side of the pump until the desired pressure reading appears in the window. Unscrew the cap on the tire valve and press the air hose nozzle firmly against the tire valve stem until air stops flowing and the air pump bell stops ringing. Double-check the pressure with your gauge.

If one tire loses pressure slowly and there's no obvious problem (like a nail or piece of glass in the tread), have a gas station attendant remove the wheel and check the tire and valve for leaks and the wheel for cracks.

Tread Check

Since bald tires will skid even in a drizzle, you should never let them get to that stage. To prevent this, wear bars (slightly raised areas) are cast into the tire tread at regular intervals during manufacturing.

When the tread wears down to $1/16$ inch, these bars will appear as gaps in the tread. If wear bars appear between two or more adjacent tread grooves, it's time for new tires. Tread depth of $1/16$ inch or less is unsafe and illegal in most states.

Brake Fluid

Check the brake fluid every month. If the fluid is low, braking power is diminished. Hydraulic brake fluid is stored in a small reservoir attached to the brake master cylinder (see pages 258–259 for the location).

Some reservoirs are translucent plastic, so you can see the level of the fluid inside without removing the cap. If you have to remove the cap, wipe it off first with paper towel, so no dirt gets into the reservoir and clogs the tubes.

Brake fluid should be up to the Full level marked on the reservoir, or within $1/2$ inch of the top. If it's not, add fresh fluid from a new container. Always use fresh fluid as old fluid absorbs moisture and loses its effectiveness. If the fluid level is low every time you check it, have a mechanic inspect the system for leaks.

Power-Steering Fluid

Check the power-steering fluid once a month with the engine at normal operating temperature (after driving 20 minutes or more).

Power-steering systems are run by a belt-driven hydraulic pump mounted near the engine. This pump has a fluid reservoir with a screw cap on it.

On many cars, there's a dipstick attached to the cap so you can read the level of fluid in the reservoir (it's similar to the oil dipstick). If the fluid is below the Full mark, add some to fill. On pumps without a dipstick, the fluid should be $1/2$ to 1 inch from the top of the reservoir.

Transmission Fluid

If you have an automatic transmission, you will need to check the level of the fluid in it once a month. This is also measured with a dipstick. Check the level with the engine running and the transmission at normal operating temperature (after driving 20 minutes or more).

Park the car on level ground, and move the shift lever through all its positions, then put on the parking brake and shift the trans-

A Kit for the Car

Tools to Carry

Flashlight
Funnel (flexible neck)
Ice scraper
Jack
Jumper cables
Locking pliers
Lug wrench

Penknife
Pliers (adjustable)
Screwdrivers (slotted blade and Phillips head)
Tire pressure gauge
Tow strap or chain
Wrench set (small)

Supplies to Have

Aerosol tire inflator (nonflammable brand)
Antifreeze (or 50/50 coolant mix)
Blanket
Board (to put under jack on soft ground)
Brake fluid (new, unopened can)
"Call Police" sign (for window)
Can opener
Drive belts (assorted sizes specified for your car model)

Gloves
Hand cleaner (foil packs or a tube)
Fire extinguisher
First aid kit (see page 294)
Flares
Gallon jugs (empty; to hold water or gas in an emergency)
Paper towels
Safety glasses
Spare tire

Documents to Keep Handy

Auto club membership card
Credit card or emergency cash
Driver's license (keep on person)
Emergency phone numbers
Insurance ID card

Maps
Owner's manual
Service record or log
Vehicle registration

mission into Neutral or Park (read your owner's manual).

Open the hood and, being careful not to touch any moving or hot parts, remove the transmission dipstick (see pages 258–259 for the location). Wipe it clean with a paper towel and insert it all the way back into its tube. Pull the dipstick out again, and note the level of fluid clinging to it. The fluid should be between the Full and Add marks.

If the level is below the Add mark, pour fluid through the dipstick hole using a funnel with a flexible neck; add one pint at a time until the dipstick reads Full.

Adding transmission fluid

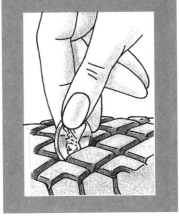

TREAD TEST

To check if your tires are worn, stick a penny head first into the tread grooves. If you can see the top of Lincoln's hair, the tread is worn and you need to replace the tire.

SHIFT FOR YOURSELF?

☛ There are two types of transmissions: manual and automatic.

☛ As its name implies, you must shift gears by hand with a manual transmission, sometimes called a standard transmission, or stick shift.

☛ A *manual transmission* generally gives better gas mileage. Some drivers feel they have more control of a car with a manual, but it's also more work to drive, especially in stop-and-go traffic.

☛ An *automatic* shifts for you once you place it in Drive. This offers greater convenience, but uses more fuel.

Fresh transmission fluid is red or pink. If the fluid on the dipstick is brown or black, or has a burned smell, the transmission needs service. Consult your mechanic.

Changing the Engine Oil and Air Filter

Oil never wears out, but the chemical additives in it that slow the corrosion of engine parts, neutralize acids, and hold dirt in suspension become exhausted as the months and miles add up. When you change the oil and filter, you remove this dirt and replenish the chemical additive supply.

For typical stop-and-go, around-town driving, most car manufacturers recommend changing the oil every 3,000 miles or three months, whichever comes first. If you drive on unpaved or dusty roads, or have a diesel or turbocharged engine,

you need to change the oil and filter even more often.

Your owner's manual will tell you how often to change the oil and filter and what type of oil you need for various driving conditions. Some specify different weights for winter and summer.

There are two classifications of oil: a service classification by the American Petroleum Institute (API) and a weight classification by the Society of Automotive Engineers (SAE). Never consider an oil without both ratings.

The API service ratings of oil for gasoline engines run from SA (now obsolete) to SG, which is used in modern cars. Oil for diesel engines is rated CC or CD.

The SAE weight classifications are also called viscosity grades. They run from 5 (the thinnest oil) to 90 or more (the thickest, used in rear axles). Most motor oils include additives called viscosity improvers, which allow one oil to cover several weight ratings. A 10W–30 oil, for example, covers the ratings 10–30; the W means the oil is suitable for low-temperature winter use.

Although 10W–40 is the most popular oil, it is not necessarily the best because it contains so much viscosity improver that it may leave damaging deposits inside the engine.

A relatively thin 5W–30 oil is recommended in many new cars for better fuel economy, because thinner oil puts less drag on an engine's internal parts.

Drive Belts

Drive belts are the modern equivalent of the old-fashioned single fan belt. Most cars have three to six drive belts; these turn pulleys that transfer power from the engine to the water pump and fan (which cool the engine) and such accessories as the alternator (which charges the battery), the power-steering pump, air-conditioner compressor, and the air pump used in some pollution-control systems.

There are three kinds of drive belts. Most have a V-shaped cross section and are called V belts. Other belts have a

TRANSMISSION TIPS

☞ Don't ride the brakes.

☞ If you need to add transmission fluid, check for leakage.

☞ If you do heavy hauling (trailer towing or other heavy loads) consider installing an auxiliary transmission cooler.

AS THE SEASONS CHANGE

FOR WINTER

Your car requires special maintenance before cold weather so it will operate smoothly all winter long. Be sure to do the following:

- Tune the engine.

- Check the battery cables and have a mechanic determine if the battery itself is fully charged.

- Check all lights for working bulbs and clean lenses.

- Inspect wipers and washers, and make sure the washer reservoir is filled with fluid that contains windshield washer antifreeze (not engine antifreeze). Put a jug of extra washer fluid in the trunk.

- Check defrosters and defoggers.

- Rotate the tires.

- Have the exhaust system checked. It must be in perfect shape when

you drive with the windows closed. The smallest leak in the muffler or exhaust pipes can lead to carbon monoxide poisoning.

- Stock your trunk with galoshes, extra gloves, an ice scraper and brush, aerosol de-icer, tire chains, jumper cables, a bag of sand, and a small shovel.

FOR SUMMER

Avoid warm weather problems by preparing ahead of time:

- Check all belts and hoses.

- Check the antifreeze concentration. If necessary, have the cooling system flushed, the pressure tested, and the thermostat checked.

- Have the air-conditioning system tested.

CHANGING YOUR AIR FILTER

THE AIR YOUR ENGINE BREATHES has to be filtered to screen out dust, grit, insects, and other harmful infiltrators. After several thousand miles of driving, the air filter might become clogged, which can lead to hard starting, stalling, or poor gas mileage. On most cars, it should be replaced every 15,000 miles; to be sure, check your owner's manual.

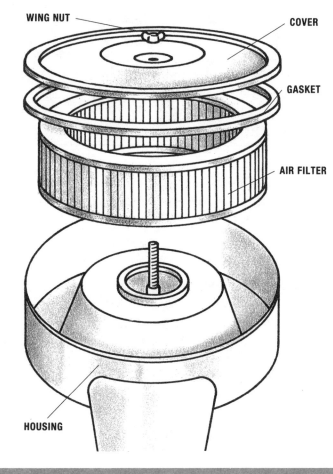

WING NUT

COVER

GASKET

AIR FILTER

HOUSING

Aside from the engine itself, the air filter housing is one of the bigger things under the hood so it should be easy to find. On today's pollution-controlled cars, it is mounted inside a metal or plastic housing with vacuum hoses and ducts connected to it. The housing is oval or rectangular, and it may be located on top or alongside the engine. On older cars, the air filter is mounted inside a circular housing at the top of the engine.

To change the filter, open the clips or unscrew the wing nuts that hold down the cover, remove it, and lift out the filter. If it is wet, damaged, or caked with dirt, insert a new filter of the same size. Replace the housing cover and refit the screws or clips.

If you don't have a new filter on hand, you can dislodge some of the dirt from the old air filter by tapping it gently on the pavement; then replace it as soon as possible.

number of grooves that fit into special pulleys. A third kind of belt zigzags between all the accessories.

Loose belts can squeal annoyingly. Slipping belts don't transmit full power to the accessories and can make steering difficult, drain the battery, or lead to overheating. A cracked or worn-out belt may snap, leaving you stranded on the highway when the accessory it drives stops working.

With the engine off and cool, check both sides of all belts every six months—in spring and fall—to make sure they're not brittle, cracked, glazed, or soaked with oil. If they are, have them replaced.

Also check belt tension. Press down on each belt in the middle of the longest span between pulleys. If you can move the belt more than ½ to ¾ of an inch, it needs to be tightened; consult a mechanic.

HOSES

☞ A typical engine has four coolant hoses—two each to the radiator and heater. Check all hoses every six months. If any hose is brittle, cracked, spongy, or oil soaked, have it replaced. A burst radiator hose will cause the engine to overheat and leave you stranded. Replace all hoses every four years.

COMMON PROBLEMS

The most common causes of car failure are usually quite basic. You can save time and money by troubleshooting problems yourself before taking your car to a mechanic.

CAR WON'T START

If the starter cranks normally, slowly, or not at all and the engine won't start, you may have one or more of the following problems:

- Out of fuel: Check the gauge, and add fuel if needed.

- Improperly set transmission: Put the shift lever in Park or Neutral in an automatic transmission. Make sure the clutch is fully depressed in a manual transmission. Follow starting procedures in your owner's manual.

- Dead battery: Jump-start the car (see opposite), recharge or replace the battery, or check cables and battery terminals for corrosion.

If your starter cranks slowly or if the headlights or the lights on the instrument panel seem dim, the battery may need to be recharged. A service station or repair shop can quick-charge a dead battery in less than an hour. If your battery needs frequent charging, the charging system may be faulty. Have a mechanic check it.

Corrosion on the battery terminals—greenish-white deposits at the ends of the battery cables—can slow or block the flow of current.

To remove corrosion, loosen the nuts on the cable clamps with a small wrench, and remove the cables from the battery terminals.

Clean the terminals and the insides of the cable clamps with a wire brush or sandpaper until the metal is shiny.

Then reinstall the cables. Put a small dab of petroleum jelly on top of each terminal to slow future corrosion.

- Loose or defective spark plug cables: Open the hood, locate the distributor and spark plugs, then push the cables running between them into their terminals until they are tight. If that doesn't help, see a mechanic.

Major defects in the electrical or starter system, the carburetor, fuel injection, or fuel pump require the services of a mechanic.

ENGINE STALLS

Many of the same problems that keep an engine from starting can also cause it to stall. First, check for the problems listed in "Car Won't Start." If these don't help, check for and solve the following problems:

- Clogged air filter: Inspect and replace, if necessary.

- Disconnected vacuum hose: Check under the hood and reconnect any hoses that have come loose.

Other problems may include incorrect ignition timing, fouled spark plugs, clogged fuel filter or line, dirt or water in the gas, or the need for a tune-up. See a mechanic.

Engine Stalls When Cold

- Iced-over fuel system: Add fuel line antifreeze fluid to the gas tank.

If the choke needs adjustment (on older cars with carburetors), see a mechanic.

HOW TO JUMP-START A CAR

WHEN YOUR BATTERY IS DEAD, all you need to start it is a set of jumper cables and access to a running car, which will act as a booster. It's a good precaution to wear safety glasses and gloves. If your car doesn't start with this method, you need a mechanic.

1. Park the cars nose to nose without touching bumpers. Shut off the engines and open the hoods. Set both parking brakes and put automatic transmissions into Park, manuals into Neutral.

2. Identify the positive and negative posts on each battery (usually marked POS. or + and NEG. or –). Attach the red clamps to positive posts on each battery. Attach one black clamp to the negative post of the good booster battery and the other to a clean metal part on the engine with the dead battery.

Never attach the black clamp to the negative post of the dead battery or to a part of the engine near the dead battery. The negative cable can spark and ignite the explosive hydrogen gas given off when a battery is being charged.

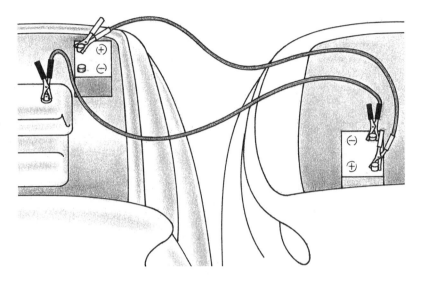

3. Keep hands and cables clear of all fans, pulleys, and belts. Start the engine of the booster car. Then start the engine with the dead battery.

4. Remove the black cable from both cars, starting with the booster car. Then remove the red cable. Drive the car that was jump-started for at least 20 minutes so the alternator can recharge the battery.

Engine Stalls When Hot

- Flooded carburetor (older cars only): Wait 5 minutes, turn on the ignition, then push the gas pedal down to the floor without pumping it. The car should start. If it doesn't, you need a mechanic.

- Vapor lock (in hot weather): Open the hood and let the fuel pump and lines cool off for 10 to 15 minutes. The car should start. If it doesn't, you need a mechanic.

ENGINE OVERHEATS

Cars overheat for several reasons, including mechanical and electrical faults, igni-

tion problems (spark plug system), or an inadequate cooling system.

The water temperature gauge can warn you if you notice it moving toward the danger zone. However, the TEMP light on the dash usually doesn't signal until it's too late.

If you ignore the warning light, you'll soon see steam coming out from underneath the hood, grille, or wheel wells. Check for the following problems:

- Low coolant level: Add a 50/50 mixture of water and antifreeze to the radiator and coolant recovery tank after the engine has cooled (see page 273).

- Slipped or broken fan belt: Adjust or replace as necessary.

KEEP YOUR BATTERY WARM

☞ Heating a weak battery overnight will keep up its strength. Electric battery heaters that run on house current are sold in auto parts stores. You can also heat a battery by placing a mechanic's drop lamp with a 100-watt bulb under the battery overnight. If the engine still won't crank in the morning, get a jump-start from another car (see above) or a charge.

- Burst or leaking radiator hose: Check all hoses, and replace those that are damaged.

- Bad radiator cap: Check the pressure cap on the radiator or coolant recovery tank. Replace it if the gaskets are damaged or the spring is broken or badly corroded.

Other problems, including an inaccurate thermostat and a leaking radiator, require a mechanic.

CAR STARTS BUT WON'T MOVE

When the engine revs with the transmission in gear but the car won't move, there may be a problem with the transmission.

Automatic Transmission

Check the fluid level and add some if necessary.

Other problems, including burned or contaminated transmission fluid, leaking or disconnected vacuum hoses, damage to internal transmission parts, and adjustment of transmission bands, require the services of a mechanic.

Manual Transmission

Any number of things can go wrong with a clutch. It can go out of adjustment, become worn, damaged, or contaminated with oil or grease, or the shift linkage may need adjustment. In all cases, see a mechanic.

MINOR BRAKE TROUBLE

If your car pulls to one side when you brake, is hard to stop, or the brake warning light stays on after the engine has started, you may have one of the following problems:

- Incorrect tire pressure: Check and adjust.

- Low brake fluid level: Check the fluid level and add more if it's low. If it

stays too low, have the car towed to a mechanic.

- Overheated and faded brakes: Stop your car and let the brakes cool for 15 or 20 minutes before driving.

- Wet brakes after driving through deep puddles: Dry them by putting light pressure on the brake pedal as you drive.

If none of these seems to be the problem, your brakes may have worn or defective parts, grease or fluid buildup, or need adjusting; there may also be air in hydraulic brake lines. In any case, see a mechanic.

Squealing brakes may signal worn or defective brake parts. Always have a mechanic inspect noisy brakes; don't drive until they fail completely.

STEERING TROUBLE

If your car pulls to one side or the steering wheel shimmies while you're driving along a flat smooth highway, you probably have one of the following problems:

- Incorrect tire pressure: Check and adjust.

- Mismatched or unevenly worn tires: Replace them.

Other problems include out-of-balance or misaligned wheels, defective suspension, steering mechanism or brake parts, a bent frame, loose wheel bearings, or worn ball joints and shock absorbers. See a mechanic.

If the steering wheel is unusually hard to turn, check for the following problems:

- Incorrect tire pressure: Check and adjust.

- Low power-steering fluid: Add some.

Otherwise, it could be that your steering linkage needs lubrication, your wheels are misaligned, worn, or damaged, or the suspension or wheel bearings are loose. See a mechanic.

SQUEALING BRAKES

☞ On some disc brakes, a loud squeal indicates low or worn linings. Have a mechanic check the linings and replace them, if necessary.

☞ A high-pitched squeal during light braking is normal on some disc brake designs. Ask the dealer to check to see if the car maker has found a cure since the car was manufactured.

BULBS BURN OUT

Most cars have at least a dozen exterior lights set under plastic lenses. The taillight cluster often contains separate bulbs for the turn signal, brake light, backup light, and taillight itself.

There are three ways to get at an exterior light bulb:

1. If the lens has visible screws, remove the screws and lens. Then remove the bulb by pushing it into its spring-loaded socket and turning it counter-clockwise about a quarter turn.

2. If the entire light housing, or unit, comes off with the lens, the bulb and socket can usually be removed from the back of the housing. Twist the socket, then remove the bulb by pushing and twisting.

3. Some sockets can be reached without removing the housing from the car body. Check inside the trunk or behind the bumper or fender to see if you can reach and remove the socket. You can often find the sockets for taillights through access panels in the trunk.

Take the used bulb to an auto parts store to make sure you buy a replacement with the same model number. To insert a new bulb, align the pins on the sides of the bulb with the slots in the socket. Push in and twist clockwise to seat the bulb. Refit the socket or lens.

FUSES BURN OUT

Your car has an electrical system protected by fuses, just as your house does. A short-circuit or overload will burn up the filament inside a fuse. The fuse box may be under the dash or the hood (see your owner's manual). Most new cars have plug-in plastic fuses with two metal tangs. Many older cars have cylindrical glass fuses.

When an electrical accessory such as the fan or power door lock quits, check the fuse box. Labels in the box may tell you which components each fuse protects. If not, check the manual.

You must remove a plug-in plastic fuse to check its filament. To replace glass fuses, you need a fuse puller, available at auto supply shops.

Always use a fuse with the correct amperage (the blown one could have been the wrong amperage). The correct amperage is usually printed next to the slot on the fuse box. If not, look it up in your owner's manual.

If the fuse blows repeatedly, there's a short in the system. See a mechanic.

SAVING DOLLARS ON YOUR CAR

These preventive measures will help you reduce the amount of money you need to spend.

- Be assertive when it comes to service checkups. Read your manual and follow the frequent-service schedule detailed there.

- Call around to find the dealer who follows the factory schedule most closely. Visit the service manager before leaving your car and discuss the exact services you want and the estimated cost. Don't agree to any extra services.

- Beware of "ghost" (unessential) services:

  Adjusting valves—many are now designed to be self-adjusting.

  Chassis lubrication—most newer vehicles have sealed suspension bearings and ball joints.

  Adjusting the timing or idle speed—computer controlled on many cars.

  Cleaning and adjusting the choke on fuel-injected cars—these don't have chokes.

TREADING SMARTLY

There are different kinds of tires for different driving conditions.

☛ *All-season tires:* the best compromise for multiple road conditions.

☛ *High-performance tires:* the best handling on dry roads but are not so good on snow.

☛ *Snow tires:* good on snow but are noisy on dry roads.

☛ *Studded snow tires:* the best traction on ice and hard-packed snow but are illegal in some states.

HOW TO CHANGE A TIRE

TIRE CHANGING IS A BASIC skill that every driver needs, whether for fixing a flat, putting on snow tires, or rotating tires, which should be done periodically to equalize tread wear. When making an emergency repair beside a busy road, always park the car on firm level ground, well off the road, and work quickly.
NOTE: *Keep your hands and feet out from under the car at all times in case the jack slips.*

1. Set the parking brake, and put an automatic transmission into Park, a manual transmission into Reverse. Wedge a rock or a piece of lumber against the tire that is diagonally across from the one you want to change, so the car can't roll off the jack. (For example, when changing the right rear tire, chock the left front tire.)

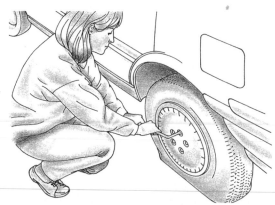

LOOSENING LUG NUTS

2. Take the jack and spare tire out of the trunk. Use the tapered end of the jack handle or a big screwdriver to pry the hubcap (if any) off the wheel and expose the lug nuts. If the car has a special tool for removing custom wire wheel covers, follow the instructions packed with the tool.

JACKING UP THE CAR

3. Use a lug wrench to loosen the lug nuts before you raise the car. On most cars they are loosened counterclockwise. If they loosen clockwise they should be marked.

4. Assemble the jack. Jacking instructions should be written in your owner's manual, on labels affixed to the jack, or under the trunk lid of your car.

POSITIONING THE REPLACEMENT WHEEL

5. Position the jack at the jacking point nearest the tire to be changed. (Jacking points are listed in the jacking instructions.) Insert the handle, crank it clockwise, and raise the car until the tire is 3 to 4 inches off the ground.

6. Make sure the car is steady on the jack and doesn't wobble if you push on it gently. If it does wobble, lower the car to the ground and start over. Make sure you're using the correct jacking point and that the jack is on firm ground. If the ground is soft, place a wide board or piece of plywood under the jack.

7. Once the car is steady on the jack, remove the lug nuts and the wheel. Put the lug nuts in a clean, safe place, such as inside the hubcap.

8. Position the replacement wheel on the wheel studs. Make sure the mounting holes are aligned with the studs and the correct side of the wheel is facing out. If the wheel is too heavy to lift with your arms, squat and use your leg muscles to lift it.

9. Push the wheel flat against the mounting surface, and screw on the lug nuts by hand, starting at the bottom. The tapered side of each nut must face the wheel. When the nuts are fingertight, use the lug wrench to gently tighten them until they are snug. Be careful not to exert too much pressure or you could knock the car off the jack.

10. To lower the car to the ground, turn the crank on the jack counterclockwise. Remove the jack. Now use the wrench to make the nuts as tight as possible. Work in a criss-cross pattern to avoid cracking the wheel.

11. If the roadside is very busy, toss the flat, jack, and hubcap into the trunk, remove the wheel chock, and drive to a safer spot. Then secure the jack properly, and refit the hubcap. Hold the hubcap in position and pound it into place with the heel of your hand or with firm but gentle kicks.

12. Have the flat fixed or replaced as soon as possible.

DONUT DON'TS

☞ If your car has a small emergency spare (often called a donut) instead of a full-sized tire, don't drive faster than 50 mph or more than 50 miles on it.

GETTING LOOSE

If the six-sided lug nuts are too tight to loosen by hand, position the lug wrench horizontally and push down on it with your foot.

If they still won't budge, steady yourself on a fender and stand on the wrench. Bounce a little if necessary, but be careful not to slip off the wrench.

If that doesn't work, call a mechanic.

If you lose one of the lug nuts during the tire change, drive slowly to the nearest service station.

ROAD EMERGENCIES

Emergencies do happen, but they won't be so traumatic if you know what to do ahead of time. As a precaution, carry a flashlight with good batteries and flares in the glove compartment. Make sure your spare tire is in good condition and has the correct pressure. If your car becomes disabled for any reason, get it well off the road, if possible.

ROAD SERVICE PLANS

The AAA (Automobile Association of America) is the oldest, best-known organization offering 24-hour emergency road service to its members. Today, many oil companies, car makers, and other firms also offer similar plans.

The services offered by different plans vary greatly. Check all the fine print in the membership application before you sign it.

Some plans are offered free for several years when you purchase a new car. Others have a modest annual membership fee for which they will dispatch a tow truck or mechanic when you call a toll-free emergency number. The service or tow may be free, discounted, or reimbursed later (up to certain limits) depending on the provisions of your plan.

A road service plan with extra features is well worth the typical $30 to $50 annual fee.

Many plans also include extra features:

- Accident insurance.

- Discount coupons for hotels, restaurants, rental cars, and popular tourist attractions.

- Emergency check-cashing privileges.

- Guaranteed arrest bond.

- Limited reimbursement of legal defense fees for traffic violations and of food and lodging costs if your car is disabled in an accident far from home.

- Personalized trip planning and maps.

- Rewards for recovery of your car if it's stolen.

ACCIDENTS

Even though any accident is upsetting, it's important to remain calm and think clearly. Always keep the legal aspects of an accident in mind. Don't leave the scene until you do the following:

- If the accident is minor and in the city, park at the curb to get the car out of the flow of traffic. If a serious injury has occurred, you probably shouldn't alter the positions of the cars involved.

- Turn off the ignitions in all the cars to reduce the chance of fire.

- Place flares or reflective triangles along a highway against oncoming traffic to warn other drivers.

- If you have certified first aid training, treat the injured until professional help arrives. If not, leave them alone and send for help. Never move an injured person unless he or she is in danger from fire, leaking gasoline, or traffic (see pages 294–323).

- Send for the police if there are injuries, if there is serious damage, or if other drivers involved are hostile. Request an ambulance if there are injuries and a fire truck if there is leaking fuel or a fire.

- Take down the names, addresses, and phone numbers of everyone involved, including passengers and witnesses.

- Exchange licenses and registrations with all the other drivers and write down the following information for each: driver's license number and expiration date, registration number, car's license plate number, make, model, year, color, and body style (such as sedan or wagon) of the car. Note which driver was in which car.

- Get the name and phone number of each driver's insurance company and, if available, copy the information on any insurance ID cards.
- Record the names and badge numbers of all police officers.
- Make a sketch of the scene, showing all street names, each car involved, and its direction of travel.

ACCIDENT REPORTS

In many areas of the country, you have to file an accident report with the police if you've had an accident that involves more than one car, if there are any injuries, or if damages exceed a given amount. If you are unsure, ask the police or your insurance agent if you need to file one and how much time you have to do it.

You also have to file a report with your insurance company, whether or not you intend to file a claim or sue the other driver(s). Both police and insurance reports may be used in court, so they should agree in every detail. Refer to the notes you made at the scene. Filing a report doesn't automatically mean your insurance rates will go up (especially if you don't file a claim).

It's a good idea to keep a blank accident report form in the glove compartment. Ask the local police department or your insurance agent for one.

BREAKDOWNS

If your car breaks down, immediately turn on the emergency flashers and try to coast off the road. If you can't get the car off the road, don't sit in it. Get out, and set up flares at least a hundred feet in the direction of oncoming traffic.

If possible, tie a white cloth to the door handle or radio antenna to signal other drivers that you need help. Have them phone the police or your auto club or alert toll-booth personnel. While you wait out of the car, be sure to stay well off the road.

If your car is off the road and you're in a familiar area, lock your car and walk for help. Bring with you your emergency road service materials and auto registration. On a secondary road, walk facing traffic. If you're stuck in a strange area, stay inside the locked car with a white cloth on the door, and only open the window a slight crack to ask for help.

OVERHEATING

Your car is more likely to overheat if it's stuck in traffic than if it's moving at a constant speed. If you have a belt-driven (not electric) fan and you're stuck in a jam, shift into Neutral and rev the engine periodically. This increases coolant flow through the engine and draws more air through the radiator. Turn off the air conditioner. As a last resort, turn the heater on high to draw heat away from the engine.

If the radiator does boil over, pull off the road and call for help. Wait at least 15 minutes before opening the hood. Look for coolant leaks, burst hoses, or broken fan belts.

If there are no obvious faults, place a heavy towel over the radiator cap, and without pressing down, slowly turn it to the first stop. Be careful: Boiling water may shoot out of the overflow tube. When the steam stops, press down on the radiator cap and unscrew it.

After the system is thoroughly cool, slowly add a 50-50 mix of water and antifreeze. If no antifreeze is available, add plain water. Then drive slowly to a garage to have the cooling system drained and a proper coolant mixture added.

STUCK IN SNOW, ICE, SAND, OR MUD

If your car loses traction and starts to spin its wheels on snow, ice, sand, or mud, the only way to get unstuck is to gently rock the car back and forth. Shift

COLD-WEATHER DRIVING TIPS

☞ Check tire pressures during cold weather and adjust to recommended levels.

☞ Never reduce tire pressure for increased traction in snow or ice. This doesn't work and might damage the tires.

☞ Snow tires should be used in pairs (two front or two back) if not on all four wheels and should be the same size and construction type as the other tires.

between Drive and Reverse on an automatic transmission; shift between First gear and Reverse on a manual transmission. Keep the front wheels pointed straight ahead to reduce resistance.

Successful rocking requires a definite rhythm and feel. Apply as little gas as possible. As the car begins to move, time each shift so it's at the high point of each rock, which increases momentum.

You can increase the traction of a rear-drive vehicle by placing more weight over the rear wheels. Ask passengers to sit in the rear or load the trunk with plastic garbage bags filled with sand or rocks. Install snow chains—if you have them and can get them onto the wheels. In sand or snow, dig long ramps from the wheels to create a pathway.

If you can jack up the car safely, place some carpet, wood, metal screening, or other traction aid under the stuck tires. Have bystanders move aside; traction aids can fly out if the wheels begin to spin.

If you're not free after a dozen rocks, either try other methods described above or call for a tow truck. Excessive rocking can overheat the engine and damage an automatic transmission.

DRIVING ON ICE OR SNOW

Your ability to gain traction and stop decreases on snow and ice, making driving more difficult. Leave extra distance for stopping and passing, and avoid sudden acceleration, sharp turns, or hard braking, which can cause skids. Pump the brakes lightly and rapidly instead.

To climb a steep hill, you must gain enough momentum before you reach the hill to get to the top and then cruise uphill without accelerating further. If you have to accelerate partway up the hill, the wheels will spin and you may lose control.

If your wipers clog with ice, they will streak and you won't be able to see. Pull off the road in a safe, clear, level spot (if you can find one), and bang the blades

against the windshield several times to dislodge the ice. If you can't find a good spot, don't stop.

DRIVING IN RAIN OR FOG

Most accidents occur when it first begins to rain after a dry spell because the water lifts accumulated oil from the pores of the pavement and brings it to the surface, making the road slippery.

It's always a good idea to wipe the soles of your shoes dry on the floor mat before you start the engine so your feet will not slip from the pedals. Use all the controls gently and leave a larger margin than usual for miscalculations and errors so you won't have to slam on the brakes or wrench the steering wheel.

Good visibility is also a must. Use the defrosters (front and rear) and the air conditioner on the recirculate setting (labeled REC or MAX). If you don't have A/C, make sure the defroster is not on the REC setting. Using a defroster on the REC setting without having A/C will only recirculate old air, which will fog up your windows.

Wiper Blades
Clean the wiper blades periodically with paper towels and washer solution to remove road grime. If they still streak, smear, or chatter, replace them.

In heavy rain, the faster you drive, the more water hits the windshield and the harder it is for the wipers to clear it. If the wipers can't clear the windshield, slow down until they do.

Puddles
Deep puddles can cause your tires to hydroplane (lose contact with the road) and you will skid. The less tread on your tires and the faster you drive, the more likely you are to hydroplane. If your steering suddenly feels light, the front tires are hydroplaning. Slow down until you regain steering control.

FOG-FREE WINDOWS

☞ The air conditioner will clear up fog faster than the heater's drying action.
You often can wipe moisture from the side windows by opening and closing them.

TURN ON THOSE LIGHTS!

☞ In some states, by law you must turn on your headlights in daylight if conditions require you to use your windshield wipers. It is always a good idea to keep headlights on, night or day, when the weather is bad.

CONTROLLING SKIDS

IF YOU EXCEED the traction limits of your tires when steering, braking, or accelerating, your car has a good chance of going into a skid. Avoiding skids requires "reading" the road conditions, having a good feel for the car's handling, and using common sense. If you're going too fast, however, none of this will work.

Although most people know to lift off the gas pedal if a car starts to skid, few realize you should do the same with the brake. After reducing pressure on the brake, try again using a gentle pumping action.

Controlling a skid in a turn is more difficult. There's often no room for corrective maneuvers. If the back of the car slides to one side, take your foot off the gas and brake pedal and steer in the direction of the skid. For example, steer to the left if the rear is sliding to the left. When the car has straightened out, try again to gently steer in the right direction. When you correct a skid, however, the car will often slide in the other direction. Be prepared to steer quickly back and forth several times if the car fishtails.

Sometimes a car will skid straight ahead when you're braking for a turn. Stop braking, straighten the wheel slightly, then gently try again.

CARJACKING

☞ An increasing problem, carjacking can happen on a street just as easily as in a remote area.
☞ Drive with the doors locked and the windows up, and be aware of who is around you when you are parked or waiting at a light.
☞ Never resist if confronted. It's better to lose your car than your life.

Visibility is even more of a problem in fog than in rain. Turn on your headlights so other cars can see you. At night, your own bright lights may bounce off the fog and cut your vision. Use fog lights or low beams if this happens.

In thick fog, open your windows, even if it's cold. You may be able to hear approaching cars before you see them. Use the right edge of the road as a guide. Drive slowly so you can stop in the distance visible ahead. If you have to creep along, turn on your hazard flashers. If conditions get too bad, pull well off the road.

BRAKE FAILURE

All cars have split system brakes. Some are split between the front and the back wheels; others are split diagonally, with one front and one back wheel linked.

In cars split between the front and the back wheels, the front brakes provide most of your stopping power. If both front brakes fail, it will take a long distance to stop the car. Don't continue to drive. Call for a tow truck.

If both rear brakes fail, you may hardly notice a loss except for the warning light. You should be able to drive

CHILD SAFETY

*ALL FIFTY STATES require safety seats or belts
for children riding in automobiles.*

Infant seats are
designed for babies
too young to sit up by
themselves.

Child seats are for
children up to five
years of age. Children over five can
use adult lap belts.

Seats are available in department
and children's stores, and at some
car dealers.

Choose the seat with the most
straightforward instructions. It
should be easy to
strap onto the car's
safety belt; the safest
spot is in the middle
of the backseat.

The more compli-
cated the instructions,
the less likely you will be to make
use of the seat, and the more likely
you will make a mistake in adjusting
the straps.

There are safety seats that work facing either forward or backward.
Infant seats tend to face backward
while child seats tend to face forward.

AVOIDING CARSICKNESS

☞ Get plenty of rest before a
trip.

☞ Eat a light, easy-to-digest
meal.

☞ Wear comfortable clothing.

☞ Sit in the front seat and, in
summer, turn on the air conditioner. (Heat and humidity
contribute to motion sickness.)
In winter, open your window
a bit to let in cool air.

slowly and carefully to the nearest gas
station for repairs.

If one circuit of a diagonally split
system fails, you will notice some loss of
stopping power and the car may pull to
one side as you brake. Call a tow truck
if the car is difficult to drive.

When brakes do fail noticeably, they
do it in one of two ways: The pedal may
go all the way to the floor with no effect
or it may feel rock hard and almost
impossible to press. The latter is less
serious and signals a failure of the power
brake booster, not the brakes themselves. If you push on the pedal with all
your strength—use both feet if the pedal
is wide enough—you should be able to
slow the car.

If the pedal sinks to the floor with no
resistance, there's probably a leak in the
hydraulic system. The red BRAKE warning light on the dash will come on. On
modern dual-circuit brake systems, half
the brake system should still work, even
if there's a leak in the other half.

If the brakes fail completely, pump
the pedal. You may be able to build up
pressure temporarily. Apply the parking
brake gently and increase pressure gradually; jerking on the parking brake can
throw you into a skid. Release it immediately if the car begins to skid.

Shift the car into lower gears, one at
a time, and let the engine's drag slow
the car. If you have a manual transmission, ease your foot off the clutch
(engage the clutch) after shifting down.
Popping the clutch may lock the drive
wheels and cause a skid. On an automatic transmission, be careful to shift
down only one gear at a time, from Drive
to Second, then First. Use of the parking brake will be more effective when
you are in a lower gear.

If all else fails, try to slow the car by
scraping it along a guard rail, wall, hedge,
snow bank, or dense shrubbery. The rule
of thumb is: Better to hit something soft
than something hard; better to hit something hard than something living.

KEEPING UP APPEARANCES

Keeping your car in top working order is a priority, but you'll also want it to look its best. This is as good for its health as for its resale value.

Regular washing and waxing are essential to minimize rust and ensure a long life for the finish. You should also check your paint often for chips and scratches and repair them immediately.

Washing

You can wash your car by hand or take it to a car wash. In areas where roads are salted to remove snow, make sure the car wash rinses the underside.

If you wash your car by hand, do it in the shade (sunlight on water will bake and damage the finish) and use plenty of rinse water before, during, and after washing.

Start by hosing out the wheel wells and the underside of the car. Use a soft brush, mild household detergent, and a garden hose to remove all salt and impacted road dirt from the wheel wells, under the bumpers and doors, and inside each door opening.

SPECIAL FINISHERS

IF HOUSEHOLD DETERGENT doesn't seem to do the cleaning job, try these special products, available at a hardware or auto supply store.

Automotive cleaner or polish: a very mild abrasive that removes "dead" oxidized paint (chalk) caused by exposure to the elements.

Polishing compound: a stronger abrasive used to restore badly chalked and faded paint. It's a paste (usually white). Apply it by hand, not machine, using a damp cloth and light pressure to avoid removing too much paint, especially on sharp edges.

Rubbing compound: a harsh abrasive (usually red or pink) used as a last resort before a new paint job is required. Use it very carefully, especially on metallic and clear-coat paint jobs. If you rub away the color coat and penetrate the primer, you'll need to repaint the car.

Polymer sealant: a hard wax that is fairly difficult to apply but is extra long-lasting.

Silicone protectant: gives a satisfying shine to leather, rubber, and plastics, including vinyl. It repels water, oxygen, ozone, and ultraviolet rays, forming an antistatic film that helps repel dust.

TIME TO WAX

☞ Rain forms almost spherical droplets on a newly waxed car. As the wax wears off, water beads become larger and flatter, indicating it's time to rewax.

EASY TOUCH-UP

☞ If the primer or touch-up paint you need is available only in an aerosol can, spray a little bit into a paper cup and apply it with a small artist's brush. You can use a cotton swab for small nicks.

A soft old toothbrush will help you get into the grille and other crevices. Do a small area at a time, rinse off all soap, and check for rust spots. Dry the car with a clean chamois that's been soaked in clear water and wrung out well. (You can buy this soft leather cloth in an auto supply store.)

Waxing

Wax provides a waterproof barrier that seals out moisture, prevents chalking ("dying" paint), and makes the finish shine. Apply a thin layer with a clean, soft cloth (old T-shirts work particularly well) and buff it off with a clean, dry cloth.

Wax comes in solid, paste, liquid, and spray forms. The harder the wax, the more difficult it is to apply. Most types last about the same amount of time under similar driving and weather conditions, except for sprays, which have a shorter life because they are diluted.

Cleaning the Interior

Remove the floor mats for hosing off or cleaning and vacuum the carpet. You can clean fabric seats with a special foaming shampoo. To remove stains, follow the directions for cleaning household upholstery (see pages 33–34). Use a glass cleaner on all windows to remove film caused by smoking or by vapors that escape from vinyl and other plastics.

Repairing Vinyl

You can patch small tears or scratches in vinyl seats, dashes, and tops with a special vinyl paste that hardens to match the vinyl when heated with a special tool.

To fix a larger tear in vinyl upholstery, slip a patch of vinyl between the upholstery and the foam padding underneath. Apply plastic or auto trim adhesive to the patch and upholstery, then press the torn upholstery gently into place and let it dry.

If seats are badly torn or worn out, cover them with seat covers or have them professionally reupholstered.

PAINT POINTERS

CHECK YOUR CAR often for nicks, scratches, and blisters in paint; these are an invitation to rust that can spread and ruin an otherwise good car.

You can repair minor paint damage yourself with touch-up primer and paint.

Buy only primer and paint labeled for your make, model, and color of car. (It still may not match exactly, because your car's paint has weathered.)

You will also need rust converter, which changes the chemical composition of the rust so it no longer eats into the bodywork. All these supplies are available in auto parts stores and dealer showrooms.

For small chips and blisters, use a small bottle of primer and paint. Scrape away loose paint and rust with the corner of a razor blade, then wipe the area with rust converter.

Clean the area with a mild detergent mixed with plenty of water,

rinse well, and dry completely. Apply primer with an artist's brush. Let it dry thoroughly, then apply the touch-up paint with a small brush.

For bigger blisters or long scratches, use aerosol primer and paint. Sand away rust with a superfine (400 grade) sandpaper (see page 211), treat it with converter, clean and dry the area, then spray on the primer and paint.

To apply, cut a 1-inch hole in a piece of cardboard, hold it 1 or 2 inches from the car, and spray through the hole. This confines the spray without leaving a ridge of paint around the edge.

Wait several days, then rub out the repaired area with polishing compound. Do not wax the repaired area for 90 days.

CHAPTER 8

SAFETY AND HEALTH

Sheets into Curt... ...HANDY TIPS: For Buffing Wood Fl... ...king Rooms Look Larger, Ironing ... ...ning Tile Grout, Creating a ☛ *M... ...e on Car Repairs, Buy Produce, C... ...reventing Carpet Dents, Unsticking Stacked Glasses, Making Rooms Look Larger, Ironing Pleated Skirts, Arranging Flowers, Jump-Starting a Car, Cleaning Tile Grout, Creating a Home Office, Fixing a Leaky Faucet* ☛ STEP-BY-STEP GUIDES: *To Checkbook Security, Unblocking a Sink, Buying a Home, Successful Decorating* ☛ SAFETY FIRST: *Preventing falls inside and outside your home. Steps for fireproofing your home. Emergency phone numbers to keep on hand. Precautions for a safe pool. Preventing electrical accidents. Children and the elderly: safety suggestions. Safeguarding against household mishaps.* ☛ EMERGENCIES IN THE HOME: *Fire hazards: planning and using escape routes. How to put out small fires. All about fire extinguishers. Smoke detector features. Minimizing water damage. Ways to prepare for a major storm. What to do when you smell gas.* ☛ INDOOR POLLUTANTS: *Mildew, molds, and mites. Using air circulation to lower formaldehyde levels. Avoiding carbon monoxide poisoning. Plants that absorb pollution. Asbestos, lead, and radon: discovering and disposing of harmful amounts. Getting rid of potentially hazardous material. Burglar deterrents for your home. Components of a basic or complete first aid kit.* ☛ FIRST AID: *Dos and don'ts for helping. Calling for emergency aid. Preventing and treating fainting. Taking a pulse. Handling an unconscious person. Helping a choking victim. Treating heat exhaustion, hypothermia, and heat stroke. Caring for victims of electric shock. Diagnosing and treating allergic reactions. Steps for treating poisoning. Heart attack symptoms and care. CPR step by step. The Heimlich maneuver step by step for adults, the obese or pregnant, and infants.* ☛ INJURIES: *Controlling bleeding. Applying a pressure bandage. Spotting and treating injury-induced shock. Covering cuts and scrapes. Step-by-step tourniquet instructions. Making slings and splints. Immobilizing injured limbs. Treating sprains and fractures. All about first-, second-, and third-degree burns. Caring for eye injuries. Removing splinters. How to treat animal bites. Identifying poisonous snakes. Insect bites and infection.* ☛ EVERYTHING YOU NEED TO KNOW: *About Choosing Pots and Pans, Front-Wheel-Drive Cars, Making Healthier Meals, Vacuum Cleaners, Garden Tools, Upholstered Furniture, Your Credit Card Statement, Curtain Styles* ☛ MONEY-SAVING HINTS: *How to Turn Bed Sheets into Curtains, Save on Car Repairs, Buy*

Safety First

Post these numbers near your telephone:
- ☞ Emergency medical service (in many communities it's not 911)
- ☞ Fire and police departments
- ☞ Ambulance and nearest hospital; physician and pharmacist
- ☞ Poison control center (usually administered by your local health department)
- ☞ Gas, electric, and water companies (customer and 24-hour service numbers)
- ☞ Dependable neighbors

HEALTH UPDATE

- ☞ State and local health departments provide information on asbestos, formaldehyde, lead, radon, water, and other environmental concerns. (Ask your state health department for a list of the agencies to contact in your area.)

ON THE ALERT

- ☞ Everyone in your family who is responsible enough to cope with an emergency should know where circuits, fuse boxes, water and gas line shutoffs are located and how to operate them.

Falls, fires, and electrical mishaps, in that order, are the major types of home accidents. By understanding these potential risks and taking the proper precautions, you can go a long way toward ensuring that your home is safe.

AVOIDING FALLS

Most household falls occur on wet floors and slippery or uneven sidewalks or when trying to reach high places. Here's how to avoid them:

Indoors
- Keep floors dry.
- Wipe up spills immediately.
- Keep stairs and other traffic areas free of obstacles.
- Place area rugs carefully. Don't use them at the top of the stairs, in entrance halls or other high-traffic areas, or in the bathroom, where a fall against ceramic surfaces can cause serious injury.
- Use a nonskid pad beneath area rugs or put nonskid adhesive strips on the backs to prevent slippage.
- Use only code-approved stepladders or step stools to reach high shelves, curtain rods, or light fixtures. Never use chairs.

Outdoors
- Replace broken paving stones and fill in pavement cracks.
- Always keep sidewalks clear of snow.
- Salt icy walkways.
- Install sturdy railings on steps.
- Make sure walkways, porches, and steps are well lit and maintained.
- Don't let leaves gather on walks, steps, and porches.

- Use a sturdy nonslip doormat.
- Paint the edges of outdoor steps white so they are easy to see in the dark.
- To reach high places, use only code-approved ladders and carefully observe the rules on the caution decal (see page 207).

PREVENTING FIRES

While fire is one of the most frightening and potentially devastating household disasters, basic, easy-to-implement prevention techniques can be a powerful defense. (For information on what to do if fire does break out, see page 286.) Follow these basic recommendations:

- Place at least one smoke detector on every level of your house or apartment. Make sure there is one at the top of each stairway, because this is where rising smoke is likely to accumulate first.
  Check the batteries regularly and change them yearly. Consider having them interconnected and hard wired to your house's electrical system. That way if one sounds off, they all sound off and dead batteries are no longer a factor.
- Have your furnace cleaned and checked once a year (see pages 228). Filters should be changed regularly (follow the manufacturer's recommendations) to avoid overheating.
- Keep broilers and other grease-gathering parts of your stove clean (see pages 51–52).
- Use fireplace screens and always make sure the chimneys are functioning properly (see pages 229–230).
- Store flammable paints and cleaning fluids well away from furnaces, fire-

WHERE TO GET SAFETY INFORMATION

NUMEROUS PUBLIC AGENCIES AND COUNCILS provide valuable safety information free of charge. Keep their phone numbers on hand.

ASSOCIATION	INFORMATION
American Council of Independent Laboratories (202) 887-5872	Lists labs that test for lead, radon, other contaminants around the house.
Centers for Disease Control and Prevention (404) 332-4555	How to recognize symptoms of Lyme disease.
Federal Emergency Management Agency (202) 646-2500	How to protect your home from fire, severe storms, flooding, and other emergencies.
Household Products Disposal Council (202) 659-5535	How to safely dispose of potentially hazardous household products.
National Fire Protection Association (800) 344-3555	How to prevent household fires.
National Lead Abatement Council (609) 520-1414	How to deal with lead; lists by region contractors who treat home lead problems.
National Lead Information Center Hotline (800) LEADFYI	How to deal with lead.
National Pesticides Telecommunications Network Hotline (800) 858-PEST or (806) 743-3091 in TX	How to use pesticides safely.

ASSOCIATION	INFORMATION
National Poison Control Center Hotline (202) 625-3333	How to treat accidental ingestion of chemicals, drugs, and poisons (operated by Georgetown University Hospital, Washington, D.C.).
National Safety Council (800) 621-7619 or (708) 285-1121 in IL	Fire safety, radon, and other household hazards; accident prevention; and first aid.
Safe Drinking Water Hotline (800) 426-4791 or (202) 382-5533 in Washington, D.C.	How to detect and deal with lead, radon, and other contaminants in drinking water; lists government-certified laboratories that test water and/or sell testing kits.
Toxic Substances Control Act Assistance Information Service Hotline (202) 554-1404	How to deal with asbestos and other toxic substances.
U.S. Consumer Product Safety Commission (800) 638-CPSC	Potential hazards associated with products used around the home and how to avoid risks (does not handle boats, cars, food, drugs, cosmetics, firearms, or pesticides).
U.S. Environmental Protection Agency Public Information Center (202) 475-7751	How to test for and handle asbestos, formaldehyde, lead, radon, and other household toxins.
U.S. Environmental Protection Agency Radon Hotline (800) SOS-RADON	How to test for and handle radon.

If you have a swimming pool, check local ordinances for proper safety regulations.

- Enclose the pool with a fence at least 5 feet high.

- Install gates that latch automatically.

- Install alarms on the gate or turn on pool alarms (which are activated when anyone falls in the water), when you are indoors or away.

- Keep the water level at least 3 inches from the top so a child can grasp the side and get air.

- Cover the pool during off season but remove the cover completely when the pool is in use.

- Keep a first aid kit and phone near the pool.

- Take a course in CPR and water safety at your local YMCA or chapter of the American Red Cross.

- Keep electrical appliances and glass away from the pool area.

- Store pool chemicals in a locked cabinet.

places, and stoves. A detached garage or toolshed is the safest place for them.

- Keep any rags saturated with furniture polish, oil, or other flammable material in sealed metal containers.

- Never use space heaters to dry clothes.

- Make sure space heaters are throwing heat into the open room, not toward draperies or flammable furniture.

- Be very careful with ashtrays and lit cigarettes, and never smoke in bed.

- Don't dry oily rags in the dryer; the heat can ignite them if they aren't completely clean.

- Be sure the dryer is properly vented to avoid lint buildup.

- Don't cook near drapes or when wearing flowing sleeves.

PREVENTING ELECTRICAL MISHAPS

It's not necessary to know all the ins and outs of your home electrical system to operate it safely. Common sense and some basic knowledge will help you avoid burns, shocks, and fires, the most common electricity-related problems. Be aware that:

- If your lights flicker and your appliances run sluggishly, your electrical system might be overloaded or switches and outlets may be faulty. An electrician can correct this poten-

tial fire hazard. Also, never overload an outlet with extension cords. Multioutlet extension bars are safer than extension cords because they are equipped with built-in safety shut-offs that cut off power if the socket becomes overloaded.

- To avoid shocks, make sure your hands are dry before you use, plug in, or unplug appliances. Never use an electrical appliance near a tub or basin of water. If it falls into the water, even if it is turned off, it can create an electrical field that will electrocute anyone who is in the water or who reaches into the water.

  In your bathroom and kitchen, consider installing outlets with ground-fault circuit interrupters (see page 242). These outlets cut off power automatically as soon as they sense electrical current leaking from the power tool or appliance, as it does when dropped in water.

- When buying power tools and appliances, check to make sure they are listed by Underwriters Laboratories (they will be marked with "UL"). This assures they have met rigorous safety standards set by this nationally recognized authority.

- Replace worn and frayed wires and cords and plugs that become hot when the appliance is in use.

HOME SAFETY FOR CHILDREN AND THE ELDERLY

EVERYONE NEEDS TO BE CAREFUL around the house, but the young and old have special needs. The only way to ensure your child's safety is to stay vigilant. However, childproofing areas of the house that can be especially dangerous will make your job easier. Older people are vulnerable to falls and broken bones, so take precautions.

CHILDREN

THROUGHOUT THE HOUSE

- Put covers on unused electrical outlets.
- Be alert to young children who might chew on cords. Biting through an electrical cord can cause severe burns.
- Use child safety gates with small openings at the top and bottom of stairways and install window guards in rooms above the ground floor.
- Don't leave partially filled buckets of water around the house; a child can drown in them.
- Be alert to long cords on appliances.

IN THE KITCHEN

- Keep all sharp and breakable objects, as well as cleaners and other hazardous substances, in cabinets and drawers equipped with child safety locks.
- Childproof appliance knobs.
- Try to use back burners and turn handles toward the wall, so a child can't reach up and grab a hot pot.
- Don't consider high shelves or cabinets to be childproof—they may simply be challenging an adventurous child to attempt a dangerous climb.

IN THE BATHROOM

- Never leave a child unattended in the bathtub.
- Don't leave the toilet seat up; a young child could fall in and drown.
- Install child safety locks on the medicine chest and on all other cabinets and cupboards.
- Make sure the water heater is set to no higher than 130°F to prevent scalds.
- Teach children to test the water before washing their hands or climbing into the bath or shower.

ELDERLY

THROUGHOUT THE HOUSE

- Install extra stair railings and secure carpets and rugs.
- Check for adequate lighting on stairs, landings, and porches.
- Install emergency alert buttons around the house to summon help.
- Install photosensitive night-lights in the hallways and bathrooms.
- Make sure the house is warm in the winter to avoid the risk of hypothermia, which can be caused by temperatures less than 55°F. Keep the house cool in summer to lessen the risk of heat exhaustion.

IN THE KITCHEN

- Use electric kettles, coffeemakers, and irons that switch off automatically, especially if anyone is forgetful.
- Kitchen utensils with sure-grip handles make cooking easier and safer, especially for arthritis sufferers.
- Install lights that shine directly onto the stove and countertops to help avoid accidents.

IN THE BATHROOM

- Install lights that provide sufficient illumination for those with poor eyesight.
- Strategically place sturdy handrails both inside and outside the shower and tub.
- Provide sturdy and secured steps to help bathtub users safely in and out.
- Use nonskid bath mats in both shower and tub.
- Make sure the water heater is set to no higher than 130°F to prevent scalds.

THE SAFE HOUSE

You can go a long way toward preventing common household mishaps—which can lead to serious injury—by following these recommendations:

THE KITCHEN:

• Keep all areas on and around the stove free of grease to avoid fires.

• Keep containers of drippings and grease well away from the stove.

• Check that your hot-water heater is set at 130°F or less to prevent scalds.

• Make sure the pilot light, if there is one, on a gas stove is always lit.

• When cooking, rely on insulated heating pads, pot holders, and oven mitts—a dish cloth won't protect you from a burn and can ignite easily.

• Keep your stove, sink, and countertops well lit.

• Keep a fire extinguisher handy.

THE STAIRS:

• Use bright lights, and install light switches at the top and bottom of the stairs.

• Make sure handrails are secure and run the entire length of the stairs. For extra safety, install a handrail on each side of the steps.

• Carpeting must be tight fitting and secure. Repair frayed and threadbare carpet immediately. Dense, short-pile carpet provides the surest footing.

• Metal or vinyl guards fitted onto the edge of steps make it easy to see each step and provide a nonslip surface.

THE BATHROOM:

- Keep a window open or use a ventilation fan to control moisture and prevent mildew and other allergy-triggering molds.
- Keep electrical appliances well away from water.
- Use nonskid rugs.
- Make sure medicines are clearly labeled. Look at "expiration" or "use by" dates and dispose of all old medicine and cosmetics.
- Store all breakable bottles in places where they can't easily be knocked over.
- Use a night-light to avoid stumbles in the dark.
- Use nonskid mats in the bath and shower.
- Install a handrail near the bathtub to minimize the risk of falling as you climb in and out.

THE GARAGE AND BASEMENT:

- For stairs in the basement and other dark places, paint the top and bottom steps yellow or white.
- Store paints, chemicals, and other toxins, such as pesticides, neatly in their original containers.
- Keep all tools, especially those with sharp edges, where they can't be stepped on or tripped over.
- Make sure light switches are easily accessible.
- Label gas and water lines and their shutoff points, and tag fuses or circuit breakers to show which rooms they control.

SAFE HOUSE DON'TS

☛ Don't hang frequently used items at the back of the stove top, where you may have to reach across hot burners to grab them.

☛ Don't turn on a microwave oven if the door is damaged. After heating anything in a microwave, open the containers carefully—the escaping steam can cause severe burns.

☛ Don't leave any pans unattended when cooking.

☛ Don't let objects clutter the stairs or landings.

☛ Don't polish wooden stair surfaces.

☛ Don't leave oily rags, wood shavings, and other flammable material lying around.

CLOSE ENCOUNTERS

☛ If you have an electric garage door opener, equip it with a monitor that stops or reverses the motor when the door encounters an object.

If a fire has occurred in
your home:

☛ Contact your insurance
agent and the financial institution
holding your mortgage.

☛ Secure your house against
intruders.

☛ Itemize the damaged and
destroyed items. Be sure to ask
your agent how much detail
is needed.

☛ If the electricity or gas has
been turned off, call the utility to
restore the service. Ask a service
person to check your appliances
for water and wiring damage
before using them.

EMERGENCIES IN THE HOME

No one likes to contemplate accidents, but they can happen anytime. If you know what to do in case of an emergency, it may mean the difference between life and death for you and your family and can save your home from extensive damage.

FIRE

Precautions: No matter how many precautions you take against fire, knowing what to do if one does break out can save lives and minimize property damage (see pages 280 and 282 for basic fire-prevention steps).

Everyone in your household should know the fastest routes out of the house, and it's a good idea to practice fire drills.

When considering escape routes, be aware that any room in the house could be completely cut off by fire, trapping people inside. At least one window in every room must open wide enough so an adult can squeeze through it. All rooms on the second floor or higher should be equipped with a fire ladder or a knotted rope.

Think carefully about how you would get an elderly or handicapped member of the family out in the event of a fire. Remember, it will take someone who's disabled much longer to get out, so plan accordingly.

If Fire Breaks Out

The most important thing to do in a fire is to get everyone out of the house quickly. No one should take the time to dress, gather valuables, or even look for a family pet in another part of the house. Have an assigned meeting place outside the house, such as a tree or the end of the driveway. This way, you will be able to account for all family members at a glance. Call the fire company from a neighbor's house.

Beware of smoke: Smoke and gases can be more deadly than flames. If you are surrounded by smoke, tie a rag (preferably wet) around your nose and mouth to filter the fumes. Smoke rises, so crouch on the floor on your hands and knees. Don't lie prone on the floor, though, because lethal gases can collect there, too.

Check doors: If you are in a closed room, check the door before opening

---

PUTTING OUT FIRES

You should only try to fight small, contained fires that can be put out in less than two minutes. Call the fire department immediately for anything larger.

GREASE

Never throw water on a grease fire. Turn off the heat beneath the pan and smother the flames with a lid or a damp towel. You may also use a fire extinguisher that's filled with chemicals appropriate for flammable liquids.

ELECTRIC

Unplug the appliance and use a fire extinguisher intended to douse electric fires. If you don't have one, smother the burning appliance in a rug or heavy blanket. Don't throw water on a burning appliance, even if it's unplugged, because residual current could give you an electric shock.

MATTRESSES AND UPHOLSTERY

Pour water on a mattress or piece of upholstered furniture that is smoldering and carry it outside away from the house. If you are not able to control the fire, leave the house immediately because some upholstery contains material that emits lethal fumes when burning. Be aware that mattresses and upholstery can reignite if not completely doused.

FIRE EXTINGUISHERS

A RELIABLE, WELL-maintained fire extinguisher can put out a small fire before it becomes a disastrous blaze. Water-based extinguishers are for fires in upholstery, wood, and most other household materials. Chemical and foam extinguishers are for grease and electrical fires and should not be used on fabrics and wood.

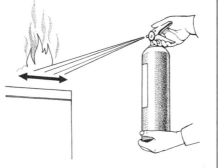

- Keep an extinguisher on every level of the house, near the locations where a fire is most likely to occur—in the kitchen, for instance, or near the furnace.

- Keep extinguishers easily accessible; they are useless if tucked away in drawers or cluttered cabinets.

- Check extinguishers regularly, according to the manufacturer's instructions, to make sure nozzles aren't clogged, the pressure is high enough, and they are otherwise in good working order.

PROPER USE:

Stand six feet from the flames and sweep the nozzle back and forth, aiming the spray at the base of the fire. If the flames don't go out by the time the fire extinguisher is empty, get out of the house and call for help.

RECOMMENDED TYPES:

- For the kitchen: Buy a 5BC type.

- For the basement: Buy a 1A or a 10BC type.

Note:

A fires = wood, rags, and paper

B fires = grease, gas, and flammable liquids

C fires = electrical

When you buy a smoke detector, look for these features for use in specific rooms:

- **In the kitchen:** A silencer or "hush" feature lets you shut off the smoke detector during preset times when cooking may set off a false alarm. It will cycle back to "on" after the allotted time period.

- **In hallways and bedrooms:** Built-in emergency lights come on when the alarm is triggered.

it—fire could rush through the door as soon as you open it and engulf the room in seconds.

First, touch the door with your hands to see if it's hot. Be sure to check the top of the door, because heat rises. If it's hot, don't open it. Then check to make sure smoke isn't curling under the bottom. Make sure everyone in your family knows how to check a door in this way. Many people

are killed or injured when they open a door to an inferno on the other side.

If the door is hot or smoke is seeping through the cracks from the other side:

- Do not open it. Stuff towels, blankets, rugs, or whatever else is on hand at the bottom of the door to keep out smoke and fumes.

- Open the window and call for help or let yourself out on an emergency ladder.

If you are in the path of an oncoming major storm:

☛ Bring indoors or secure lawn furniture, garbage cans, tools, and other objects that might be blown or washed away.

☛ Clean sinks and bathtubs and fill them with water as a reserve in case you lose your water supply.

☛ Make sure your car is filled with gas and stock the trunk with water, blankets, a first aid kit, and nonperishable food.

☛ Board up windows with plywood or heavy cardboard or latch shutters over them securely.

☛ Keep flashlights and radios on hand; be sure their batteries are fresh.

BEFORE THE DELUGE

☛ One of the first things to do if you anticipate flooding is to switch off circuits, fuse boxes, and gas mains. If water has reached the level of electrical outlets and appliance motors, don't walk into a room until the the power has been turned off.

If it seems safe to open the door:

- Do so cautiously and pay careful attention to the air temperature on the other side—if it isn't suspiciously hot, it may be safe to leave the room and take the fastest route out of the house.

If you can't get out of the room:

- Hang a sheet out the window to alert fire fighters that someone is trapped inside. Get down on your hands and knees to avoid smoke and fumes. **As a last resort,** you can tie sheets together to use as a ladder, attaching them firmly to a radiator or other fixture. Before you do so, though, throw a mattress, pillows, or even coats out the window to cushion a fall.

FLOODS

Water can be very destructive, so it is important to act quickly. Even a minor flood in your home can destroy furniture, floors, and structural members. Water has disastrous effects on electric circuits, gas lines and appliances, triggering fires and gas leaks and posing the risk of electrocution. Know the location of your main water valve (see page 236).

If a Pipe Bursts:

- Turn off water at the main valve.
- Close the doors to the room where the pipe has burst and put towels over the door jamb to keep water out.
- Repair the pipe if you know how or call a plumber (see page 237).
- Mop up the water; thick towels are especially efficient because they are so absorbent.

If Water Floods Outside:

- Turn off gas and electricity to the house.
- Put rolled up blankets and towels at the bottom of doors to the outside to keep as much water out of the house as possible.

- If there's time, move valuables to an upper floor.
- If it's prudent, leave the house by a safe route to dry land. If not, take food, bottled water, a flashlight, candles and matches, and a battery-operated radio to an upper floor and wait for help. If the telephone is still working, alert your local emergency service of your situation and whereabouts.

GAS LEAKS

Gas furnaces, water heaters, stoves and other appliances should be serviced regularly, according to the manufacturer's recommendations. It's also important that gas appliances, such as a gas dryer, are installed properly. Gas furnaces, for instance, require sufficient air space around them so there is enough oxygen for the gas to burn properly. Some gas appliances may require vents or flues. Follow the manufacturer's installation instructions carefully and if in doubt call your local utility company. Know where the main gas valve is located.

If You Smell Gas:

Don't take the smell of gas casually—a gas leak can cause an explosion, start a fire, or cause asphyxiation. Calmly follow these steps:

- **If the odor is strong,** get everyone out of the house at once. Immediately call the emergency service of your utility company from a neighbor's house.
- **If the odor is relatively slight,** open doors and windows to air out the house.
- Put out fires, cigarettes, candles, and other open flames.
- Don't operate electrical appliances, use the telephone, or turn on lights.
- Check pilot lights. If one has gone out, wait for the gas smell to diminish, then relight.
- If the source is unknown, call for emergency service.

INDOOR POLLUTANTS

SPIDER PLANT

Pollutants lurking around the house can trigger coughs, runny noses, watery eyes and, in some cases, even serious illness. Be familiar with common pollutants so you can protect yourself.

MILDEW, MOLDS, AND DUST MITES

These organisms grow in bathrooms, the kitchen, and other areas of your home with high humidity and often account for persistent sneezing, watery eyes, and other allergylike symptoms.

To reduce the level, keep bathroom tiles and other surfaces free of mildew (see page 57), clean air conditioners and humidifiers frequently, and open a window or install a fan in bathrooms and the kitchen to reduce humidity. (If your window panes sweat, the humidity in your house is too high and you are creating ideal living conditions for these irritants.)

Many allergy sufferers react to dust mites, tiny creatures that live in carpets, bedding and upholstered furniture and require moisture to live. Regularly clean furniture, cushions, and mattresses to eliminate them (see box page 30), and reduce the level of humidity in your house.

FORMALDEHYDE

While it is often not a problem, formaldehyde does emit a gas that can cause skin rashes, runny noses, watery eyes, and other reactions. Formaldehyde is used in insulation, paneling, pressed plywood, carpeting, fabrics, cabinets, and countless household products, including facial tissue and toothpaste.

You can usually lower formaldehyde levels considerably simply by keeping windows open to circulate fresh air through the house. Your state health agency or local EPA office can also inspect your home or recommend private inspectors.

It may be necessary to remove material containing formaldehyde or take such measures as covering paneling that emits formaldehyde with a vinyl wall covering. Airing dry cleaning before putting it in the closet helps too.

CARBON MONOXIDE

A surprising number of household devices, including wood-burning stoves, fireplaces, furnaces, barbecues, kerosene lamps, and gas-fired water and space heaters, can release carbon monoxide if they burn without enough oxygen.

When fresh air is restricted, carbon monoxide can build up in your home and cause fatigue, irregular heart beat, headaches, and—in cases of very high concentrations—unconsciousness and death. This gas is especially threatening in winter, when your house is often sealed up tight against the cold.

Carbon monoxide is tasteless and odorless, so you are not likely to know if it is building up until you begin suffering from its ill effects. Therefore, it is important to take some commonsense precautions.

- Be sure adequate air is available to any room containing a gas-burning appliance. Have your building code inspector check if in doubt.

- Have your furnace, chimneys, and flues checked regularly for cracks and leaks that can release carbon monoxide into your home.

NATURE'S POLLUTION FIGHTERS

☞ Houseplants—especially spider plants—offer some help in your fight against household air pollution, according to NASA scientists who have been investigating ways to clear the air in space stations. A philodendron can absorb much of the formaldehyde that builds up in a room, while a chrysanthemum will reduce some of the harmful chemicals in tobacco smoke.

PHILODENDRON

CHRYSANTHEMUM

☞ Air out the house after new carpeting is installed or fresh paint is applied.

☞ Limit the use of air fresheners and perfumes.

☞ Use solvents and bathroom cleaners only in well-ventilated areas.

- When buying a wood-burning stove, choose one that meets EPA safety standards. (The stove should be labeled as such; if not, ask the retailer or dealer.) It should be installed to meet local installation codes.

- Make sure the door and stovepipe connections on all old wood-burning stoves fit tightly.

- Use a range hood with a fan if you have a gas range, or install an exhaust fan in a nearby window.

- Open a window slightly or make sure a door is open to the rest of the house when using a space heater that operates on oil, gas, or kerosene.

- Never barbecue in the house or garage.

- Make sure the garage door is open whenever the car is running.

ASBESTOS

This durable, fibrous material was once widely used in flooring, ceiling tiles, shingles, and insulation. Because prolonged exposure to asbestos fibers has been found to cause cancer, the material was banned 20 years ago. If your home was built before then it's quite possible that the pipes and heating ducts in your basement are wrapped in asbestos.

However, the asbestos in your house is not necessarily dangerous. If the material is in good condition and is not leaking fibers as it crumbles and flakes, the rule of thumb is to leave it in place. Be extremely careful when working around asbestos, however.

- Never tear the asbestos coating from around a pipe, for instance, when brushing or vacuuming it, and don't saw or drill into asbestos when remodeling.

- Never remove the material yourself. If you are concerned that asbestos in your home poses a hazard, contact your state health agency or local EPA office (see page 281) for a list of inspectors and contractors who specialize in asbestos removal.

GET THE LEAD OUT

IF THERE IS LEAD PAINT
IN YOUR HOUSE:

- Don't remove it yourself, because you risk exposing yourself and your family to harmful lead-dust particles. Ask your local health department for names of contractors who specialize in lead paint removal.

- Don't simply paint over lead paint, because the lead will continue to chip and fill the air with particles.

- Don't sweep floors. Wash them with a wet mop so you stir up as little dust as possible.

- To keep children away, use

furniture to block window sills and other areas where paint might be chipping; repair as soon as possible.

- Have children wash their hands to remove any lead residue.

- Install vinyl siding over exterior lead paint as a less expensive alternative to costly scraping and repainting.

- Wash toys and any large objects children might put in their mouths.

IF THERE IS LEAD IN YOUR WATER:

- Run tap water for 30 to 60 seconds to drain off lead that accumulates

in the pipes in your house. (If lead is entering your water supply from street mains and connections—many municipalities used lead in water systems up until the 1930s—you will not be able to flush lead from your pipes simply by letting the water run for a while. Use bottled water for drinking and cooking or install a water filter registered for lead reduction.)

- Use cold water rather than hot for cooking and drinking. Hot water accumulates more lead from pipes.

- When in doubt, call the EPA Hotline: (800) 426-4791.

LEAD

Lead poisoning, a major home health concern, can occur when this metallic element leaches into drinking water through lead pipes. Dust particles from flaking lead paint are another hazard.

If you live in a house built before 1978, when lead paint was banned, have the paint tested. Have the water tested for lead if your house was built prior to 1988, when the government prohibited the use of lead in plumbing materials.

Even if your home is equipped with copper water pipes, your water is not necessarily lead free. Pipe connections may contain lead solder, and brass and bronze faucets often contain lead that can leach into the water.

RADON

This odorless, colorless, tasteless gas occurs naturally when uranium in rocks and soil decays. It is found all over the United States and may be entering your house undetected through cracks in the basement floor, pores in concrete-block basement walls, and through other openings between the earth and the house.

Radon can occur randomly. Just because a neighbor's house is radon-free doesn't mean that yours is.

Recent studies indicate that exposure to high levels of radon over extended periods can cause lung cancer, making radon one of the most hazardous indoor pollutants. Fortunately, it's easy to identify a radon problem and it's usually easy and fairly inexpensive to lower levels.

All states now have offices that provide information on radon, and some states will test your home for radon free of charge (call your local health department to locate the nearest office). Inexpensive, do-it-yourself radon test kits, usually less than $50, are also available at supermarkets and hardware stores. Your state radon office can provide a list of test-kit companies that have met EPA requirements for reliability or are state certified.

DISPOSING OF TOXIC HOUSEHOLD PRODUCTS

Many communities now sponsor programs to recycle and/or safely dispose of household waste materials that can be dangerous if not taken care of properly. Some communities support recycling centers where home owners can bring drain cleaners, car batteries, motor oil, paints and thinners, pesticides, houshold cleaners, and other potentially hazardous materials.

Ask your local health department or EPA office (see page 281) to provide information and advise you on services available in your community to get rid of questionable substances. While you are waiting to dispose of these items, store them safely.

- Keep flammable items in the garage or tool-shed, where they will be far from the furnace, stove, and other heat sources.

- Lock up hazardous materials securely to keep them out of the reach of children.

- Keep materials in their original containers so you don't confuse them with other products.

Be aware, however, that the EPA cautions against do-it-yourself repairs, so you may want to have these problems fixed by a qualified contractor. If the problem persists, consult the state's radon office to determine the best way to respond.

Testing involves placing a device—usually a small canister or plastic strip—to collect samples in the basement for a specific time period. (If you do not have a basement, place the device in the lowest lived-in area.) Then send the device to a laboratory for analysis. You need to test only once. If you have a well, you should also test your water for radon.

If you do have radon, you can try to correct the problem by caulking cracks in basement concrete and masonry through which the gas can enter (see page 234) and sealing floors and walls with latex paint. Sometimes you can reduce radon levels simply by keeping your basement windows open or installing fans to circulate fresh air from outside. Be sure to test again.

THE SECURE HOUSE

No house is 100 percent burglarproof. It's reassuring to know, though, that the more precautions you take to prevent a break-in, the less likely a burglar will be to target your house. This illustration shows some basic ways to increase the security of your house. If you are frequently away from home and live in an area where break-ins are common, a burglar alarm system may be in order.

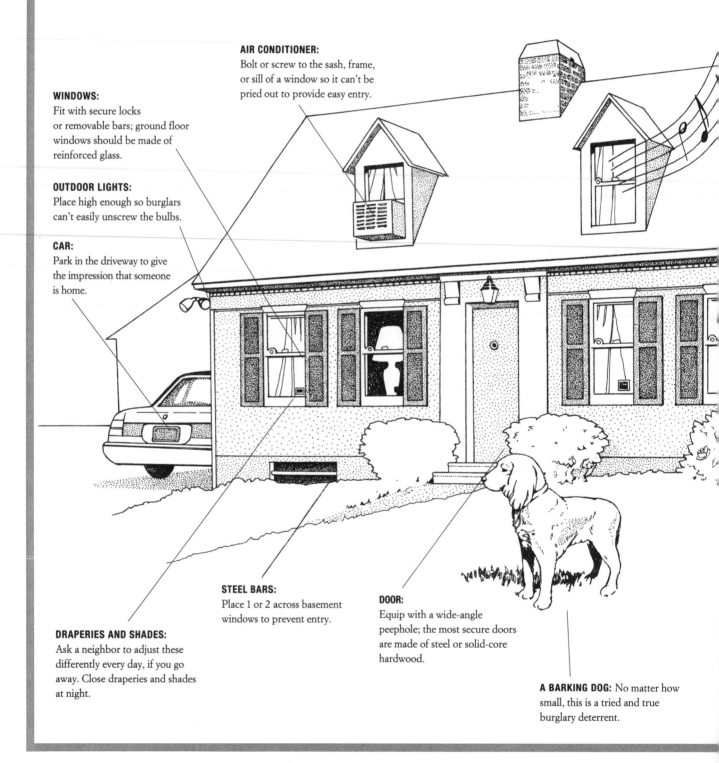

AIR CONDITIONER:
Bolt or screw to the sash, frame, or sill of a window so it can't be pried out to provide easy entry.

WINDOWS:
Fit with secure locks or removable bars; ground floor windows should be made of reinforced glass.

OUTDOOR LIGHTS:
Place high enough so burglars can't easily unscrew the bulbs.

CAR:
Park in the driveway to give the impression that someone is home.

STEEL BARS:
Place 1 or 2 across basement windows to prevent entry.

DOOR:
Equip with a wide-angle peephole; the most secure doors are made of steel or solid-core hardwood.

DRAPERIES AND SHADES:
Ask a neighbor to adjust these differently every day, if you go away. Close draperies and shades at night.

A BARKING DOG: No matter how small, this is a tried and true burglary deterrent.

SOUND:
Use timers to turn on a radio or TV at different times when you are gone.

LIGHT:
Use timers, for lights as well, to turn on and off when you are away.

PORCH LIGHTS:
Turn on at night.

GLASS DOORS:
Fit with double cylinder locks that are opened with keys from both inside and out. This way, a burglar can't just knock out the glass and reach in and turn the knob. Insert a dowel cut to fit in the track of a sliding glass door to prevent the door from sliding. Keep a key handy to exit in emergencies.

NATURAL DETERRENTS:
Plant holly, roses, and other prickly plants at the bottom of drain pipes.

WINDOW DECALS:
These say you have an alarm system, whether you do or not.

SECURE HOUSE DON'TS

☞ Don't leave electronic equipment, jewelry, money and checkbooks, silver services, and other valuables visible or within reach through a window.

☞ Don't let shrubs and trees obscure doors and windows, affording a burglar concealment.

☞ Don't let mail and deliveries pile up outside the house.

☞ Don't leave notes on the door saying you're away, no matter how short the time.

ANATOMY OF A LOCK

THE LOCKS ON your doors are your first line of defense against a break-in. Check the following in all locks:

CYLINDER:
The part of the lock that accepts the key—should be covered with a guard plate to protect it from prying.

ANGLE IRON:
This piece of the lock is made up of two L-shaped bars attached to the door and the door frame. It prevents a burglar from wedging a crowbar between the frame and door to jimmy the lock.

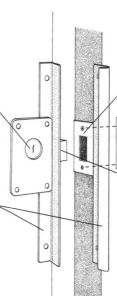

STRIKE:
The receptacle that's mounted on the door frame to accept the bolt and keep the door locked tight—must be mounted securely to the frame with long screws; otherwise a burglar can kick in a locked door.

BOLT:
The piece of the lock that slides into a receptacle on the door frame—should be made of high-grade steel and be at least an inch long, so it can't be easily jimmied.

THE FIRST AID KIT

*ALWAYS KEEP A WELL-STOCKED first aid kit in an easily
accessible place. Make sure everyone in the family knows where it is; keep
a complete first aid manual handy.*

BASIC KIT

BANDAGES

- Adhesive bandages of assorted sizes (for minor cuts or scrapes)
- Bandages and gauze pads of assorted sizes (to dress wounds)

MEDICATIONS

- After-sun lotion
- Antibiotic ointment
- Antiseptic solution and wipes (to clean wounds)
- Aspirin or a nonaspirin pain killer like acetaminophen
- Calamine lotion (to apply to insect bites)
- Cough syrup
- Sunscreen

EQUIPMENT

- Adhesive tape
- Blanket made of Mylar or some other lightweight material
- Cotton balls and swabs
- Safety pins (to fasten bandages)
- Scissors (to cut bandages)
- Thermometer
- Tweezers (to remove splinters and objects from wounds)

COMPLETE KIT

FOR A COMPLETE KIT, ADD the following to your basics:

BANDAGES

- Butterfly bandages
- Elastic bandages, 3 inches wide (for sprains)
- Eye patches
- Triangular bandage (to make a sling)

MEDICATIONS

- Antacid
- Diarrhea medicine
- Eyewash (sterile saline solution)
- Hydrocortisone cream (to soothe skin irritations)
- Insect repellent
- Laxative
- Syrup of ipecac (to induce vomiting)

EQUIPMENT

- Bottled water
- Flashlight
- Latex gloves
- Matches (to sterilize instruments)
- Paper and pencil
- Paper cups (for fluids, to flush wounds, to use as a protective covering for eyes or wounds)
- Petroleum jelly (to remove ticks)
- Sewing needle (for splinters beneath the skin)
- Snakebite kit (suction cup, sterile blade, tourniquet)
- Soap

EMERGENCY FIRST AID

Knowing how to administer first aid in an emergency may
mean the difference between life and death.

When administering first aid:

Do check the ABCs:

>   Is the **airway** clear so the
>   victim can breathe?
>
>   Is **breathing** normal?
>
>   Is **circulation** adequate?

Do call for help.

Do stay calm—it's very important to
make rational decisions.

Do proceed carefully; the last thing you
want to do is make an injury worse.

Do care for the most serious injuries first.

Don't leave the victim alone—the one excep-
tion is to get help.

Don't assume that the noticeable injuries are
the only ones.

Don't assume the victim is making rational
decisions or using sound judgment.

Don't move the victim if broken bones or
back, neck, or head injuries are suspected.

IN THIS SECTION:

Fainting 297
Unconsciousness 298
Choking 299
Heat Exhaustion 300
Hypothermia...300
Heat Stroke...301
Electric Shock 302
Anaphylactic Shock......................................303
Poisoning..304
Heart Attack...305
Cardiopulmonary Resuscitation (CPR) 306
The Heimlich Maneuver 310

BE A GOOD SAMARITAN

☞ Nearly all states have Good Samaritan
laws, which are meant to encourage citizens
to stop and help in an emergency. While the
laws vary state to state, most protect the lay
rescuer from liability as long as he or she
doesn't do anything that can be defined as
grossly negligent or that shows willful
misconduct. Check with your local police
department, public library, or attorney to
know the law in your state.

CALL EMS

In many communities "911" is not the emergency number. If you don't know the local EMS *(emergency medical service)* number, dial the operator for assistance.

Call if the victim:

- Is not breathing or is having difficulty breathing. (Do not delay mouth-to-mouth resuscitation [see page 306].)

- Has (or might have) suffered a heart attack or stroke.

- Is unconscious, having convulsions, or in shock (see pages 298–299, 302–303, and 316).

- Has (or might have) suffered a back, neck, or head injury.

- Has a serious fracture.

- Is bleeding profusely.

- Cannot easily be moved.

Be prepared to state:

- Exactly what happened.

- Exactly where you are (the street address as well as nearby landmarks, the name of the district and/or building, floor, office, or apartment number, etc.).

- The telephone number from which you are calling.

- How many people need help and their condition (conscious or unconscious, bleeding, suffering a heart attack, have been poisoned, etc.).

- What help victims have received.

It is very important to stay on the line; the dispatcher will be able to help you care for the victim.

EMERGENCY:
FAINTING

If someone is feeling faint:

1. Instruct the person to lie down.

2. Raise his or her legs at the knees or elevate them slightly.

3. Help the person up gradually to avoid another episode.

4. Call EMS if recovery is not prompt.

If someone has already fainted:

1. Lay the person on a flat surface, face up. (A person almost always regains consciousness when in a reclining position.)

2. Elevate his or her feet 8 to 12 inches to promote blood circulation. Don't put a pillow under the head as this can block the airway. If the person vomits, quickly put him or her in the recovery position (see page 298).

3. Apply a cloth soaked in cool water to the victim's face.

Since fainting can often be a symptom of a serious condition, someone who faints should see a physician as soon as possible.

TAKING A PULSE

Press two fingertips against the radial artery in the wrist just below the base of the thumb or against the carotid artery on the right side of the neck. (Don't use your thumb, because it has a pulse point that can interfere with your reading.) Count the number of beats for 20 seconds and multiply by 3 to obtain the beats per minute. The norm for adults is anywhere from 60 to 100 beats a minute.

A heart rate significantly above that may be an indication that someone has gone into shock (see pages 302–303 and 316). If you cannot detect a pulse, it may be necessary to administer cardiopulmonary resuscitation (see pages 306–309).

An accelerated heart rate may also be the sign of a serious condition, such as heat stroke (see page 301).

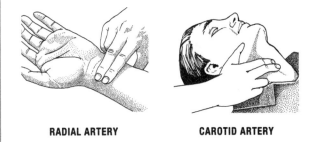

RADIAL ARTERY   **CAROTID ARTERY**

Emergency:

Unconsciousness

The signs of unconsciousness are obvious: lack of motion and a comalike state. Also look for these signs of flagging consciousness:

- Disorientation
- Drowsiness
- Incoherence
- Slipping in and out of alertness
- Stupor

If someone is unconscious or semiconscious:

1. Check the pulse immediately (see page 297). Administer cardiopulmonary resuscitation if necessary (see pages 306–309).

2. Check for a Medic Alert tag on a bracelet or chain around the neck; it may explain why the person has lost consciousness.

3. Call EMS if the person doesn't wake up within five minutes.

Do not move someone who you suspect might have head or neck injuries.

If breathing is normal and you feel it is safe to do so, take the following steps to place the victim in the **Recovery Position:**

1. Position the victim so he or she is lying face up.

2. Loosen any tight clothing around the neck and chest.

3. Kneel on one side of the person. Bring the far arm across the chest and the far leg across the near one.

4. Using the crossed arm and leg, gently pull the person onto his or her side, facing you.

5. Bring the knee of the leg closest to you slightly forward and bring the arms above the head.

The person will now be lying on his or her stomach with his or her head slightly tilted to the side and one leg bent at the knee. This position will facilitate breathing and blood flow.

EMERGENCY:

CHOKING

Always seek professional emergency medical help for a choking victim, even after recovery. Complications can arise not only from the choking incident but also from the first aid maneuvers.

Symptoms include:

- Convulsions or loss of consciousness
- Gagging
- Grasping the throat
- High-pitched crowing sound
- Noisy breathing
- Pale or bluish skin, especially on the face
- Weak, ineffective coughing

If someone displays the above signs, ask if he or she is choking.

If the person can speak or cough forcefully,

the blockage is partial and the obstruction might be dislodged. Ask the person to cough strongly. If the airway remains blocked, explain that you are going to do the Heimlich maneuver.

If the person can't respond,

the airway might be totally blocked and the obstruction could be life threatening. Administer the Heimlich maneuver immediately then call EMS.

See pages 310–314 for the Heimlich maneuver.

HEAT EXHAUSTION

Heat exhaustion is the result of inadequate fluid and salt intake to balance losses. *Symptoms include:*

- Dizziness
- Faintness
- Fast, shallow breathing
- Headache
- Nausea
- Pale, clammy skin
- Rapid pulse

If someone suffers from heat exhaustion:

1. Have the victim lie down in a cool place with his or her feet raised about 12 inches.

2. Add ¼ teaspoon of salt to a pint of water for the victim to drink.

3. Keep the victim still and give him or her plenty of liquids.

HYPOTHERMIA

Hypothermia, caused by prolonged exposure to cold conditions, occurs when body temperature falls to 95°F or lower. The elderly are especially vulnerable to hypothermia and can succumb to the condition by spending long periods in a poorly heated house. *Symptoms include:*

- Cold skin, especially in areas that are normally warm, such as the groin and armpits
- Confusion
- Drowsiness
- Paleness
- Slow heart rate

Call for medical attention immediately, then:

1. Move the victim to a warm place.

2. Remove any wet clothing and cover the victim with a blanket.

3. Give the victim a warm nonalcoholic drink.

EMERGENCY:

HEAT STROKE

Heat exhaustion can develop into heat stroke (sometimes called sunstroke), a serious, sometimes fatal condition. With the onset of heat stroke, sweating stops; the skin becomes dry, hot, and flushed; breathing becomes increasingly shallow; the pulse becomes more rapid; and body temperature rises dramatically.

The most important thing to do is to bring the body temperature down as quickly as possible.

Call for medical attention immediately, then:

1. Move the victim into the shade.

2. Remove clothing.

3. Cover the victim with cool towels or sheets or apply cold packs to the body.

4. Fan the victim.

5. If possible, spray the victim with cool water or put the victim in a tub filled with cold water and ice cubes.

The victim is not out of danger until body temperature drops to 101°F. (At this temperature, the skin will begin to feel cool to the touch.)

EMERGENCY:

ELECTRIC SHOCK

Electrocution can have severe effects on the body, so you may have to administer artificial respiration or CPR, treat the victim for shock, or treat burns (see below and page 316 for shock procedures).

If the victim has come in contact with an appliance:

1. Don't touch him or her until you've switched off the current. Electricity can flow from the victim to you, giving you a serious shock as well.

2. If possible, unplug the appliance or turn off the power at the circuit breaker or fuse box.

3. If you can't switch off the power, use a nonmetal object such as a broom, a belt with a nonmetal belt buckle, or a branch to pry the source of electricity away from the victim. Make sure you are not standing in a wet area and if possible, stand on a rubber mat or some other insulating surface.

4. Call for medical attention immediately.

If the victim has come in contact with a high-voltage power line (almost always fatal):

Stay at least 60 feet away because power can jump. Call for medical help and stay nearby to warn others of the danger.

EMERGENCY:

ANAPHYLACTIC SHOCK

Some individuals who are allergic to insect bites, stings, certain foods and/or plants can experience a severe life-threatening allergic reaction known as anaphylactic shock. *Symptoms include:*

- Coughing and breathing difficulties
- Dizziness and possible unconsciousness
- Nausea and vomiting
- Severe swelling at the site of the bite as well as around the eyes, lips, and tongue

To treat someone who has gone into anaphylactic shock:

1. Administer mouth-to-mouth resuscitation if necessary (see pages 306–307).
2. Call for medical help immediately.
3. Remove the stinger by scraping it with a fingernail or credit card.
4. Place a cold pack on the sting.
5. Keep the victim still until medical help arrives.

EMERGENCY:

POISONING

Poisons can have delayed effects as they are absorbed by the body, so it is important to get medical attention. Don't take statements like "I feel better" as signals that the victim is out of danger.

If the victim is unconscious:

1. Get him or her to the hospital as soon as possible.

2. Take with you any poisonous fluids, pills, plants, or other substances found near the victim, along with samples of vomit for analysis.

If the victim is conscious:

1. Try to determine what the poisonous substance is.

2. Call your local poison control center immediately; personnel there will walk you through the proper procedures. In some poisoning cases, it may be necessary to administer mouth-to-mouth resuscitation or CPR (see pages 306–309).

3. If the victim has been poisoned by toxic substances that are absorbed through the skin, such as a pesticide, wash the skin with soap and water. Wear rubber gloves to avoid contaminating yourself.

4. If the victim has inhaled carbon monoxide or another poisonous gas, get him or her into the fresh air as quickly as possible. Loosen constricting clothing.

5. If the victim has ingested a corrosive substance, such as drain cleaner (indicated by burns around the mouth and intense stomach pains), do not induce vomiting, because the substance will burn the digestive tract on its way up to the mouth. Instead, have the victim drink a glass of water or milk to dilute the poison. Discontinue dilution if it nauseates the victim. Daub mouth burns with milk or water and get the victim to the hospital.

6. If the victim has eaten a poisonous plant or swallowed an overdose of drugs, the poison control center may ask you to induce vomiting with a glass of salty water.

EMERGENCY:

HEART ATTACK

Prompt medical attention is essential for anyone suffering a heart attack.

Symptoms include:

- Agonizing pain and pressure in the center of the chest (often described as like being in a vise) that may extend to the arms, shoulders, and jaws

- Dizziness

- Irregular heartbeat

- Nausea

- Sense of impending death

- Shock

- Shortness of breath

- Sweating

- Unconsciousness

For someone who is conscious and having a heart attack:

1. Call EMS.

2. Administer CPR (see pages 306–309) if required.

3. Calm the victim and help him or her into a comfortable position.

4. Loosen clothing around the neck, chest, and waist.

5. Help the victim take angina medicine if it's been prescribed and is on hand.

6. Stay with the victim until help arrives.

For someone who is unconscious and having a heart attack:

1. Administer CPR if required (see pages 306–309), then call EMS.

2. Treat for unconsciousness (see page 298).

3. Stay with the victim until help arrives.

BE PREPARED

☞ Preparedness is one of the most valuable things you can bring to an emergency situation. Take a course in CPR or first aid; lots of organizations such as the YMCA and the Red Cross offer them regularly.

CARDIOPULMONARY RESUSCITATION (CPR)

STEP BY STEP

This life-saving technique restores breathing and restarts the heart in a victim experiencing cardiac or respiratory arrest. CPR involves two processes:

1. **Rescue breathing** (mouth-to-mouth resuscitation) fills the victim's lungs with oxygen, and

2. **Chest compressions** exert external pressure on the chest to force blood out of the heart into the arteries.

Note: The best way to learn CPR techniques is with a trained instructor, and to practice them on a mannequin, not a person. Organizations such as the YMCA and Red Cross regularly offer classes.

Before performing CPR:

You must determine that the victim is not breathing and has no pulse.

Never perform chest compressions if there is a pulse (see taking a pulse page 297).

1. Check to see if the victim is conscious.

2. Do not delay in performing CPR.

3. Call EMS—even if CPR works, swift medical attention is essential.

Rescue breathing
(mouth-to-mouth resuscitation):

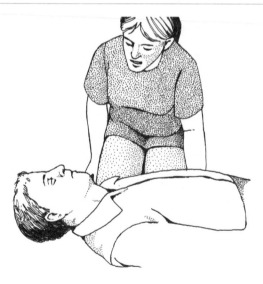

1. Place the victim on his or her back, with legs straight and the head at the same level as the heart.

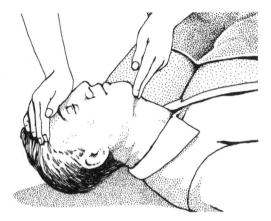

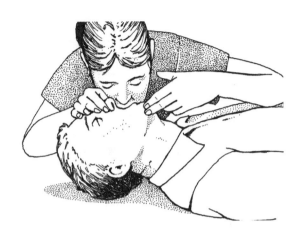

2. Kneel next to the victim's chest.

3. To open the airway, place one hand on the victim's forehead and two fingers under the chin. Push on the forehead and lift the chin at the same time, tilting the head back.

4. To check breathing, put your ear to the victim's mouth for 3 to 5 seconds; you may hear or feel a breath. If you do, stop and wait for EMS to arrive. If you don't, administer mouth-to-mouth resuscitation.

5. Pinch the victim's nose shut and put your lips tightly to the victim's mouth. Blow hard 2 times into the victim's mouth; each breath should last for 1 to 1½ seconds. Watch the victim's chest rise and fall before giving another breath.

6. If the victim does not begin to breathe, repeat the steps to open the airway and repeat mouth-to-mouth resuscitation. If the victim still doesn't begin breathing, administer the Heimlich maneuver, using the procedure for someone who is unconscious (see page 311).

(continued)

(continued)

Checking Circulation:

7. **If the victim is not breathing,** check his or her circulation. Place one hand on his or her forehead and gently tilt the head back while taking the pulse in the carotid artery in the groove between the voice box and the muscle on the side of the neck with the other hand for 5 to 10 seconds (see page 297).

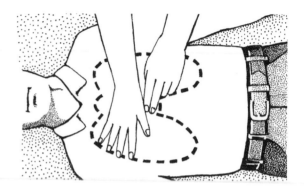

    If the victim has a pulse and is breathing, administer first aid for any injuries and wait for help to arrive.

    If the victim has a pulse but is not breathing, continue mouth-to-mouth resuscitation, giving 1 breath every 5 seconds and rechecking the pulse after every 12 breaths, until medical help arrives.

    If the victim has no pulse and is not breathing, proceed with CPR.

8. Locate the notch where the victim's ribs meet the breastbone in the center of the chest. Place the middle and index fingers of one hand on the notch, then place the other hand in the center of the victim's chest next to and above your index finger.

9. Lift your fingers from the notch and place the heel of that hand on top of the other hand. Interlace your fingers so as to keep them off the victim's chest.

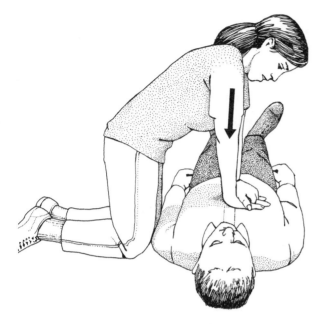

11. Repeat the procedure to open the airway by pushing on the forehead and lifting the chin, then use mouth-to-mouth resuscitation to give 2 more breaths.

12. Repeat 4 times the cycle of 15 compressions followed by 2 breaths, then check the pulse.

If the victim has a pulse and is breathing, administer first aid for any injuries and wait for help to arrive.

If the victim has a pulse but is not breathing, continue mouth-to-mouth resuscitation, giving 1 breath every 5 seconds. After 12 breaths, listen for breathing and check the pulse. Resume chest compressions if the pulse stops.

If the victim has no pulse and is not breathing, continue the cycles of 15 compressions and 2 breaths until he or she revives or help arrives.

10. Lean over the victim so your shoulders are directly above his or her breastbone. Keeping your arms straight, press forcefully down on the breastbone, which should depress about 1½ to 2 inches. Release by lifting up, but keep your hands firmly in place on the victim's breastbone. Push straight down and do not pause between compressions. Repeat 15 times, counting out loud, "One and two and three and…" at the rate of 80 to 100 a minute.

THE HEIMLICH MANEUVER

FOR ADULTS AND CHILDREN OVER ONE YEAR OLD

Be persistent when administering the Heimlich maneuver. When deprived of oxygen, a victim's muscles may relax and moves that were previously unsuccessful may work. Never push or poke an object stuck in the victim's throat; you may make the situation worse.

Do not delay in performing the Heimlich maneuver. Then call EMS.

If the victim is conscious:

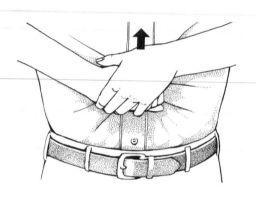

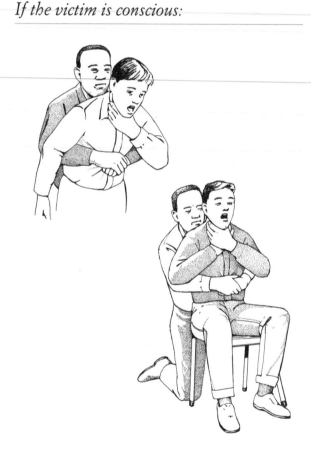

1. Stand behind the person; if the victim is seated, kneel behind the chair.

2. Wrap your arms around the victim.

3. Make a fist with one hand.

4. Place the fist so the thumb is against the victim's abdomen, just above the navel.

5. Grab your fist with your other hand.

6. Press your fist forcefully inward and upward with one quick thrust. Repeat the thrusts until the victim expels the object or becomes unconscious. If the victim becomes unconscious, follow the instructions for an unconscious choking victim (see opposite).

If the victim is unconscious:

1. Don't push or poke any object lodged in the victim's throat; you might force it farther down the airway.

2. Lower the victim to the ground onto his or her back.

3. Put one hand on his or her forehead, and gently tilt the head back with the fingers of your other hand under the victim's chin.

4. Pinch the nose shut, seal your lips around the victim's mouth, and give 2 breaths, each lasting at least a second. Let the chest rise and fall between breaths. If the breaths do not work, tilt the victim's head farther back and try again. If you are still unable to breathe air into the victim, begin abdominal thrusts:

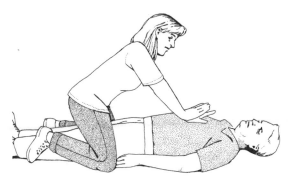

5. Kneel astride his or her thighs.

6. Place the heel of your hand on the abdomen just above the navel and place your other hand on top of it with fingers pointing toward the victim's head.

7. Press into the abdomen with 6 to 10 quick, forceful upward thrusts.

If these efforts fail:

8. Grasp the victim's tongue and jaw between your thumb and fingers, lift the jaw and probe the victim's mouth with your index finger, starting at the cheeks and moving to the back of the mouth. Don't push or poke any object lodged in the victim's throat; you might force it farther down the airway.

9. If you find the object, sweep it out gently.

10. If you can't find the object, repeat the breaths and the abdominal thrusts.

If you are alone and begin to choke:

Press your own fist against your upper abdomen with a quick upward thrust. Or lean forward and press your abdomen over any firm object, such as the back of a chair.

(continued)

THE HEIMLICH MANEUVER

(continued)

FOR THE PREGNANT OR OBESE

Do not delay in performing the Heimlich maneuver. Then call EMS.

If the victim is pregnant or obese and conscious:

1. Stand behind the victim and bring your arms around under the armpits. (If the victim is seated, kneel behind the chair.)

2. Place your fist so the thumb is directly in the *middle* of the breastbone. Place your other hand on top of your fist and apply thrusts as you would to the abdomen.

If the victim is pregnant or obese and unconscious:

1. Lay the victim flat on his or her back.

2. Kneel next to the victim and place the heel of one hand in the middle of the breastbone. Then place the heel of your other hand on top of the hand you've placed on the victim's breastbone and give quick, repeated thrusts.

3. Probe the victim's mouth with your finger (see step 8, page 311). If you find the object, sweep it out gently with your index finger. If you don't find the object, give 2 breaths then 6 to 10 more thrusts; repeat the sequence until the object is dislodged or medical help arrives.

FOR CONSCIOUS INFANTS

If the infant cannot cough, breathe, or cry, or is coughing weakly, the obstruction is life threatening. If a child is older than one year, you can use the thrusts as you would for an adult, but with gentler force (see pages 310–311). For a child under age one:

Do not delay in performing the Heimlich maneuver. Then call EMS.

1. Drape the infant facedown so his or her abdomen rests on your forearm with the head lower than the rest of the body. Support the head and neck firmly with one hand under the jaw. Rest your arm on your thigh.

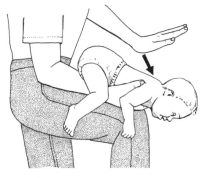

2. Deliver 4 blows directly between the shoulder blades with the heel of your free hand.

3. Immediately lay the infant flat on his or her back against your thigh or on a firm surface with the head lower than the chest.

4. With the heel of your hand or several fingers, press straight down on the breastbone with 4 quick thrusts, depressing the breast ½ to 1 inch each time.

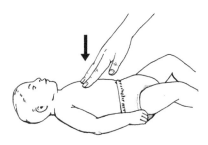

5. Continue this series of 4 back blows and 4 chest thrusts until the object is dislodged or the infant loses consciousness. If the infant loses consciousness, continue as you would for an unconscious infant (see page 314).

(continued)

THE HEIMLICH MANEUVER

(continued)

FOR UNCONSCIOUS INFANTS

Do not delay in performing the Heimlich maneuver. Then call EMS.

1. Lay the infant on his or her back.

2. Cup the forehead in one hand, place a finger under the chin, and, gently pressing on the forehead, lift the chin.

3. Put your ear to the infant's mouth for 5 seconds and listen for breathing. If the infant isn't breathing, keep the head tilted, seal your mouth around the infant's nose and mouth, and give 2 breaths that last at least 1 second each; wait for the infant's chest to rise and fall before you give another breath.

4. If you are unable to breathe air into the infant, tilt the head farther back and repeat the breaths.

5. If these breaths don't work, apply 4 back blows and 4 chest thrusts as you would for a conscious infant.

6. Check the infant's mouth to see if the object has been dislodged by depressing the tongue with your thumb while you lift the jaw back with your fingers. If the object has been dislodged, sweep it out with your little finger.

7. If the infant is not breathing, continue to breathe air into the mouth and nose. If the object has not been dislodged, repeat the sequence of breaths, back blows, and chest thrusts, checking the mouth for the object after each cycle.

8. Continue until the object is dislodged or medical help arrives.

INJURIES

BLEEDING

External

Don't assume that a wound that is not bleeding severely is not serious: The rate of blood flow is not a good gauge of the severity of the injury because certain areas of the body, such as the scalp, bleed more than others.

A minor wound will stop bleeding when a clot forms. With more serious wounds, however, blood can flow too quickly for clots to form. Bleeding from the arteries, which carry blood from the heart, tends to occur in spurts and is extremely serious because the victim can lose blood rapidly. Bleeding from the veins, which carry blood back to the heart, is usually steadier and easier to control.

To stop severe bleeding: Blood loss can cause shock or lead to death. In all but the most severe cases, these measures should stabilize the situation until you can get medical help.

1. Place sterile gauze or the cleanest cloth you can find on the wound and apply direct pressure.

2. If possible, raise the wound to a point above the heart to minimize the flow of blood to the injured area.

If bleeding continues, apply firm pressure to the body's pressure points.

- *The brachial point,* on the inside of the arm just above the elbow: for bleeding from an artery in the arm.

- *The femoral point,* at the juncture of the thighs and torso in the groin: for bleeding from an artery in the leg.

- *The superficial temporal artery,* at the sides of the head directly in front of the ears: for scalp wounds.

"STERILE" DEFINED

☞ Sterile dressings (gauze pads) are free from germs before use. If a dressing accidentally brushes the victim's skin while you're positioning it, discard it and use a fresh dressing. The skin's bacteria have probably contaminated the dressing.

HOW TO MAKE A PRESSURE BANDAGE

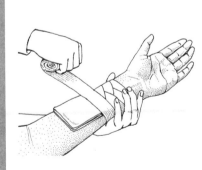

1. Wrap a large strip of gauze bandage or lengths of cloth firmly around any dressings you are holding on a wound.

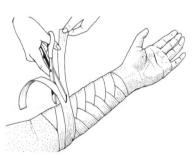

2. Split the end of the bandage into two strips and, placing one end around and under the wound, tie a knot.

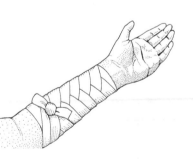

3. The bandage should be tight enough to control the bleeding but not so tight it cuts off circulation. Check the pulse at a point below the bandage; if there is no pulse or if the pulse is faint, the pressure bandage is too tight and must be loosened.

RECOGNIZING SHOCK

Someone who is bleeding profusely, has been burned severely, suffered multiple fractures, or is otherwise injured may go into shock. This is a potentially fatal condition.

SYMPTOMS INCLUDE:

- Drowsiness or confusion.
- Dull, sunken eyes.
- Moist and clammy skin or very pale and cold skin.
- Unusual thirst.
- Vomiting.
- Weak, rapid pulse.

Call EMS immediately and take the following steps:

1. If possible, lay the victim flat, face up, and elevate the legs about a foot.

2. Put blankets under and around the victim to prevent the loss of body heat, but do not overheat.

3. Don't give the victim anything to eat or drink. This can trigger vomiting.

SPECIAL CASES:

- If someone has incurred head, neck, or chest injuries or suffered a stroke, keep the head and chest elevated to relieve pressure on the brain.

- Place someone who's suffered a heart attack in a sitting position to make breathing easier.

- Lay someone who is vomiting on his or her side to avoid choking.

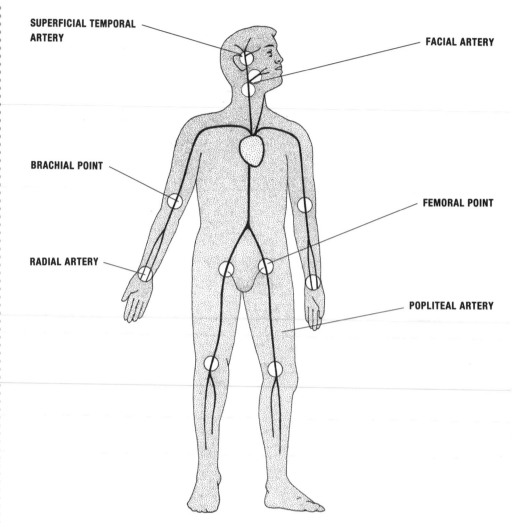

THE BODY'S PRESSURE POINTS

SUPERFICIAL TEMPORAL ARTERY

FACIAL ARTERY

BRACHIAL POINT

FEMORAL POINT

RADIAL ARTERY

POPLITEAL ARTERY

- *The facial artery,* at the lower edge of the jawbone: for bleeding from the lower part of the face.

- *The radial artery,* on the inside of the wrist near the base of the hand: for bleeding from the hand and fingers.

- *The popliteal artery,* at the back of the knee: for bleeding from the lower legs and feet.

When the bleeding stops or you need to free your hands, you can apply a pressure bandage (see page 315) until you are able to get medical help.

Internal

Someone who has been in an automobile accident, fallen, been struck, or suffered other injuries may develop internal bleeding. Symptoms include:

- Bruising
- Pale, clammy skin
- Severe chest pain
- Swelling or severe pain in the abdomen
- Vomiting or coughing up blood

If you suspect internal bleeding:

1. Call EMS immediately.

2. Lay the victim flat, with feet elevated about a foot. Cover with a blanket.

3. Keep the victim still.

CUTS AND ABRASIONS

Cuts and scrapes should always be treated thoroughly to avoid infection and speed healing. Wash your hands first.

1. Stop external bleeding if necessary (see page 315).

2. Rinse the wound with running water to remove dirt and other foreign material.

3. Pat the wound dry with a sterile pad and cover with a sterile dressing.

4. Seek medical attention if the wound seems serious.

PUNCTURE WOUNDS

Don't remove any embedded object; you could damage nerves, tendons, and blood vessels.

1 Stop the external bleeding (see page 315).

2. Flush the wound with running water.

3. See a physician, because these wounds may cause more tissue damage than you suspect.

SPRAINS AND FRACTURES

A **sprain** is an injury to the ligaments and tendons around a joint. A **fracture** is a break in the bone. To tell the difference, check for these signs:

Signs of Sprains:
- Localized pain and tenderness
- Redness
- Swelling

Signs of Fractures:
1. Bruising.

2. Deformed appearance of a limb or joint (compare the area with the same area on the other side of the body).

3. Exposed bone ends protruding through the skin (this is a compound fracture).

4. Inability to move or feel a bone or joint.

5. Localized pain and tenderness.

6. Swelling.

Treating Sprains and Fractures
If the injury appears to be a minor sprain, elevate the limb and call a physician;

APPLYING A TOURNIQUET

USE A TOURNIQUET ONLY IN emergencies when nothing else will stop the bleeding because it cuts off the blood supply and can result in the loss of the limb. After you apply a tourniquet, rush the victim to a doctor. Only a physician should remove a tourniquet, because the sudden flow of blood and possible blood loss can immediately send the person into severe shock.

 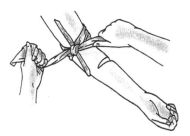 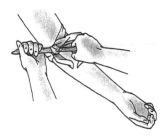

1. Wrap a wide piece of strong cloth around the limb above the wound, and tie it loosely in place with a half knot.

2. Place a short stick across the knot and tighten a full knot over it.

3. Twist the stick in a circle to tighten the tourniquet until the bleeding stops.

HOMEMADE SPLINTS AND SLINGS

☞ Keep a mental checklist of things around the house that may come in handy if you have to treat a fracture or sprain. Umbrellas, rulers, and scrap lumber can be used as splints. Scarves, napkins, and handkerchiefs can be used as slings. An old door or a table leaf is a makeshift stretcher. Sanitary napkins and disposable diapers can stanch heavy bleeding.

aspirin, rest, and occasional ice packs may be the only treatment necessary. However, it may be difficult to tell the difference between a sprain and a fracture without an X ray. Therefore, a serious sprain and a fracture require the same immediate attention: Immobilize the affected limb with a splint or sling and see a physician.

• Do not attempt to move an injured person if you suspect that bones in the neck, back, skull, or pelvis are affected; call EMS for help.

• Exposed bones are prone to severely damaging infection. Don't touch a bone that has broken through the skin or try to push it back into position; cover the area with a sterile dressing.

• If the wounded limb is bleeding, take measures to stop the bleeding (see pages 315–316) and elevate the limb slightly with pillows to lessen the flow of blood.

Making Splints and Slings

Immobilize a limb where you suspect a bone is fractured. Administer treatment at the scene of the injury. Walking even a few feet with a broken bone can cause damage and severe pain.

Almost any rigid material can be used as a splint: a stick, branch, ski, piece of board, or even a rolled-up newspaper. The material should be long enough to extend beyond the joints above and below the suspected fracture.

For Wrist and Lower Arm Injuries:

1. Place the injured arm across the upper abdomen at a right angle, palm inward.

2. Using folded newspaper or another soft material as a splint, wrap the lower arm from the elbow to the wrist.

3. Tie the splint in place with bandages or pieces of cloth.

4. Place the arm in a sling, making sure the hand is elevated several inches above the elbow. This will help reduce swelling.

For Upper Arm Injuries:

1. Place a small towel or other kind of padding under the victim's armpit.

2. Place the injured arm across the upper abdomen at a right angle, palm inward.

3. Wrap the outside of the upper arm in folded newspapers or another soft material and tie in place with pieces of cloth. Knots should be on the outside of the arm.

HOW TO MAKE A SLING

YOU CAN BUY or make slings for your emergency medical kit.

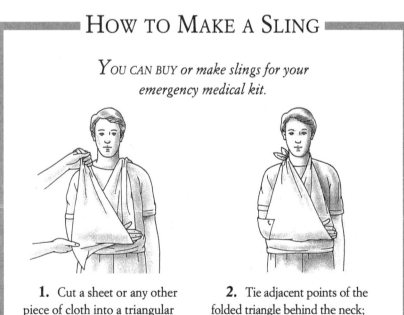

1. Cut a sheet or any other piece of cloth into a triangular shape. Two sides should be about 40 inches long and the third about 55 inches long.

2. Tie adjacent points of the folded triangle behind the neck; fasten the second point to the front of the sling near the elbow.

4. Place the lower arm in a sling for support, then create a larger sling by wrapping a towel around the injured arm and chest, bringing it across the back, and tying it under the uninjured arm.

For Hand Injuries:
Follow the same splint and sling procedures as you would for an upper arm injury. In this case, however, the splint will extend from the elbow to the end of the hand.

For Elbow Injuries:
If the elbow is bent, do not try to unbend it. Instead, support the arm with the two slings you would make for an upper arm injury and see a physician.

If the elbow is not bent, keep the arm straight and apply padded splints to the inside and outside of the arm.

1. Place folded newspaper or towels on either side of the arm.

2. Place rulers, sticks, or other stiff materials on the outside of the padding.

3. Wrap cloth strips around the arm and tie.

If materials for a splint are not available, put a pillow between the injured arm and the torso and secure by bringing several strips of cloth around the injured arm and across the torso.

For Ankle or Foot Injuries:
1. Remove the shoe.

2. Wrap a pillow, a rolled towel, or a folded blanket around the leg from the calf to the end of the foot.

3. Tie the material in place with strips of cloth.

For Leg Injuries:
Use the uninjured leg to support the injured leg.
1. Gently straighten the injured leg so it is parallel to the uninjured leg.

2. Place padding (a rolled towel, folded blanket, or other soft material) between the legs, from the crotch to the heels.

3. Tie the legs together with bands of cloth, avoiding the injured area of the leg.

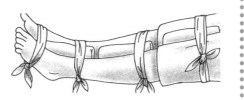

For Kneecap Injuries:

Find a board or other flat, stiff material that is at least 4 inches wide and long enough to reach from the heel to beyond the buttocks. Wrap towels or sheets around it for padding.

1. Gently straighten the leg and place the padded splint beneath it.

2. Tie the splint in place by wrapping pieces of cloth around the board and leg at the thigh, above and below the knee, and the ankle.

For Finger Injuries:

You can put a piece of gauze between the injured finger and the next digit and tape them together, or use a flat piece of wood, such as a Popsicle stick or an emery board, as a splint.

1. Gently straighten the finger.

2. Place the splint under the finger and tie it in place by wrapping tape or cloth around the splint and finger.

BURNS

The severity of a burn determines the kind of aid that should be administered. Keep a burned limb elevated to reduce swelling.

The effect of any burn can be reduced by immediate and sustained cooling with cold water.

First-Degree Burns

The burn you might get when you briefly touch a hot pot or iron is a first-degree burn. These burns affect the epidermis, the outer layer of skin, and cause blistering, peeling, and redness. They generally don't require professional medical attention.

1. Run cold water over the burned area. Don't apply butter or other fats because these may trigger an infection. It is especially important to flush a burn caused by contact with chemicals with cold running water.

2. Remove rings, watches, shoes, and constrictive clothing from a burned area immediately; it may be hard to do so once the area begins to swell.

3. Lightly cover the burn with a non-fluffy, nonadhesive sterile bandage.

Second-Degree Burns

These burns damage the epidermis and the layer of skin beneath it, the dermis. Second-degree burns can be very painful but they usually do not cause scarring.

Seek medical attention if the burn is especially painful, seems severe, or is dirty. Don't break the blisters that often appear soon after the skin is burned, and don't try to pick off pieces of clothing that may adhere to the burned flesh.

1. Soak the burned area in cold water.

2. Remove jewelry and constrictive clothing before the area begins to swell.

3. Lightly cover the burn with a non-fluffy, nonadhesive sterile bandage.

Third-Degree Burns

These burns destroy all layers of skin and may even reach underlying muscle and bones. It may be necessary to treat a severe burn victim for shock (see pages 302 and 316); check to see if the victim is unusually clammy and pale or if breathing has become shallow.

1. Call EMS.

2. Lay the victim down, feet propped up.

3. Pour cold water over the burn.

EYE INJURIES

Burns
1. Flush the eye with sterile saline solution or cool water.
2. Lay a cool compress over the eye but do not apply pressure.
3. Call EMS or see a doctor.

Chemical Exposure
1. Try to determine the substance involved and call your local poison control center for advice; if the injury is serious, call EMS.
2. Hold the eyelid open and flush the affected eye for 10 minutes by pouring a steady stream of sterile saline solution or water from the inside of the eye (next to the nose) to the outside.
3. Cover both eyes with patches or gauze bandaged loosely in place.
4. Seek medical help.

Cuts and Blows
1. If the injury is serious, call EMS.
2. Apply cold compresses to reduce swelling.
3. Apply sterile dressings to cuts around the eyes.
4. Seek medical help if the eyeball seems to have been injured or if blood is visible inside the eye.

Penetration
1. Call EMS.
2. Leave the object in place.
3. Wash your hands.
4. For a large puncture, put a paper cup or a similar object over the eye and tape it in place. Cover the uninjured eye with an eye patch or sterile dressing. By covering both eyes, you will minimize eye movement that might damage the injured eye.

Removing a Foreign Object
1. Wash your hands with soap and water.
2. Seat the victim in good light and gently pull the upper eyelid down. Tears may wash the object out.
3. If the object remains in the eye, pour a steady stream of sterile saline solution or water over the eyeball from the inside of the eye (inner corner) to the outside.
4. If the object remains, pull down the lower eyelid. If the object is visible, remove it with a clean moistened cloth or tissue.
5. If the object is not visible, lay a cotton swab or similar object across the outside of the upper eyelid. Have the victim look down. Gently grasp the eyelashes, and fold the eyelid back over the swab. You should be able to see the object. Remove it with a clean moistened cloth or tissue, or the corner of a folded piece of clean paper.

SPLINTERS

These common nuisances must be removed carefully to avoid infection. Seek medical attention if the splinter is deeply embedded, breaks off beneath the skin, or if redness, pus, or red streaks (signs of infection) appear near the wound.

If the splinter protrudes from the skin, grasp it with sterilized tweezers as close to the point of entry as possible and pull it out at the same angle at which it entered the body.

If the splinter is beneath the skin, use the tip of a sterilized needle to loosen the skin and lift the splinter out. You can sterilize a needle by holding it over an open flame for a few seconds, by boiling it in water, or by pouring antiseptic over it.

1. When the splinter has been removed, squeeze the wound until it bleeds, which will wash out bacteria and dirt.
2. Wash the area with soap and water and apply a clean adhesive bandage.

ANIMAL BITES

The bite of any animal can cause serious infection, so take first aid seriously. Call EMS if the bites are deep. If the bite was inflicted by a wild animal or an unfamiliar domestic animal, be prepared to describe it to animal-control authorities. They may be able to capture the animal and observe it for rabies. If the animal can't be captured, the victim may have to undergo a series of rabies vaccinations.

After a bite, a victim should watch for signs of serious infection, such as redness, discharge, and red streaks spreading from the wound toward the heart, and get medical help immediately if they appear.

1. Wash your hands or put on sterile latex gloves.

2. If the wound is not bleeding seriously, wash it carefully with soap and water.

3. If the bleeding is severe, control the blood flow (see pages 315–316). Get medical help.

SNAKEBITES

Although snakebites are fairly common, most are inflicted by nonpoisonous snakes and only rarely cause serious injury or death. Swift medical attention is essential for any snakebite, but especially for bites by poisonous snakes, because snake venom can destroy tissue and cause death.

Four venomous snakes inhabit the United States: rattlesnakes, water moccasins, copperheads, and coral snakes (see box).

If someone is bitten by any venomous snake other than a coral snake:

1. Help the victim into a comfortable position.

2. Tie a belt or other band about 2 to 4 inches above the bite. The band must not cut off circulation. You should be able to slip a finger under the band and feel a pulse in the limb beneath the band.

3. Immobilize the limb with a splint.

4. If medical help is not readily available, use a snakebite kit to flush out the wound. With the blade provided or a sterilized knife or razor blade, make a cut no deeper than half an inch through each fang mark. Use the suction cups in the kit to draw out venom. You may also suck out the venom, but only if you do not have cuts or sores in your mouth. Spit out the venom as you suck it out. Whether you remove the venom orally or with the suction cups, allow at least half an hour to suction the wound.

5. Apply a sterile dressing to the wound.

6. Bandage the area.

7. Seek medical attention quickly, alerting the facility ahead of time to have the proper antivenom serum handy.

POISONOUS SNAKES

Know what poisonous snakes look like, so you and medical authorities can administer the proper treatment. Rattlesnakes, copperheads, and water moccasins are known as pit vipers, because they have deep pits between their eyes and their nostrils. These snakes also have triangular-shaped heads and slitlike eyes. Coral snakes have roundish heads, round eyes, and black nostrils. They have yellow, red, and black rings.

RATTLESNAKE

WATER MOCCASIN

COPPERHEAD

CORAL SNAKE

If someone is bitten by a coral snake (the venom of the coral snake can be more potent than that of other snakes):

1. Wash the area immediately.

2. Immobilize the limb with a splint.

3. Keep the bitten area below the victim's heart and **seek medical attention immediately.**

INSECT BITES

Insect bites cause a reaction that can range from slight redness to extreme swelling and itching. If the reaction seems to be severe, contact a physician.

- Wash the area with soap and water.

- Apply calamine lotion to relieve discomfort.

- Avoid scratching the area.

Insect stings
Bees, wasps, hornets, and yellow jackets inject venom that can cause pain, redness, and swelling for up to 48 hours. They can also cause anaphylactic shock (see page 303).

1. Using a sterilized needle, knife blade, or a fingernail, gently pry from beneath the skin the stinger and the sting sac that insects often leave behind. Be especially careful while removing the sting sac so you don't press on it and force more venom into the skin.

2. Wash the area with soap and water.

3. Apply hydrocortisone cream and cold compresses to reduce swelling.

Tick Bites
To avoid tick bites, wear long-sleeved shirts and long pants tucked into socks when walking through heavily wooded or grassy areas.

Because ticks carry various diseases, including Lyme disease, it is important to try to avoid them or to remove them immediately if bitten. To dislodge a tick:

1. Cover the tick with petroleum jelly, salad oil, or some other heavy oil to close its breathing pores. If the tick does not disengage at once, wait half an hour, then remove it carefully with tweezers. If the head remains embedded in the skin, have a physician remove it to avoid infection.

2. Wash the area with hot, soapy water and rubbing alcohol.

3. Apply hydrocortisone cream.

Tick

Spider Bites
For most spider bites, it is necessary only to clean the area with soap and water. However, the bites of black widow and brown recluse spiders can be very serious. The bite of a brown recluse produces a stinging sensation followed by severe pain and tissue damage. Black widow bites cause pain, swelling, severe nausea, and breathing difficulties. To treat these bites:

1. Keep the bitten area at a level lower than the heart.

2. Place a cold compress on the bite.

3. Get medical attention immediately.

Scorpion Stings
These stings can cause intense burning pain followed by tingling, numbness, seizures, and severe nausea.

1. Keep the area affected by the sting at a level lower than the heart.

2. Place a cold compress on the sting.

3. Get medical attention immediately.

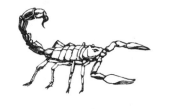

Scorpion

TO CATCH AN INSECT

☛ Proper insect identification can determine the kind of treatment that's administered to a bite victim. Capture the offending insect or spider by placing a cup or glass over it and sliding a piece of paper underneath. Hand it over to the medical unit attending the victim.

INDEX

Numbers in italic indicate illustrations.

A AA (Automobile Association of
   America), 272
abrasions, first aid for, 317
abrasive cleaners, 31
acoustical tile, 48
acrylic furniture, 34
air conditioners, 231, 232, 243
   home security and, 293
   mildew and molds in, 289
   reverse-cycle, 229, 231
air filter, car, 264, 265, *265*
air fresheners, 31, 290
alcoholic beverages, 105
allergic reactions, 22, 30, 285, 289
   anaphylactic shock, 303, 323
altering clothes, 84–86
aluminum furniture, 60
aluminum utensils, 53, 55, 135
ammonia, 30, 31
anaphylactic shock, 303, 323
anchors, 216, 217, *217*
animal bites, 322
animal pests, 255
antifreeze, 261
antiques, 185
ants, 254
appliances, 128, 140, 196
   buying of, 196
   carbon monoxide and, 289
   circuit breakers and, 241
   fires and, 282, 286, 288
   gas, 288, 289, 290
   hot weather and, 232
   installation of, 196, 288
   maintenance of, 140
   safety and, 143, 282, 283, 285
   small, 54–55, 130
   warranties on, 20
   see also specific appliances
appliquéd garments, 82

art, framed, 189
asbestos, 280, 290
ashes, fireplace, 45
asphalt floors, 39
attics:
   animal pests and, 255
   fans in, 232, *232*
   leaks in, 243-44
automobile, *see* car
Automobile Association of America
   (AAA), 272
awnings, 60, 232

B aby's room, 59
baking soda, 31
bamboo furniture, 35
bandage, pressure, 315, *315*
bank accounts, 11
   checking, 4, 5, *5*, 17, 293
   insurance and, 19
   statements of, 2, 4, 5
bar, setting up of, 153, 154
barbecues, 60, 121, 290
   carbon monoxide and, 289
basement, 60
   animal pests and, 255
   cleaning of, 60
   safety in, 285, *285*
   security and, 292
bathrooms:
   checklist for safety and efficiency in,
      199
   cleaning of, 23, 24, 32, 57-59, 290
   decorating of, 199–200
   exhaust fans in, 233
   fixtures in, 199–200; *see also* bathtubs;
      showers; sinks; toilets
   framed art in, 189
   mildew and molds in, 289
   painting of, 169
   safety in, 199, 282, 283, 285, *285*

bathtubs, 199
   cleaning of, 32, 57, 58
   clogged drains in, 238–39
   safety and, 283, 285
battery, car, 266, 267, 291
beaded garments, 78, 81, 82, 94
beans, 96, 97, 103, 104
   in Food Guide Pyramid, 98, 99
bedding, 30, 72, 78
   dust mites and, 289
bedrooms, painting of, 169
beds, *188*
   buying of, 187
bed sheets, curtains from, 176, 179
beef, 106, 115
   food safety and, 116, 117–18
   lowering fat intake and, 103
   microwave cooking of, 123
   refrigeration of, 131
   roasting of, 116
bee stings, 323
belt buckles, 94
belts, 90
bidets, 200
birds, 255
bites:
   animal, 322
   insect, 323
   snake, 322–23
blankets, 72
bleaches, 30, 32, 63, 64, 68, 75
bleaching, dos and don'ts for, 64
bleeding, 315–16
blenders, 54, 138
blinds, window, 45–46, 60, 178, *178*, 232
blouses, ironing of, 80, *80*
bluing, 65, 68
boilers, 228–29
bolts, *206*
   expansion and toggle, 216, *216*
bookcases, 203
bookshelves, putting up, 216, 217, *217*

boots, 89–90, 94
boot trees, 94
box springs, 187
    standard sizes of, 188
brake fluid, 262
brakes, car, 264
    problems with, 268, 275–76
bran, 96, 103
brass, 56
brass and copper cleaner, 56
    homemade, 55
breads, 96, 97, 104
    in Food Guide Pyramid, 98, 99
breakers, circuit, 241, 280, 285
brick, 40, 48, 184
briefcases, 90
broilers, broiling, 51, 280
brooms, 28, 28, 29
brushes:
    for cleaning, 28, 28, 29
    for painting, 166, 246
budget, 2–4
    home buying and, 13
    sample, 3
burglars, 286, 292
burners, 50–51, 51
    safety and, 120, 283, 285
burns:
    first aid for, 320
    prevention of, 282
    shock and, 316
buttons, 87
    dry cleaning and, 82
    sewing of, 83, 83, 87, 87

Cabinets and cupboards:
    children and, 283
    cleaning of, 49
    decorating and, 192–93
    formaldehyde in, 289
    organization of, 198, 198, 203
cane furniture, 35
Canned Food Information Council, 134
canned goods, 122, 128, 131
canning, 134, 135
can openers, 54, 138
canvas furniture, 60
capons, 106
    roasting of, 119
car, 257–78, 290, 292
    accidents, 272–73
    anatomy of, 259
    batteries of, 267, 291
    brake problems in, 268, 275–76
    bulbs in, 268–69
    checklist for maintenance of, 260

changing air filter of, 264, 265, 265
changing tires of, 270–71, 270
children in, 276
cold weather driving and, 273
controlling skidding in, 275
drive system in, 261
driving in rain or fog, 274
driving on ice or snow, 274
engine problems in, 266–67
exterior appearance of, 277–78
failure of, 266–69
fogged windows in, 274
fuses in, 269
insurance for, 12, 19–20, 269
jump-starting of, 267, 267
kit for, 263
overheating of, 273
paint touch-ups for, 277, 278
preventive maintenance for, 258–65, 269
road emergencies and, 272–76
safety and, 258, 276
seasonal care for, 264
self-service checks for, 261–65, 261, 263
spills and drippings from, 60
starting problems in, 266, 268
steering problems in, 268
stuck, 273–74
used, 258
vinyl repair for, 278
warranties on, 20
washing of, 277–78
waxing of, 277, 278
carbohydrates, 96, 97
    increasing intake of, 104
carbon monoxide, 289–90
cardiopulmonary resuscitation (CPR), 282, 305, 306–9
carjacking, 275
carpenter ants, 254
carpet beetles, 254
carpet fresheners, 25, 31
carpets, carpeting:
    area rugs and, 156, 180
    backing of, 180
    cleaning of, 32, 40–43
    color and, 157
    decorating and, 180–82
    dents in, 41
    dry-cleaning powders for, 43
    dust mites and, 289
    formaldehyde in, 289
    heating system and, 229
    indoor pollutants and, 290
    longevity of, 159

padding for, 182
pile of, 181, 181
protection for, 156
quality of, 181
repairing burns and holes in, 224, 225, 225
safety and, 283, 284
    see also rugs
carpet sweeper, 29
carsickness, 276
cast iron utensils, 55, 137
caulking air leaks, 234
cedar, 93, 254
ceiling fans, 48, 233, 243
ceilings:
    asbestos in, 290
    cleaning of, 47–48
    repair of, 214–15
ceramic pots and pans, 137
ceramic tiles, 40, 184
    repair of, 215, 215, 225, 226
cereals, 97, 104, 128, 129
    in Food Guide Pyramid, 98, 99
chairs, repair of, 211–12, 212
champagne, 154
    uncorking of, 152, 152
chandeliers, 48
checking accounts, 4, 17
    security and, 5, 5, 293
cheese:
    in Food Guide Pyramid, 98, 99
    food safety and, 122
    refrigeration of, 128, 130
chemicals, 252, 285
    disposal of, 291
    pool, 282
chests and trunks, 203
chicken, 106, 115
    food safety and, 120
    microwave cooking of, 123
    roasting of, 119
children:
    cleaning and, 59
    decorating and, 158
    parties for, 150–51
    storage and, 203, 204
children, safety and, 283
    in car, 276
    electrical outlets and, 243
    grills and, 121
    in kitchen, 120, 123, 143, 283
    lawn chemicals and, 252
    tools and, 206
chimneys, 229–30

carbon monoxide and, 289
fire prevention and, 280
china, 145
chipping of, 145
cleaning of, 55-56
mending of, 210
storage of, 56
choking, 299
cholesterol, 97
chopping blocks, 49
chrome, 34
chrysanthemums, 289
cigarette smoking, 282, 289
circuit breakers, 241, 280, 285
cleaning, 21-60
allergies and, 22, 30, 289
of barbecue grills, 60
of bathroom, 23, 24, 32, 57-59,
290
of ceilings, 47-48
clutter and, 9, 22, 156, 203, 283
cooking habits and, 53
of curtains and draperies, 46
of dishes, cookware, and utensils,
55-56
of doors, 44-46
of electronic equipment, 37-38
equipment for, 25-30
of floors, 38-43
of furniture, 33-38, 60
of glass, 32, 34, 37, 44
of kitchen, 23, 24, 49-56
of lamps and lamp shades, 37
of mirrors, 37, 58
of nursery, 59
of porches, decks, and patios, 60
products for, 30, 31-32, 291
professional help for, 22
of rugs and carpets, 29, 32, 40-43,
72
saving time and, 22
timetable for, 23-24
of upholstery, 33-34
of walls, 47-48
of windows, 44-46
cleansers, 30
closets, 203, 204, 204
clothes, 78-94
camouflaging tears in, 86
dry cleaning of, 82
fur, see fur

ironing of, 78-81, 80-81, 87
jewelry, 91, 293
leather, 82, 89-90
sewing of, see sewing
storage of, 93-94, 204, 204
suitcase packing, 92-93, 92
see also laundry
clothes dryers, see dryers, clothes
clutter, 9, 22, 156, 203, 283
cobwebs, 47
cockroaches, 254
coffeemakers, 54, 138
cold weather maintenance, 256
color, 156-59, 162, 165
wheel, 157, 157
color bleeding, in fabric, 74
comforters, 72
computers, 201
cleaning of, 37, 38
cooking, 115-27
cleaning and, 53
equivalents used in, 126-27
fire prevention and, 282, 284
ingredient substitution in, 127
lowering fat intake and, 103
microwave, 122, 123; see also
microwave ovens
nutrition and, 115
safety and, 143, 285
terms used in, 124-25
see also food
cooking utensils, see utensils
cook tops, 50-51, 144, 196
cookware, 135-37, 144
for baking, 143
basic, 136, 136
burned, 56
buying of, 135
cleaning of, 55-56
nonstick, 56, 137
safety and, 143, 285
storage of, 193, 198
cooling systems, 231-33
see also air conditioners; fans
cooperative buying, 105
copper and brass cleaner, 56
homemade, 55
copper cookware, 56, 137
cosmetics, 285
cottons, 70-72, 78
storage of, 93-94

countertops, 49, 193, 198, 283
coupons, 106
CPR (cardiopulmonary resuscitation),
282, 305, 306-9
crabgrass, 252
cream, 128, 130
credit, 2, 6-7
for furniture purchases, 186
home equity line of, 17
records of, 11
credit cards, 2, 6, 7, 11
credit rating, 6-7
crystal, 55-56
caring for, 149
chipping of, 145
lead, 146
cupboards, see cabinets and
cupboards
curtains and draperies:
from bed sheets, 176, 179
cleaning of, 46
decorating and, 156, 176, 177
fire prevention and, 282
for glass doors, 176
home security and, 292, 293
measuring windows for, 176
styles of, 179
weather and, 228, 232
cushions, 34, 186, 187
dust mites and, 289
cuts, first aid for, 317
cutting boards, 49, 198

Dairy products, 96, 97
in Food Guide Pyramid, 98, 99
food safety and, 121-22
labels on, 107
lowering fat intake and, 103
refrigeration of, 128, 130
storage of, 128
darning, 84, 84
debt, 2, 6, 13
decks, 60
decorating, 155-204
of bathroom, 199-200
checklist for, 158
closet organization, 204, 204
color in, 156-59, 162, 165
floor plan in, 156, 160, 160
floors in, 180-84
flowers in, 190, 191

furniture arrangement in, 159-62
furniture selection in, 185-88
of home office, 201, 202
of kitchen, 192-98
lighting in, 162-64
painting in, *see* paint; painting
with professional designers, 161
storage and, 203
style and, 159
time and money-saving hints for, 156
traffic patterns and, 161, 162
wall coverings in, *see* wallpaper; wallpapering
wall decorations in, 189–90
window treatments in, 176–79
deer, 255
den furniture, 186
desk, 201
detergents, 30, 63, 68, 74
diapers, 64
dimmer switches, 162, 163, 243
dirt, 22
dishes, 55–56
see also china
dishwashers, 53–54, 144, 145, 196
loading of, 54, 55
disposers, food, 50, 236
door locks, 218, 220, *220*
anatomy of, 293, *293*
doors:
anatomy of, *219*
cleaning of, 44–46
glass, 176, 293
hinges of, 218, 220
home security and, 292, 293
painting frames of, 156
rattling doorknobs on, 220
repair of, 218–20
squeaky, 218
door sweeps, 234, *234*
down jackets, coats, and comforters, 72
drafts, 234
drain cleaners, 30, 32, 291
drains, 236
clogs in, 50, 238–39
draperies, *see* curtains and draperies
drawers, 49
dresses, ironing of, 81, *81*
drive belts, 264–65

drop cloths, 169, 170
drowning, 283
dry cleaning, 82
dryers, clothes, 62–63, 70
fire prevention and, 282
gas leaks from, 288
hot weather and, 232
troubleshooting chart for, 71
drywall, holes in, 215
duck, duckling, 106
microwave cooking of, 123
roasting of, 119
dust, 22
dusting, 30, 38
products for, 29, 30, 32, 35
dust mites, 30, 289
dustpans, 29

Eggs, 96, 97
in Food Guide Pyramid, 98, 99
food safety and, 121
labels on, 107
lowering fat intake and, 103
refrigeration of, 130
elderly, safety and, 283
electrical accidents:
fires, 286
prevention of, 282, 283
shock, 302
electricity, electrical system, 241–43
circuit breakers and fuses in, 241, 242, 280, 285
outlets in, 242, *242*, 243, 282, 283
surges in, 201
switches in, 243, 282
electrolytic cleaning, 56
electronic equipment, 37–38, 293
emergencies, 280, 286–88
preparedness in, 305
telephone numbers for, 280
when to call EMS in, 296
see also first aid; injuries
Emergency Medical Services (EMS), 296
emergency road service plans, 272
enamel-on-steel pots and pans, 137
engine, car, 264
coolant hoses in, 265
problems with, 266–67
entertaining, 150–54

timetable for, 151
equity, 2, 17
estate planning, 2, 12
exhaust fans, 233, 290
expansion bolts, 216, *216*
extension cords, 282
exterior painting, 246
eye injuries, 321

Fabric(s):
color bleeding in, 74
formaldehyde in, 289
scraps, uses for, 84
swatches, 162
fabric softeners, 63, 65, 68, 70
fainting, 297
falls, avoiding of, 280
fans, 231–32, 285
attic, 232, *232*
ceiling, 48, 233, 243
exhaust, 233, 290
fasteners (clothing), 83, *83*
fasteners (hardware), *206*
fats, 97, 104
in Food Guide Pyramid, 98
lowering intake of, 97, 103–4
faucets, 196, 199, 200
cartridge, 238, *239*
cleaning of, 49–50, 57
leaky, 236, 237–38
with washers, 237–38, *238*
feather dusters, 29
fences, 293
fertilizers, 248, 252
fiber, dietary, 96, 103
files and records, 8–9, 8, 9, 11–12
finances, 1–20
checkbook security, 5, 5
credit, 2, 6–7
file organization, 8–9, *8, 9*
home buying, 13–17
important papers, 10–12
money management, 2–4
mortgages, 15–17
property insurance, 18–20
fire extinguishers, 284, 287
fireplace inserts, 229
fireplaces, 45, 229–30
anatomy of, *230*
animal pests and, 255
carbon monoxide and, 289

fire prevention and, 280
fires:
  grilling and, 121
  kitchen, 120
  prevention of, 280–82, 284
  putting out, 286
  smoke and, 286–87
  types of, 286
  what to do in case of, 286–88
firewood, 230
first aid, 295–314
  for anaphylactic shock, 303
  cardiopulmonary resuscitation (CPR), 306–9
  for choking, 299
  for electric shock, 302
  for fainting, 297
  for heart attack, 305
  for heat exhaustion, 300
  for heat stroke, 301
  Heimlich maneuver, 310–14
  for hypothermia, 300
  for poisoning, 304
  preparedness and, 305
  for unconsciousness, 298
  see also injuries
fish, 96, 97
  buying of, 106
  in Food Guide Pyramid, 98, 99
  food safety and, 120–21
  labels on, 107
  odors from, 116
  refrigeration of, 128, 131
fixtures, wall, 48
flammable materials, 280, 282, 285, 291
  laundry and, 70
flavorings, 97, 112–14
fleas, 255
flies, 254
floods, 288
floor plans, 156, 160, 160
floors, flooring:
  asbestos in, 290
  brick, 40, 184
  ceramic tile, 40, 184, 225, 226
  cleaning of, 38–43
  decorating and, 180–84
  falls and, 280
  nonresilient, 40, 184
  removing polish from, 40

repair of, 224–27
resilient, 38, 39–40
in small spaces, 193
stone, 40, 184
vinyl, 39, 40, 182, 183
waxed, removing stains from, 39
wood, 38–39, 40, 182–83, 183, 224–25, 226, 227
floor scrubber/polisher, 29
flowers, 190, 191, 191
fluorescent bulbs, 162
food, 96–135
  canned, 122, 128, 131
  canning of, 134, 135
  eating well, 96–105
  labels on, 103, 107, 128, 134
  nutrients in, 100–102
  odors from, 116
  preparation space for, 193
  safety and, 116–22
  shopping for, 105–14, 117, 132
  storage of, 128–35
  see also cooking; kitchen
food disposers, 50, 236
Food Guide Pyramid, 98–99
food processors, 54, 138
formaldehyde, 280, 289
fractures, first aid for, 317–20
frames, framing, 189–90
freezers, 52–53, 140–44
freezing, 105, 128–29
  hints for, 129
frozen foods, 132, 133
fruits, 96, 97, 103, 104
  buying of, 110–11
  in Food Guide Pyramid, 98, 99
  food safety and, 122
  freezing of, 129
  refrigeration of, 128, 130
  ripening of, 111
fur, 89–90, 94
  dry cleaning of, 82
  insect pests and, 254
furnaces, 30, 228
  carbon monoxide and, 289
  fire prevention and, 280
  gas leaks from, 288
furniture:
  antique, 185
  arrangement of, 159–62
  buying of, 185, 186

care of, 33, 185
cleaning of, 33–38, 60
decorating and, 159–62, 185–88
fire prevention and, 282
heating system and, 229
for home office, 201
longevity of, 159
multipurpose, 187
outdoor, 60
porch or den, refurbishing of, 186
traffic patterns and, 159, 161, 162
upholstered, 30
wood, see wood furniture
furniture polish, 30, 34, 35
fuses:
  in car, 269
  in home, 241, 242, 280, 285

Garage, 60, 290
  car supplies to keep in, 258
  dooropeners, 285
  flammable fluids and, 280
  safety in, 285, 285
garage door openers, electric, 285
garden, see yard
garlic, 49
gas-burning appliances, 289, 290
  leaks from, 288
gas lines, 280, 285
gasoline, 70, 262
gas stations, 262
  self-service car care at, 261–65, 261, 263
gems, precious, 91
glass:
  cleaning of, 32, 34, 37, 44
  doors, 176, 293
  picture, 37
  pool safety and, 282
  removing paint from, 44
  window, replacement of, 223, 223
glass-fiber textiles, 72
glassware, 55–56, 146–49
  cookware, 143
  crystal, 55–56, 145, 146, 149
  mending of, 210
  pots and pans, 137
  stacked, unsticking of, 56
  storage of, 56
  types of, 148, 148
  white deposits on, 55

gloves:
   leather, care of, 90, 94
   work, 46, 248
glue:
   application of, 210, *210*
   for mending furniture, 212
   spilled, 210
   types of, 210
goggles, safety, 248, 252
gold jewelry, 91
Good Samaritan laws, 295
goose, 106
   roasting of, 119
grains, 96, 103, 104, 129
   complete proteins from vegetables
      and, 99
   in Food Guide Pyramid, 98
grass:
   varieties of, 250
   see also lawns
grease fires, 286
grills, grilling, 60, 121, 290
   carbon monoxide and, 289
grocery lists, 105, 115
grocery shopping, 105–14, 117
   frozen foods and, 132
ground-fault circuit interrupters
   (GFCI), 242, 282
grout, 57
   stained, 49
gutter guards, 245–46, *246*
gutters, 245–46
   anatomy of, *246*
   leaky, 245, *245*
gypsum board, holes in, 215

Halogen bulbs, 162
handbags, 90, 94
hand washing, 74
hanging decorative objects, 189, 190,
   216–17
hard water:
   determining of, 65
   removing buildup from, 65
   soaps and, 64
   softening of, 63. 65, 68, 240
hazardous products, 252, 285
   disposal of, 291
headlights, 274
health, 279–323
   first aid kit, 294

indoor pollutants and, 289–91
information agencies for, 280
   see also emergencies, medical;
      injuries
health insurance, 12
health records, 12
heart attack, 305
heart rate, 297
heaters, space, 282, 290
heat exhaustion, 283, 300
heating ducts, 290
heating systems, 228–30
   carbon monoxide and, 289
heat pumps (reverse-cycle air
   conditioners), 229, 231
heat stroke, 301
hedges, 293
Heimlich maneuver, 310–14
   for infants, 313–14
   for the pregnant or obese, 312
hemming garments, 86
herbs, 97, 105, 112, 113
hinges, 218, 220
home buying, 2, 13–17
   checklist for, 14
home-owner's insurance, 18–19
hook-and-eye fasteners, sewing of, 83,
   83
hook scraper, 169
hornet stings, 323
hot-water boilers, 228
hot-water heaters, 284
houseflies, 254
household linens, 78
houseplants, 289
   hanging of, 216, 217
housing records, 12
humidifiers, 289
humidity, 289
hydronic heaters, 228
hypothermia, 283, 300

Incandescent bulbs, 162
income tax records, 12
injuries, 315–23
   animal bites, 322
   bleeding from, 315–16
   burns, 320
   cuts and abrasions, 317
   eye, 321
   insect bites and stings, 323

puncture wounds, 317
shock and, 316
snakebites, 322–23
splinters, 321
splints and slings for, 318–20, *318,
   319, 320*
sprains and fractures, 317–20
insects, 254, 255
   bites and stings from, 323
insulation:
   asbestos in, 290
   formaldehyde in, 289
   pipe, 233
   where to put, 235, *235*
   window, 234
insurance, 13, 18–20
   automobile, 12, 19–20, 269
   filing a claim, 18
   fires and, 286
   home-owner's, 18–19
   records of, 9, 12
   renter's, 19
   warranties, 20
insurance agents, 20
interest, interest rates, 13, 17
interior designers, 161
investment plans, 2, 9, 12
ironing, 78–81, *80–81*
   buttons and, 87
   organization and, 78
irons, 78, 79

Jewelry, 293
   care of, 91
juicers, 54
jump-starting a car, 267, *267*

Kitchen, 135–54
   cabinets in, *see* cabinets and
      cupboards
   cleaning of, 23, 24, 49–56
   countertops in, 49, 193, 198, 283
   decorating of, 192–98
   electrical safety in, 282
   equipment in, 126, 135–44
   exhaust fans in, 233
   framed art in, 189
   mildew and molds in, 289
   painting of, 169
   safety in, 120, 283, 284, *284*

saving space in, 193
sink types for, *197*
storage in, 193, *198*
windowless, 192
work triangle in, 194, *194–95*
see also food; utensils
knit clothing, 70–72, 93
knives, 137–38
    care of, 139
    essential, 139, *139*
    sharpening of, 138, *138*

Labels, food, 103, 107, 128, 134
lace, 78
    vintage, 73, *73*
ladders, 169, 207, *207*
    falls and, 280
    ratings of, 207
    safety and, 280
lamb, 106
    food safety and, 120
    microwave cooking of, 123
    refrigeration of, 131
    roasting of, 118
lamps, 164
    anatomy of, *241*
    cleaning of, 37
    cords of, 161
    energy saving and, 243
    rewiring of, 241–42
lamp shades, 156, 164, 172
    cleaning of, 37
    styles of, *164*
laundry, 59, 62–77
    air drying, 70
    care label symbols and, 72, *72*
    cleaning method chart for, 66–67
    colorfastness and, 64, *64*
    and decals on clothing, 62
    equipment for, 62–63
    hand, 74
    machine drying, 70
    machine washing, 68–70
    pretreating of, 65, 68, 70, *70*
    procedure for, 68–74
    products for, 63–65
    setting up room for, 69
    special-care clothes and, 70–74
    stain removal, 64, 65, 68, 70, *70*,
      75–77, 82
    vintage linens and lace, 73, *73*

lawn furniture, 60
lawn mowers:
    maintenance of, 249, *249*
    safety and, 208, 248
lawns:
    chemicals and pesticides used on,
      252
    fertilizing of, 248
    maintenance of, 253
    mowing of, 248, 249
    seeding of, 248–49
    sprinklers and, 251
    water pooling on, 251
lead, 280, 290–91
    in crystal, 146
    in paint, 290, 291
    in water, 290, 291
leaks, roof, 243
leather, 89–90
    accessories, 94
    dry cleaning of, 82
    furniture, cleaning of, 34
leftovers, 115 128, 131
legumes, 97, 99, 103, 104
lentils, 103
liability insurance, 19
life insurance, 12
light bulbs, 162
    for bathrooms, 200
    energy saving and, 243
    types of, *163*
    wattages of, 163
light fixtures cleaning of, 48
lighting:
    bathroom, 199, 200
    decorating and, 162–64
    dimmer switches for, 162, 163, 243
    energy saving and, 243
    flickering of, 282
    for home office, 201
    home security and, 292
    safety and, 283, 284, 285
    see also lamps
linens, 78, 93–94
    vintage, 73, *73*
linseed oil, boiled, 37
lint, 68, 70, 82
    fire prevention and, 282
loans, 6, 7, 13
    home equity, 17
    mortgages, 13, 15–17

locks, door, 218
    anatomy of, 293, *293*
    installation of, 220, *220*
locks, window, 292
logs, prefabricated, 230
lucite, 34
Lyme disease, 255, 323

Machine oil, 70
maintenance, 205–56
    car, 258–65
    cooling system, 231–33
    electrical, 241–43
    gutter, 245–46
    heating system, 228–30
    lawn, 253
    mower, 249, *249*
    plumbing, 236–40
    weatherproofing, 233–35
    workshop and, 206–9
    yard, 248–56
marble, 35, 40
masonry, 40
mattresses:
    allergies and, 30, 289
    buying of, 187
    fire and, 286
    standard sizes of, 188
meal planning, 115–16
measurements, equivalent, 126
measuring ingredients, 127
meats, 96, 97, 115
    buying of, 106
    in Food Guide Pyramid, 98, 99
    food safety and, 116
    labels on, 107
    lowering fat intake and, 103
    microwave cooking of, 123
    refrigeration of, 131
    storage of, 128
medicines, 285
mending clothes, 84–86
menu planning, for parties, 152
metal cleaner/polish, 32
mice, 255
microwave ovens, 54, 122, 123, 144
    adapting recipes to, 122
    china and, 145
    cooking table for, 123
    hot weather and, 232
    safety and, 123, 285

mildew, 285, 289
  damp clothes and, 78
  removal of, 57, 169
milk:
  in Food Guide Pyramid, 98, 99
  labels on, 107
  refrigeration of, 128, 130
minerals, 97, 102
mirrors:
  cleaning of, 37, 58
  hanging of, 190, 216–17
mites, dust, 30, 289
mixers, food, 54, 138
molds, 122, 285, 289
Molly bolts, 216, 216
money, see finances
mops, 29–30, 38
mortgages, 6, 13, 15–17
  adjustable rate, 16
  FHA and VA, 15
  fires and, 286
  fixed rate, 16
  no-points, 13
  rollover or renegotiated rate, 16
mosquitoes, 254
moths, 93, 254
motion sickness, 276
motor oil, 261
  disposal of, 291
mowers, see lawn mowers

Nails, 206, 206, 208
napkins, 78
  folding of, 149, 149
National Wood Flooring Association,
  40
nursery, 59
nutrition labeling, 103, 107
nuts, 103
  in Food Guide Pyramid, 98, 99

Oats, 96
office, home, 201, 202
oils, 97
  in Food Guide Pyramid, 98
onions, 49
opals, 91
organization, 203
  of closets, 204, 204
  of files, 8–9, 8, 9

outdoor furniture, 60
outlets, electrical, 243, 282, 283
  replacement of, 242, 242
oven cleaners, 30, 32
ovens, see stoves and ovens

Paint:
  car, repair of, 277, 278
  chip samples of, 162, 165
  disposal of, 291
  exterior, 246
  finishes of, 156, 166, 168
  for furniture, 213
  gold, 170
  how much to buy, 165–66
  laundry and, 70
  lead, 290, 291
  longevity of, 159
  primer and finish, 165, 246
  removing from window glass, 44
  safety and, 285, 290
painting, 165–71
  color and, 157, 165
  decorative techniques in, 170
  dos and don'ts for, 167
  equipment for, 166–69
  exterior, 246
  masked areas and, 246
  preparation for, 169, 169, 246
  procedure for, 170, 170, 246
  stenciling, 171, 171
  time needed for, 165
  of window trim, 246
paneling, wood, 48
pans, see cookware
pantry, 49
pants:
  ironing of, 80, 80
  shortening of, 86, 86
papers, important, 10–12
  filing of, 8–9, 8, 9, 11–12
parties, 150–54
  timetable for, 151
pasta, 96, 97, 104, 128
  in Food Guide Pyramid, 98, 99
patios, 60
pearls, 91
peas, 99, 103
pest control, 254–55
pesticides, 252, 285
  disposal of, 291

pewter, 56
philodendrons, 289
picture hanging, 189, 190, 216–17
pillowcases, 78
pillows, 30, 72, 156, 188
pipes:
  asbestos and, 290
  bursting, 288
  insulation for, 233
  lead in, 291
  temporary patches for leaks in,
    237, 237
  thawing ice in, 236–37
  see also plumbing
place settings, 146
plants:
  indoor, 216, 217, 289
  outdoor, 232, 293
plaster, patching of, 214–15, 214
plasterboard, holes in, 215
plastic cookware and utensils, 56, 122
plastic furniture, 35, 60
plexiglas, 34
plumbing, 236–40
  dos and don'ts for, 236
  drains, 50, 236, 238–39
  see also faucets; pipes; toilets
poisoning, 304
poison ivy, 252
polish, floor, removal of, 40
polish, furniture, 30, 34, 35
polishing, 211
pollutants, indoor, 289–91
polyurethane, 224
pool safety, 282
porches, 60, 293
  furniture for, 186
  safety and, 280, 283
pork, 106
  food safety and, 116, 118
  microwave cooking of, 123
  refrigeration of, 131
  roasting of, 117
potatoes, 96, 99, 103, 104
pots and pans, see cookware
poultry, 96, 97
  buying of, 106
  in Food Guide Pyramid, 98, 99
  food safety and, 116, 120
  labels on, 107
  lowering fat intake and, 103

microwave cooking of, 123
  refrigeration of, 128, 131
  roasting of, 119
power failure, 128
power-steering fluid, 262
pressing, 78
pressing cloth, 79
pressure bandage, 315, *315*
prewash stain removers, 65, 68, 70,
  70
produce, *see* fruits; vegetables
property documents, 9
property insurance, 12, 18–20
proteins, 96, 97, 99, 104
pulse, taking of, 297
pumice, 37
puncture wounds, 317
purchases, proofs of, 9
putty knife, 169

Quarry tile, 40, 184
quilts, 72, 73

Raccoons, 255
radon, 280, 291
range hoods, 290
range tops, 50–51, 144, 196
rattan furniture, 35
razor scraper, 169
real estate records, 9
recipes, 117
  adapting to microwave, 122
  for leftovers, 115
records and files, 8–9, *8, 9,* 11–12
refrigeration, 105, 128, 130–31
refrigerators, 52–53, 142, 144, 196
  moving of, 196
  storage capacity of, 196
  work triangle and, 194, *194–95*
renter's insurance, 19
repairs, 205–56
  carpet, 224, 225, *225*
  china and glass, 210
  door, 218–20
  electrical, 241–43
  floor, 224–27
  gutter, 245–46
  hiring professionals for, 247
  plumbing, 236–40
  roof, 243–44

wall and ceiling, 214–15
  window and screen, 221–23
  wood furniture, 211–13
  workshop and, 206–9
restaurants, 96
reverse-cycle air conditioners (heat
pumps), 229
rice, 96, 97, 104
  in Food Guide Pyramid, 98, 99
road emergencies, 272–76
Rock Cornish hen, roasting of, 119
roofs:
  anatomy of, *244*
  gutters and, 245–46
  repair of, 243–44
room fresheners, 31
rottenstone, 37
rubber mats, 58
rugs:
  carpet beetles and, 254
  from carpet remnants, 180
  cleaning of, 29, 40–43, 72
  decorating and, 156, 182, 184
  falls and, 280
  longevity of, 159
  Oriental, 41, 182
  safety and, 161, 283, 285
  shampooing of, 29
  standard sizes of, 181
  see also carpets, carpeting

Safe-deposit box, 10
safety, 279–323, *284–85*
  appliances and, 143, 282, 283, 285
  basement, 285, *285*
  bathroom, 199, 282, 283, 285, *285*
  car, 258, 276
  carpets and, 283, 284
  children and, *see* children, safety
    and
  cooking and, 143, 285
  don'ts for, 285
  elderly and, 283
  electrical, 243, 282
  emergencies, 286–88
  falls and, 280
  fire prevention, 280–82; *see also*
    fires
  first aid kit, 294
  gas leaks and, 288
  grilling, 121

home security, 292–93, *292–93*
  indoor pollutants and, 289–91
  information agencies for, 280, 281
  kitchen, 120, 123, 143, 283
  ladder, 207
  lawn chemicals and, 252
  in microwaving, 123
  mowers and, 208, 248
  pool, 282
  with snow blowers, 256
  stair coverings and, 226
  storms and, 288
  telephone emergency numbers,
    280
  tool, 206, 208
  water damage and, 288
  workshop, 206, 248
  see also emergencies; first aid
safety goggles, 248, 252
safety seats and belts, 276
salads, 96, 103
salt (sodium), 102, 104–5
salt stains, on shoes, 89
sanders, 224
  electric hand, 212
sanding, 211
  of wood floors, 224–25, *225*
sandpaper, 224
  grades of, 211
sauces, 96, 97, 115
  thickening of, 121
savings account, 19
scorpion stings, 323
scouring pads, 32
scrapes, first aid for, 317
screens, window and door, 44, 45
  repair of, 221–23
screws, 206, *206*
seafood:
  buying of, 106
  food safety and, 120–21
seasonings, 97, 112–14
security, home, 292–93, *292–93*
seeds, 103
  in Food Guide Pyramid, 99
sequined garments, 78, 81, 82
sewing, 83–88
  alternatives to, 83
  basic stitches in, 88, *88*
  of buttons and fasteners, 83, *83,*
    87, *87*

darning, 84, 84
mending and altering, 84–86
repairing sweaters, 83, *83*
shortening trousers, 86, *86*
sewing basket, 85
shade energy efficiency and, 232
shades, window, 45, 46, 172, 177, *177*, 293
sheets, 78
making curtains from, 176, 179
shelf life, 134
shellfish:
buying of, 106
food safety and, 120, 121
refrigeration of, 131
shelves, 203
children and, 283
putting up, 216, 217, *217*
shingles, asbestos in, 290
shirts, ironing of, 80, 80
shock:
anaphylactic, 303, 323
recognizing of, 316
shock, electric:
first aid for, 302
prevention of, 282
shoebags, 59
shoe rack, 203
shoes, 89–90, 94
fabric, washing of, 72–74
scuffed, 90
wet, 89–90
wooden heels on, 90
shoe trees, 90, *90*, 94
shopping, grocery, 105–14, 117
frozen foods and, 132
shower curtains and liners, 58
showers, 57–58, 199
safety and, 283, 285
shrinking minimizing of, 68
shrubs, 232, 293
shutters, 178, *178*
wood, 46
sidewalks, falls and, 280
silk, 78, 82
silver, 56, 293
electrolytic cleaning for, 56
flatware, 55, 145–46
jewelry, 91
tarnishing of, 52, 53
silver dip, 53

silverfish, 254
sink cleaners, 32
sinks, 196, 199, 200, 236
cleaning of, 49–50, 57
clogged drains in, 238–39
height for, 200
materials for, 196
removing rust and mineral stains from, 57
storage under, *198*
types of, *197*
work triangle and, 194, 194–95
sizings, fabric, 63, 65
skid protection strips, removal of, 59
skirts:
changing hemlines of, 86
ironing of, 81, *81*
sliding doors, curtains and, 176
slings, 318–19, *318, 319*
slipcovers, 156, 187, *187*
slow cookers, 138
smoke, 286–87
smoke detectors, 128, 280, 287
smoking, 282, 289
snacks, 97, 99
snakebites, 322–23
snakes, 322, *322*
snaps, sewing of, 83, *83*
sneakers, 72–74
snow blowers, 256
safety and, 208
snow removal, 256
soap dishes, 57, 58
soaps, 63–64, 68, 74
Social Security benefits, 6
socks, darning of, 84, *84*
sodium (salt), 102, 104–5
solvents, 290
soups, 115
space heaters, 229, 282, 290
carbon monoxide and, 289
spackling, 214, *214*
spices, 105, 113–14
spider bites, 323
spider plants, 289
spills, 22, 38
falls and, 280
splinters, 321
splints, 318–20, *318, 319, 320*
sprains, first aid for, 317–20
sprinklers, 251

squeegees, 44
squirrels, 255
stainless steel:
cookware and utensils, 56, 135–37, 146
furniture, 34
sinks, 196
stains:
on carpets, 42–43
on countertops, 49
in grout, 49
on painted surfaces, 48
in tubs and sinks, 57
on wall coverings, 48
on waxed floors, 39
on wood furniture, 37, 211; see *also* cleaning
stains, clothing, 68, 75–77
bleaches and, 64
dry cleaning and, 82
mystery, 68
pretreating of, 65, 68, 70
supplies for removing, 77
stairs and steps:
safety and, 226, 280, 283, 284, *284*, 285, *285*
vacuuming of, 41
starches, dietary, 96
starches, fabric, 63, 65, 68, 70, 94
steam boilers, 228–29
steel wool, grades of, 211
stenciling, 171, *171*
stereo equipment, cleaning of, 37–38
sterile dressings, 320
sterling silver flatware, 145
stings, insect, 323
stocks, 115
stone, 48
flooring, 40, 184
stone flooring, 184
storage, 203
of cleaning products and equipment, 30
closet organization, 204, *204*
of clothes, 93–94, 204, *204*
of food, 128–35
kitchen, 193, *198*
of toys, 59
storms, 288
stoves and ovens, 128, 141, 144, 196
burners of, 50–51, *51*, 120, 283, 285

carbon monoxide and, 289
cook tops, 50–51, 144. 196
energy efficiency and, 144
fire prevention and, 280, 284
gas leaks from, 288
hot weather and, 232
microwave, *see* microwave ovens
safety and, 120, 283, 285
wood-burning, 290
work triangle and, 194, *194–95*
studs walls, 216
styles, decorating, 159
suede, 89
dry cleaning of, 82
shoes, 90
sugars, 96, 105
in Food Guide Pyramid, 98
limiting intake of, 104
suitcase, packing of, 92–93, *92*
suits, 82
surge suppressors, 201
sweaters, 70
darning of, 84, *84*
repairing runs in, 83, *83*
wool, drying of, 74, *74*
sweeping, 38
swimming pool safety, 282
switches, electrical, 243, 282

Table settings, 149
tableware, 145–49
glossary of, 147
silverware, 53, 55, 145–46
see also china; glassware
tarnish, 52, 53
on belts and handbags, 94
on copper and brass, 56
taxes, 13
tax records, 9, 12
teakettles, removing lime deposits
from, 51
telephone numbers:
emergency, 280
for safety information, 281
telephones, 292
cleaning of, 38
televisions, 292
cleaning of, 37
termites, 254
terra-cotta tiles, 183, 184
terrazzo, 40

thermoses, 49
thermostats, 228, 232
ticks, 255, 323
tile cleaners, 32
tiles, 199
acoustical, 48
asbestos in, 290
buying extra, 40, 183, 226
ceramic, 40, 184, 215, *215*, 225,
226
cleaning of, 32, 40, 57
floor protection for, 40
quarry, 40, 184
replacement of,185, 215, *215*,
225–26
rubber, 39
stained grout and, 49
terra-cotta, 183, 184
vinyl, 183, 225, 226; *see also* vinyl
flooring
time saving, 22
tires:
changing of, 270–71, *270*
checking treads of, 262, 263, *263*
emergency spare, 271
pressure in, 262, 273
snow, 273
steering trouble and, 268
types of, 269
toasters and toaster ovens, 55, 138
toggle bolts, 216, *216*
toilet boil cleaners, 32
toilets, 199, 200, 236
anatomy of, 240
children and, 283
problems with, 239–40
tools, 208–9, *208, 209*
car care, 263
garden, 251, *251*
power, 208, 282
safety and, 206, 208, 282, 285
tips for using, 208
toolshed, 251, *251*, 280
tourniquet, application of, 317, *317*
towels hard water and, 65
toxins, 252, 285
disposal of products containing,
291
toys, 59, 72, 203
traffic patterns, in house, 159, 161,
162
transmission, car, 264, 266

problems with, 268
two types of, 263
transmission fluid, 262–63, *263*, 264
trash containers, 50
trees, 232
triangular shave hook, 169
trousers, shortening of, 86, *86*
trunks and chests, 203
tubs, *see* bathtubs
turkey, 106, 115
food safety and, 120
lowering fat intake and, 103
roasting of, 119
typewriters, cleaning of, 38

Unconsciousness, 298
underwriter's knot, 242–43, 242
upholstered furniture, upholstery, 30
anatomy of, *186*
cleaning of, 30, 32, 33–34
cushions of, *186*
dust mites and, 289
fire and, 286
longevity of, 159
quality of, 187
slipcovers for, 156, 187, *187*
upholstery cleaners, 32, 33–34
utensils, 142–43
cleaning of, 55–56
elderly and, 283
knives, 137–38, *138*, 139, *139*
nonstick, 56
plastic, 122
storage of, 193
see also cookware; tableware

Vacuum cleaners, 25–27
attachments for, 26, *26*
hand-held and stick, 27, *27*
maintenance of, 25
preventing backup in, 27
types of, 25, *25*, 27,*27*
vacuuming:
allergies and, 30, 289
of cobwebs, 47
of floors, 38, 40, 41
of stairs, 41
of upholstery, 30, 33–34, 289
of walls and ceilings, 47
VCRs, cleaning of, 37

veal, 106
    food safety and, 120
    refrigeration of, 131
vegetables, 96, 97, 103, 104, 115
    buying of, 108–9, 111
    complete proteins from grains and, 99
    in Food Guide Pyramid, 98, 99
    food safety and, 122
    freezing of, 129
    refrigeration of, 128, 130
vegetarians, 96, 104
velvet and velveteen, 78
ventilation, 231, 285
vinegar, 30, 32, 74
vinyl, 35
    repair of, in car, 278
vinyl flooring, 39, 182, 183
    buying extra, 40, 226
    tiles, 183, 225, 226
vitamins, 97, 100–101

Wall decorations, 189–90
wall fixtures, cleaning of, 48
wallpaper, 172
    cleaning of, 47, 47
    complementary patterns of, 173
    longevity of, 159
    old, removing of, 173
    sample books, 172
wallpapering, 172
    of bathrooms, 199
    equipment for, 174, 174
    procedure for, 174–75, 174, 175
    time needed for, 165
walls:
    cleaning of, 47–48
    repair of, 214–15
wall storage systems, 203
wardrobe, organization of, 204, 204
warranties, 20
washers, clothes, 62, 68–70
    troubleshooting chart for, 71
washing soda, 63
wasp stings, 323
wastebaskets, 59
water, 63, 64, 65, 68, 240
    electrical safety and, 282, 285
    hard, softening of, 240
    lead in, 290, 291
    as nutrient, 97

water damage, 288
water heaters, 283
    carbon monoxide and, 289
    gas leaks from, 288
water lines, 280, 285
water safety, 282
waxes, furniture, 34, 35, 213
weatherproofing, 233–35
weather stripping, 233–34
    for windows, 233–34, 233
weed killers, 252
wicker furniture, 35
window(s):
    anatomy of, 221
    blinds for, 45–46, 60, 178, 178, 232
    child safety and, 283
    cleaning of, 44–46
    curtains, see curtains and draperies
    decorating and, 176–79
    insulation for, 234
    measuring for curtains, 176
    painting of, 156, 246
    repair of, 221–23
    replacing glass in, 223, 223
    security and, 292
    shades, 45, 46, 172, 177, 177, 293
    shutters, 178, 178
    stuck, 221
    weather stripping for, 233–34, 233
wine, 153, 154
winter:
    car care in, 264
    house maintenance in, 256
wood:
    blinds and shutters, 46
    counters and cutting boards, 49
    paneling, 48
    parquet tiles, replacement of, 225–26, 226
wood-burning stoves, 290
wood floors, 38–39, 182–83, 183
    new, treatment of, 224
    restoration of, 224–25, 226
    treatment guide for, 227
wood furniture:
    caring for, 185
    cleaning of, 34
    finishes, 213
    longevity of, 159
    outdoor, 60

restoration of, 35, 36, 37, 211–13
woodwork, cleaning of, 48
wool, 70, 72, 78, 82
    insect pests and, 254
    repairing runs in, 83, 83
    sweaters, drying of, 74, 74
    wrinkles in, 92
word processors, cleaning of, 38
work gloves, 46, 248
workshop, home, 206–9
    safety in, 248
    see also tools
work triangle, 194, 194–95
wounds:
    bleeding from, 315–16
    puncture, 317
wrought iron, 34

Yard, 248–56
    pests in, 254–55
    snow removal in, 256
    toolshed in, 251, 251, 280
    see also lawns
yellow jacket stings, 323
yogurt:
    in Food Guide Pyramid, 98, 99
    lowering fat intake and, 103
    refrigeration of, 130

CREDITS

FOR SMALLWOOD AND STEWART:

Writers
Melanie Barnard
Stephen Brewer
Linda Hetzer
Wade Hoyt
John H. Ingersoll
Barbara Mayer
Diane Nelson
Rita Marie Schneider
Dorothy B. Schoenfeld

Editorial
Kathy Belden
Maryann Brinley
Rachel Carley
Susan E. Davis
Victoria Klose
Judith McQuown
Sophia Nardin
Andrew Neusner
Matthew Vogel
Daniel Weaver
Dr. Robert Youngson

Illustrators
Wendy Frost
John Gist
Edward Lam
Tomo Narashima

Art/Production
Carole Desnoes
Clarence Feng
Marie Nicole Haniph
Rosalind Lord
Annemarie McMullan